Gender and Development

From Sam:

To Alex Wallisch and Sakura Reyes, for being constant sources of education and learning

From Rae:

To Valerie and David Blumberg, with love and appreciation for the joy you bring to my life

Sara Miller McCune founded SAGE Publishing in 1965 to support the dissemination of usable knowledge and educate a global community. SAGE publishes more than 1000 journals and over 800 new books each year, spanning a wide range of subject areas. Our growing selection of library products includes archives, data, case studies and video. SAGE remains majority owned by our founder and after her lifetime will become owned by a charitable trust that secures the company's continued independence.

Los Angeles | London | New Delhi | Singapore | Washington DC | Melbourne

Gender and Development

The Economic Basis of Women's Power

Samuel Cohn

Texas A&M University

Rae Lesser Blumberg

University of Virginia

Los Angeles | London | New Delhi
Singapore | Washington DC | Melbourne

FOR INFORMATION:

SAGE Publications, Inc.
2455 Teller Road
Thousand Oaks, California 91320
E-mail: order@sagepub.com

SAGE Publications Ltd.
1 Oliver's Yard
55 City Road
London, EC1Y 1SP
United Kingdom

SAGE Publications India Pvt. Ltd.
B 1/I 1 Mohan Cooperative Industrial Area
Mathura Road, New Delhi 110 044
India

SAGE Publications Asia-Pacific Pte Ltd
18 Cross Street #10-10/11/12
China Square Central
Singapore 048423

Printed in the United States of America

Library of Congress Cataloging-in-Publication Data

Names: Cohn, Samuel, 1954- editor. | Blumberg, Rae Lesser, editor.

Title: Gender and development : the economic basis of women's power / [edited by] Samuel Cohn, Texas A&M University, Rae Lesser Blumberg, University of Virginia.

Description: Thousand Oaks, California : SAGE, [2020] | Includes bibliographical references and index.

Identifiers: LCCN 2018054396 | ISBN 978-1-5063-9663-7 (pbk. : alk. paper)

Subjects: LCSH: Women in development. | Women—Economic conditions.

Classification: LCC HQ1240 .G428 2020 | DDC 330.90082—dc23 LC record available at https://lccn.loc.gov/2018054396

This book is printed on acid-free paper.

Acquisitions Editor: Jeff Lasser
Editorial Assistant: Tiara Beatty
Production Editor: Rebecca Lee
Copy Editor: Meg Granger
Typesetter: Hurix Digital
Proofreader: Penny Sippel
Indexer: Kathy Paparchontis
Cover Designer: Candice Harman
Marketing Manager: Kara Kindstrom

19 20 21 22 23 10 9 8 7 6 5 4 3 2 1

Table of Contents

Acknowledgments

SAGE would like to thank the following reviewers for their time and editorial insight:

Lloyd J. Dumas, *University of Texas at Dallas*
Dr. Elise LoBue, *University of Illinois-Springfield*

About the Editors

Samuel Cohn (contributing author and coeditor) is professor of sociology at Texas A&M University. He is the founder and first president of the American Sociological Association section on development. He has won the American Sociological Association's Jessie Barnard Award for the best book on gender, his *Process of Occupational Sex-Typing* (Temple, 1985). Among his other works are a general book on race and gender discrimination in the United States, studies of race discrimination in American cities, a book on Brazilian economic development, and studies of development processes in 19th century Norway and the British Celtic fringe. He recently won a prize from the American Sociological Association for his service to development sociology.

Rae Lesser Blumberg (contributing author and coeditor) is the William R. Kenan, Jr., Professor of Sociology at the University of Virginia. Much of her academic work involves her general theory of gender stratification and theory of gender and development. In both, women's versus men's relative economic power (defined as control of income and other assets) is posited as the key—but not sole—factor affecting gender equality and many other development-related outcomes. She has worked in 48 countries in virtually all sectors of development, beginning with the Peace Corps in Venezuela. Her work includes time with the World Bank, USAID, UNESCO, UNDP and other UN agencies, the African Development Bank, Inter-American Development Bank, various international nongovernmental organizations, and several individual governments. She was president of the Sociology of Development Section of the American Sociological Association in 2014–2015. Her BS, MA, and PhD are from Northwestern University, and she is the author/coauthor of more than 100 publications, including eight books.

About the Contributors

Phyllis L. Baker is Professor Emerita of Sociology from the University of Northern Iowa and is special assistant to the president, Office of the President, University of Illinois System. She is an affiliate faculty in the Women and Gender in Global Perspectives Program at the University of Illinois Urbana-Champaign. Her most recent research focuses on public gendered violence in cross-cultural contexts. Guiding her work are her theoretical interests at the intersection of institutional contexts and gender and interpersonal interaction.

Marie E. Berry is an assistant professor at the Josef Korbel School of International Studies at the University of Denver, where she is an affiliate of the Sié Chéou-Kang Center for International Security and Diplomacy. She is a political sociologist with a focus on mass violence, gender, politics, and development. She is the director of the Inclusive Global Leadership Initiative, an effort to catalyze research, education, and programming aimed at elevating and amplifying the work that women activists are doing at the grassroots to advance peace and security across the world. Her first book, *War, Women, and Power: From Violence to Mobilization in Rwanda and Bosnia-Herzegovina* (Cambridge University Press, 2018), examines the impact of war and genocide on women's political mobilization in those countries. Her work has been published in *Gender & Society*, *Democratization*, *Signs*, *New Political Economy*, *Mobilization*, *Politics & Gender*, *Foreign Policy*, *The Society Pages*, and *Political Violence @ a Glance*.

Manuela Boatcă is professor of sociology with a focus on macrosociology and head of the school of the Global Studies Programme at the Albert Ludwigs University of Freiburg, Germany. She was Visiting Professor at IUPERJ, Rio de Janeiro, in 2007–2008 and professor of sociology of global inequalities at the Latin American Institute of the Freie Universität Berlin from 2012 to 2015. Her work on world-systems analysis, postcolonial and decolonial perspectives, gender in modernity/coloniality, racialization, and the geopolitics of knowledge in Eastern Europe and Latin America has appeared in the *Journal of World-Systems Research*, *Cultural Studies*, *South Atlantic Quarterly*, *Political Power and Social Theory*, *Berliner Journal für Soziologie*, *Social Identities*, *Current Sociology*, and *Theory, Culture and Society*. She is author of *Global Inequalities Beyond Occidentalism* (Routledge, 2016) and coeditor (with E. Gutiérrez Rodríguez and S. Costa) of *Decolonizing European Sociology: Transdisciplinary Approaches* (Ashgate, 2010) and of the monograph issue, "Dynamics of Inequalities in a Global Perspective" (with V. Treitler; *Current Sociology*, 2016).

Jennifer N. Fish is professor and chair of the Department of Women's Studies at Old Dominion University. She is a sociologist who focuses on women's labor and migration in the informal economy, with an emphasis on transnational activism and development. Her ethnographic research forms the foundation of four books, numerous journal articles, and a series of organizational reports. For the past 15 years, Dr. Fish has worked with migrant domestic workers' organizations throughout the world. Her recent book *Domestic Workers of the World Unite! A Global Movement for Dignity and Human Rights* (New York University Press, 2017) chronicles the achievement of the first UN policy to protect domestic workers through the accounts of women activists.

Jasmin Hristov is assistant professor of sociology at the Department of History and Sociology and associate member of the Gender and Women's Studies Program at the University of British Columbia, Okanagan. She is the author of *Paramilitarism and Neoliberalism: Violent Systems of Capital Accumulation in Colombia and Beyond* (Pluto Press, 2014) and *Blood and Capital: The Paramilitarization of Colombia* (Ohio University Press, 2009). Her work includes refereed articles featured in the *Canadian Review of Sociology*; *Journal of Peasant Studies*; *Latin American Perspectives*; *Journal of Peacebuilding and Development*; *Journal of Islamic Studies and Humanities*; *Labour, Capital and Society*; and *Social Justice*, as well as a forthcoming chapter in *Gendering Globalization, Globalizing Gender: Post-Colonial Perspectives*, with Oxford University Press. Her field of research is in political and global sociology with a focus on development and conflict, state violence, irregular armed groups, social movements, gender-based violence, and sex trafficking. She is presently the principal investigator for the project Violence and Land Dispossession in Central America and Mexico, funded by the Social Sciences and Humanities Research Council of Canada.

Rita Jalali is Scholar in Residence in the Department of Sociology and Center on Health, Risk, and Society at American University. Her research has focused on cross-national issues of race and ethnicity, social movements, civil society, gender inequalities, and water and sanitation deprivation. Her work has been published in numerous peer-reviewed journals. Her current work in the field of water, sanitation, and hygiene (WASH) focuses on four research areas: (1) historical examination of water, sanitation, and hygiene issues in multilateral development organizations, using quantitative and qualitative methods; (2) quantitative study of household expenditure on sanitation and hygiene in India to examine gender bias in the intra-household allocation of resources; (3) a conceptual analysis of the gendered nature of WASH-related diseases; and (4) field studies on menstrual and other personal hygiene practices of poor women in India and its social and health impact. She received her PhD in sociology from Stanford University.

Kevin T. Leicht is professor of sociology at the University of Illinois Urbana-Champaign, former sociology program officer for the National Science Foundation, and former chair of the Department of Sociology and director of the Iowa Social Science Research Center at the University of Iowa. He has written extensively on issues relating to economic development, globalization, and political sociology; his work has been funded by the National Science Foundation, National Institutes of Health, Spencer Foundation, and the Ford Foundation; and his published articles have appeared in the *American*

Sociological Review, *American Journal of Sociology*, *Academy of Management Journal*, *Law and Society Review*, and other outlets. He is the current editor of the *Journal of Professions and Organization* and past editor of *The Sociological Quarterly* (official journal of the Midwest Sociological Society) and *Research in Social Stratification and Mobility* (official journal of the social stratification section of the International Sociological Association).

Valentine M. Moghadam is professor of sociology and international affairs and director of the Middle East Studies Program at Northeastern University. She was formerly at Purdue University, where she directed the Women's Studies Program, at UNU/WIDER in Helsinki, and at UNESCO in Paris. Born in Tehran, Iran, Dr. Moghadam received her higher education in Canada and the United States. Dr. Moghadam's areas of research are globalization; revolutions and social movements; transnational feminist networks; and gender, development, and democratization in the Middle East and North Africa. Among her many publications are *Modernizing Women: Gender and Social Change in the Middle East* (1993, 2003, 2013), *Globalizing Women: Transnational Feminist Networks* (2005, winner of the American Political Science Association's Victoria Schuck Award), and *Globalization and Social Movements: Islamism, Feminism, and the Global Justice Movement* (2009, 2013). Her current research is on prospects for a women-friendly democratization after the Arab Spring.

Julia Roth is professor of American studies with a focus on gender studies and inter-American studies at Bielefeld University, Germany. She was postdoctoral fellow on the research project The Americas as Space of Entanglements and at the interdisciplinary network desiguALdades.net: Interdependent Inequalities in Latin America at Freie Universität Berlin, as well as lecturer at Humboldt University Berlin, the University of Potsdam, and the Universidad de Guadalajara, Mexico. Her research focuses on postcolonial and gender approaches, intersectionality, and global inequalities, and has led her to the United States, Cuba, Mexico, Puerto Rico, Nigeria, and Peru. Her work currently focuses on antiracist feminist knowledge from the Caribbean, hip hop, intersectionality theorizing, and right-wing populism and gender. Alongside her academic work, she organizes and curates cultural–political events (e.g., the theater-festival Women/Images of the Americas in Movement in Berlin, 2010; BE.BOP: Black Europe Body Politics with Alanna Lockward, 2014 and 2016).

Jennifer Rothchild is associate professor of sociology and coordinator of the Gender, Women, & Sexuality Studies program at the University of Minnesota, Morris. Her current research centers on gender and development, childhoods, reproductive health, and social inequalities, particularly in relation to menstrual health and hygiene. For more than 20 years, Rothchild has conducted community-based research in South Asia and the United States, and she is considered one of the leading scholars on gender and development in Nepal. She is the author of the book *Gender Trouble Makers: Education and Empowerment in Nepal* (Routledge, 2006), as well as book chapters, essays, and policy reports. Her expertise has been sought out by community development and outreach organizations, international non-governmental organizations, and government sectors in the United States and abroad, and she has won several awards for her activism and public sociology work.

Priti Shrestha studies gender and development, reproductive health, and women's economic status in the Global South. She has conducted fieldwork throughout her home country of Nepal. Her work has been featured in research publications, grassroots organization reports, and policy briefs. She holds a master's degree in sociology and an MA in social change and development studies.

Justin Sprague holds a PhD in women's studies from the University of Maryland, College Park. He received an MA in women's studies from the University of Maryland and an MA in humanities from Old Dominion University in Norfolk, Virginia. His dissertation, *Cooking With Mama Kim: The Legacy of Women (Re)Defining Korean-American Authenticity Through Food*, positions women as gatekeepers of cultural authenticity. His larger research explores affect and the social construction of gender representations, with a focus on maternal figures as symbols of authenticity and collective cultural nostalgia, and an intersectional analysis of the racial and ethnic identity construction of multiracial subjects.

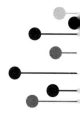

CHAPTER 1

"Power of the Purse": The Importance of Women's Economic Power

Why Women's Economic Power Is Absolutely Essential

Rae Lesser Blumberg and Samuel Cohn

Globally, countries are losing $160 trillion in wealth because of differences in lifetime earnings between women and men.

— World Bank, May 30, 2018

The increase in female employment in the rich world has been the main driving force of growth in the last couple of decades. Those women have contributed more to global GDP growth than has either new technology or the new giants, China and India.

— *The Economist*, "Forget China, India and the Internet: Economic Growth Is Driven by Women" (Special Report: The Importance of Sex), April 12, 2006 (16)

The central thread in this book is about the causes and effects of women's economic power, defined as *control* of economic resources—income, wealth, credit and/or assets such as real property, land, livestock, stocks and bonds, and the like.

Women's economic power matters not only because power is the key to gender equality but also because we argue that when it comes to gender equality or inequality, it's the most *important* of the five main types of power: political, force/violence, economic, ideology, and information/education. It's also the only one of those five types that varies for *both* women and men from near 100% to near 0%, although there are many more male than female cases of near-total economic power. But there are no cases where women have full 50/50 equality or better in any of the other four types of power. Here are two empirical cases of extreme economic power:

- In Colonial North America, the women of the six tribes of the Iroquois Confederation controlled essentially the entire economy: land, crops (which they cultivated), and the storehouses where food was kept. It gave the Matrons, the women leaders, the power to nominate male chiefs, as well as to recall them and nominate a replacement; the Matrons also could veto a military expedition by not giving the men the stored trail food needed.

Men and women also had equal power in the religious sphere. There is no mention of *any* wife beating or violence against women (Brown 1970, 1975).

- In today's Afghanistan, men control almost all the wealth. A study by Grace (2005:16) found that men owned more than 98% of the land—in a country that is about three fourths rural. The dominant ideology views women akin to property and "not quite human beings." Overwhelmingly, women wear near-identical face-covering burqas with *no* individual touches when they go out lest they be recognized and harmed by disapproving men (Blumberg 2016b). UNIFEM estimates that 87% of Afghan women face abuse and violence (UNIFEM 2006; Khan 2012:2). Yet, via a U.S.-promoted quota system, women are 27.7% of members of Parliament (Inter-Parliamentary Union 2018). Some are brave and speak out, but none wield any real clout.

Another reason that women's economic power is important is that it—and the greater gender equality it fosters—spurs the best kind of development: not merely economic growth but also improved human well-being. Conversely, its absence is linked to the worst kind of development, including violence and armed conflict, as well as malnutrition and ill health of children and their mothers (Blumberg 2016a).

So, what *causes* women to attain economic power? This is the key question. It is one thing to explain the adverse treatment of women by claiming they lack economic power; it is another to explain how women can gain economic power so they can increase gender equity.

The Two Primary Causes of Women's Economic Power

There are many ways women can acquire economic power. Most fall into one of two broader categories, however: "strategic indispensability" (Blumberg 1984) and "strategic alliances."[1]

Strategic indispensability. Strategic indispensability is the *essence* of power (Pfeffer 1981). Being indispensable gives a worker a credible exit threat. If the worker leaves, the organization cannot go on without her. Lady Gaga is essential to a Lady Gaga concert. You can replace a roadie or a bass player but not the main attraction. If Lady Gaga is unhappy and threatens not to go onstage, the show will not go on. Lady Gaga's strategic indispensability makes it likely she will get exactly what she wants.

Hirschman (1970) made this argument compellingly in *Exit, Voice and Loyalty*. If management does something that workers don't like, the workers have a choice of exit, voice, or loyalty. They can leave, they can protest, or they can suck it up and take it. Voice (protest) works only if acting on the exit threat would actually hurt management. If the firm can operate perfectly well with replacement workers, the exit threat is meaningless: the workers have no power to force significant change in policy or practice.

Strategic indispensability is particularly important for *women's* economic power. To be indispensable, women must work in key production activities. That is the *prerequisite* (Blumberg 1984). To transform their work into economic power, the activity has to be important and valued. The women cannot be easy to replace. Could the society or the power elite do without female production? If the answer is "not easily," women have crucial strategic indispensability and, with it, some level of economic power.[2]

Strategic alliances. Power is not strictly based on one's own resources. Victories are won by coalitions of people working together. Having powerful allies matters. If women receive the support of key gatekeepers and power holders in society, they can leverage this assistance into women's victories. If every significant societal actor favors male domination, the women are outnumbered and outflanked. Regardless of their own resources, they are likely to lose.

Resource mobilization theorists make this argument compellingly. Tilly (1988) and McCarthy and Zald (1977) argue that the success of protests depends on whether elite forces contribute resources to the cause. Wealthy sponsors can donate money. Government officials can provide parliamentary votes, favorable administrative decisions, victories in court, or protection from police repression. Moral authorities and celebrities can provide publicity or can frame women's case in a manner that increases public approval. Movements with sponsors win. Movements without sponsors are crushed. Comparable arguments are made in the literature on organizational power where worker autonomy and access to decision making are linked to alliances with key outsiders (Pfeffer 1981).

In today's world, what kinds of resources are necessary to get strategic indispensability? The most common resources are money, property, and skills. In some cases, availability to work makes one indispensable when no one else is available.

What kinds of people must one connect with to get strategic alliances? Economic gatekeepers matter. Women in business, from micro to large-scale, need alliances with customers, vendors, and lenders. If male, they may have strong preferences on gender issues, including whether or not they will do business with women. The state is of fundamental importance, too. If the law is biased against women, then regulators, the police, and even customs officials all can hamper women's economic activities. Moral, cultural, and religious authorities also can create or destroy public support for women.

The 10 Supporting Causes of Women's Economic Power

There are many ways to obtain strategic indispensability and strategic alliances. You probably can think of a dozen right now. We propose five determinants of women's strategic indispensability and five of strategic alliances. These 10 undergird women's economic empowerment. It is easy to demonstrate their importance in helping women solidify their economic power in numerous empirical settings in both the Global North and Global South.

Table 1.1 Ten Supporting Causes of Women's Economic Power	Strategic Indispensability	Strategic Alliances
Absence of patrilineal inheritance	X	
Absence of patrilocality		X
Absence of non-irrigated plow agriculture	X	
Labor scarcity	X	
Access to human capital	X	
Commercialization of women's home-based production/enterprise	X	
Absence of male preference by controllers of capital or sales		X
Women's economic organization		X
Favorable balance of nondiscriminatory versus patriarchal noneconomic institutions		X
Absence of armed conflict near women's homes		X

Here is a brief overview of how the 10 factors listed in Table 1.1 work.

1. *Absence of patrilineal inheritance.* Patrilineal inheritance is inheriting property or money strictly between males, especially from father to son. Wives and daughters are intentionally bypassed. Cutting women off from inherited assets weakens them economically.

2. *Absence of patrilocality.* Patrilocality is having women go to live with their husband's family when they marry. When women are forced to live exclusively with their husband's family, surrounded by his male-side kin, contact with and support from their family of birth typically plummets or disappears. This leaves them with no allies in a marital dispute. Everyone else in the household and his relatives will support the husband.

3. *Absence of non-irrigated ("dry") plow agriculture.* Men have been far more likely to use the plow than women, given that human- or animal-drawn plows require considerable upper-body strength and, biologically, men have roughly one half more. In dry plow agriculture, plowing the earth to plant the seeds may be seen as the single most important phase of the food production process. In these cases, men, not women, have strategic indispensability and male power is high. In fact, women have little role from plowing to harvest. The next section adds more detail. (Blumberg's chapter gives a fuller treatment of dry plow agriculture; Blumberg 2004b, 2009 offers more detail on points 1, 2, and 3.)

4. *Labor scarcity.* Keeping women out of powerful positions requires that there be enough men available to fill those powerful positions. When men are either scarce or insufficient to meet rising demand and alternative labor forces (e.g., male migrants or even robots) are not readily available, there are jobs that will go undone unless one allows women to do them. Scarcity of men can come from warfare when men leave their homes to fight distant battles. It can also come from men migrating to other places. Such male absence often leaves the women to handle all the normal business at home (although sometimes older men who stay behind can prevent women from gaining economic autonomy). Overall labor scarcity can come from economic expansion or business booms. These scenarios increase women's prospects for becoming strategically indispensable.

5. *Access to human capital. Human capital* is economic jargon for skill. Human capital generally comes from education and work experience; good health and nutrition also enhance it. In a modern industrialized economy, skilled jobs pay more than unskilled jobs. Having human capital is essential to attaining positions of responsibility and status.

6. *Commercialization of women's home-based production/enterprise.* Prior to industrialization, most people lived on farms and produced the bulk of goods at home. When industrialization comes, some of that work can become valuable in the market. If women make textiles or art objects or do market trading—and are lucky enough to have that sector take off—they can find themselves in a lucrative niche in the economy.

7. *Absence of male preference by controllers of capital or sales.* It is hard for women to become economically powerful if men won't do business with them. If credit institutions and banks won't loan to women, then the only businesses with significant assets will be those controlled by men. If strategic buyers won't negotiate with women or buy their products, then marketing and dealmaking will be male monopolies.

8. *Women's economic organization.* Women can make alliances with each other to increase their mutual power. Female business associations, cooperatives, trading groups, traditional rotating savings and credit groups (especially among traders in sub-Saharan Africa and Southeast Asia), as well as informal cooperation among women in business, all increase women's economic power relative to men. Microfinance institutions, too, often prefer women as microloan clients because they usually repay better than men.

9. *Favorable balance of nondiscriminatory versus patriarchal noneconomic institutions.* Women need societal support if they are to attain positions of power. To the extent the government or the law is antifeminist and discriminates against women, women seeking power will face legal and political obstacles. The same applies if religious organizations, schools, or the mass media are patriarchal,

discriminating, and antifeminist. Under those circumstances, women will face hostile public opinion, as well as organized resistance from gatekeepers enforcing traditional moral codes.

10. *Absence of armed conflict near women's homes.* War and violence close to home foster male control over women. Women who want positions of power must be able to go about their business. If the streets are unsafe, women either must stay home or find armed male escorts if they wish to go out. Limited mobility severely constrains what women can do on their own behalf. In warlike conditions today, power devolves on those people who carry guns. Disproportionately, gun carriers tend to be males.

Now we consider these points in greater detail, illustrating their operations with examples from the empirical literature, including studies of gender and development.

Absence of Patrilineal Inheritance, Patrilocality, and Non-Irrigated Plow Agriculture

We consider the first three factors together: absence of (1) patrilineal inheritance, (2) patrilocal residence for newlyweds, and (3) a farming system based on non-irrigated plow agriculture. We do so by looking at the *opposite* side of the coin: When all three factors are *simultaneously present*, women's position falls to its geographic and historic low point. Caldwell (1982) described a "patriarchal belt" stretching across the Middle East/North Africa (MENA), as well as much of South Asia and (pre-Revolutionary) China, based solely on patriarchal kinship. (Note that this encompasses Muslim, Hindu, and Confucianist areas.) The "patriarchal belt" also led to a "patriarchal bargain" (Kandiyoti 1988) whereby women accepted being largely confined to the home, acting submissively and with propriety, in return for male support and protection. With no importance in dry plow agriculture or way to earn income, what else could they do?

Patrilineal Inheritance

When men receive most or all inheritance in a patrilineal kinship system, including of crucial resources such as land in rural areas, women have to create their own livelihoods by alternative means—or end up in highly subordinated positions. Conversely, when patrilineal inheritance is absent, women's chances for greater equality rise.

Patrilineal inheritance is prevalent de facto, if not de jure, in the following world areas:

1. *The "patriarchal belt"* delineated by Caldwell (1982)—MENA, much of South Asia, and (pre-Revolutionary) China. It has long traditions of this—for example, half-share inheritance for women under Islamic Sharia; male inheritance in Hindu-majority India,

where there are still problems despite legal changes; and in pre-Communist China.

2. *Sub-Saharan Africa,* where 75% of ethnic groups have a male-dominated kinship/property system (Elondou-Enyegye and Calves 2006). Presently, in rural areas among these groups, there still is considerable de facto male inheritance of land even in nations where a land law has been passed giving women rights to inherit it. Mainly, this is because the legal code has yet to be scrubbed of remaining "customary law." In contrast to the "patriarchal belt," however, most of those African women long have been important in horticultural cultivation (see the section on "Horticulture"), as well as in trade. These pursuits have given most of them the ability to earn—and control—income on their own, even if they don't inherit. Where women do control income, especially in West Africa, which has the strongest, longest traditions of female entrepreneurship, women and men keep "separate purses" (Hill 1969; Treas 1991); that is, neither husband nor wife knows what the other is earning—which protects women's income from possible male designs.

This leaves much of the world (Europe, the Western Hemisphere, Southeast Asia, and Australia/New Zealand) with less patriarchal modes of transmitting property and wealth.

Patrilocality

Women do better in economic and well-being terms when they have allies. This is easiest where patrilocal residence is absent. Some nonpatrilocal groups (mostly in sub-Saharan Africa) have full matrilineal descent, inheritance, and postmarital residence.[3] Most *nonpatrilocal* peoples of the world, however, have *bilateral* kinship: mother's and father's kin are given fairly equal weight, although different groups may lean toward male or female kin to varying degrees. A female tilt is called *matrifocality* (women favoring women relatives, preferring to live near them, and exchanging help from childcare to making ends meet). In today's Global South, bilateral kinship with a matrifocal tilt is found mainly in the Caribbean and Southeast Asia. In both regions, women have long-standing traditions as market traders.[4] In Southeast Asia, in particular, women traders and entrepreneurs often have another advantage: nearby female kin they can rely on (Ireson 1996). This further increases the security of their livelihoods. Strong kin-based alliances among women traders also are found among members of Southeast Asian groups with full matrilineality, such as the Minangkabau of Sumatra, Indonesia, and part of Malaysia. Nor is patrilocality always a big obstacle for women with deeply rooted entrepreneurial traditions and their own economic organizations (e.g., in West Africa).

"Dry" Plow Agriculture

To understand why non-irrigated ("dry") plow agriculture pushed women out of production, ushering in the world's highest levels of gender inequality (especially when combined with patrilineal inheritance and patrilocal residence), it is necessary to look across human history at the four alternatives to dry plow agriculture.

Chronologically, the main ways human societies have made their living off the planet[5] are:

1. foraging (i.e., hunting and gathering);

2. hoe horticulture (cultivating garden-size plots, each containing a variety of crops);

3. plow agriculture (growing single crops on large individual fields, which can be [a] "dry," non-irrigated cultivation of field crops or [b] "wet," which involves cultivation of irrigated rice; Blumberg 2004a, 2015); and

4. industrial production, whereby livelihoods are obtained not from nature but from products and services created by humans.

To reiterate, of these, dry plow agriculture has proven the worst for women.

1. *Foraging (hunting and gathering)*. This is the way we lived as big-brained *Homo sapiens* from the time we arose in Africa about 315,000 years ago (Hublin et al. 2017) until about 13,000 years ago when cultivation likely first emerged. Archeological and anthropological research shows that gender inequality was low among hunter-gatherers. This is because economically, all members of the foraging band were basically equal: Few foragers owned many possessions. Also, foragers were often nomadic and possessions are heavy to carry. Moreover, *sharing* has been found in *every* foraging band ever studied, with people giving when there was surplus and getting in times of scarcity. Women were very important economic actors: 20th century research on still-intact bands found that except at Arctic latitudes, females gathered about 60% or more of the food supply (Lee 1968, 1969). The rules of sharing also tended to be stricter for the products of the men's hunts, which were less reliable than the women's gathering. (Animals run away, but plants don't.) This means non-Arctic women generally had at least as much control of economic resources as men and that foragers living traditionally were mostly gender-egalitarian. It also helped that the kinship system was predominantly bilateral (recognizing both mother's and father's kin).

2. *Horticulture*. Between about 13,000 and 6,000 years ago, cultivation had emerged on every large land mass except Australia (which had no suitable plant species that mutated easily and gradually could be tailored into a basic staple; Blumberg 2009). Women gatherers were the botanical specialists. Men hunters were the zoological experts. Women were the ones who experimented with plants and transformed a few into today's top staple foods: wheat, rice, and corn. Thus, women deserve the credit for the cultivation revolution (Childe 1942), arguably the most important in human history. They first used digging sticks but soon changed to the hoe. Most farming was in small garden-size plots having a variety of plants, using *shifting "slash and burn"*[6] techniques (after about 3 years, more weeds than food come up and it's time to clear a new plot).

Much of sub-Saharan Africa (except for the areas of Southern and Eastern Africa that became white settler colonies) has shallow soils that aren't deep enough for the plow (see the next section, on "Agriculture"), so cultivation in those areas remains horticultural to this day. Women still produce up to 70% (or more) of basic food crops in the region (Saito and Weidemann 1990) and typically have income sources of their own. This allows them to overcome the fact that 75% of sub-Saharan ethnic groups still have male-dominated kin/property systems (Elondou-Enyegye and Calves 2006).[7]

3. *Agriculture.* The plow was invented 5,000 to 6,000 years ago in the Middle East and diffused across the vast Eurasian land mass and nearby North Africa.[8] Plow agriculture has had a major impact on gender equality. From the start, it required a lot of upper-body strength. Men have one third to one half more upper-body strength than women do, thus putting females at a great disadvantage in plowing. Non-irrigated wheat, rye, barley, oats, and the like, however, don't require much labor per unit of land area (especially compared with irrigated rice; see the next paragraph). So if a field can be plowed by one man with a mule or two, you don't need many people to have a successful farm. This means there's not enough work for all the men, and women are pushed out. The surplus men grew up as farmers and easily could replace a male peasant, thus undercutting the peasantry's bargaining power (Lenski 1966).[9]

In contrast, "wet" agriculture means irrigated rice. Everyone creates economic value, men and women alike. As long as you add workers *gradually*, each new person's hands raise more rice than the person's mouth eats. This permits such high labor intensity that areas with small rice paddies could support very dense populations with enough left over to send to the cities of dry agrarian states (e.g., from "wet" Southern to "dry" Northern China and from "wet" Southern to "dry" Northern India).[10] In sum, in irrigated rice, "everybody works": men, women, girls, boys, and large domestic animals that pull the plow (Blumberg 2015). Even if the kin/property system favored men, as in southern China, women's work was recognized. Where the kin/property system was bilateral/matrifocal or matrilineal, and women inherited and traded, as in most of Southeast Asia, women in wet rice areas kept economic clout and local level near equality.

Overall, though, plow agriculture—especially if "dry" and with a male-tilted kin/property system—has been linked to history's highest levels of economic and gender inequality. Plows vastly increase the value of fixed plots of land by bringing up nutrients from deep in the soil; they also break up or bury weeds. With the help of manure from domestic animals, the plow permits *permanent cultivation.* The same plot or field can be used for centuries if soil fertility is maintained by use of manure from livestock and good farming practices.[11] Permanent cultivation also facilitated *permanent settlement.* Once people were tied to the land, they couldn't escape, and if some ruler wanted to rule over them, they had to accept it (Mann 1986). Eviction meant social—and often physical—death. In sum, the agrarian era saw the rise of very high levels of social and economic inequality (Lenski 1966). Many folk proverbs say something like, "When the plow enters, so, too, does servitude." In dry agriculture, women suffered the double blow of losing their strategic indispensability just when social systems became more oppressive, with dictatorial landlords and nobles who could enforce patriar-chal laws that favored men.

4. *Industrial*. Industrialization generally has been good for women. Industrial economies pay workers wages. Women work for lower wages than men. This has meant that women are the labor force of choice in many work settings where cheap labor is economically important to the employer. The low-wage factor was irrelevant in earlier economies. Foraging and tra-ditional farming did not pay wages. Workers were "paid" with the food they hunted, collected, or grew.[12] Once employers started to pay their employees with cash, however, they started to look for ways to save cash. Hiring cheap female workers has been a common—and profitable—strategy.

Women working for lower wages than men has been a near universal under capitalism (England 1992; Seguino 2000). Why this is so is under debate.[13] But lower female wages make women the workers of preference if wages represent a high percentage of total expenses (Cohn 1999). In the early days of the Industrial Revolution, women were in demand because their wages were lower than men's. They entered into textile production despite opposition from male workers that slowed their hiring (Huber 1991). Soon they moved into other paid work: In the United States by 1900, clerical and many service jobs had become sex-segregated into "women's jobs." These were the types of work destined to grow the most since then. Most recently, in East Asia and later in Southeast Asia, women were recruited—sometimes out of the rice paddies—into the rising, mostly labor-intensive export-oriented industries, such as textiles/clothing, electronics assembly, and toys.

Labor Scarcity

Women are more likely to attain positions of power when there simply are no men available to fill those positions in their stead. This can occur either from an acute shortage of men or from a general shortage of labor all around.

Many of the most important female occupations became female because they grew so quickly as to exhaust the available male labor supply. Clerical work and elementary school teaching now are nearly all-female jobs. They were created in the 19th century, and demand for these positions simply exploded. When no—or not enough—men were available to do the work, male resistance to women taking those jobs was futile.

A good example of failed male resistance occurred in the British Postal Savings Bank, a bank actually run by the British Post Office. Banks needed vast numbers of accountants and financial clerks. Male Post Office managers did not want to give these jobs to women because working with numbers was a "masculine" intellectual skill. The Postal Savings Bank was growing as more and more people began using banks rather than keeping their money at home. The Post Office simply could not fill its vacancies. So in the 1870s, the Post Office instructed its Savings Bank managers to start hiring women. The male managers resisted this fiercely. They orchestrated their resistance by finding doctors who testified that female clerks were medically incapable of keeping accounts! Keeping accounts would involve lifting ledger books.

What would happen if a woman tried to do this while she was ill or having her period? The doctors and male managers argued the strain of such lifting might easily make women infertile.

The men's arguments went no place. The Post Office simply had too many positions to fill. Women became employed in the Savings Bank and were allowed to reach high-level managerial positions. The women in the Post Office became some of the highest paid women in Britain (Cohn 1985).

Labor scarcity helped women even more in jobs where there were no strong objections to women working: They were readily accepted as schoolteachers because of cultural stereotypes linking women to working with children. However, as with clerical work, the occupation was expanding rapidly. Large numbers would be required as teachers. The dynamic economies in that era were in the northeastern cities. In places like Boston and New York, business booms and the rapid expansion of manufacturing soaked up the supply of male workers. Thus, women became schoolteachers in East Coast cities simply because male schoolteachers could not be found.

This had major economic consequences (Goldin 1986; Blumberg 1989). Had women not been willing to teach for low wages, when men generally were not, mass education might have been too expensive to be politically feasible (Fishlow 1966:435). And mass education increased real U.S. national income some 12% to 23% over the first 60 years of the 20th century (Denison 1962). Thus, U.S. women, through their paid work plus the human capital created by their teaching, have contributed formidably to the "wealth of their nation."

Men migrating away from home to seek work in distant places has often (but not always) facilitated women gaining economic power. Many men are gone. Labor is scarce. Women are the only workers available to do any job, high status or low status. In the MENA region, an area where women's labor force participation and status traditionally have been very low, male out-migration from non-oil nations to oil-rich nations has been a force promoting women's work in the oil-poor countries. Female labor force participation goes up in periods when men are away working—giving women jobs and, sometimes, money (in this region, many women have to turn over part or all of their pay to their families). When the oil-rich Gulf states shed labor and the men return home, they reclaim their old jobs and female labor force participation diminishes (Hammam 1986; Hijab 2003).

Male absence in the oil-poor countries of the region, however, doesn't always improve women's economic power (Blumberg 1989). Howe (1985) studied the impact of male migration from Yemen to the oil-rich Gulf countries. National statistics showed that, due to male absence, 45% of rural Yemeni women were engaged in agriculture full-time as *unpaid family labor*. It was the older, nonmigrating males, though, who controlled all the income from agriculture.[14]

Men going away to war can also lead to economic power for women. The longer and/or more often men are away, the more likely that arrangements have evolved so that others are taking care of the males' economic affairs. Consider the following examples: (a) the Viking era in Scandinavia and (b) U.S. women during World War II.

a. The women of the Viking era (about 800 to about 1100 A.D.) had considerable autonomy. Women ran the farms in their husbands' absence. They were allowed to inherit land. Many widows in fact became important landowners (Hurstwic n.d.). Other women were involved with trade: Mierswa (2017:6) cites Stalsberg (2001) and Stig Sorensen (2009:261), stating, "Women all around Scandinavia and Norse settlements have been found to be buried with [merchant's] scales and weighing equipment." They also had legal protection from unwanted sexual attention (Hurstwic n.d.; Jesch 1991, 2011). A striking example of female autonomy was Aud the Deep Minded. When both her husband and son died, she took the family assets and moved herself and her daughters to Iceland. There she distributed land to her followers, becoming one of Iceland's most important settlers (Jesch 1991, 2011; Pruitt 2016).

b. During World War II, American women worked in war industries in large numbers, holding jobs that previously had been filled by white men. They earned higher salaries than "women's work" paid. Women also worked in many other capacities in niches that had opened due to the conflict. These ranged from mail carriers to professional athletes. Women in the labor force rose from 27% to 37% of the workforce from 1940 to 1944, and the number of women working for pay almost doubled, to 20 million workers. By 1945, 4.5 million women worked as factory operatives, a 112% increase (Schweitzer 1980:89–90). But factories converted to peacetime production and refused to rehire women; they were replaced by (white) men returning from the war. This pushed women back into their female-typed jobs. Without question, women during the war had considerably more freedom—and income—than in the postwar period through the 1950s (Kessler-Harris 1993).

Access to Human Capital

Women are more likely to have strategic indispensability when they have skills that are economically valuable. Women with more education and more experience are paid more than other women (England 1992). This applies both to their years of education and to the years they have worked continuously for one employer. Working for one employer matters because this gives you *firm-specific* skills, skills that you learn exclusively from on-the-job experience with your present employer. England found that education and continuous experience explain about one third of the pay differential between men and women.

Education has been the key to women entering many strategic occupations. Women's historical entrance into nursing, social work, teaching, and clerical work was predicated on their having the education that would allow them to fill these positions. In MENA and South Asian societies that are otherwise hostile to women's employment, education often has been the key to getting women into the small number of occupations open to them. For example, Saudi Arabia makes exceptions to its constraints on women working to allow women to take jobs in nursing and teaching other females (El-Sahabary 2003).

Sometimes women obtained skills from being married to a man in a skilled occupation or coming from a family with a traditional family occupation. This allowed women to participate in the family business. In 18th century Paris, women were often the active operating partner in businesses that were nominally controlled by men. They sold goods and services, kept accounts, arranged for credit, paid the workers, and in some cases, arranged for the use of force in collecting debts from deadbeat creditors (Melish 2015). When her husband died, a woman could often take over the business in his absence. In preindustrial Europe as a whole, widows often maintained their financial independence by continuing the operation of the family trade. This prevented economic necessity from forcing them to remarry (Leyser 2002; Ogilvie 2003).

The importance of education in determining women's access to occupational power can be shown by the extent to which men have resisted women's education until quite recently, because they wished to maintain exclusive male access to desirable jobs.

One of the clearest historical examples, however, occurred here in the United States: restricting women's access to medical school. Women were systematically denied entry into most of the major American medical schools. For a woman to obtain medical training, she had to be foreign-born or had to travel overseas to get an education. Zurich and Paris became particularly important locations for the training of American women doctors, but the openings in these locations were limited. There were a number of women's medical colleges in the United States. These institutions had problems attracting qualified faculty because men wouldn't teach there. As a result, many of these schools earned a legitimate reputation for providing substandard training, further limiting women's capacity to obtain necessary skills (Walsh 1977).

Some of the antifeminist campaigns were more colorful than others. When, in 1869, some nonchauvinistic male doctors invited female colleagues to clinical lectures at Philadelphia's Pennsylvania Hospital, male medical students objected. During the first class, the male students waited until the last hour of lecture and then showered the women with a nonstop barrage of paper projectiles, tinfoil balls, and tobacco quids. After all attempts to maintain order failed, the hospital canceled any further attempt to coeducate clinical sections.

The first years of the 20th century actually produced retrogression rather than progress. The handful of medical schools that had opened to women in the 19th century reduced their offerings in the early 1900s. At Tufts, the faculty found that their top medical students were all women and that the men were forced into shyness and awkwardness having to compete with females. Their solution was to ban women from the main medical program and put them in an inferior, underfunded female college. More commonly, medical schools opened up their ranks de jure to women but in practice maintained strict quotas limiting female admissions. Some medical schools, Yale and Emory among them, cited explicit discriminatory policies against women in their promotional literature (Walsh 1977).

This exclusionary strategy basically worked. Until 1900 in the United States, fewer than 5% of all physicians were women. That number had risen only to 7.2% by 1970 (although now there are about equal numbers of women and men in U.S. medical schools). Today, school is a key to women's economic power. Taking away that key can be devastating.

Commercialization of Women's Home-Based Production/ Enterprise (Ideal Circumstances Required)

Women can gain significant economic power when their domestic activities become commercially valuable, if they are able to keep the money. The most obvious example of this occurred in the Industrial Revolution. The first modern factories were textile factories. They hired spinners and weavers. Women spun thread and wove cloth in the home. When they needed cheap labor for the factories, the bosses could just take pretrained women and put them on the job. Factory jobs were relatively well paid. In return for longer hours, women got substantial autonomy and the ability to live on their own, independent of fathers and brothers (Pinchbeck 1981; Kessler-Harris 1993). What happened in the Industrial Revolution has been replicated in nearly every country in Europe, the Americas, or Asia that started industrializing. In all cases, the earliest factories were textile factories; the workers in them were mainly women (Chapkis and Enloe 1983).

More generally, a great deal of women's entrepreneurial activity in the Global South is home-based (Blumberg 2001b). It saves them spending money for rent and both time and money commuting, while it keeps them in the place where their children can help them when not in school. Moreover, the older children or nearby female kin typically help with childcare and domestic chores, which the woman entrepreneur can quickly check in on and supervise while running her business. In a large-scale study of Ecuador's informal sector (Blumberg 1991a; Magill et al. 1991),[15] one of the biggest differences between women and men clients of microfinance programs proved to be the much greater likelihood that the women's businesses started out—and often remained—home-based.

This source of economic power is very fragile, however. Attempts to empower women through the use of traditional female activities have often failed. The problem is that basic female domestic skills are widely held and are not scarce. There may be very few trained oncological nurses. So those nurses have economic power. There are a lot more trained piano teachers. Those women have less power. Virtually all women can do basic housework tasks. Therefore, even if these tasks become commercially valuable, there is an immediate glut of qualified women who can do this—which keeps the occupation oversupplied and underpaid.

Even worse is when men exploit women's domestic skills for their own benefit. This was the case in Maria Mies's *The Lace Makers of Narsapur* (1982). In Andhra Pradesh, India, most (except the lowest castes) observed purdah (female seclusion). The husband dealt with the middlemen who brought the materials and picked up the finished product. He kept the income. The women got nothing for their intense labor. But their lacemaking also meant they didn't have to experience the loss of face for themselves and their family of having to go out on the street to earn income the family needed.

Domestic textile skills produced significant female power in the early Industrial Revolution because the industry was linked to a gigantic economic expansion. There was massive demand for machine-made textiles, and wages were excellent. When the demand for women's services is more marginal, the payoff to women with domestic skills is much lower. There have been various attempts by economic developers to empower women by creating industries where women commercially sell traditional products made in the home. Often these projects are linked to the tourist industry. These domestic empowerment projects often fail miserably. There are few more pathetic spectacles than going to some new expensive "farmer's market" in a city in the Global South to see 70 or 80 women sitting around a plaza trying to sell identical bottles of hot sauce or jam to the handful of tourists passing through.

That said, when there is a female domestic skill that is relatively scarce, or the demand for domestic skills is extremely high, then the commercialization of women's domestic activities can be a meaningful source of economic power. But this only works under ideal circumstances.

An example of such favorable circumstances was found in a Colombian public housing complex. Apartments were assigned at random. Women who, by luck, got a ground-floor apartment were able to run home-based businesses that gave them twice as much income as that of women on upper floors who had businesses. The lucky ground-floor women closed the gender earnings gap by 58.5% and earned an income above the poverty line (Doering and Liu forthcoming).

This is an exception. The huge number of women who can flood the market for "women's services" dooms most such endeavors to economic marginality, at best, or failure.

Absence of Male Preference by Controllers of Capital or Sales

Economic power often is linked to the ability to play a key role in a successful business. If women have less access to capital and sales than men, women's businesses will be less successful than men's businesses. If the strategic players in large businesses are those that bring in capital or sales, women will be less likely to be those key individuals.

It is often harder for women than men to obtain business loans. There is significant evidence of credit discrimination against female-owned businesses in the United States (Cavalluzzo, Cavalluzzo, and Wolken 2002; Mijid 2014), although some counter studies exist (Orser, Riding, and Manley 2006). Gender discrimination in business lending seems to be less of an issue in Europe (Ogena and Popov 2015).

Credit discrimination against women has been a far more severe problem in the Global South. In the Belgian Congo, a woman could not get a loan without her husband signing for her (MacGaffey 1988). In Tanzania, village elders would typically refuse to cosign loans for women, while they would freely do so for men (Ishengoma 2005). The resulting credit constraints could be fairly severe. In a study of 242 households in Mongoro, Tanzania, lack of access to credit was the single largest factor leading to gender inequities in business success. Sixty-eight percent of women reported being held back by inadequate access to capital. No other factor of production came even close (Ishengoma 2005). The exception is microcredit, discussed in the next section, on "Women's Economic Organization."

In the Global South, where farming is a particularly important activity, access to money can be less important than access to land. At the most basic level, without access to land, there can be no farming. At a secondary level, without clear ownership of their land, farmers have no collateral with which to get agricultural loans. Before colonialism, women in parts of the Global South owned land and were farmers in their own right (e.g., in Southeast Asia and some West African ethnic groups). European colonial administrators' consistent policy was to reorganize land tenure, taking land away from women and giving it to men (Boserup 1970; Lewis 1984). Much of this was part of an explicit European strategy to make women dependent on men so that export crops could be grown with cheap unpaid family labor (Henn 1995). In some cases, local men could be just as vigorous as Europeans in favoring men for land ownership. In Zimbabwe, where the Shona and the Ndebele, the main ethnic groups, are patrilineal/patrilocal, land traditionally passed from male to male. One of the early actions of the post-independence government was distributing formerly European lands to *male* Zimbabwean owners (Folbre 1988). Even where formal law was not particularly discriminatory, entrenched local customs could limit women's access to land, as Bashaw (2005) illustrates for Ethiopia (which has patrilineal ethnic groups with male land inheritance). Large international land deals also concentrate land in male hands; women are less capable of mobilizing social networks to protect their lands from predatory speculators (Behrman, Meinzen-Dick, and Quisumbing 2012).

Women's success in many businesses depends on being able to sell their merchandise. Somali women were not so lucky. They had been the traditional marketers of sheep and goats. However, when the Italians colonized Somalia, they insisted on trading exclusively with men (Kapteijns 1993). In Zimbabwe, all African participation in marketing was reduced by colonial policies giving Europeans a monopoly on wholesale trading. This disproportionately hurt women, who had been particularly active in this sector (Folbre 1988).

Ironically, one of the sectors where U.S. women still have restricted access to marketing is in the selling of financial services in elite Wall Street firms. The function of bringing in wealthy individual or corporate clients is called "rainmaking." Women may not be assigned major clients for fear that these clients would rather deal with men. Louise Roth describes the logic of this as "homophily": assuming that customers are more likely to trust and respect individuals like themselves. Women are sent to meet with female clients. Men are sent to meet with men. Because most of the American corporate elite is male, using homophily to pick the salesperson cuts women off from some of the most lucrative clients in the industry. Women find their compensation reduced and their strategic power limited because they are not the key players in working with the customers that matter (Roth 2004).

Women's Economic Organization

Where women in the Global South have long histories of economic activities that give them resources under their control (i.e., economic power), they seem to create some fairly similar ways of aggregating that power in the form of organizations that advance their interests. They also tend to create entities that provide working capital for members. Sometimes, both functions are served in a single entity. In other cases, there are separate associations or groups handling their professional interests on the one hand and their working capital needs on the other. These economically active women—rural and urban and at all levels from microenterprises to high-level or international businesses—are found mostly in the Andes, the Caribbean, Southeast Asia, and in the parts of sub-Saharan Africa where women long have been traders (especially in West Africa), whether in a local market or by selling and buying in widely dispersed sites.[16]

Working three times in Nigeria in the latter 1980s, where most traders are women, Blumberg was told the length of the week in the traditional calendar in different areas depended on whether the local market was held every 4 days or every 5 days. Women traders also said that during the colonial wars, women traders banded together and traveled in armed convoys, staying in business. Although Yoruba and Igbo women are famed traders, the most striking group of businesswomen she met in 1986 were secluded Hausa women in Northern Nigeria (Blumberg 1987; Gamble et al. 1988). Around 1800, the patrilineal/patrilocal Hausa were conquered by mounted jihadi Fulani warriors; 80% were converted to Islam. This included a form of seclusion marriage, *kulle*, which was seen as high status. Almost all secluded Muslim Hausa women operate home-based businesses (Blumberg 1987).[17] As the sole woman on a four-person team, however, Blumberg was the only one who could enter Hausa family compounds where there were secluded women. She saw the separate huts the women kept for their own "women's currency," white enamel or brass basins (*kwane*), piled to the ceiling. They used it among themselves—and for their daughters' start-up capital (a kind of dowry) when they married and moved to their husbands' villages.

Entrepreneurial women with fewer constraints to their mobility, in sub-Saharan Africa, Southeast Asia, and elsewhere (e.g., the Andes, the Caribbean), often used a simpler system: They would belong to one or more traditional rotating savings and credit associations (ROSCAs), which had differing numbers of members and different levels of weekly (or biweekly or monthly) contributions. All had a "kitty" system: every X weeks or months, a different woman would get the kitty from that meeting.

One ethnic group of women Blumberg studied in Guinea-Bissau, the Muslim Saracule, made a good living from informal cross-border trade with the Gambia, buying fine cloth and the mordents, dyes, and other ingredients for dying their purchases back home, and then selling the finished product wholesale and/or retail in Bissau. Most belonged to one ROSCA that gave them a few fairly small payouts a year for working capital and another where they got only one—but large—payout a year (these had 48 to 50 members with weekly distribution meetings except during holidays). When they got their payout, they bought capital goods and most of their stock. Another multiethnic group of mostly Muslim women dominated the wholesale deepwater (pelagic) fish trade, selling a ton a week in season, a huge transaction in one of the world's poorest countries.

The businesswomen of Guinea-Bissau also had their own organization, *Associaciao das Mulheres de Actividade Economica* (Association of Economically Active Women; Blumberg 1998). It was so well-led and well-organized, that the USAID Trade and Investment project Blumberg worked with[18] chose it over male, mixed, and other female economic organizations to help create and run a non-bank financial institution in a country that essentially had no banking system for anyone below the top elites.

More recently, Blumberg and Malaba (2016) studied informal cross-border traders (ICBTs) at six borders in Southern Africa.

ICBTs were overwhelmingly female. In addition to belonging to a national organization, many traveled in groups of two or, often, three (that way, on the overnight international buses, they could take turns sleeping and watching their possessions, and they would stay very close as each went through customs, hoping to reduce bribe seeking). More dangerously, women crossing from Zambia or Zimbabwe to Kasane, Northern Botswana, said they rarely got visas long enough to sell their goods, so some braved the wild animal corridors at night, crossing with solitary male elephants, buffalo, hyenas, lions, and other predators and prey.

These professional traders and entrepreneurs are at one end of a continuum. At the other end are the mostly women clients of microcredit groups. Many of these are microfinance institutions (MFIs), which have evolved sets of "best practices" since the early 1980s. These microcredit providers have matured into the largest program in the world offering small loans to women (via individual loans or solidarity group loans, where about five women mutually guarantee each other's debt). The best known MFI is the Grameen Bank, founded in Bangladesh by Mohammad Yunus (who got the 2006 Nobel Peace Prize for his work). The latest data show 211,119,547 borrowers (about 75% women) and 114,311,586 *poorest* borrowers (about 83% women; Microcredit Summit Campaign 2015).[19] Why so many women? They have been found to be better than men at repaying their loans—and making their payments on time. This is why the clients of microfinance have been so disproportionately female in the past several decades.

Favorable Balance of Nondiscriminatory Versus Patriarchal Noneconomic Institutions

Women's economic power is linked to political power. When government and cultural institutions support women, they usually have easier access to economic opportunities. If these same institutions are patriarchal, women often face multiple obstacles to earning and controlling income.

Colonialism often worked to the disadvantage of women. But many precolonial societies were patriarchal, too. Their traditional village rulers could be more antifeminist than official European administrators (Henn 1995; Bashaw 2005). Even so, the Global South contained some regions with more equitable gender relations (e.g., some ethnic groups in sub-Saharan Africa, most of Southeast Asia)—until the Europeans arrived, dispossessing women and granting power to men (Boserup 1970). Folbre (1988), writing about Zimbabwe, dominated by the patrilineal Shona and Ndebele, argues that colonial women faced three separate institutions that favored patriarchy.

European administrators preferred dealing with males. They wanted unpaid family labor to work on plantations, which was difficult to implement if women had their own businesses. *Christian missionaries* were opposed to women working, because free women were more likely to become "immoral." *Traditional elders* worried that women would migrate to the cities, allowing them to escape the elders' control. All three groups agreed on the undesirability of giving women access to new Western economic opportunities.

This led to a systematic exclusion of women from education and technical training. The situation in the Belgian Congo was typical. Here, women were barred from formal education past the minimum level. Six years of education were offered for boys but only three for girls. Girls received no instruction in French even though it was the language of colonial administration and Western business. Girls received no training in commercial agriculture (MacGaffey 1988).

The agricultural education exclusion is significant. Most colonial administrations sought to introduce modern technologically advanced agriculture. Agricultural extension services were created to train local farmers in Western methods. Women were nearly always excluded from these training projects (Lewis 1984; Heyzer 1986). Some of this exclusion continued under post-Independence governments. Ishengoma (2005) notes that in Tanzania, agricultural extension agents still avoid training women.

Governments and institutions can have beneficial effects on women's status even when they are in no way feminist. Consider the case of Singapore.

Singapore has vacillated between traditional gender roles and vigorous support for women working (Lee, Campbell, and Chia 1999). In the early 20th century, it was a rubber-growing colony. Sexism ruled. Women were confined to traditional sex-typed roles (e.g., cooking, childcare, and prostitution). As Singapore became independent, its economy evolved toward financial services and light export manufacture. At this point, the government decided that women working was desirable. In 1971, the prime minister suggested to the Singapore Employer's Federation that industry hire more women. Singapore was an authoritarian state; following the prime minister's suggestions was not optional. Factories were moved near the housing estates so that women would have short commutes. The government trained older women returning to work (Kazeno 2004) and created a public day care program (Lee, Campbell, and Chia 1999). The new jobs were fairly well-paid skilled or semi-skilled work. In 2015, Singapore ranked the 15th most gender equal among 155 countries (United Nations Development Programme 2015).

Still, Singapore, with a 74.3% ethnic Chinese population (Central Intelligence Agency 2018), who have a more patriarchal history, is less gender egalitarian than Buddhist Southeast Asian nations such as Laos, Thailand, and Myanmar (Burma), with thousands of years of local-level gender equality (White 1982, 1988, 1990, 1992a, 1992b).

Currently, many international nongovernmental organizations (INGOs) and international and local feminist organizations promote women's economic power. Much of the international development community, including the United Nations and the World Bank, also has embraced gender equality as a strategy to promote economic development (World Bank 2015; United Nations Development Programme 2017). Indeed, the only purpose of some single-focus transnational organizations, such as the Global Fund for Women and the International Women's Tribune Center, is to promote global women's empowerment. Local women's organizations in most of the world's countries do so as well: The *International Directory of Women's Organizations* lists more than 2,000 feminist organizations in nations ranging from Afghanistan to Zimbabwe (Asian Pacific Infoserve 2018).

International and national feminism have real effects. Moghadam's (2010) discussion of women's struggles in North Africa describes a quite successful example.

The 1990s and 2000s saw a big upsurge in women's welfare in Morocco, Tunisia, and Algeria. Women's employment share rose in law, medicine, banking, tourism, and business ownership. This was at a time of neoliberal reform when all three countries were aligning their economic policies with the West and working to increase exports to Europe. This increased their receptivity to large international campaigns for women's rights. Each nation signed the 1979 Convention on the Elimination of All Forms of Discrimination Against Women (CEDAW) and the 1995 Beijing Declaration on women's rights.

Local feminist organizations were important, too. They agitated for changes in family and labor law and won concessions. They were able to prevent women's employment from being a negative factor in child custody cases. They obtained restrictions on sexual harassment, safety regulations for pregnant workers, and a toughening of antidiscrimination laws. International organizations could not have done the lobbying that led to these changes; local organizations would not have succeeded if global opinion makers were not on their side. Together they had a coalition that increased women's economic power.

El Salvador is another example of local women's cooperation and success: After the 1992 Peace Accords ended the 12-year civil war, right-wing ARENA and left-wing FMLN women members of parliament—against the odds—got a law passed against gender-based violence while the men continued to squabble on other issues (Blumberg 2001a).

Absence of Armed Conflict Near Women's Homes

War is bad for women's power. When women cannot go into the street without risk of being attacked or killed, their mobility is greatly restricted. This impedes or stymies their ability to carry out their activities. In armed conflict, physical security depends on the protection of armed males. If bodyguards give women orders, they have limited ability to disobey men.[20]

This is not to say that the absence of war guarantees women's economic power. Most settings in the world are peaceful, including those where women are under male economic domination. However, being in constant physical danger is a devastating experience. Women living under these conditions often find their power is severely constrained, even if other factors that would have been operating in civilian life would have made them relatively autonomous.

How war affects women can vary dramatically. Women respond differently to the *presence* of armed conflict *near* their homes, depending on

- the length and intensity of the conflict;
- how subjugated or not women had been before the conflict;

- the extent to which women participate in a wide variety of roles with the combatants;

- whether women are linked by geography, kinship, or common suffering with combatants; and

- whether the soldiers on the women's side are committed to gender egalitarian goals.

War rarely leaves women in good positions. Consider two very opposite, long-duration wars: Afghanistan, where men wholly dominate women, and El Salvador, where the FMLN rebels proclaimed themselves the protectors of women from rape by government soldiers.[21]

In both countries, the war involved widespread fighting that affected high proportions of the rural populace. Both have a rural techno-economic base of non-irrigated plow agriculture in which men are the primary cultivators and women have high levels of economic dependency. Both have ideologies of machismo/male superiority.

There are significant differences, however. The first one is the kinship/property system. Afghanistan's kinship system is completely male-dominated. El Salvador has bilateral kinship. Rural Afghanistan women have *very* limited freedom of movement. When Afghan women leave the house, they almost invariably wear head-to-toe burqas designed for total anonymity. The heavy mesh eyeholes produce blurring and limited peripheral vision. There are no identifying decorations. Women have to be inconspicuous and anonymous, since they are intruding on men's public space (Blumberg 2016b).

In comparison, rural El Salvador women wear light, practical, hot-climate clothing. They have few sources of income but are usually free to move about, including going to the market to buy or sell food.

War affected Afghanistan and El Salvador in profoundly different ways.

In Afghanistan, the typical household is multigenerational, with a senior male in charge. Men dominate women's lives and actions. Afghan women with older males living in the home would have far less occasion to go out than women in a household without adult males.

Viterna (2013) argues that in the El Salvador war, men soon vanished from the rural villages. As the war intensified, more and more of the men went to the guerrilla camps. The women were left behind to cope. In rebel areas, able-bodied women were expected to provide logistical aid to the guerrillas, bringing food or transporting arms and materiel. This started with women purchasing agents in cities and extended to women living near combat zones who helped deliver needed arms, ammunition, equipment, clothing, and everything else required to support the war. The rebels sent women with young children, the old, and the infirm to refugee camps in Honduras. These camps were run with great competence by women, many of whom had little education or prior work experience.

Young people, both male and female, were recruited for the FMLN camps as combatants. The FMLN guaranteed young women that they would be safe from rape. This gave the rebels the reputation of being protectors of women, the "good guys" in the war—versus the Government troops' notorious reputation for violent rapes.

After the war, the rural economy became somewhat less unequal. Rural male combatants received land because of the 1992 Peace Accords. Few female combatants—although they composed 30% of demobilized FMLN at the time—received land. Economic opportunities for rural women have been limited. On the plus side, some microfinance programs came to the countryside. Women could still earn some seasonal money harvesting coffee (Blumberg 2001a). Viterna (2013) describes only two women ex-combatants who got well-paid jobs after demobilization: One had worked with a high-level male military commander who helped her get the job; the other was hired by a gender-focused NGO she had worked with during the war. These were the *only* two cases where the women said they had egalitarian relationships with their male partners, including in decision making. Viterna describes other women who were frontline fighters for years, then went back to the rural milieu and became full-time housewives whose husbands were the decision makers in the household.

War did not bring any notable increase in the "power of the purse" for women in either nation. In the absence of widespread economic opportunities for women, men continue to dominate both nations—although women in El Salvador have a far better position than their Afghan counterparts.

Conclusions

The conclusions tell a very simple story: The power of the purse is positive. In its absence, negative consequences emerge, from the level of individual women to the future of planet Earth.

- With more economic power for women, good things happen (with one generally short-term exception discussed later in this chapter). With less economic power for women, bad things happen.

- The *micro-level* effects of economic power or its absence affect individuals and families.

- Economic power or its absence also affects the *macro level* of large groups—social classes, racial/ethnic groups, whole countries, regions, the global economy, and the planet.

The Micro Level

The first boon of an increase in income or other economic resources is increased self-confidence. Many studies have found this (Blumberg 2016a cites references). And with the increased self-confidence that comes from a rise in one's economic resources, women and men alike tend to translate this into speaking up and getting more say in household decisions.

People with increased economic power tend to be more assertive—and successfully so—about *household decisions* concerning:

1. family *economic affairs*: decisions about buying, saving, and selling—what income *should* be devoted to and what it *should not* be devoted to;

2. family *domestic well-being*: how much attention and resources should be devoted to children's (a) *education,* (b) *health,* and

(c) *nutrition* and whether this should vary if the children are boys or girls;

3. family *fertility and composition*: how many children and the breakdown by sex—and how to achieve this, from specific contraceptive methods to sex-selective abortion to accepting "all the children that God gives us" (Blumberg 1984 discusses these "life options"); and

4. family *division of childcare and domestic labor.* Unfortunately, unlike (1), (2), and (3), there is only a modest relationship between a woman's income earned and contributed to the household and the amount and type of childcare and housework each partner does (Blumstein and Schwartz 1991). So a woman who has just gotten a raise or a tidy profit from a business will probably be disappointed. It's tough to translate that boost in income into a mutually agreed-on new split of "who does what." Diapering the baby? Ironing the clothes? Changing the light bulbs? Taking the kids to a movie? It's surprising how little that bonus or big sale helps reduce women's housework burden.

Increased economic power also tends to improve a person's outcomes on a set of *life options* found in all known human societies (Blumberg 1984), including, for example, women versus men's say in

- marriage (whether, when, and with whom);

- divorce (whether, for what reasons);

- sexual activity (and, if yes, whether both partners are pleasured);

- fertility (whether, when, how many, how far apart, and, if sex preference is for males, how to achieve it), and

- freedom of movement (Blumberg 1984 discusses a more complete list of life options).

More economic power should increase one's voice in all of the above. But for women, sometimes it doesn't happen or happens only a little, due to individual traits or the norms and laws of the larger society. These "discount factors" (Blumberg 1991b) can be negative or positive for either gender at the *micro* level but are still negative to varying degrees for women in *all* contemporary nations at the *macro* level.[22]

There are two more micro-level considerations:

1. Differential spending patterns that have been empirically well-documented for women versus men with provider obligations: *Women tend to spend disproportionately on the education, health, and nutrition of their children compared with counterpart men.*

2. When a woman first starts increasing her economic power, the more the men in her life—husband or partner, father,

brothers—view her gaining income as a zero-sum game in which *they* lose, the more likely there will be a (usually) short-term spike in violence. This is the *only* negative effect of women increasing "the power of the purse." In the longer term, however, the strongest factor predicting male violence against women is the women's *economic dependency*, according to David Levinson's (1989) 90-society study.[23] Women without income are the most likely to be beaten.

The Macro Level

1. The most consequential outcome of women's economic power is the aggregated impact of women spending disproportionately more than men on children's education, health, and nutrition. These are three of the principal components of human capital. *Increasing human capital increases (a) national income growth and (b) indicators of national well-being.*

2. Almost as consequential are the macro impacts of fertility— although it's now falling almost worldwide. Even so, recent research (Das Gupta, Bongaarts, and Cleland 2011) has found there *still is an inverse relationship between fertility and national income growth.* Nine of the ten highest-fertility countries in the world are in sub-Saharan Africa, where access to modern contraception, especially in rural areas, is the lowest. The tenth is Afghanistan, where availability is low and economically dependent women have no say if a man wants more children.

3. There is a very high *inverse correlation* (no causation is claimed) between women's labor force participation (LFP) and armed conflict, within or across international borders. Specifically, every 5% drop in women's LFP is linked to an almost *500% rise* in armed conflict (Caprioli 2000, 2005; Hudson et al. 2009). Moreover, *all* seven of the nations with the lowest women's LFP are presently engaged in armed conflict: Algeria, Afghanistan, Iran, Iraq, Jordan, Syria, and Saudi Arabia (Blumberg 2016a).

4. South Asia has a serious problem: It has the world's highest rate of malnutrition among children 5 and under even though it is far from being the poorest region. That problem is linked to the low female LFP/lack of economic power of its women (Blumberg, Dewhurst, and Sen 2013a, 2013b). Because young women are seen as liabilities, their families marry them off very young— often, shortly after puberty. Then their in-laws expect a child within a year. South Asia has the highest proportion of women who marry and give birth as teenagers compared with any other region (Blumberg et al. 2013a, 2013b). But if the bride gives birth at 18 or younger, she has a 200% to 500% increased risk of maternal mortality (Sethuraman and Duvvury 2007). She also has a 25% to 50% chance of delivering a low birth weight (LBW) baby (Sethuraman and Duvvury 2007). Worse yet, LBW babies are

likely to have lifelong cognitive and health problems (e.g., early onset male heart disease, which is quite prevalent in South Asia).

5. The planet has an even more serious problem: environmental degradation, increasing water scarcity, and increasing land and ocean temperatures. In most of the Global South's rural areas, women still are the primary collectors of firewood and haulers of water. They generally are very aware of the relationship between deforestation and their increasing difficulty in getting both firewood and water. Where they have economic power, they have more voice in household as well as community decisions about deforestation, which lowers both the water table and the total amount of rainfall (Blumberg 2008). Without economic power, they have little or no voice. Deforestation is neither the only nor the principal cause of climate change. But it is one that could be better addressed and perhaps ameliorated where women have more economic power.

The bottom line is that increasing women's power of the purse will not only increase gender equality, but it will help reduce the imminence and impact of some of the world's worst challenges and increase key measures of wealth and well-being.

NOTES

1. The following discussion draws heavily from previous work by the editors. See Blumberg (1984, 1988, 2015, 2016a) and Cohn (1985).

2. If the women producers also have other strategic indispensability factors (e.g., organizing on their own behalf, control of technical expertise, and competition for their services; Blumberg 1984), this further increases the likelihood that their work will translate into economic power.

3. This doesn't guarantee that women will have economic power, however. In Alice Schlegel's (1972) 66-society sample of matrilineal societies, women inherited but brothers and/or husbands often had acquired more economic power. In a community-based natural resource management project in mostly matrilineal

Central/Southern Malawi, Blumberg (2004b) found women did almost all the very hard work in the project-promoted aquaculture fishponds but rarely controlled the proceeds. The husbands sold the fish in the market, keeping most of the cash, telling the wives they would be cheated since they were illiterate; women didn't know market prices but knew they were shortchanged.

4. Most Caribbean women have varying levels of West African ancestry; West African women are renowned traders.

5. Blumberg (1978) calls them "techno-economic bases"; Lenski's (1966) term is "modes of subsistence."

6. At the end of the dry season, underbrush, bushes, and small trees were cut down and left to dry. Next, a carefully controlled burn

left ashes that contained all the nutrients found in the plants. The first year, there would be few weeds and high yields, but within several years, weeds multiplied and yields fell and a new plot was cleared. Now, as sub-Saharan Africa populations rise, plots often are used too long, especially where women don't own land.

7. Archeological evidence indicates that early horticultural societies were generally peaceful and gender-egalitarian (e.g., in "Old Europe," including present-day Romania, Bulgaria, and Greece, before the first invasion by mounted Kurgan herders about 6,300 years ago; Gimbutas 1980, 1982; Eisler 1987). Later, many horticulturalists switched voluntarily or by conquest to patrilineal–patrilocal kin/property systems that allowed high-level men to have more than one wife, increasing their resources since women were key cultivators. Women's position then depended on whether they had resources of their own.

8. Millennia later, it was brought to the rest of the world by European conquerors and colonizers.

9. There is evidence that some farm women in northwestern Europe kept control of small economic resources (e.g., taking their butter, eggs, handicrafts, and occasional chickens to the fairs and markets; see Ward 2006 about medieval England).

10. This is why China and India have populations of about 1.4 billion each and Southeast Asia has 620+ million people (vs. about 509 million in the full 28-country European Union, including the United Kingdom; Blumberg, 2016a).

11. As Diamond (1997) describes (and Engels 1884 also discussed in *The Origin of the Family, Private Property and the State*), the Eurasian landmass got almost all the world's important domesticatable animals, including those used to pull the plow.

These animals deposited their manure as fertilizer on the large, single-crop fields.

12. Wage labor on farms (i.e., paid in money, not food) came only after the Industrial Revolution (Cochrane 1979).

13. See England (1992) and Cohn (1999) for discussions of the causes of gendered wage differentials.

14. Howe wrote that providing women with water availability closer to home and kerosene for cooking would free enough time for the women to increase their time in agriculture and for daughters to start school (if the men in their lives permitted it).

15. She was the sole woman and social scientist on a team of 11. She has worked in 48 countries since Peace Corps in Venezuela, in all major sectors of development. She uses her own version of Rapid Appraisal (Blumberg 2002).

16. Blumberg has worked with women traders/ entrepreneurs in many nations, starting in the Dominican Republic and Guatemala in 1985; Nigeria starting in 1986; Ecuador starting in 1989; Southeast Asia starting in 1992–1993; and Guinea-Bissau in 1997–1998. The most recent was in 2016, with informal cross-border traders in five Southern African nations (Blumberg and Malaba 2016).

17. Many prepared street foods sold by preadolescent nonsecluded daughters; others, operating at a larger scale, worked with a brother who handled the "outside" work with suppliers and customers. Polly Hill (1969) described the "separate purses" kept by West African economically active women and their husbands.

18. All of July and August 1997 and late December 1997 to end of February 1998.

19. The average client household has five members, so a billion+ people are affected. MFIs try to be self-sustaining. They usually charge an interest rate sufficient to, at minimum, cover full operating costs.

But the alternative, subsidized credit has a miserable record of loans "trickling up" to more affluent people who don't repay, leading donors to end the program after replenishing the loan fund several times (Adams 1984; Blumberg 2001b).

20. In most military situations, men will be armed and women will be unarmed. There are settings where women carry weapons as well. But even in these settings, the commanders overwhelmingly are men, and women are directly under male military control (see Viterna 2013, about women in war in El Salvador).

21. The Afghan war is still ongoing; it began in 2001 after the 9/11 attacks on the United States when a U.S.-headed coalition toppled the Taliban regime (1996–2001) that prohibited females from working and going to school. Their position is slightly better now (Blumberg 2016b). The 1980–1992 El Salvador war between a right-wing government and the left-wing FMLN has not led to a big rise in the position of still-subordinated rural women, even the ex-combatants (Viterna 2013).

22. At the micro level, the greater a person's assertiveness or relative attractiveness, the better their leverage. But the less a person cares about the partner or needs the other partner's income also leads to more leverage. At the macro level, the discount factors are still negative today for every nation, though far less in Sweden than in Saudi Arabia.

23. Blumberg (1978), using a 61-society sample, found that where women had well-established economic power, they were less likely to be beaten by their husbands.

Guide to the Book

Samuel Cohn and Rae Lesser Blumberg

Women's economic power is the strongest underpinning of women's level of equality in general—and a fundamental determinant of the dynamics of development. All too often, it is a backdrop in the study of gender and development and not the main focus. The purpose of this book, and the purpose of the leadoff chapter, is to put women's economic power back in the center of the analysis. The chapter "Power of the Purse" is Blumberg and Cohn's attempt to lay out a general theory of women's power. The chapter argues for the importance of women's strategic indispensability. It argues for the importance of women's strategic alliances. The rest of the chapter elaborates each of those two critical concepts, identifying the social correlates of both women's indispensability and women's alliances.

The causes and effects of gendered power are complex. The interrelation between gender and development is even more complex. There are far more causes and far more effects of women's economic power than can be listed in one chapter. This book is a fuller analysis of the causes and effects of women's power and its linkages to the development process. About one third of the invited chapters discuss the causes of women's economic power. The remainder cover the effects of such power. There are tie-ins to a broad variety of social changes both in the Global North and in the Global South.

The authors in this collection are some of the most prestigious and most important writing in the sociology of gender and development. Each was invited in because of his or her distinguished past contributions to gender analysis and because of her or his distinctive personalized point of view. The chapters are, by design, very different from one another. Nearly all of them extend the study of women's power, gender, and development in new and interesting directions that go beyond the already broad scope of our introductory chapter. As a result, this book is full of surprises. Surprises are good.

What does the book have above and beyond the Blumberg and Cohn general theory of women's economic power?

The *Hristov* piece is bloody. It shows how women in the Global South become disempowered during campaigns of rural proletarianization. In Colombia, there is a gigantic land grab as local capitalists and military men expel peasants from their lands and homes so the capitalists and military men can create agribusinesses and development projects for themselves. Women are pawns in this brutal game of dispossession. Rape is a standard tool for punishing women who refuse to abandon their lands. Sexual access to poor women is the reward for the men in death squads and paramilitary units who do the dirty work of forcing people off the land.

Blumberg builds on her theories of gender stratification and gender and development, introducing a new concept: "the created biology of gender stratification." Where women have economic power, the "created biology" helps them "be all that they can be" and often aids men as well. Where they don't, consequences can extend from malnutrition to murder. She examines females' equal economic position and gender equality among hunter-gatherers (about 96% of our *Homo sapiens* history) and shows that bonobo females' economic power and peaceful leadership undercut the view that men and all our close primate kin are "nasty animals." She traces women's economic power through history to today, providing new insights into horticultural and agrarian societies and today's Global North versus South.

The *Moghadam* piece is a double lesson on the evils of petroleum and the beneficent power of women's organizations. Moghadam contrasts Iran, where women are relatively powerless, with Tunisia, where women are relatively empowered. Iran's economic development is based on oil, an industry that marginalizes women. Tunisia has a more diversified development plan that emphasizes export industries in which women play a key role. Women are strategic assets in Tunisia because the economy needs their labor. Women are also better organized in Tunisia. Women's organizations produce a more favorable legal and political environment for women, which in turn gives women further economic and social advantages.

Jalali describes the economic and social consequences in India of women's lack of access to basic facilities of menstrual hygiene. It is difficult to maintain feminine sanitation in environments where women have no economic power. Furthermore, in rural India, sanitation is hard to maintain due to the lack of running water and sewage systems. However, cultural taboos, women's lack of or insufficient income, and restriction of their freedom of action are crucial factors that deprive women of access to modern sanitary napkins, washing facilities, and secure places for performing bodily functions. Women are at increased risk of gynecological problems and infections. Women's participation in work and education is restricted in much of rural India, especially. Powerlessness produces sanitation problems, which further increase women's powerlessness.

The *Cohn* piece shows how men's choices affect the economic power available to women. Most employers are male. They decide what occupations will be male and what occupations will be female. When do they let in women? When they need to economize on labor. When they need to export. When they have to work with other companies with women in strategic decision-making positions. Other special cases exist as well. These decisions to offer jobs to women reflect the different economics of different types of firms. The economics shape men's willingness to hire women. Men's willingness to hire women shapes the ability of women to enter occupations with organizational power.

The *Boatcă and Roth* article is a powerful reminder that economic power is shaped by those arbitrary social constructions known as national borders. Citizenship grants massive economic opportunities to some women while denying them to others. Ability to negotiate or contravene national borders becomes an important strategy for gaining economic power. Boatcă and Roth discuss migration, as well as how gender creates narrow and idiosyncratic roads to upward mobility through changing the legal definition of one's citizenship. Obtaining the legal right to migrate is often extremely sexual; the negotiation of national status occasionally must be done on one's back.

The *Leicht and Baker* piece has a contrarian but serious alternative view of women's power. Superficially, it would seem that women would be better off if they were economically powerful and men were less powerful. Leicht and Baker argue that this is not necessarily so. When men lose status, they become resentful and dangerous. They take their frustration out in greater violence against women. Leicht and Baker review the global consequences of males' resentment of their declining economic position. Not only do women face increased personal victimization, but they also face increased political powerlessness as men work to regain their lost status by supporting ever more antifeminist political movements.

Berry discusses how war affects women's power by considering the aftermath of civil wars in Rwanda, Bosnia, and Nepal. Losing family in warfare is always tragic. However, she points out that the loss of husbands and fathers can mean the loss of significant protection for women and daughters. In patriarchal societies, women who have lost their men are vulnerable to exploiters hoping to seize their lands and resources. Women in Rwanda, Bosnia, and Nepal had to respond to postwar threats by organizing among themselves for their own protection. This led not only to the creation of significant women's organizations but also to the greater inclusion of women in national politics.

Rothchild and Shrestha show that despite the progress documented for Nepali women in Berry's piece, life for females continues to be difficult in this poor country. Patriarchal norms are deeply ingrained. The authors interview Nepali women of various castes and ethnic groups to learn how this affects individual women's lives. Women have limited access to education and credit. Limited opportunities for women's employment lead to poverty and hunger. Nongovernmental organizations have been less than successful in providing meaningful alternatives. Migrating from Nepal is often one of the few good options. However, men who migrate limit women's access to foreign money. Women face legal barriers to migrating themselves. Women become trapped in lives of powerless drudgery with few meaningful economic prospects.

The *Fish and Sprague* piece covers an organizational attempt to improve the situation of one of the world's largest economically vulnerable populations of working women—domestic workers—by gaining them the support of the International Labor Organization. Women who work in homes as cleaners, cooks, or nursemaids are absolutely subject to low pay, long hours, arbitrary bad treatment, and too often, sexual assault at the hands of employers. Strange but true, there are now international conventions and accords to protect the union and legal rights of these workers. Fish and Sprague tell the story of how these implausible protections came about. Strategic allies and supportive organizations play a big role here.

* * *

Some of the chapters are theoretical. Some are graphic and violent. Some chapters discuss great victories. Others cover appalling defeats. Some chapters show women cleverly working the system. Others show the system utterly crushing women. All the chapters show something new and unexpected about gender, development, and women's economic power.

CHAPTER 3

Armed Actors, the Commodification of Women, and the Destruction of Childhood

Understanding the Connections Between Predatory Sexuality and the Violence of Capital in Colombia

Jasmin Hristov

When people hear the term *forced marriage* or *child brides*, they typically associate it with traditional practices in societies across Southeast Asia or Africa. This is not surprising given that best sellers in the field of women's oppression, such as *Half the Sky: Turning Oppression Into Opportunities for Women Worldwide* (2008), bring to us shocking stories of brutal violent acts against women and girls in countries such as Pakistan, India, Afghanistan, the Congo, Nigeria, and others. Nevertheless, Latin America's rate of child marriage, for instance, rivals that in high-prevalence countries in Africa and Asia (Barr 2017). Consider for a moment the following story that comes from 21st century Colombia. Hernan Giraldo, was a former paramilitary chief of the United Self-Defense Forces[1] (Autodefensas Unidas de Colombia, or AUC) and a large-scale landowner from the Department of Santa Marta.[2] In the early 2000s he was involved in 50 cases of sexual violence that he carried out on his ranch, against girls 14 years old and younger, including some who were as young as 9. In many of the cases, he kept the girls on his property as his "wives" or girlfriends. Many of the victims became pregnant as a result, and nine of them gave birth before they were 14. The youngest got pregnant at 12. Present-day paramilitary groups in Colombia continue to prey on children from low-income families in rural and urban areas where girls are coerced into sexual relationships and boys are recruited into the armed organizations as informants and gunmen. For instance, in the Uraba region across the Department of Antioquia and Choco, leaders of one of the most notorious present-day paramilitary groups, Autodefensas Gaitanistas de Colombia-Urabenos (also known as Clan del Golfo), openly announce to families that they will take their daughters away once they turn 10 years old (CODHES 2017). The consumption of girls as sexual objects who are appropriated and later discarded is one of the important expressions of paramilitary territorial domination, the consequences of which have been unwanted early pregnancies, forced plastic surgeries and abortions at unlicensed facilities, sexually transmitted diseases, disappearances, and even deaths. Sexual violence against children (under 12 years of age) in Colombia has reached epidemic proportions. Between 2008 and 2012, 48,915 children were victims of sexual abuse by armed actors. In 2012 alone the number was 13,230—of them 2,412 boys and 10,812 girls (Verdad Abierta 2014). In April 2017, a 4-month-old baby girl was sexually abused by a soldier from the Battalion 21 Vargas of the Colombian Armed Forces in Granada, Department of Meta (*El Colombiano* 2017). Sexual violence against children[3] and teens is part of a much more profound, widespread, and long-standing problem of violence against women.[4] In 2016, more than 15,000 girls and women were victims of sexual violence; 85% of them were under 17 years of age (CODHES 2017). Colombia is not an exceptional case. Latin America and the Caribbean is the region with the highest levels of non-intimate partner sexual violence[5] against women and the second highest in intimate partner violence. Seven out of the ten countries with the highest rates of femicide[6] in the world are in Latin America and the Caribbean (Yagoub 2016). This region also happens to have the highest income inequality and the highest rate of homicide in the world. Thirty-eight percent of the world's homicides take place here even though Latin America represents just over 8% of the world's population (UN Office on Drugs and Crime 2014; World Health Organization 2014).

It is interesting to note that Colombia is the country with the highest number of internally displaced people in the world—7.2 million (Norwegian Refugee Council 2018)—and ranks as having the second highest femicide rate in the world (Yagoub 2016). The intersection of forced displacement, poverty, and the normalization of violence against women has produced lethal outcomes exemplified by the emblematic case of the death of the indigenous 7-year-old girl Yuliana Samboni in Bogota. Yuliana's family was forcibly displaced from the Department of Cauca, a place ridden with paramilitary violence. She was living with her parents in Bogota when she was abducted, tortured, raped, and killed by the 38-year-old upper-class architect Rafael Uribe Noguera in 2016 (BBC Mundo 2016).

While it is useful to categorize violence for analytical purposes, it is important to remember that the way people experience or perpetrate violence is a lot more complex and multifaceted. For example, it is difficult to imagine a case scenario where sexual violence occurs without any elements of physical or emotional/psychological violence. Often one form of violence, such as structural violence, creates conditions conducive to another, such as domestic abuse. We must also consider the fact that violence can be categorized according to many different criteria, such as the form (e.g., sexual, physical), the scale (interpersonal, collective), the objectives or conditions out of which it arises (e.g., political, domestic, structural), the type of victim according to age (e.g., women, children), the motivation (e.g., gender-based, a tool of war), and so on. These categories can intersect or overlap; for instance, sexual violence may be used as a form of political violence if the victim is a woman who is a political activist. Therefore, looking not only at the form of violence but also at the people targeted, as well as those who benefit from it, can reveal larger power structures that are reliant on violence. Additionally, categories that differentiate violence against women from violence against children must be considered as fluid and in relation to each other, given that conditions characterized by high levels of violence against women also present high risk for violence against children and, on the other hand, children who have been victims of violence have a higher likelihood of becoming victims or perpetrators of violence as adults (Buvinic, Morrison, and Shifter 1999; Bott et al. 2012). Along the same lines, interpersonal and collective violence may feed off each other; for example, experience of political violence increases the likelihood of violence in intimate spaces, while at the same time poor male youths' willingness to use violence may be harnessed for political purposes (Pearce 2009). Last, violence by men against women is inseparable from violence by men against other men. For example, it is not uncommon that the men who use rape as a weapon of war have themselves experienced gender-based violence such as forced recruitment (Carpenter 2006) and are coerced into performing sexual violence against women. "Violence gives birth to itself, so we can rightly speak of chains, spirals, and mirrors of violence or as we prefer—a continuum of violence" (Scheper-Hughes and Bourgois 2004, cited in Pearce 2009). Hence, it is essential to recognize the complex linkages and interactions among the different modes of violence to arrive at a more holistic understanding of the mechanisms that can make violence so endemic. With this in mind, the central focus of the chapter is on the impact of the relationship between global capital and coercion on women's bodies and sexuality as manifested specifically in the relationship between sexual violence and land dispossession. Interwoven throughout the analysis are issues of violence for the purpose of repression (i.e., political violence), violence for the purpose of land dispossession, violence as an enabling instrument in sex trafficking, and entrenched harmful ideologies of masculinity and femininity in which all these violences are embedded.

Central to understanding the deeply rooted drivers of chronic violence[7] in Latin America is the question of violent regimes of capital accumulation, the most important expression of which has been land dispossession. Land is a vital source of subsistence for the rural population in most of the developing world. It is also intertwined with the social and cultural fabric of communities. Struggles for control over land rights and land use have become particularly acute since the onset of economic globalization over the past 35 years. Since the 1980s, there has been a global pattern of market-oriented agrarian restructuring characterized by a shift from (1) publicly, indigenously, and family-owned land used for subsistence food production and sale in local markets to (2) land used for large-scale industry, including agribusiness, mining, fossil fuel exploration and extraction, tourism, and infrastructure construction. Ample evidence exists of the destructive consequences of this policy for the livelihoods of millions of small-scale farmers and their children: loss of income and home; growing landlessness; profound inequality in landownership; food insecurity; rising poverty; declining health; disintegration of communities; and loss of culture (Lewontin 2000; Kay 2001; De Medeiros 2007; Bello 2009; Li 2009, 2011; McMichael and Schneider 2011; Kerssen 2013). Many communities of small-scale farmers, indigenous peoples, and Afro-descendants resist land dispossession (McMichael 2006); however, their struggles have been met with violent responses by state forces and paramilitary (parastatal) groups (Paley 2014; Solano 2015; Shipley 2017).

Paramilitary violence, exercised by non-state and/or state actors operating outside the boundaries of legality, is present in varying degrees across Latin America and other parts of the world. Commonly employed by economically and politically powerful groups, paramilitary violence targets social movements, human rights activists, and others who challenge the established political-economic model. It has also been instrumental in displacing small-scale farmers from land of strategic economic importance. The pro-capitalist violence that dispossesses people from the land and silences voices that seek social justice is of particular significance not only because of the quantity of direct victims it produces (people with no livelihood) but because it generates social conditions characterized by propensity for structural violence, femicide, sexual violence, human trafficking, organized crime, and gang membership as sustainable livelihoods are destroyed and people are forced to migrate or sell their labor/bodies at any price to survive.

Sexual violence against women in the Global South has been most frequently analyzed by the literature in the context of intimate partner violence while giving secondary importance to other conditions that place women at high levels of vulnerability, including armed conflict, forced displacement, and political repression. This chapter is intended to offer a new way of thinking about violence and gender that transgresses disciplinary boundaries and captures the complex interactions among multiple modes of violence by interweaving two seemingly unrelated themes: (1) land dispossession and (2) sexual violence with its underlying ideologies that objectify women, sexualize children, and commodify sexuality. The central objective is to shed light on how the symbiotic relationship between capital accumulation and coercion creates a fertile ground for the objectification of women, the appropriation of their sexuality, and the destruction of childhood. The discussion centers on three main arguments. First, increasing landlessness and land-ownership inequality in Colombia is dialectically related to violence against women. Second, paramilitarism (as the violent counterpart of capital) and patriarchy are part of a vicious cycle where each feeds into the reproduction of the other while continuously evolving and taking on increasingly harmful expressions. Third, global capital, both legal and illegal, in the way it is embodied locally in Colombia and interacts with the local patriarchal structure, has given rise to pervasive destructive ideologies that dominate gender relations; lead to the further commodification of human beings, including children; promote gross consumerism; and normalize the use of violence against women. It is important to make clear at this point that this is not a study about the ways women are victimized in the midst of armed conflicts and forced displacement or about the use of rape as a tool of war. The realities behind these facts are horrifying but already well-known and adequately documented. The scholarship that deals with sexual violence in the midst of armed conflicts focuses predominantly on violence as an instrument used by armed actors to terrorize people and make them flee the land, as well as the vulnerability of victims of forced displacement to sexual violence. What I would like to contribute here is a perspective that captures the intersection between the material as well as nontangible consequences of land dispossession that go beyond the act of violence itself and encompass ideologies of femininity and masculinity arising from the gender roles imposed by armed actors on youths. Through such an approach we can discover a dialectic between the dispossession of people from their land and the dispossession of women from their sexuality. The latter is a process that begins with the destruction of childhood and the conversion of children into instruments for violence and sex.

The chapter is organized in the following way. I begin with some background on the Colombian armed conflict and, particularly, the ways land dispossession has been exacerbated by the relationship between neoliberal restructuring and the consolidation of paramilitarism. This is followed by an overview of the types of violence against women and the legal mechanisms in place to address this problem. Next, the chapter provides an overview of the main clusters of literature on the subject of sexual violence against women in the Global South. The chapter then draws on several theoretical traditions—Marx's theory of "primitive accumulation," Federici's (2004) feminist perspective on primitive accumulation, Marxist feminist views of the interrelatedness of gender and class, and Bourdieu's concepts of "habitus" and "symbolic violence"—to analyze the permissive conditions for the reproduction of violence against women in Colombia and particularly the connection between control over land and control over women's sexuality. Here I explore the interrelatedness between class and gender by looking at the material conditions of these forms of inequality as well as the mutually reinforcing corresponding ideologies of counterinsurgency/anticommunism and machismo. I conclude by reflecting on the implications of all this for peace and gender equality in Colombia.

Land Dispossession and the Rise of Paramilitarism in Colombia

Paramilitary organizations are armed groups, created and funded by sectors of the capitalist classes, with military and logistical support provided unofficially by a capitalist state. In a society where the economically powerful sectors are also the dominant political forces, paramilitary violence has the political objective of preserving the status quo and, thus, guaranteeing and supplementing the state's functioning. Paramilitary violence has a clear class objective: to secure conditions for capital accumulation. So far this objective has been typically pursued in two ways: repression (attacking social movements from below, activists, intellectuals, and any individuals/groups who represent a challenge to the interests of the elites) and dispossession. Colombia is the Latin American country with the most advanced form of paramilitary violence. Many, however, are tempted to view Colombia as an isolated case with peculiar extremes of violence related to drug trafficking that are not generalizable to the rest of the region. I argue that the Colombian experience represents merely a fully developed expression of a phenomenon that is otherwise in the making in other parts of the Global South. Let's take a brief look at the political–economic conditions out of which paramilitarism has emerged.

The relationship between the concentration of wealth and the use of violence has a long history and is rooted in the question of ownership and control of land. The latter has always been of great importance to local and foreign capital, given that the integration of Colombia into the world capitalist economy took place through primary sector-based exports such as coffee, sugar, bananas, meat, gold, and fossil fuels (Perez-Rincon 2006). By the 1960s, most of the traditional haciendas (large landed estates) were transformed into highly mechanized capitalist agribusinesses for the cultivation of cash crops and stockbreeding for export. Many tenant farmers had been evicted and replaced with wage laborers, and the demand for rural wage laborers became lower and of a more temporary nature. By 1970, farms under 10 hectares had diminished substantially in number and size. In the Department of Nariño, Cauca, Antioquia, Caldas, Cundinamarca, Boyacá, Santander, and Norte de Santander, peasants tried to survive on diminishing plots of land alongside modern mechanized agriculture and cattle-ranching estates. In 1984 there were 1,504,215 *minifundistas* (small-scale farmers) with an average of 2 hectares of land. Of these, 636,255 properties had less than 1 hectare. At the same time, 10 million hectares of land were in estates of more than 500 hectares each owned by an estimated 12,000 landowners, most of whom were cattle barons (Pearce 1990). Richani (2010) uses the term "de-agriculturalization" to refer to the decrease of agricultural production as a share of the GDP, the decrease in the land suitable for agricultural production, and increase in the land dedicated to pasture (from 20.5 million hectares in 1978 to 40.1 million in 1987). While there was an attempt at agrarian reform in 1961, its implementation was sluggish and inefficient, and under the subsequent administration in 1967, the laws pertaining to agrarian reform were repealed or reversed, members of the peasant movement were persecuted and imprisoned, and the dispossession of *minifundistas* resumed. By the 1980s, the agrarian political economy rested mainly on cattle ranching and agribusinesses. Agricultural production was increasingly based on cash crops for export (such as coffee, plantain, banana, African oil palm, flowers, and sugar cane) while less and less was used to grow crops for local food consumption, such as potatoes, beans, and maize (Richani 2010). Since the early 1990s, when the Colombian economy was subjected to a massive neoliberal restructuring aimed at opening up its resources to global capital, the above pattern intensified, leading to what many have described as a "counter-agrarian reform" as more and more land was transferred away from small-scale farming for subsistence and local markets, to agribusiness, mining, industries, infrastructure construction, tourism, and others. Another contributing factor to the concentration of land was the new sector of the capitalist class that emerged in the 1980s as a consequence of the illegal drug trade. Drug traffickers invested their revenues in large parcels of arable land[8] used to raise cattle and horses in the Department of Antioquia, Meta, Córdoba, Cauca, and along the Caribbean coast (Holmes, Gutierrez de Pineres, and Curtin 2008). Eventually narco-capital was also invested in industry, commerce, and finance, converting drug traffickers into an economically powerful and politically influential actor (Medina 1990). Starting in 2000, in addition to agribusiness, the other predominant sector of Colombia's rural political economy became mineral resource extraction. In 2001, the Colombian Congress approved Mining Code Law 685,·which erased restrictions on foreign ownership of concessions, liberalized the cadastral system, and removed restrictions on licensed corporate mining activity on public lands (O'Connor and Bohorquez 2010). Currently, around 40% of the national territory is used for mining and energy exploitation. In the Department of Cauca, 84% of the territory has been handed over to foreign investors (Zamora 2013). The cumulative impact of all this is that between 1990 and

2009 land titles for about 10 million hectares of land were transferred into the hands of the elite and some foreign companies (Hristov 2014).

Present land distribution in Colombia is among the most unequal in the world. Sixty-two percent of the country's best farmland is owned by 0.4% of landowners (USAID 2010). Close to 30% of the population nationwide lives in poverty, 8% of which live in extreme poverty. In rural areas, the poverty rate is over 50%, with 18% living in extreme poverty. In 2015 predictions were made that poverty would rise up to 35% in the next 2 years (*El Espectador* 2015; *El Tiempo* 2016). Around 45% of Colombians work in the informal economy unprotected by labor laws (*Prensa Latina* 2012). As Araghi (2009, cited in Thomson 2011) has put it, neoliberal reforms created a "massive process of dispossession by displacement of the world's peasantries, which has produced a gigantic reserve army of migratory labour" (112).

Let's now look at the role of violence in impoverishing the greater part of the population, dispossessing small-scale farmers from the land, and keeping people inside exploitative social relations. The Colombian armed conflict, which has left over 220,000 dead, is typically identified as dating back to the birth of the leftist guerrilla organization the Revolutionary Armed Forces of Colombia (Fuerzas Armadas Revolucionarias de Colombia-Ejercito Popular, or FARC-EP) in the early 1960s. The conflict is depicted as one between the state and the guerrillas, leaving out the most important actor in the armed conflict: the paramilitary, which according to many reputable human rights agencies, including those of the United Nations, has been responsible for the greatest portion of human rights violations. Thus, an end to the conflict between the Colombian state and the FARC-EP has been almost always wrongly equated with an end to the violence in Colombia. Unfortunately, as we can see, after the signing of the Peace Accords between the Santos administration and the FARC-EP in September 2016 and the subsequent disarmament of this guerrilla organization, various forms of human rights violations, including forced displacement and the assassination of social movements' leaders and activists, have not only not ceased but actually escalated. Between September 2016 and June 2017, 82 human rights defenders were murdered (Programa Somos Defensores 2017). Hence, it is crucial to understand the role of the paramilitary as the central driver of violence.

The legal foundation for the establishment of paramilitarism in Colombia was laid by Decree 2298, which was passed in 1965, converted into Law 48 in 1968, and remained in effect until 1989, authorizing the executive branch to create civil patrols by decree and ordering the Ministry of Defense to supply them with weapons normally restricted to the exclusive use of the armed forces. Subsequently, paramilitary bodies called "civil defense forces" were designed by and incorporated within the Colombian military system (Stokes 2005). This was part of the military project Plan Lazo, launched by the Colombian and U.S. administrations, which was designed to defeat the guerrillas and also eliminate the potential for subversion by targeting sectors of the civilian population that were considered fertile ground for communist indoctrination and guerrilla support. The target for paramilitary actions was the "internal enemy" that extended beyond armed insurgents and encompassed legal political organizations demanding real democratic reforms, educators, leaders of dissident groups, peasant movements, and labor unions (Hristov 2009).

Starting in the 1980s, the capitalist class of Colombia played a more direct role in the setting up of paramilitary bodies and used the same term as the state had given them in the 1960s: "self-defense" forces. Nevertheless, the state promoted and supported these initiatives, and state actors frequently participated directly. This second wave of creation was enacted by large-scale landowners, cattle ranchers, agribusiness owners, the mining entrepreneurs, and drug traffickers. A key factor that facilitated this process was the legal framework established in the 1960s, which paved the way for nonstate armed groups to attain legitimacy. The alliances among sectors of the capitalist classes, politicians, and the military gave rise to the emergence and territorial expansion of various groups[9] throughout different parts of the country, accompanied by a progressive growth in their financial and military strength, despite the outlawing of paramilitarism in 1989.

Paramilitary groups in Colombia typically attack any social forces that emerge as an obstacle or a challenge to the interests of local and foreign capitalists. Their targets include trade unions; indigenous women, youths, and peasant organizations; educators, journalists, and students; and human rights defenders. Between 1993 and 2006, the paramilitary carried out 1,528 massacres that left 8,449 people dead (Semana Multimedia 2012). Since the late 1990s, more than 3,500 trade unionists have been murdered (ICFTU 2005). Colombia continues to be the most dangerous country in the world for unionists. Paramilitary groups have power and influence over the operations of most state institutions, including the military, the justice system, and the government. Of course, it is important not to dismiss the role of the state military in human rights violations. For instance, under former president Alvaro Uribe (2002–2010), the military murdered more civilians than FARC guerrillas did in more than 30 years (Alsema 2017). In 2006, the Uribe government announced the demobilization of the largest paramilitary organization, the AUC. Over the past 10 years the government has categorized any non-guerrilla armed groups as criminal gangs (*bandas criminales*, or BACRIM) and has firmly denied the existence of paramilitarism. Contrary to state discourse, paramilitarism in Colombia has not been eradicated. Old groups have restructured, and new groups have emerged. In 2010, there were about six organizations of paramilitary nature exercising territorial and military control on a national level (Verdad Abierta 2010a). Paramilitaries continue to be the principal actors behind forced displacement and repression. Presently, their targets include leaders of peasant, indigenous, Afro-Colombian, and other community organizations; movements for land rights by victims and/or displaced people; labor unions; environmentalists; human rights lawyers; youth organizations; and LGBTQ[10] activists (all of which are regarded as human rights defenders by nongovernmental organizations and other violence monitoring initiatives). Death threats issued frequently in the form of pamphlets or phone voice/text messages to social movements and organizations come from groups that identify themselves as anti-leftist/anticommunist and pro-business and have included Aguilas Negras, Los Rastrojos, and Los Urabeños/Autodefensas Gaitanistas,[11] among others. The leaders of these groups come from the former AUC structure, and some of the members are former or active military or police officers. Given all the above factors, it is crucial to distinguish these groups from actors involved merely in drug-related violence, which is what the state and its international allies

Table 3.1 Aggressions Against Human Rights Defenders in Colombia 2015 to 2016

Year	Number of Assassinations	Number of Attempted Assassinations	Total Number of Aggressions	% of Victims Male	% of Victims Female	% of Aggressions Carried Out by Each Type of Armed Actor
2015	63	35	682	61	39	66% paramilitary 25% unknown 7% armed forces 1.5% public prosecutor (Fiscalia) 0.5% guerrilla
2016	80	49	481	68	32	66% paramilitary 25% unknown 8% armed forces 0.1% guerrilla

Source: Sistema de Informacion Sobre Agresiones Contra Defensores de Derechos Humanos (2015, 2016)

would like the public to believe. The primary forms of aggressions/violations include murder, attempted murder, threats, and torture. In the first 5 years after the demobilization, 1.5 million people were displaced and 205 unionists were murdered (Hristov 2014). Over the past 3 years, paramilitary violations have been increasing progressively. In 2015, two human rights defenders were attacked every day on average. In 2016, a human rights defender was killed every 4 days. The following table illustrates the increase in assassinations of human rights defenders by the paramilitary between 2015 and 2016.

The increase in assassinations from 2014 to 2015 was 13%, and from 2015 to 2016, it was 22%. Between January and October 2017, 81 leaders of popular organizations were assassinated. A comparison of the first half of 2017 with that of 2016 shows a 31% increase in homicides against human rights defenders and a 6% overall increase in all types of aggressions against such individuals. In 2017 paramilitary groups were responsible for 67% of all aggressions, unknown actors for 22, state armed forces for 7, Public Prosecutor's Office (Fiscalia) for 3, and the guerrillas for 0.1 (Programa Somos Defensores 2017).

Paramilitary violence continues to play a central role in securing land for large-scale industries such as agribusiness, cattle ranching, and mining. For instance, 87% of displaced people come from mining regions even though only 35% of municipalities are covered by mining (Webster 2012). Map 1 shows the areas that had the highest concentration of internally displaced people in 2000.

It is not a coincidence that today these happen to be the areas with a concentration of agribusiness properties, such as Uraba region (bananas, cattle, African palm); Departments of Cesar and Guajira (cotton, cattle, African palm); southeast of Bogota (corn, biofuel, African palm, cattle); and Department of Valle del Cauca (sugar, corn). For instance, Afro-Colombian communities in the Department of Choco who had been given collective

Map 3.1 Areas of Forced Displacement

Source: UNHCR Mapping Unit. June 2000.

titles to land under the 1991 Constitution were forced to flee their lands in the late 1990s due to paramilitary invasion of the region. Presently, in the Department of Choco, 29,000 hectares of land to which Afro-Colombian communities still hold collective titles is occupied by agribusinesses; 7,000 hectares of it is cultivated with African oil palm (Semana 2009).

We can see that the consequences of paramilitary activities stretch beyond the individuals directly harmed by their violence. These nonstate actors shape the relations of production (the creation of masses of landless workers and the concentration of land in the hands of large-scale industrial farms and mining companies) in a way that is synchronized with the prevailing mode of capital accumulation of the global economy as a whole, which is based on a logic of maximizing profit by creating cheap labor, securing control over natural resources, and generating markets for the commodities coming out of global production chains—all with little to no concern for human and environmental well-being. As Giles and Hyndman (2004) have put it, "Globalization is not a unitary or unified project . . . but a composite of processes that generate patterns of exclusion, pockets of wealth and sites of violence" (302). The paramilitary, as a nonstate armed actor, therefore emerges out of a social structure that requires violent measures in order to be reproduced and at the same time generates the human resources to enact those violent measures. This is the vicious cycle of neoliberalism and paramilitarism, which can be described as follows: Market-oriented restructuring of agrarian relations generates poverty and intensifies inequality. The struggle of the poor to improve their situation takes different forms, many of which are favorable to the formation and sustainability of groups of paramilitary nature as impoverished people form social movements that challenge the status quo or are available for recruitment by armed groups. The vicious cycle that makes paramilitary violence an aggravator of class structures is replicated within the realm of gender inequality. It is to this subject that I turn next.

Violence Against Women and Children in Colombia

Women in Colombia represent 51% of the victims of forced displacement, 43.8% of the victims of torture, 46.8% of those disappeared, and 51% of those threatened with death. Between 2001 and 2009, on average, 170 women were sexually abused daily (Verdad Abierta 2010b). Between 2011 and 2012, there was a 103% increase in femicides. In 2012, every half hour a woman was a victim of sexual violence. Between 2015 and 2016, there was a 7.5% increase in sexual violence, and even more disturbing is the fact that the increase has been primarily in the 10-to-14-year-old category. Between 2005 and 2015, the largest proportion of all sexual violence against girls was in the 10-to-14 age category, followed by the 5-to-9 age category (CODHES 2017). The following are the types of physical and sexual violence that women in Colombia face, according to the motivation of the perpetrator and/or the context within which it occurs. The first is instrumental violence[12] for the purpose of land dispossession. Here the violence is carried out against women due to their objective position of residing on land of strategic economic importance. This is accomplished by tactics such as torturing women and men in the presence of others, leaving corpses grossly mutilated, and engaging in practices that lead the victims to experience a painful death. The following is a testimony of a person forcibly displaced by paramilitary terror who was interviewed by Amnesty International (AI) in 2003:

A stick was pushed into the private parts of an 18 year-old pregnant girl and it appeared through [the abdomen]. She was torn apart. . . . They [army-backed paramilitaries] stripped the women and made them dance in front of their husbands. Several were raped. You could hear the screams coming from a ranch near El Salado [Department of Bolívar]. (AI 2004)

The second purpose of violence against women is to humiliate, demoralize, or punish the "enemy," where the latter includes real or suspected guerrilla supporters or sympathizers. In this sense, the bodies of women become a terrain of war (AI 2004) as they are tortured and mutilated. Along the same lines, Cockburn (2004) argues that violence against women in the conquered territory is conceded to the victor. This has a long history in Colombia, dating back to colonial conquest and later the period known as La Violencia, where "women's bodies were seen as objects of war, mutilated and killed because they symbolized the enemy, and its honour, identity and reproductive force, all of which had to be exterminated in its seeds" (Meertens 2010:151). Armed actors in other parts of Latin America and the world have also been known to engage in such heinous acts. For instance, the paramilitary group responsible for the 1997 massacre in Acteal, Chiapas, "mocked the symbols of maternity by hacking the women's breasts with machetes and extracting the fetuses from those who were pregnant" (Olivera and Cardenas 1998, cited in Olivera and Furio 2006:111). Similarly, gangs such as the Mara Salvatrucha are known to carve the gang's insignia on the women's dead bodies (Olivera and Furio 2006), and one of the explanations for the notorious case of murdered women in Ciudad Juarez, Mexico, has been "the use of [women's] damaged bodies as coded languages among powerful men, businessmen, or among criminals and their gangs" (Fregoso and Bejarano 2010:14).

The third purpose of violence against women in Colombia has been to repress their political participation, activism, or leadership. Here the targets have been leaders of social movements, political parties, human rights defenders, lawyers, and judges, all of whom are targeted due to their progressive or politicized subjectivity. Between 2011 and 2012, the number of women victims of sexual violence for political reasons increased by 81%. In 2013, every 4 days a woman human rights defender suffered some form of violent attack (Semana 2013). Piedad Cordoba, a female senator and an Afro-Colombian, stated, "I am the archetype of political violence against women. . . . I am attacked for being a woman, being Afro and my progressive ideas" (Semana 2017a). Similarly, Claudia Lopez, a senator and member of the LGBTI community, sees herself as a victim of political violence given the numerous death threats she has received. The following are just a few of the latest examples from 2017. On January 26, 2017, Yoryanis Isabel Bernal was shot and murdered in Valledupar, Department of Cesar. She was a member of the indigenous community Wiwa Golkuche and a defender of women's rights. On February 11, 2017, Danna Mendez, a trans woman, was raped and murdered in Chaparral, Department of Tolima. She was working with the organization Asociacion Chaparral LGTBI Diversa to fight homophobia. On March 2, 2017, Ruth Alicia Lopez was murdered in Medellín. She was a peasant leader, a human rights defender, a member of the Agroecological

Interethnic Intercultural Association, and a strong advocate for food sovereignty in the Department of Choco. Prior to her death, her family had suffered forced displacement by the paramilitary several times. On June 15, 2017, Narda Barchilon was shot in her home in the town of Arauca, Department of Arauca. She was an advocate for women's health and a member of the organization Apoyar, which works to support displaced families (Programa Somos Defensores 2017).

Another type of violence occurs in the context of human trafficking, for the purpose of coerced or voluntary prostitution where women are supplied as merchandise to paramilitary training camps, military bases, entertainment establishments for those employed along drug-trafficking routes, private parties of paramilitary and drug-trafficking bosses, and other such occasions. Various scholars have recognized that warlike conditions promote sex industries (Enloe 2003; Cohn 2012; Raven-Roberts 2012). As Raven-Roberts (2012) puts it: "War time sex trades are not just anomaly or an effect of war but crucial to the part of the political economic and sexual production of conflict" (47). This author draws examples from the armed conflict in Kashmir where the Indian military imported prostitutes to tend to the needs of Indian soldiers with the purpose of decreasing mental instability and suicide among soldiers (Raven-Roberts 2012). The trafficking of women for the purpose of prostitution under conditions of armed conflict can occur in different variants. A former participant in a sex-trafficking network that traffics women from Colombia to Western Europe with the use of deception describes how traffickers take advantage of not only the economic necessities of low-income or unemployed young women, many of whom are single mothers, but also their need for protection and security in the context of violent environments. "Among the girls employed at the hotel, the one who was the chosen one, the one who was told that the owner wanted her to be his girlfriend, would become ecstatic at the thought of having a secured livelihood and a powerful partner who would take care of her." This interviewee explained how the girls were lured to travel to Spain to meet with their "boyfriend." Upon arrival their documents were confiscated, they were forced to have sex with the man who they were told was their boyfriend, and then against their will they were placed to work at a brothel. Those who demanded to return to Colombia were told that they had to first pay the debt incurred in the process of getting them from Colombia to Europe and threatened that if they attempted to escape, their families in Colombia would be murdered (interview, August 2017). Similarly, Wilson (2014) has found that many of the illegal migrants trafficked from Mexico into the United States are women who may be forced into prostitution in places of destination. The above two examples illustrate that sex trafficking adds a transnational dimension to the problem of violence against women.

Another type of violence women in Colombia face is for the purpose of forced recruitment into armed groups where women may be forced to clean, cook, take care of kids, fight, gather intelligence, provide sexual services, and so on. Last, the most well-known or frequently cited motivation behind violent acts is passion/sentimental reasons in the context of domestic/intimate partner violence. In Colombia in 2012, every 11 minutes a woman was a victim of intimate partner physical abuse, and every 3 days a woman was killed in intimate partner violence (Semana 2013). The problem with this category of violence is that it covers up many revealing details that point in the direction of more structural causes. For instance, women who have been traumatized at a young age in the hands of armed actors may end up in abusive relationships due to lack of other options, especially if they have children to raise, or due to a perception that this is a normal part of being in a relationship (Bott et al. 2012). Alternatively, what is reported as intimate partner violence may be in reality an intimate relationship in which the perpetrator of violence is an armed actor.

The Constitution of 1991 gave the Constitutional Court of Colombia a prominent role in protecting women's rights as well as addressing the needs of internally displaced populations (Meertens 2010). Law 1257 of 2008 introduced new elements in the definition of violence against women: economic damages and the restriction of freedom. The Constitutional Court's Act 092 of 2008 addressed the necessity to assess the disproportionate impact of the armed conflict on women by creating a classification system of types of violence against women, such as forced recruitment, persecution due to leadership in human rights matters, loss of economic provider, and vulnerability due to being identified as a member of a particular ethnic group (Ruiz and Valencia 2016). According to the present Criminal Code, the crime of femicide is given 40 years in prison and more if the victim is a minor (BBC Mundo 2016). However, as is no secret, Colombia suffers from structural nonimplementation; what is outlined by law is a world away from what happens on the ground. Shame, fear, corruption, and lack of awareness of women's rights are some of the reasons why many of the crimes remain unreported and many of those reported remain in impunity. For instance, Alzate (2007) points out that ignorance about rights is endemic among internally displaced people, the majority of whom have a very low level of education and low literacy or are completely illiterate. Under these circumstances, navigating through the bureaucratic procedures necessary to access services has been nearly impossible in most cases.

Overview of the Literature on Sexual Violence in the Global South

Aside from the extensive literature that deals with intimate partner violence against women, there are several clusters of scholarship that address sexual violence in relation to larger political and economic structures and actors. The first focuses on gender-based violence among conflict-affected populations. Within this field, there are scholars who stress the use of sexual violence by armed actors as a weapon of war, drawing on examples from El Salvador, Peru, Haiti, Argentina, Chile, Paraguay, Uruguay, Honduras, Guatemala, Rwanda, Sierra Leone, Liberia, China, Japan, and Nazi Germany (e.g., Giles and Hyndman 2004; Carpenter 2006; Fregoso and Bejarano 2010; Meertens 2010; Cohn 2012). Wilson (2014) argues that rape during war is a strategy used to psychologically attack men by demasculinizing their identities. There are also others who still support the overall argument that women experience war differently than men, but shift the focus to the frequently ensuing sexual violence in contexts of forced displacement and sex work (Cockburn 2004; Alzate 2007; Meertens 2010; Raven-Roberts 2012; Ruta Pacifica de las Mujeres 2013; Wirtz et al. 2014). Raven-Roberts (2012) argues that we need a political economy approach to war to better understand gendered impacts of armed conflict, given that violence may be used to generate economic gains and sustain political power (Cramer 2006, cited in Raven-Roberts 2012). War feeds off existing inequalities and often aggravates them. One example of this is the informal economies that develop during wartime, particularly sex work, which lead to the commodification of women and children as resources to be trafficked and exploited as indentured servants and sex workers. "There is a gender idealization that women selling themselves for money is 'natural'" (Raven-Roberts 2012:47).

Another focus within the field of literature on violence against women under conditions of war has been on forced displacement and the vulnerability of women to various forms of violence in the post-displacement period. Among internally displaced populations, argue Wirtz et al. (2014), there is an increased likelihood of abductions, rape, forced recruitment, trafficking, and an exacerbation of intimate partner violence, including control of the woman's reproductive decisions, unintended pregnancy, forced abortions, and violence during pregnancy. Cockburn (2004) advances the same argument by pointing out the precarious living conditions of displaced populations where female bodily processes such as "menstruation, gestation, parturition, and lactation become more burdensome, uncomfortable and dangerous" and women and girls are at risk of rape and molestation (48). For instance, in Colombia, it is estimated that one in five internally displaced women has been raped and 30% of adolescent internally displaced women are mothers or pregnant, compared with the national figure of 20% for this age cohort (Alzate 2007). Eighty-one percent of sexually active male and female displaced youths do not use contraception (Pacheco Sanchez and Enriquez 2004, cited in Alzate 2007). Other types of damages, such as economic ones, including the loss of home, crops, and farm animals (Ruta Pacifica de las Mujeres 2013), and psychological ones such as the trauma associated with being "homeless" (Alzate 2007), combined with the financial difficulties of having to support themselves and their children in a new urban setting (Wirtz et al. 2014) where women are economically coerced to offer sexual services (Alzate 2007), deepen women's subordination in society and their vulnerability to more violence.

Another cluster of literature that approaches sexual violence through a political economy perspective revolves around militarism, nationalism, and imperialism. Chaterjee (1996, cited in Giles and Hyndman 2004) argues that nationalism, gender, and sexuality are mutually constitutive. Hegemonic notions of what it means to be a man or a woman are intertwined with strategies that generate violence against civilians in the name of the nation, the state, the economy, or the family (Giles and Hyndman 2004). In the same vein, Mohanty, Pratt, and Riley (2009) point to the racist, heterosexist, masculinized, and gendered practices and ideologies of U.S. imperialist wars, which further consolidate patriarchy and exacerbate women's subordination. Among the works on nationalism and imperialism, we see a common theme, which is the recognition that gender relations and identities are reproduced by governments, militaries, and other armed actors and are then exploited in the pursuit of political and economic hegemony (Giles and Hyndman

2004; Mohanty et al. 2009). Particularly influential here has been the work of Enloe (2000, 2007) in encouraging us to recognize the interrelatedness between the construction of dominant ideas of masculinity and femininity on one hand and militarism on the other.

One of the important contributions to the literature that links violence against women to larger political and economic structures is made by works that look at how violence against women is exacerbated by the use of violence to secure conditions for capital accumulation. One such work is by Preston and Wong (2004), who look at how structural adjustment programs in Ghana interacted with the armed conflict in a way that intensified the vulnerability of women to sexual violence. In the same vein, Giles and Hyndman (2004) reveal the correlation of the international diamonds trade with violence against women in Sierra Leone. A number of works dedicated to the case of murdered and disappeared women in Ciudad Juarez and Chihuahua, Mexico, have drawn a connection between the feminicides[13] on one hand and the neoliberal restructuring resulting in the privatization of communal lands, the flexibilization of labor, the feminization of poverty, and the growth in *maquilas* (Olivera and Furio 2006; Fregoso and Bejarano 2010). "The feminicides can be seen as a result of the economic processes in the region (the 'maquilas'), and the machismo culture in Mexico" (Fregoso and Bejarano 2010:14). Aside from the femicides, Muñoz (2007) and Salzinger (2003, cited in Wilson 2014) very eloquently establish a link between the sexual objectification and economic exploitation of female *maquiladora* workers. In the same vein, Tovar-Restrepo and Irazábal (2014) contextualize the violence experienced by indigenous women in Colombia in the context of threats to territorial autonomy by looking at the forced displacement that has been caused by the activities of mining companies and transnational corporations.

A very different field of literature, yet highly relevant to the endeavors of this chapter, focuses on the ideological and cultural dimensions of masculinity, machismo, and patriarchy that serve to normalize violence against women (Viveros 2001; Cockburn 2004; Giles and Hyndman 2004; Olivera and Furio 2006; Mohanty et al. 2009; Fregoso and Bejarano 2010; Baird 2012; Cohn 2012; Raven-Roberts 2012). According to Cockburn (2004), it is the power imbalances of gender relations in most societies that generate cultures of masculinity prone to violence. It is important to acknowledge here that there is no such thing as "masculinity" in general but, rather, multiple masculinities. The harmful masculine identity is one that is inscribed with hegemony over other masculinities as well as over femininity, since its essence presupposes domination over other human beings (men and women). This hegemonic masculinity legitimates men's power vis-à-vis women, as well as "men having greater power than other men, those with 'subordinate masculinities'" (Connel 1987, cited in Cohn 2012). There is a large literature that demonstrates the association between hegemonic masculinity and violence (e.g., Viveros 2001; Fregoso and Bejarano 2010; Raven-Roberts 2012). Raven-Roberts (2012) uses the term *predatory patriarchy* to refer to masculine identities infused with and constituted through violence and aggression.

In this context, particular attention has been given to the relationship between social exclusion/poverty on one hand and the prevalence of such masculine identities on the other. Baird (2012) argues that under conditions of economic deprivation, boys tend to join gangs because the latter becomes a vehicle for "doing masculinity" and a pathway to manhood. In turn, such violent masculinities play an integral role in the reproduction of violence. Similarly, in a 2006 documentary titled *Hip Hop: Beyond Beats and Rhymes*, producer Byron Hurt demonstrates how male African American youths from low-income, crime-ridden neighborhoods can rely on two sources of power: One is their physical strength, which implies being capable of inflicting violence or "putting fear into other men's hearts," and the other is their domination over female sexuality, which is only possible through the objectification and degradation of women.

In Latin America, masculinity is rooted in the hegemonic positioning over women and on competition between males (Viveros 2001). The hegemonic masculinity takes the form of machismo, "the belief that women should be subordinate to the needs and desires of their male partners, taking care of them, providing them with pleasure (either as wives or partners or as approached in predatory fashion by men who would not consider marrying them) and bearing their children" (Wilson 2014:4). Of course machismo is not limited to Latin American societies. Viveros (2001) outlines the main elements of machismo, which include expansive sexual appetite (demonstrated by having sex with a variety of women in addition to their spouses), viewing female sexuality as an object over which the male has control, and proving manliness by displaying sexual dominance. Machismo is sustained by cultural models that assign women positions that subordinate them to the personal and institutionalized power of men. This paves the way to violence through insinuations, offensive comparisons, harassment, threats, abuse, and intimidation that eventually lead to beatings, rape, and persecution (Olivera and Furio 2006). It is also important to note that those whose gender or sexuality deviate from the heterosexual model also become targets for violence, as in the case of trans, bisexual, or queer individuals. Latin American states' history of violence is intertwined with the consolidation of violent patriarchies, the contemporary extreme expression of this being femicide (Fregoso and Bejarano 2010).

Land, Sexuality, and Capitalism's Commodification of Bodies: A Never-Ending Dispossession

There are striking parallels in the way the logic of dispossession operates when it comes to land and sexuality. Dispossession makes people conceive of work and sexuality in capitalist terms. According to MacKinnon (1989), sexuality is to feminism what work is to Marxism: most one's own yet most taken away. Marxists question the way the labor power of workers is expropriated for the benefit of capitalists and workers are deprived of control over work relations, and feminists criticize the expropriation of women's sexuality for the benefits of men and the way women are deprived of control over sexual relations. MacKinnon (1989) defines sexuality here as "not confined to that which is done as pleasure in bed or as an ostensible reproductive act . . . it does not refer exclusively to genital contact or . . . narrowly to sexual desire. . . . Sexuality is conceived as a far broader social phenomenon, as nothing less than the dynamic of sex as social hierarchy" (xiii). Even though the author eventually develops the argument that a synthesis or a reconciliation between Marxism and feminism is impossible, the above statements are a solid point of departure for thinking about the violence entrenched in the processes that lead to the objectification of human labor and female sexuality under capitalism. In fact, the parallels that MacKinnon (1989) draws between Marxist and feminist theories have led me to think about the interrelatedness between the actual process described by those theories—the creation of wage labor on one hand and the creation of women's subordination and femininity (defined by MacKinnon as a female identity that consists of men's standard of desirability). Even though the implication of violence in the proletarianization (or de-peasantization)[14] of peasants and women's subordination in Colombia precedes contemporary paramilitary groups, I argue that the acts of violence of these nonstate armed actors, as well as the corresponding misogynist and degrading ideologies, norms, and practices, have exacerbated dispossession and given it a grotesque expression.

Class, Gender, and Violence in Primitive Accumulation: Historical Continuities

Let me begin with the core concept that captures the crucial importance of land dispossession and the violence it entails to the reproduction of capitalist relations—primitive accumulation. In his work *Capital Vol. I* Marx (1867/1990) argues that the departure point of capitalism is the forcible separation of people from their means of subsistence (i.e., land). The process that divorces the worker from the ownership of the conditions of his own labor "is a process which operates two transformations, whereby the social means of subsistence and production are turned into capital, and the immediate producers are turned into wage-labourers" (874). Once the direct producers have been expropriated (robbed of all other ways of survival), they have only one option: to enter the exploitative relationship offered by those who have now come to monopolize the means of production. "So-called primitive accumulation, therefore, is nothing else than the historical process of divorcing the producer from the means of production" (874–875). After the Civil War of 1642, most of the landed ruling class in England was no longer feudal in nature, and there was a drive toward a transformation of what used to be feudal property into commercial farms (capitalist property). Peasants either became employed as agricultural wage laborers, became tenants on such farms, or migrated to towns. Legislation and armed force were two very important instruments that were employed to expropriate peasants and to subsequently convert them into proletariat. In the 15th and 16th centuries, small peasant properties and common lands were usurped through individual acts of violence. Marx rightfully describes capitalism as "dripping from head to toe, from every pore, with blood and dirt" (926). By the 18th century, the law itself became "the instrument by which the people's land is stolen" (885).

Legislation and armed force were not only applied during the process of separating the rural population from the land but also in the transformation of expropriated people into wage earners. We should note here Marx's recognition of the crucial role played by the state in enforcing mechanisms of primitive accumulation and protecting the interests of the bourgeois class in general. To address the issue of social order as the number of expropriated increased, legislation was used to criminalize those who did not participate in the capitalist system of production (such as beggars or anyone who sought a livelihood outside the capitalist relations of production) and ordered the use of most horrifying forms of physical punishment. Marx (1867/1990) provides a long list of examples of this "bloody legislation" from the late 15th to 17th centuries, such as "whipping and imprisonment for sturdy vagabonds. They are to be tied to the cart-tail and whipped until the blood streams from their bodies" (899) and "the ear-clipping and branding of those whom no one was willing to take into service" (901).

Marx's account illustrates that the process of primitive accumulation is vital to the creation and survival of the capitalist mode of production since it generates the principal elements necessary for its functioning—the availability of wage labor, natural resources, and markets for commodities. "As soon as capitalist production stands on its own feet, it not only maintains this separation, but reproduces it on a constantly extending scale" (Marx 1867/1990:874). Given that working class struggles, which represent a refusal to accept capital's requirements as natural laws, are a continuous element of the capitalist relations of production, capital must continuously engage in strategies of primitive accumulation to re-create the basis of accumulation. In other words, the inherent continuity of social conflict within capitalist production therefore implies capital's inherent need for processes of primitive accumulation. Even within established capitalist relations, methods of primitive accumulation are put into use every time the producers set themselves as an obstacle to the reproduction of their separation from the means of production (De Angelis 2001). The case of Colombia, as illustrated earlier in the chapter, is a typical example of present-day primitive accumulation where the expansion of agribusiness and mining (two of the pillars of the global economy) has led to the dispossession of small-scale farmers from their land and has left them with no other option but to sell their labor at any price to survive. The abundance of people with no livelihood not only generates conditions of desperation, frustration, or ultra-exploitation (which on their own are sufficient enough to spur domestic violence against women) but also provides a reserve army for paramilitary groups and organized crime (which I described earlier as the vicious cycle between paramilitarism and neoliberalism).

An analysis of the creation of wage labor through primitive accumulation would be incomplete without a consideration of how gender inequality intersects with class. According to Marxist feminism, the subordination of women has always been associated with economic inequality. As McNally (2002) observes, gender inequality did not exist in truly egalitarian societies, but it has always been a feature of class-divided societies. Thus, while gender inequality preceded capitalism, "Western capitalism preserved structures of female oppression and compounded them with new forms of suffering and hardship" (127). It is essential, therefore, to examine the ways gender inequality has been affected by the process of primitive accumulation. This question is best answered in the work of the historian Silvia Federici, whose compelling feminist analysis of primitive accumulation demonstrates that male-centered systems of exploitation have always relied on violence to discipline and appropriate the female body. In the following paragraphs, I trace the historical continuities in the relationship between land dispossession and violence against women by drawing parallels between developments during the early stages of capitalism, as documented by Federici (2004), and those during its global stage, with particular attention to their present-day manifestation in the case of Colombia.

Federici (2004) argues that the rise of capitalism was coeval with a war against women. In feudal society, production relations on serfs' plots of land were organized for the purpose of subsistence primarily and the market only secondarily. Thus, she explains, there was no social separation between the production of goods and the reproduction of the workforce given that all work contributed to the family's subsistence. As a result of that, the sexual division of labor was less pronounced and less discriminating than in the capitalist farm. Even more important is the fact that land was given to the family unit; the man possessed the land in partnership with the wife. Women not only worked on the farm but could dispose of the products of their labor and did not have to depend on their husbands for support. Moreover, women worked in cooperation with other women, which meant that the sexual division of labor was a source of power and protection for women as well as the basis for solidarity (Federici 2004). With the transition to capitalism and the commercialization of life, women became excluded from land possession. By the 1700s, with the rise of factory production, a sharper demarcation between the household sphere and the economic sphere was developed, leaving women entirely responsible for social reproduction, in addition to their work as wage laborers (McNally 2002).

The expansion of capitalism through colonialism generally degraded the status of women in non-Western societies and made them more vulnerable to violence. In societies characterized by existing gender inequality, colonial capitalism exacerbated patriarchal features through new property relations that adversely affected women, as well as through systems of labor that increased women's responsibility for raising children. In egalitarian societies, such as the Tsimshian people in Northwest Canada (Fisk 1991) or present-day Nigeria, the dispossession of local people from the land and the introduction of private property led to the loss of access to land for women and their subjection to sexual violence from the colonizers (McNally 2002).

In the era of globalization, the dispossession of small-scale farmers from the land and the degradation of women continue to be conditions that favor capital accumulation. The importance of women's lack of land rights has become even more pronounced today. According to the Food and Agriculture Organization of the United Nations, fewer than 2% of landholders worldwide are women, even though women constitute more than 60% of the labor force on small-scale farms (GRAIN 2014). Numerous scholars and development organizations have recognized the positive impacts that securing land-title rights for women has on human development. According to USAID (2017), women who have access to land are 8 times less likely to experience gender-based violence and 60% less likely to experience domestic abuse.

As stated previously, the development of capitalism has from the very beginning been reliant on the state's legal, violent, and ideological mechanisms. Not surprisingly then, violence against women during the transition to capitalism was state-sanctioned and intertwined with the project of class domination. Federici (2004) documents how throughout Europe between the 14th and 16th centuries political authorities coopted the "youngest most rebellious male workers, by means of a vicious sexual politics that gave them access to free sex and turned class antagonisms into an antagonism against proletarian women" (46). This was done by the legalization of rape and the institutionalization of prostitution. States' backing of rape had a class basis to it, as it applied only if the victims were proletarian or poor women. Gang rape of unmarried proletarian women (such as poor maids or washing women) became a common practice. Women who were raped had no other option but to earn their livelihood by prostituting themselves. From the 1300s to 1500s the "sex card" helped states discipline and divide the medieval proletariat. The raping of poor women undermined class solidarity, and brothels became a remedy for social protest. Here we see a crystallization of the interrelatedness between class and gender on one hand and the mechanisms of violence, law, and ideology on the other: State-sponsored violence against women and the institutionalization of prostitution assisted in crushing communalistic social movements aimed at building an egalitarian society and facilitated the transition to capitalism by ensuring the preservation of class and male power (Federici 2004).

Class was not the only key variable in the subordination of women and the normalization of gender-based violence at the time. As Federici (2004) points out, capitalism must justify the contradictions built into its social relations by denigrating the nature of those it exploits. "All . . . non-bourgeois others—Africans, Irish, Orientals, women, homosexuals, prostitutes, and the labouring poor of Europe—were animalized, feminized and racialized" (McNally 2002:124). Sexist and racist dehumanizing ideologies depicted slave women of African descent and indigenous women in ways that justified their brutalizing sexual exploitation. Black women were portrayed as repositories of insatiable sexual energy (Simms 1992; McNally 2002) and indigenous women as "libidinous" (Stevenson 1992). These ideologies justified the violence that "covets the lands, the gold and the bodies of the others" (71).

States' complicity in violence against women during the transition to capitalism as well as its class and racial dimensions are strongly reflected in the global stage of capitalism. The deaths of thousands of women in Latin America and the failure of states to take adequate measures has led to the birth of the term *feminicide*—a conscious effort by scholars to acknowledge the state's responsibility in femicides (Fregoso and Bejarano 2010).

> Feminicide is a political term. It encompasses more than femicide because it holds responsible not only the male perpetrators but also the state and judicial structures that normalize misogyny. Feminicide connotes not only the murder of women by men because they are women but also indicates state responsibility for these murders whether through the commission of the actual killing, toleration of the perpetrators' acts of violence, or omission of state responsibility to ensure the safety of its female citizens. (Guatemala Human Rights Commission 2017)

The clear class and racial components of present-day violence against women in Latin America are evident across different contexts: the feminicides in the neoliberal era in Mexico, the counterinsurgency terror in Central

America, Argentina and Chile's Dirty War, and of course, the paramilitary war on the poor in Colombia. Feminicides occur in high frequencies in areas of extreme social, judicial, and political exclusion. In the case of Mexico, the prevailing violence affects mostly poor women with little or no schooling, women in situations of dependence where there is less social development in general. At the same time, it is important to mention that feminicides also occur when women (educated or politically active) claim their rights and/or attempt to challenge male authority (Caputi and Russell 1992, cited in Lagarde 2010), as well as where women are perceived as potential sympathizers or transmitters of leftist ideology. In El Salvador, Guatemala, Honduras, Haiti, Peru, Argentina, Chile, Uruguay, and Paraguay, security forces and death squads raped, tortured, and mutilated women and girls as part of the War on Communism. The war aimed at exterminating anything associated with the Left between the 1960s and 1990s involved campaigns that specifically targeted women, the legacy of which has been social environments highly conducive to gender-based violence (Bueno-Hansen 2010; Fregoso and Bejarano 2010). In the postconflict neoliberal periods, state, parastatal, and criminal violence have been facilitated by and at the same time served to reproduce an already misogynistic social fabric. For example, Fregoso (2010) points to the connections between the sexual violence during the internal armed conflict in Guatemala (1960–1996) and the current high levels of feminicide. It is possible to identify a strong racialized component in the feminicides in some of these countries: In Mexico most of the women tend to be *mestizas*; in Guatemala and Peru they are indigenous.

Landowners, Owners of Women: Colombian Paramilitaries as Sexual Predators

In Colombia, as already mentioned at the beginning of this chapter, paramilitary territorial expansion has entailed the violent domination or possession of the poor women residing in these territories during the process of forced displacement, as well as subsequently as paramilitary chiefs/sponsors became the new owners of the land. During the second wave of paramilitarism (1980s–2006), the modus operandi of paramilitary leaders vis-à-vis women is embodied in the story of the landowner Hernan Giraldo, mentioned at the beginning of this chapter. Giraldo's reputation as a sexual predator earned him the nickname Taladro (which literally translates to "drill") due to his preferences for virgin girls aged 9 to 14. The significance of the idea of state complicity conveyed by the concept of feminicide is particularly relevant here. Even though Giraldo was responsible for the deaths of 270 people (including social movement leaders and small-scale farmers), the forced displacement of thousands, and the rape of children and young teens (24 of whom bore his children), he was extradited to the United States in 2008 (along with other paramilitary chiefs) to face charges of drug trafficking instead of crimes against humanity. Giraldo's lawyers asked for a 12-year sentence only, arguing that he was compelled to become involved in the AUC because of patriotism and a sense of duty, honor, and obligation to protect the peasant community against leftist guerrillas (*The Guardian* 2017).[15]

During the third stage of paramilitarism in Colombia, which encompasses the post-demobilization period (2006 to present), paramilitary leaders remain the most feared sexual predators. Paramilitary bosses of the group known as Clan del Golfo (also known as Los Urabenos, Los Gaitanistas, or Clan Usuga) have been notorious for their sexual violence against young girls. Uldar Cardona (alias Pablito), Dairo Usuga (alias Otoniel), and Roberto Vargas (alias Gavilan) have been known to force peasant families living in extreme poverty in the Uraba region across the Department of Antioquia and Choco, to send their daughters aged 10 to 13 to the paramilitaries' property, where they would sexually abuse the girls and subject them to all sorts of painful and humiliating acts. If the families of the victims did not do what they were ordered, the paramilitaries ordered the murder of the girl's parents or in the best-case scenario the family would be forcibly displaced (Semana 2017b). Those families who had girls aged between 6 and 8 were told to have their daughters "ready" when they turn 10, at which point they would be taken away. For instance, in a period of 2 years Uldar Cardona abused more than 50 girls (Semana 2017d). In the same fashion, Roberto Vargas and Dario Usuga forced dozens of girls aged 8 to 15 to have sexual relations with them. They made the girls wear particular styles of lingerie and forced them to take "morning-after pills" and injections to induce abortions. Cardona and Vargas are no longer alive, but Usuga is still at large. It is important to note that these men are not isolated cases. Their treatment of girls as objects that are, to borrow a phrase from Bueno-Hansen (2010), "usable, abusable, dispensable, and disposable" (293) is still the norm among paramilitary groups and other armed actors such as those in drug-trafficking cartels, as well as state forces.

In another case, the paramilitary chief known by the alias El Oso used to organize beauty pageants at a middle school with the help of one of the teachers. At those events he would select girls whom he subsequently lured into having sexual relations (Verdad Abierta 2008). What is even more interesting and disheartening is the oppressive ideologies that support the sexual regimes installed by armed actors, which are being largely internalized by women and young children. Before I turn to this subject, let's briefly trace the historical inception of the ideologies that turn women into commodities for consumption by men and demonize all those women who resist.

The Witches

According to Federici (2004), the persecution of witches in the 16th and 17th centuries was as important as the slave trade and the enclosures of the commons, as far as the creation of wage labor is concerned. Women accused of witchcraft were often midwives, wise women, healers, those who exercised sexuality outside the bonds of marriage and procreation, those who had children out of wedlock, rebel women at the forefront of social movements, and those who challenged male authority and the Church, and were almost always of lower classes. Torture and execution of witches were public events. "According to the standard procedure, the accused were stripped naked and completely shaved . . . they were pricked with long needles all over their bodies, including their vaginas. . . . Often they were raped . . . if they did not confess . . . their limbs were torn, they were seated on a chain under which fires were lit, their bones were crushed" (Federici 2004:185). Witch hunts had a number of political and economic objectives: criminalize birth control, undermine women's control over their bodies, place the female body at the service of the production of labor power, make women economically dependent on men by destroying their self-sufficiency, and destroy women's solidarity and collective power. Federici (2004) compares the expropriation of the peasantry from the communal land through the Enclosures to the expropriation of women from their bodies through the witch hunt. "The witch-hunt was a war against women. It was an attempt to degrade them, demonize them and destroy their social power. It was in the torture chambers and on the stakes on which the witches perished that the bourgeois ideals of womanhood and domesticity were forged" (186). Given that capitalism needs a steady supply of new laborers, the dominant ideology emphasizes women's reproductive role in society by being breeders and nurturers (McNally 2002). While the reproductive role applied to women of any class, the dominant image of femininity and the standard of beauty that was imposed as a condition of social acceptability both had a clear class dimension to them. They included elements of fragility, gentleness, delicacy, and grace that were only possible to be performed by bourgeois women, not working-class women who had to work in factories, scrub floors, or take care of other women's children.

The New Witches

Dominant definitions of beauty and femininity in Latin America today still imply being gentle, weak, and dependent on a man, and generally revolve around the principal roles women have—the reproductive and nurturing role on one hand and the sexually pleasing role on the other—leaving no space for other activities that enable the autonomous development of the woman as a human being, such as education or political activism. The sexist definitions of these roles involve an inherent contradiction since all the labor that is involved in procreation and nurturing has a physical and emotional toll that is not reconcilable with the expectations for a sexual diva with a flawless physical appearance and a sexual disposition of being eager to please. Thus, a central element of machismo culture involves an assumption that these two roles are to be performed simultaneously by different women, the wife and the lover(s). This contradiction is also one of the reasons behind the way women internalize machismo culture and put it into practice. For many women the central goal in life is to improve their economic status by attaching themselves to a man with sufficient resources that would enable them to, after giving birth, dedicate their time and attention to taking care of their appearance (buying nice clothes, going to the gym, undergoing cosmetic surgeries, etc.) and thus please the man, while delegating the nurturing and housework to the *empleada domestica* (the maid).

The marriage of capitalist and patriarchal hegemony in the era of globalization has created the "new witch": the feminist, Marxist, human rights activist, lesbian, queer, *guerrillera,* and any other female who refuses to objectify her body and make procreation and pleasing men (by fitting into categories of attractiveness and desirability defined by capitalists) the main purpose of her life. The killing or rape of women activists has implications that go much further than the immediate harm caused to the victims and their families. Women are sent the message that being "political" can be dangerous or even deadly, while subjecting yourself to excessive sexual regimes on the other hand can assure you (at least short-term) access to commodities, economic security, and a comfortable living standard, where even if you are subjugated by the man, you can at least exercise power yourself by subjugating other poor women. This is why "women's life projects include things like getting buttock and breast implants rather than organizing a protest" (interview, August 2017).

Land Dispossession and the Murderous Consumption of Women: The Intersection of the Material and the Ideological

Capitalism has always relied on violent, legal, and ideological mechanisms to secure the conditions for its reproduction: resources, labor, and markets. As demonstrated, violence has been a persistent feature of capitalist social relations, but it does not work alone. It gives rise to and at the same time is reinforced by ideology. Repeated violence or threat of violence forces people to modify their behavior and internalize the new behavior as the norm. Gradually, there is no longer a constant need for physical coercion to make the new behavior occur, since it is now sustained through the ideology in place. For example, during the transition to capitalism, the dispossession of peasants from the land was violent and so was the "bloody discipline" that was put in place to destroy any independent forms of livelihood and teach the dispossessed that the only way they would be allowed to exist was if they entered the capitalist relations of production as producers and consumers. The *Poor Laws* administered poor relief (the provision of care for the destitute) in such a degrading and punitive form as to instill in the laboring masses a fear of the fate that awaited them should they relax into beggary and pauperism. "Conditions in the workhouse were intended to ensure that no one with any conceivable alternatives would seek public aid. . . . The workhouse was designed to spur men to contrive ways of supporting themselves by their own industry, to offer themselves to any employer on any terms" (Fox Piven and Cloward 1993:34). Thus, laws and violent punishment consolidated the ideology that poverty is a crime, making those without work desperately want a job even if they could not get one. This deeply ingrained ideology sustains the reserve army of labor, which in turn makes employed workers disposable, disciplined, and in competition with each other to please the boss. Four centuries later, we are grateful to have the opportunity to sell our bodies (labor power) as wage laborers. Looking for a job appears to us as the most natural thing, and so does competing with other workers.

The similarities with the period of globalization, where violence and accompanying ideologies create extreme conditions of injustice and suffering that are eventually accepted as normal, cannot be overstated. Small-scale farmers who resist dispossession are subjected to threats, imprisonment, beatings, torture, disappearances, rape, and murder. Faced with few options for survival, those who end up employed in export-processing zones, plantations, or mines quickly learn that the only way to keep the job is to be silent and not stir any trouble by starting a union. Knowing that they are easily replaceable, former and informal workers compete against each other. Working-class solidarity is very difficult to maintain and easily undermined in the era of globalization, where capital is easily mobile and has most of the planet's workers at its disposal, while workers face poverty, insecurity, militarized borders, and repressive tactics from state and nonstate armed actors.

The role of land dispossession as the great enabler of the exploitative relationship between capital and labor is replicated in the sphere of gender relations, where it encourages violence against women and facilitates the objectification of women and the commodification of their sexuality in two major ways: (1) by destroying livelihoods and generating conditions of economic deprivation and inequality—here the vicious cycle between paramilitarism and neoliberalism comes into play—and (2) by fueling harmful ideologies of masculinity and femininity. To begin with, as already discussed, land dispossession generates poverty. Displaced families are forced to migrate and start a new life with little resources or support. This is the entry point to a wide range of survival options that inevitably place the dispossessed, both men and women, in conditions of increased vulnerability and risk of violence:

1. All the stressors associated with forced migration, such as lack of proper nutrition, food insecurity, inadequate housing, and others increase the chances of domestic violence (Buvinic et al. 1999).

2. Most forcibly displaced people migrate to the shanty towns of large urban centers, where they are victims to criminal violence. The informal nature of work in which they often engage also presents higher risks of such violence.

3. Children, especially boys, in displaced families who live in urban slums are at high risk to be recruited by gangs or criminal organizations. Even if they are not forcibly recruited, often they join "voluntarily," given the conditions of high insecurity, where belonging to a gang may be perceived as a way of having some protection.

4. Children, especially girls, in displaced families who live in urban slums are at high risk of incidents of sexual violence by gangs/criminal organizations due to the dangerous social and physical environments they navigate. Girls are also at risk of human trafficking for the purpose of forced prostitution, where violence and the threat of violence are the principal instruments of control. Alternatively, girls who "voluntarily" enter sex work are still at high risk of violence due to the precarious nature of the work.

5. Displaced families who remain in rural areas often find jobs in the *fincas* of wealthy landowners, many of whom are drug traffickers and/or paramilitary commanders. Others rent a plot of land on such properties or are employed on plantations. Whatever the

case may be, such poor rural residents have no economic security. Their children are not likely to complete high school or get higher education. They are at the mercy of the *patron* (the boss or the landlord). Once again, just like in urban environments, boys are likely to be recruited by armed groups and girls are likely to be used as sexual toys by the *patron*, his security guards, friends, and so on.

6. Some of those displaced attempt to migrate illegally, especially people from countries such as Mexico, Honduras, Guatemala, and El Salvador to the United States, and in the process are victimized by human smugglers, drug cartels, corrupt police officials, and other violent actors. Once again, sexual violence is highly prevalent under such conditions.

7. Many scholars, such as Buvinic et al. (1999), have found that the trauma experienced as part of witnessing violent acts (e.g., violent forced displacement) places children at higher likelihood of becoming victims or perpetrators of violence.

The above are the direct ways a single violent act that results in land dispossession has a domino effect by creating conditions conducive to different types of violence long after the act of forced displacement has occurred and across generations. To understand the violence carried out by men against women under such conditions, it is indispensable to understand the violence carried out by men against other men. According to Carpenter (2006) there are three main forms of gender-based violence faced by men and boys in conflict situations: sex-selective massacre, forced recruitment, and sexual violence. Men can also be victims in situations of sexual violence against women if they are forced to commit rape or to watch their family members get raped. In Colombia, many of the forcibly displaced families are single-headed by women because the men were murdered during the event that led to the forced displacement, such as a massacre or selective killings. We can see how the violence against men in this case translates into conditions that place the women at higher risk of violence in the future, especially as they migrate alone to a new urban setting. Furthermore, the ability to use violence against women is seen as a natural element of the masculine identity. Those recruited into armed groups of paramilitary nature or alike, are expected to be "capable" of carrying out rape and other horrifying deeds. Among other things, such as trying human flesh[16] and mutilating bodies, rape is part of the test that new recruits must "pass" (interview, August 2017).

Let's now look at the ideological dimension: How is the vicious cycle between land dispossession and violence reflected on an ideological level where the objectification of women and children and the commodification and appropriation of women's sexuality is normalized? The idea that women's value lies in their body and physical appearance is not unique to Colombia or Latin America but is also present in the Global North. However, when combined with conditions of deep social inequalities, high levels of poverty, and chronic violence, the ugliest features of sexism become monstrous. Just as workers do not question the commodification of their labor power and compete with each other to sell their labor, women internalize and embrace machismo ideology and actively participate in the objectification of their bodies by doing all sorts of harmful things to them in order to "market" themselves as a commodity. As wage laborers compete to be employed by a capitalist, women whose survival depends on a man compete with each other for that man and are ready to hurt or even kill other women who attempt to "steal" their man. *Perra* (literally meaning "female dog") is the term used to refer to women who "steal" others' men. The *perra* is a nightmare for most women, who assume that machismo (i.e., having an insatiable sexual appetite) is part of men's nature and, thus, direct their fury stemming from their partner's infidelity at the *perra*. In Colombia, there is an abundance of cases of women murdered or disfigured with acid by a *sicario* (gunman) hired by another woman (who has the resources to pay for this "service") who perceived the victim as a threat to her livelihood (the man).

Paramilitaries involved in the trafficking of young women abroad for prostitution as well as those taking girls from poor rural families to use in their *fincas* subject their victims to risky surgical cosmetic procedures, most of the time performed at unlicensed facilities by nonmedical personnel. Girls' bodies become toys in the hands of men who can order "custom-made" dolls to satisfy their fantasies. Of course most of those who undergo plastic surgery do so voluntarily, out of the desire to attain the perfect body. It is not uncommon for a young girl to get a breast augmentation surgery as a gift for her 15th birthday.[17] Social pressure to subject one's self to such surgeries increases as this practice becomes increasingly common, even though thousands of girls and women have been disfigured and/or went through agonizing death as a result of such procedures. Girls learn to treat their bodies and sexuality as objects whose only value can be measured in terms of how well they satisfy those who will consume them.

Bourdieu's (2002) concept of symbolic violence is particularly useful to understand where the harm that women inflict on themselves comes from. According to Bourdieu (1998), symbolic violence stems from the naturalization of power relations through dehistoricization and universalization. In this context, gender inequality is not seen as a problem to be solved but a natural fact of life. Symbolic violence is lodged in an individual's habitus (durable principles of judgment and practice). In his work *Masculine Domination*, Bourdieu (2002) explains that as people absorb the existing power hierarchies into their minds, "the most intolerable conditions of existence can so often be perceived as acceptable and even natural" (1).

Even more disturbing is the fact that the pervasive ideology that makes women think of their bodies as objects to be consumed is being internalized by children. The sexualization and sexual relations of little girls with armed actors (as in the examples of the leaders of the Autodefensas Gaitanistas paramilitary group) have at times taken on the appearance of being "voluntary" due to the fact that the girls themselves appear to be seeking these experiences. In addition to death threats, members of the paramilitary approach girls under 14 years of age with gifts such as clothes, cell phones, motorbikes, and offers for paid cosmetic surgeries. One of the police officials from the investigation into the case of Dario Usuga (mentioned earlier in this chapter) reported that some of the girls Usuga had relationships with used to tell their friends at school things like "My husband gave me this Fortuner and this motorbike." This in turn attracted the attention of other schoolgirls, who felt curious to meet these "generous" men (Semana 2017c).

Let's look at the permissive conditions that intersect and produce these excessively perverted cases. The process of socialization through which human beings develop a sense of self and learn to be part of society is not disconnected from issues of class and gender inequality. The colonial and postcolonial culture rooted in deep economic inequalities, sexism, and machismo, such as the right of *derecho de pernada*—the landlord's right to have sex with the women living on his land, including the wives and daughters of the workers—is still alive today. The message that women are a resource commodity that is to be consumed and enjoyed by men is reflected in many ways across popular culture in Colombia. Songs that describe the beauty of Colombia speak of the beautiful beaches, land, and women. In everyday language we see the use of the verb *estrenar* (to try on) used in relation to a girlfriend (as in, "He is trying on a new girlfriend," or *"Esta estrenando novia"*) or the word *peluche* (stuffed animal toy) used to refer to a girl. With the rise of paramilitarism and drug trafficking, the very fabric of popular culture has become even more overtly sexist and degrading toward women. Numerous *telenovelas* (soap operas), such as *The Prepaid* (*La Prepago* 2013), *The Dolls of the Mafia* (*Las Munecas de la Mafia* 2009), *The Cartel of the Snitches* (*El Cartel de los Sapos* 2008), and *Without Breasts There Is No Paradise* (*Sin Tetas no Hay Paraiso* 2006), portray, exoticize, and reinforce the commodification of women and teenage girls' sexuality. Narco narratives in the form of *telenovelas* (which claim to be partially based on true stories) glorify the figure of the *patron* (the boss)—the wealthy man who disposes of the means of violence and who has become a role model deeply embedded in the aspirations of male youth whose life goal is to find a *patron* to work for, and possibly become one themselves. Absurdly enough, the women of the *patron*, who are as easily used and discarded as chewing gum, have become an object of attention, admiration, and envy.

Macho types of masculinity in Latin America are synonymous with social status, respect, money, sexual access to women, and violence (Baird 2012). Boys, especially those of low socioeconomic status who have no other source of power, seek to validate their masculinity through engagement in violence as well as their domination and consumption of women, while girls' femininity can be validated through being "consumed." As Baird (2012) has found in his study on poor male youths in Medellín, Colombia, "the youths in gangs admired the gang leader—the boss, duro or cacique . . . these localised signifiers of 'doing masculinity' . . . included access to material goods such as fast motorbikes, expensive clothes and trainers, . . . and sexual access to the most coveted women in the neighbourhood" (183).

Another factor that plays a role in the emergence of this harmful culture is the globalization of consumption. "Globalization is democratic and egalitarian in spreading expectations but it is inequitable in providing the means to satisfy them" (Briceno-Leon and Zubillaga 2002:28). Through the media, cultural patterns of consumption spread massively; individuals' expectations increase, but their real chances of satisfying those aspirations diminish. Consequently, poor young men in Caracas, Medellín, or Mexico City have similar aspirations and "are capable of killing someone to steal a pair of trainers" (27).

The intersection of machismo and violent masculinity, combined with a culture of consumption, growth in economic inequality, and landlessness, produces the vicious cycle between paramilitarism and the objectification of women. The idea that "women only look at a man who has a car, gun and money" (interview, August 2017) is prevalent among male youths and becomes a motivation for young men to seek employment with armed groups and drug-trafficking organizations, due to the perception that having a weapon and money gives them access to pretty women. In turn, men's access to means of violence and wealth puts them in a position to dictate norms and ideals of sexuality and femininity, where women are taken as objects to be molded to meet their fantasies. Women feel compelled to obey these norms and meet these ideals the way workers feel compelled to conform with the working conditions because they know that they can be easily replaced. The abundance of families leading precarious existences represents a supply of disposable girls, parallel to the way the mass of unemployed represents a supply of disposable workers. Dispossession from the land generates these conditions of dependency and general insecurity that are the most fertile ground for both economic and sexual exploitation. Consequently, it is not uncommon to hear a 10-year-old girl being worried about cellulite and a 10-year-old boy's mother convincing him to wear certain clothes because they will make him look like a *mafioso*.

New generations come into this world because of and in the midst of sexual violence against girls and women. The following case illustrates three

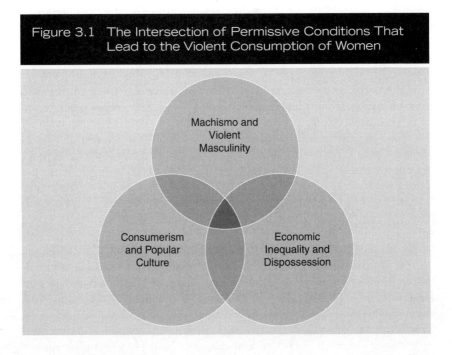

Figure 3.1   The Intersection of Permissive Conditions That Lead to the Violent Consumption of Women

Machismo and Violent Masculinity

Consumerism and Popular Culture

Economic Inequality and Dispossession

generations whose lives were destroyed by paramilitary sexual violence. Ana was born to an indigenous teenage mother who got pregnant after she was raped during a paramilitary attack on an entire community, forcing massive displacement in the Department of Cauca. Ana grew up in a slum in the city of Cali. She was lured to become a "toy girlfriend" of a para-narco when she was 14 and, soon after, was discarded and left pregnant on her own. She raised the child alone living and working as a housekeeper in the country house of a middle-class professional. When her daughter was 11 years old, she was kidnapped by members of the paramilitary group operating in the Department of Valle del Cauca. The girl's whereabouts remain unknown (interview, August 2017).

When small-scale farmers (including men and women) have ownership over land and conditions are in place to allow them to secure a livelihood by being farmers (absence of violence, infrastructure, and technical and financial support), girls can have the freedom to become autonomous human beings. An example of the difference that land makes comes from the Landless People's Movement in Brazil (Movimento dos Sem Terra, or MST). MST has made remarkable accomplishments by occupying idle land and demanding that the government grant them land titles. Once they have legal ownership over the land they organize agricultural production into cooperatives and supply local markets in nearby towns with fresh produce. This has allowed MST communities in Southern Brazil to flourish. A revealing documentary titled *Soil, Struggle and Justice: Agroecology in the Brazilian Landless Movement* (2014) shows an interview with MST youths in which one of the teenage girls says: "If it wasn't for this movement, probably our parents would have gone to live in the slums in the cities . . . and we would either be prostituting ourselves or be in the world of drugs. . . . Thanks to our parents' persistence in the movement, we are here today, I have an opportunity to study and work."

It is crucial to make the distinction between armed actors as instruments for inflicting violence against women and armed actors as creators of coercive sexual regimes maintained by violence. Armed actors may be the instrument, but they alone are not the cause of the sexual violence against women and the commodification of women's sexuality. The idea that girls and women exist to please men and that they can be used and disposed of is embedded in a capitalist consumerist social structure reliant on coercion for its reproduction. In other words, men with guns do not necessarily turn women into objects. It is when armed actors are at the service of capitalist objectives operating within a capitalist culture of consumption that we see the extreme commodification of human beings and the murderous consumption of women and girls. A helpful example to illustrate this distinction would be the FARC-EP. This was an armed movement with the objective of taking over state power and building a socialist society, with 40% of its combatants being women. While during the early stages of the movement in the 1960s to 1970s women were delegated secondary roles within the organization, as the movement continued to develop its collective consciousness and provide political education for its members, the realization that class equality was incompatible with gender inequality crystallized. By the 1980s women participated in combat and performed the same duties, routines, and drills as men. It was common to see women as first or second offi-cers of units. Most important, open discrimination and sexual violence were not tolerated. Women had the right to choose their partners and to end a relationship at their will—something that was very different from the rural reality outside of the organization. FARC celebrated women's bravery and commitment on Women's Day, Mother's Day, and International Workers' Day (Sanin and Franco 2017). As we can see, the relationship of this armed orga-nization toward women differs vastly from that of the paramilitary, where if women are recruited it is never as combatants but as sexual slaves, cooks, and cleaners.

Conclusions

Understanding the forces that make people vulnerable to multiple forms of violence requires an understanding of the structural causes that give violence what Pearce (2009) refers to as its reproductive quality across time and socialization spaces. One of these, and perhaps of most signifi-cance, has been land dispossession. Accelerated land dispossession in Colombia in the era of globalization has been made largely possible by paramilitary violence. This is a historical continuation of a long-standing dialectical relationship between capital and coercion. As Thomson (2011) agrees, capitalist development is often imposed through violent means, and at the same time capitalism generates poverty and inequality that in turn fuel violence. Modern-day primitive accumulation creates favor-able conditions for economic and sexual exploitation. The violent act of dispossessing people from the land generates bodies available to become instruments of labor, violence, or sex while contributing to the consolida-tion of the power of the wealthy. The mutually reinforcing relationship between paramilitarism and neoliberalism engulfs existing gender power hierarchies. Dispossession of people from the land and the ensuing land acquisition/land grabbing have been accompanied by the dispossession of women from their sexuality by men whose source of power is violence and territorial control. Expropriation of the land of some for the benefits of others is interrelated with the expropriation of the sexuality and bodies of some for the use of others. The objectification of women is an extension of the objectification of labor. Some may respond to this claim arguing that the main armed actors exacerbating the problem of sexual violence against women are organized crime and gangs (e.g., Yagoub 2016). While these are definitely among the culprits, there are two reasons why we need to delve deeper. The first is that in the case of Colombia, paramilitary groups work with and at times own criminal organizations. Their tentacles are entangled and compose a complex web of violence. The second is that paramilitary violence creates conditions where future generations of women are easily subjected to the reign of organized crime and gangs. In other words, wherever violence serves the purpose of capital accumulation (legal or illegal), and especially where that violence is sanctioned by the

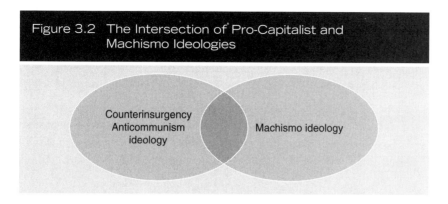

Figure 3.2   The Intersection of Pro-Capitalist and Machismo Ideologies

Counterinsurgency Anticommunism ideology

Machismo ideology

state, it also serves to deepen the subjugation of women. As Fregoso and Bejarano (2010) have put it:

> The history of violence created violent patriarchies, which lead to contemporary expressions of feminicide. . . . The widespread impunity for atrocities against women and the unfettered continuation and spread of feminicide can be seen as part of this militaristic scenario: the convergence of various coercive forces, the complicity of public officials and the organized-crime industry, in alliance with the ruling economic and political elite, all underwritten by the towering specter of state terrorism. (15)

It is useful to think about the intersection of class and gender inequality as reflected on an ideological level in the intersection of counterinsurgency/anticommunism ideology and machismo.

The anticommunist ideology and antileftist sentiment in general are highly compatible with the objectification of women. This tendency has taken on an extreme expression with the unleashed predatory sexuality encouraged by paramilitarism. Among sectors of society characterized by political awareness, militancy, collective consciousness, or activism, women have been successful in rejecting or resisting objectification, and generally speaking, the status of women within such organizations as well as within the family unit is higher. Being a member of a social movement from below has unintended positive consequences in terms of advancing women's rights and gender equality, often regardless of the movement's primary objective (one such example being the Association of Indigenous Councils of Northern Cauca). Such women do not think of their bodies as a commodity and do not desperately strive to attain an ideal that further deepens their subjugation. Hence, perhaps an important subject for future research would be the means through which political education and collective mobilization building can counter the powerful and widespread trend of objectifying women and children. However, given that under capitalist social relations, anything and everything can be commodified, thinking about the issues that poor women and children are facing in Colombia requires an interrogation of the capitalist logic itself and the violent counterpart on which it relies.

NOTES

1. The largest paramilitary organization, the AUC, was formed in 1997 and demobilized in 2006; however, paramilitary groups continue to exist in Colombia. For more on this subject see Hristov (2014).

2. He was extradited to the United States in 2008 on charges of drug trafficking and is currently serving a 16-year sentence.

3. Sexual violence in childhood can include any of the following: forced sexual intercourse before the age of 15; forced acts such as undressing, touching someone or being touched, kissing, embracing, or any other sexual act before the age of 15 (Bott et al. 2012).

4. Violence against women is defined by the United Nations as any act of gender-based violence that results in, or is likely to result in, physical, sexual, or psychological harm or suffering to women, including threats of such acts, coercion, or arbitrary deprivation of liberty, whether occurring in public or in private life (Bott et al. 2012).

5. Sexual violence is defined by the World Health Organization as "any sexual act, attempt to obtain a sexual act, unwanted sexual comments or advances, or acts to traffic or otherwise directed against a person's sexuality using coercion, by any person regardless of their relationship to the victim, in any setting, including but not limited to home and work" (Garcia-Moreno, Guedes, and Knerr 2012:2).

6. Femicide is defined as the targeted violence and killing of women based on their sex (Fregoso and Bejarano 2010).

7. Pearce (2009) defines chronic violence as the accumulated impact of intergenerational and interspacial violence.

8. It has been estimated that by 2007 Colombian drug traffickers owned 42% of the best land in the country (Holmes et al. 2008).

9. For a detailed account of the development of paramilitary groups, see Hristov (2009).

10. In Spanish the acronym equivalent to LGBTQ is LGBTI (*I* stands for *intersexual*).

11. Some of these groups are known by more than one name; for instance, the Clan Usuga/Los Urabenos/Los Gaitanistas are essentially the same organization.

12. Instrumental violence can be defined as "violence used as means to obtain a different goal. Politically motivated and drug-related violence are classic examples of instrumental violence" (Buvinic et al. 1999:10).

13. The term *feminicide* is used by these authors and others who want to emphasize the state's direct or indirect role in femicides.

14. Araghi (2009, cited in Thomson 2011) argues that in Colombia de-peasantization does not necessarily correspond to proletarianization. In other words, the dispossessed are not being absorbed into the proletariat class but remain at the margins of society (Thomson 2011).

15. In May 2017, he was sentenced to 16.5 years in prison (*El Tiempo* March 5, 2017).

16. See Hristov (2014) on the paramilitary's use of crematoriums.

17. Some have used the term *narco-aesthetics* to refer to the culture of plastic surgery created by drug traffickers in the late 1980s and 1990s (Henao 2015).

CHAPTER 4

The "Created Biology of Gender Stratification"

Links Between Economic Power
and Gender Equality From
Hunter-Gatherers to Today's
Global South and North

Rae Lesser Blumberg

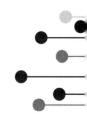

Introduction

This chapter views women's economic power—or the lack of it—as the strongest variable affecting gender equality/inequality. It looks at females' relative economic power through all of human history, from hunting and gathering to the present, as well as among our closest primate relatives, bonobos and chimps (with each of which we share 98.7% of our DNA). The data indicate not only that we humans have been relatively gender egalitarian and low in violence for all but about 4% of our roughly 315,000-year existence as *Homo sapiens* (Hublin et al. 2017) but that our closest nonhuman kin are not uniformly patriarchal and violent either. To the contrary, bonobos are the opposite: Females control the food supply (economy); the troop is female-led and peaceful. Among chimpanzees, males do *not* control the food supply, the troop is *not* invariably male-dominated, and violence is subject to checks and balances (De Waal 2005). These findings undermine assertions of "universal patriarchy" and that both men and our nearest nonhuman kin are "nasty animals."

Data also are presented—including some new studies—about gender-egalitarian hunter-gatherers, and a new twist is presented about why women began to cultivate about 13,000 years ago.

All this is linked to a concept, the "created biology of gender stratification" (Blumberg 2001b; Blumberg, Maryanski, and Ralston-Coley 2002). It posits that greater gender equality results in both women and men being better able to realize their potential—akin to the old Army recruiting slogan, "Be all that you can be." Conversely, with greater gender inequality, not only do females suffer harm ranging from discrimination to disease and death, but the well-being of men and boys also is diminished.

Considering the other 4% of human history, it is clear that there indeed are some highly patriarchal and violent peoples. Some of their actions against females—from fetuses through the life cycle—have been, in a word, horrible. But as will be discussed, not all geographic areas have been involved, and the levels of patriarchy and violence have varied over time and space. There actually are whole regions (in, e.g., Southeast Asia) where at the *village* level, gender equality was and remains relatively high and internal conflict relatively low. The "created biology of gender stratification" also can affect males who lose much or all of their economic position and power and develop—and increasingly die from—the "diseases of despair" (Case and Deaton 2015, 2017). Unfortunately, this has been happening to a fast-growing number of low-education white U.S. males. Gender is not just about women.

Here is an overview of the chapter's major thrusts:

1. For 300,000+ years—about 96% of our history as big-brained, anatomically modern *Homo sapiens*—we were hunter-gatherers (foragers). Anthropological and archeological data indicate most women and men foragers were about equal and had equal economic power, posited as the key variable affecting the level of gender equality in a group. Little evidence of violence has been found.

Today, there are still some local-level groups where women and men are roughly equal. All share a common factor: Women control 50% or more of economic resources; that is, they have *economic power*. Presently, there are far more gender-*unequal* groups. In almost all of them, males dominate economic power.

2. When the Congo River formed around 1.5 million years ago, the direct ancestors of bonobos and chimps were split into two species. Bonobos arose on the south side of the river, in lush forests loaded with fruit and other edible delights. Chimpanzees arose on the north side, in a drier habitat with fewer resources and more predators. Bonobos are little known compared with chimps. But they defy the picture of our primate "closest kin" as male-dominated and violent. Females control the bonobo food supply (equivalent to economic power). They're far better organized than males and run the show. They also use frequent sexualized contact to maintain harmony. Chimps are well-known. Males do *not* control the food supply. But though male chimp violence ranges from sporadic to frequent in different troops, they are held up as an example to "prove" that both they and human males are hopelessly "nasty animals" (De Waal 2005). Nevertheless, the very existence of female-dominated, peaceful bonobos undermines the view that men and our closest non-human kin are both inherently patriarchal and violent.

3. Next, the chapter explores the biggest revolution of all, the rise of cultivation starting about 13,000 years ago. The argument is that it was *women*, the primary gatherers and botanical specialists, *who created horticulture*, raising a variety of vegetables, grains, root crops, and fruits in small garden plots—and possibly saving humanity after a near-global catastrophe. It appears that the early horticultural period might have been the high point of women's equality, even higher, perhaps, than among female gatherers.

4. An unknown Middle Eastern man invented the plow 5,000 to 6,000 years ago (Nolan and Lenski 2015). It diffused across the Eurasian

landmass and to North Africa. Life soon became more difficult for most of the population as wars, patriarchy, and inequality rose. On the one hand, the plow permitted permanent cultivation: The same fields could be farmed for centuries if not mistreated. On the other, it meant peasants were in a cage (Mann 1986): The ruling elite had soldiers and rent collectors who demanded, on average, half the crop (Lenski 1966). Folk sayings arose, such as, "When the plow enters, so, too, does servitude."

Females fared worst in *non-irrigated* plow agriculture: "Dry" farming doesn't need much labor (except briefly at peak periods). A few people could raise large fields of a single crop such as wheat. So women and even some men were pushed out of production; they weren't needed. In my gender stratification theory (Blumberg 1984), work in important production activities is the *prerequisite* to gaining economic power. Women who were *not* producers became subjugated—especially where men ran the kinship system. (This was so in the Middle East/North Africa [MENA], most of South Asia, and northern China.)

Plow agriculture involving *irrigated rice* is very different: It *can* use a *lot* of labor, as long as it is added gradually. So men, women, girls, and boys *all* worked. Even in East Asia, where the kin/property system was run by men, rice-growing women were not as subjugated as the nonproductive women where dry agriculture prevailed. And in Southeast Asia, rice-growing women controlled income and had a female-friendly kin/property system. There, especially at the village level, gender equality was, and remains, relatively high.

5. Next, today's industrial societies in the Global North and developing nations in the Global South are considered. Women's position ranges from high to very low, affected by their economic power or lack thereof, as well as their class, race–ethnicity, and nation. But rising precariousness and inequality in our globalized world capitalist economy can hurt even dominant-group men, if they're working class or poor, as discussed in the section on Low Education U.S. White Males.

As this chapter looks at human history and the present, it views the most and least gender-equal groups through the lens of two theories: Blumberg's gender stratification theory (the 1984 article has the fullest explication) and theory of gender and development (first published in 1988). Both theories posit that women's economic power, defined as *control* of economic resources (income, land, credit, etc.), is the most important—though not the only—variable affecting female equality. It also considers the link between the presence or absence of economic power and the "created biology of gender stratification."[1]

Not only is economic power the key determinant of women's relative position, but it is also the only form of power that varies from near-zero to near-100% for *both* men and women.[2] Where women have equal—or greater—economic power, everyone benefits: women, men, boys, and girls. Within those groups, gender roles tend to be more flexible and violence, including against women, is usually low. Where women have little—if any—economic power, it's the opposite. Most people, including many men and boys, (ultimately) lose.[3]

Big-Brained Modern *Homo Sapiens* and How We Compare With Bonobos and Chimpanzees

A recent find of a *Homo sapiens* skull in Morocco dated as 315,000 years old (Hublin et al. 2017) has pushed back how long we've been big-brained, modern humans from roughly 200,000 to about 315,000 years. Other data indicate that for a little over 300,000 of those years, roughly 96% of our *Homo sapiens* history, *we lived in apparently peaceful, egalitarian hunter-gatherer (foraging) societies. Women and men were about equal,*[4] *but they had a gender division of labor where men did most of the hunting and women did most of the gathering—and everyone benefited.* In fact, I argue, the genders had equally favorable levels of the "created biology of gender stratification." Archeological evidence also shows that during the first few thousand years of cultivation, from about 13,000 to roughly 6,500 years ago, humans still remained almost equal (Gimbutas 1980, 1982). It seems that *high patriarchy is in the neighborhood of 7,000 years old.* And even now, it's neither uniform nor 100% universal.

Before we were *Homo sapiens*, our earliest hominin ancestors emerged in Africa about 6,000,000 years ago. They were small-brained but already walked upright. Even before *Homo sapiens*, they learned how to control fire and make all kinds of technological aids (from hand-axes to, probably, water-tight canteens and baby-carrying slings; Slocum 1975). They likely made their living the same way as *Homo sapiens*: by hunting and gathering. How do human survival strategies compare with those of bonobos and chimps?

1. *Human hunting-gathering versus bonobos and chimpanzees' browsing.* First, all the evidence—both archeological and anthropological studies over the past two centuries—indicates that as foragers we were quite equal socioeconomically. But it also indicates that with respect to gender, we humans had differentiated ourselves from our closest relatives—bonobos and chimpanzees, whose DNA differs from ours by only 1.3%. Specifically, we adopted a completely different system of obtaining food than theirs: We had a *gender division of labor, with men doing most of the hunting and women doing most of the gathering.* In contrast, they got their food with the sexes doing virtually the *same* thing: browsing (though chimp males did somewhat more hunting than bonobos or chimp females). This meant they meandered through their habitat, finding and eating food as they went. To understand how revolutionary our way was, we need to learn what bonobos and chimps are like—and also that our distinct gender-linked food-seeking strategy created some of humanity's most enduring institutions. These include *pair-bonding* and the *nuclear family* (Gough 1971), as well as a usually temporary *home base* where food is cooked and shared. Nothing like this is found among bonobos and chimps. To introduce our closest relatives, let's start with two facts and a picture.

The first fact is that they diverged from our common ancestor more recently than we did: about 1.5 million years ago when the Congo River arose (De Waal 2005 says hominins split off about 5.5 million to 7 million years ago). As noted, *bonobos* evolved on the south bank, amid lush forests abundant with fruits and other easily obtained foods. *Chimps* evolved on the

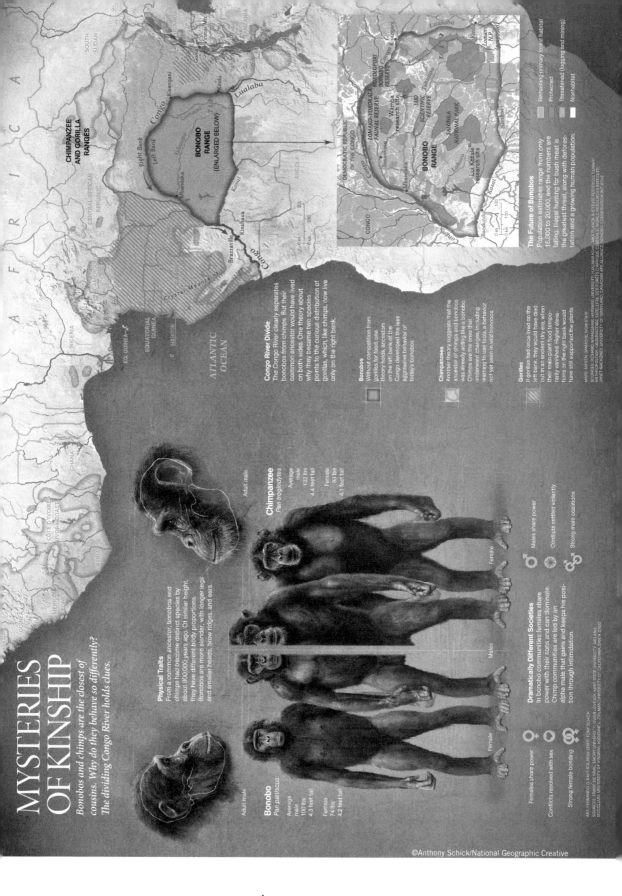

©Anthony Schick/National Geographic Creative

north bank, in much more open, dangerous terrain, with less reliable food sources and more predators. Second, their bodies became different, too.

2. *Bonobos.* Unlike chimpanzees, who are "knuckle walkers," bonobos walk upright. Their body shapes look more like ours. Also, bonobo males and females are closer to each other in size and musculature than male and female chimpanzees are (although bonobo females have the only visible breasts among any of the nonhuman great apes). More important, *females control the food supply*, the bonobo equivalent of economic power. This is due, at least in part, to the fact that bonobo females are very well *organized*. (Organization is one of the "strategic indispensability" factors, in Blumberg's general theory of gender stratification [1984],[5] that helps transform economic activities into effective economic power.) Bonobo females run the troop, maintaining internal harmony with frequent sexualized, pleasurable behaviors. These occur an average of every 90 minutes (De Waal 2005) and range from touching to intercourse, plus a whole array of practices found in the *Kama Sutra*. They rarely engage in conflict within their group. On meeting another bonobo troop, the females boldly approach the males and initiate sexual contact. Soon all are friendly. The result of this peaceful, enjoyable life is a 1:1 sex ratio; that is, bonobo males have the same survival rates as the females. This is a clear manifestation of a generally positive created biology of gender stratification.

3. *Chimpanzees.* Males are shaped more like NFL linebackers, and they are better organized than females. But they *don't* control the food supply and are more violent than bonobos or chimp females. Still, troops have a checks-and-balances system that keeps conflict within bounds. Chimps also have some sort of sexual/sexualized contact an average of every 7 hours (De Waal 2005).[6] But if two chimp troops meet, the males fight. Period. All the male conflict and stress, however, takes its toll: Among chimps, the sex ratio is 2:1—twice as many females, attesting to the males' lower rates of survival. This is an example of a negative form of created biology of gender stratification for males.

It also should be noted that most chimp troops have male leaders, but female leaders have been found (De Waal 2005). In contrast, no male-led troops of bonobos have ever been encountered.

We take it for granted that *human foragers typically specialized by gender*, with men doing most hunting and females doing most gathering.[7] But it actually was revolutionary and had enormous consequences for humanity. At this point, it's useful to take an excursion across time and space.

The "Created Biology of Gender Stratification" Across Human History and Geography
••

1. *Hunting-gathering.* We know from long-term studies of *foragers who still lived the traditional lifestyle*, getting more than 85% of their food from hunting and gathering (Nolan and Lenski 2015), that their *gender relations were equal or near equal* (Draper 1975).[8] This contrasts with the female-dominated bonobos and the usually male-dominated chimpanzees. Why? It seems to be due to two crucial facts about how we lived. (a) Animals run away but plants do not, making hunting much less reliable than gathering, and (b) *sharing* has been found

to be one of humanity's rare *cultural universals*. Every hunting-gathering group studied over the past two centuries or so has been found to share (any others presumably didn't survive to be studied). The rules for sharing vary from band to band but are always more strict and formalized for the products of the hunt than for the products of gathering. The dense, tasty protein of meat was coveted as well as unpredictable and irregular, hence the more stringent sharing rules. It also meant, however, that women had greater control over the fruits of their production than men had over theirs, since their gathering was so reliable and so rarely as mouthwatering as the men's hunted game. This, it is proposed, *equalized male–female economic power*—creating a "Goldilocks zone"[9] that was "just right" for creating both useful knowledge[10] and a successful and durable lifestyle based on *gender equality*.

Here is a well-researched example: The !Kung of the Kalahari Desert in southern Africa have been studied for several generations (e.g., by the Marshall family; see Marshall 1965 and the two-decade study led by Richard B. Lee 1968, 1969). They present a generally gender-equal picture—so long as they get almost all their food from hunting and gathering. Government-resettled !Kung forced to farm are more male-dominated and less equal (Draper 1975). Furthermore, Lee (1968, 1969) found (through input–output analysis) that the nomadic !Kung women's gathering provided 60% to 80% of the food supply; it was so much more reliable (if often considered less tasty) than hunting. As a result, women's and men's contributions to group subsistence in their traditional hunting and gathering were equally important and apparently gave them equal economic power, the foundation of overall equality (Blumberg 2009a).

Surprisingly, since the Kalahari Desert is *not* a lush habitat, they apparently also had a lot of leisure: the adult !Kung (about 65% of the population) studied by Lee (1968, 1969) and his colleagues worked perhaps 20 hours a week, with children under 15 and adults over 60 usually not going out (see also Sahlins 1968).

Another surprise is that the women were not breeding machines. How did they do this before the pill? Using a combination of passive means (low body-fat ratios and long nursing,[11] up to age 4) and active means (infanticide, abortion, and plants with contraceptive properties), women had their babies around 4 years apart (Birdsell 1968; Whiting 1968; Kolata 1974; Blumberg 1978).[12]

And here's a final example: A recent study in *Science* (Dyble et al. 2015) indicates that "sex equality can explain the unique social structure of hunter-gatherer bands." They undertook a large-scale assessment of contemporary hunter-gatherer societies and found a very unexpected but consistent pattern that bands included a good number of *unrelated* individuals. They used a modeling approach to try to explain why and found that a possible explanation was that "cohabitation choices are being governed equally by men and women" (796). In short, they noted that the social organization of mobile hunter gatherers includes male–female equality, low within-camp relatedness, and fluid "meta-groups."[13] Their "agent-based model" suggests that even if everyone in a band seeks to live with as many kin as possible, within-camp relatedness is reduced if *females and males have equal influence* in selecting camp members. Moreover, their model turned out to closely approximate the actual patterns found in two contemporary hunter-gatherer peoples, the Agta of the Philippines and the Mbendjele BaYaka of Congo-Brazzaville. They conclude that their results suggest that prevalent *pair-bonding and gender egalitarianism* in human evolutionary history may have had a transformative impact on human social organization.

Nonetheless, to survive, other factors were involved as well: We also had to be at the right place at the right time to take advantage of the often-seasonal availability of edible plants and animals (anthropologists call this "seasonality and scheduling"). Unquestionably, we were good at it. It meant, too, that we were at least seminomadic, with many groups moving around enough to be rated as fully nomadic. If you move around a lot, and have no other way to carry possessions except on your back, head, or in your arms, you can't accumulate a lot—especially of bulky, heavy items. That discourages inequality in goods among members of the foraging band. And, as noted, *100%* of hunting-gathering groups studied over the past two centuries practiced *sharing*. It was a matter of life and death. Hunting is frequently unsuccessful, whereas it is rare that extreme drought, flooding, heat, or cold can endanger *all* the plants, insects, and other edibles that are the products of gathering. In other words, people had to contend with fluctuating, sometimes scarce resources. Accordingly, they shared when they had surplus so that they would receive when they were in need.

If you add up (1) the sparse possessions and (2) the sharing, the result is a group that (3) is *socioeconomically egalitarian*. In addition to about equal female–male economic power, their prevalent kinship system also helped gender equality: It gave equal weight to mother's side and father's side relatives (i.e., most kinship was "bilateral"). Skeletons found by archeologists as well as recent anthropological studies of intact hunter-gatherers back up this picture of equality. Both genders had robust, healthy bones. After all, both ate a quite nutritious, high-fiber, low-fat, largely plant-based diet, and both exercised a lot to get it.

2. *Hoe horticulture.* The reasons for the "cultivation revolution" that began during the period from about 13,000 to 10,000 years ago used to be seen as partly mysterious. The traditional explanation is that gradually increasing population pressure was one of the factors (Meyers 1971); another explanation blaming male overhunting (e.g., Diamond 1997) hasn't held up. Now, however, many types of scientific evidence are converging to indicate that the precipitating cause may have been a comet that entered our solar system and fragmented around 12,900 years ago (+/–150 years; the original article is Firestone et al. 2007 in the *Proceedings of the National Academy of Sciences*). This was at the end of the last Ice Age, when glaciers were retreating. Evidence indicates that the fragments ignited fires in about 10 million square kilometers, an astonishing 10% of our planet's land surface (Wolbach et al. 2018a, 2018b).

Dust clogged the sky, cutting off sunlight, akin to "nuclear winter"; many plant species and about 35 megafauna (e.g., North American mastodons, mammoths, and saber-toothed tigers) were wiped out, and the North American Clovis Paleoindian culture also met its demise (Moore et al. 2017). The climate cooled rapidly, ushering in a cold period that lasted more than 1,000 years (geologists call it the Younger Dryas Boundary). The perhaps initial and biggest hit seems to have been in Quebec: Bedrock from there has been found far away in Pennsylvania (!) (Wu et al. 2013). Platinum or platinum group elements (PGEs, including osmium, presumably from the comet fragments)[14] have been found in ice cores in Greenland (Petaev et al. 2013) and across northern Europe, including Russia near the Finnish border (Andronikov et al. 2014), Lithuania (Andronikov et al. 2015), and the Netherlands and Belgium (Andronikov et al. 2016).

Sweatman and Tsikritsis (2017), in an article about a carved stone tablet found in the world's oldest known temple—the roughly 11,000-year-old Gobekli Tepe in southern Turkey—discuss what they consider its recently deciphered secrets: The tablet carvings included a headless human, indicating catastrophe, and animal symbols. These animal symbols were used to represent certain constellations. A computer program dated those constellations as shining over that part of Turkey about 12,950 years ago (+/–150). Newspaper and magazine articles (e.g., *Telegraph* 2017; *Forbes* 2017) hailed this catastrophe as leading to farming and civilization. Not one mentioned women.

But that "farming" was actually *horticulture* (from the Latin word for "garden") and it's likely that it was women who developed *cultivation* (with or without the impetus of a cosmic disaster). Many consider this the most consequential technological revolution in human history. The women may have started with the digging sticks with fire-hardened sharp points they carried for their gathering (and defense from predators). It's only a small step, however—adding a wooden blade to a sturdy wooden stick—to invent the hoe. It's more logical that it was *women* who added planting to their gathering (it's actually *harvesting*) than a sudden intervention by male hunters. V. Gordon Childe (1942), the eminent archeologist, concluded it was women—the botanical specialists—who were responsible. Since then a variety of social scientists have elaborated on women's role in early—and/or contemporary—horticultural cultivation (e.g., Boserup 1970; Boulding 1976; Martin and Voorhis 1976; Blumberg 1978; O'Kelly and Carney 1987).

These studies further bolster the case that cultivation arose from the women gatherers and their knowledge of the life cycle and characteristics (positive and negative) of a plethora of plants, not from a sudden foray into the plant world by men who specialized in knowledge about the animal world.[15] Also, women are depicted as hoeing in ancient pottery. Ester Boserup (1966), the renowned agricultural/horticultural economist, categorized horticulture as "female farming" (Boserup 1970). And to this day, women play a stronger role in cultivation in most horticultural groups, whether in sub-Saharan Africa (where Saito and Weidemann 1990 found that women horticulturalists grew up to 70% of locally produced food crops) or in other horticultural areas of the world.[16]

The early cultigens that were domesticated all were "genetically plastic" plants that could be massaged and tailored into steady food sources: *grains* such as wheat, rice, and corn (others include oats and barley) and *root crops* such as cassava, yams, and potatoes. Furthermore, within about 6,000 years after the earliest horticulture, cultivation had arisen independently on every large land mass on Earth (except Australia, which had no plants genetically plastic enough to be turned into basic food staples).[17]

Archeological evidence indicates a fairly long period of low inequality once cultivation arose. Before about 7,000 to 6,500 years ago, grave goods give no indication of gender inequality[18]—although there were large numbers of female figurines indicating possible goddess worship (Gimbutas 1980, 1982). By this time, we were living in *villages* that were moved every few years when weeds reduced yields and nearby game became scarce. We began to accumulate bigger, heavier possessions ranging from pottery and looms to more clothing, jewelry, and tools. At this point, two different paths seem to have precipitated the rise of gender inequality among horticultural-ists (Blumberg 2009b).

The first path toward patriarchy and economic inequality involved attacks on peaceful (possibly goddess-worshipping) horticultural peoples in Europe by mounted herders. Gimbutas (1980, 1982), a renowned archeologist, describes three waves of invasions by patrilineal Kurgans, who lived on the north shore of the Black Sea and invaded "Old Europe," getting all the way down to Greece. Patriarchy followed in their wake. The first wave began about 6,300 years ago, a time that Griffith (2001) describes as during a long drought that began about 7,000 years ago in dry areas of northern Africa (including the Sahara) and the vast Eurasian landmass. He argues that there is a drought-prone band from Northwest Africa across the Middle East and extending east to Mongolia and Manchuria that suffers periodic droughts. He also makes a case that starting with that drought beginning about 7,000 years ago, *after* the domestication of goats, sheep, and cattle, herders intensified its impact by not letting their ani-mals roam across enemies' territory. This was because they often rustled each other's livestock and feared revenge; instead, they created deserts.[19]

The second path was an increasing number of horticultural societies shifting from matrilineal to patrilineal kinship (Blumberg 2009a, 2009b). Women were key cultivators in early horticulture. Widespread polygyny (one man with more than one wife) was not possible with a matrilineal kin/ property system, the then-dominant type. Why would a man in a horticul-tural society want multiple wives? It was *not* for lots of sex: Clignet's (1970) answer is in the title of his book, *Many Wives, Many Powers*.

Some ambitious men, seeking power and recognition, realized that they could obtain extra resources from women's production if they had more than one wife and could persuade each to turn over part of her surplus produc-tion. The men could use this to throw lavish feasts and gain prestige, young male followers, and a leadership role. This was because generosity was still a core value (as it always has been among hunter-gatherers). These aspiring "Big Men" (Fried 1967) wouldn't have to beat their wives, just motivate them to grow enough surplus for a big feast, thereby enhancing the whole family's prestige (Blumberg 1978; prestige was much valued). There was a catch. To have more than one wife (who did not have to be a sister of his present one, an occasional exception in matrilineal societies), the kinship system would have to be changed to patrilineality. Little by little, this occurred over most of the Eurasian landmass. Women's position declined somewhat as a result.[20]

What about elsewhere? Much of sub-Saharan Africa's rainforests and some savannahs have thin, often nutrient-poor soils. As discussed next in the plow agriculture section, big, heavy plows require deep soils. There-fore, a large proportion of sub-Saharan cultivation remains horticultural to this day.[21] Over the millennia, many horticultural groups have shifted from matrilineal to patrilineal, enabling men to adopt polygyny. Men could gain from multiple wife-producers because women were primary or equal farm-ers. Elondou-Enyegye and Calves (2006) found that 75% of contemporary sub-Saharan ethnic groups are patrilineal. But this doesn't mean that most wives are oppressed and have no economic power.

Unquestionably, women are the dominant horticulturalists in sub-Saharan Africa (Boserup 1970; Saito and Weidemann 1990). That is, they meet the *pre-requisite* for economic power in my gender stratification theory: important par-ticipation in key productive activities. But despite the prevalent male-dominated kinship systems and the persistence of polygyny, to this day, there are no data showing sex-selective abortion of girls or greater malnutrition among girls or any other negative forms of the "created biology of gender stratification" in the region. Why? Especially in western and southern Africa, women earn— and *control*—income from trading and/or selling their own-account crops, by-products, or handicrafts. They have a lot of autonomy in how they acquire and spend their income. In fact, in patrilineal West African horticultural ethnic groups, women and men keep "separate purses" (Hill 1969; Treas 1991). Neither knows who earns what and how they spend their money.

Also, many horticultural groups *don't* live in sub-Saharan Africa. Negative versus positive "created biology" effects have been found among them based on (a) whether the kin/property system favors males versus females or (b) the extent to which the men traditionally were and still are engaged in warfare.

a. *Kin/property systems.* Consider two groups from northeastern India who still live mainly from shifting horticulture: the matrilineal Khasis, where the youngest daughter inherits the largest share of her mother's property (female ultimogeniture), and the patrilineal, male-dominated Karbis, where the firstborn son gets the lion's share (male primogeniture).

What's relevant for the "created biology of gender stratification" are tasks involving spatial abilities (Hoffman, Gneezy, and List 2011). In the United States, a number of studies have found that males today have better spatial abilities than females. What about these two peoples? The matrilineal Khasis proved to have *no* significant differences in men's versus women's spatial abilities performance. Conversely, among the patrilineal Karbis, men performed significantly better than women in tests of their spatial abilities.[22]

b. *Endemic, frequent warfare.* The warlike, patriarchal Yanomamo, originally called the "fierce people" by Chagnon (1968), are horticulturalists who live in dense jungles in southern Venezuela as well as across the border in Brazil. They show a key indicator of antifemale created biology: female infanticide. They kill some baby girls, saying they need many warriors. Why? They frequently fight other Yanomamo villages over women. They're always in short supply because of female infanticide and the fact that high-ranking men typically have several wives each. This leaves young warriors with poor prospects of a mate, hence the frequent raids to grab some young women from a different village. They now fight only other Yanomamos, lest the Venezuelan government attack them, with devastating consequences. Having a village with enough male warriors to hold on to its women and to raid for women living in other villages drives both female infanticide and the cycle of raids and revenge. It also leads to big villages much larger than those of nearby matrilineal peoples and frequent meat shortages that their neighbors see as the Yanomamos' own fault.[23]

One hypothesis in my still-evolving theory of gender and development is that women and men with provider responsibilities spend income under their control differently, with women disproportionately spending on the well-being of their children (i.e., their education, nutrition, and health—e.g., Blumberg 1988, 2016a—which comprise central elements of human capital). Recently, scores of empirical studies from both Global South and Global North have provided support for this proposition (Blumberg 2015 and 2016a list them). Most are by male economists, who rarely if ever read sociological studies on development. Regardless, human capital contributes to national income growth, national indicators of well-being, and development.

Thus, economically empowered women help their nations, not just their own children. Considering African development, two facts remain underappreciated: (1) Most of its farming is still horticultural (in the rain forest areas, the soil often isn't deep enough for the plow), and (2) most of its locally grown food is successfully raised by *women* horticulturalists.

3. *Plow agriculture: "Dry" versus "wet."* In terms of human history, agriculture was the third way we made a living off Mother Earth.[24] Apparently, an unknown man in the Middle East invented the plow between 5,000 and 6,000 years ago (Nolan and Lenski 2015). It diffused from there across the vast Eurasian landmass, up to Europe and across Asia, as well as down to nearby North Africa. Non-irrigated, "dry," plow agriculture is very different from "wet," which involves irrigated rice (Blumberg 2004, 2015).

"Dry" plow agriculture involves single crops usually grown on large fields. With the plow, crops such as wheat, oats, barley, rye, and the like don't need a lot of labor per unit of ground area. These crops are not "labor elastic." A labor-elastic crop is one where, if more labor is added, production rises. A non-labor-elastic crop, like many of those raised with non-irrigated plow agriculture, will *not* produce a lot more if more people are put to work. In short, if one or two men with a donkey or two to pull the plow can cultivate one such crop on a large field, it's not feasible to put 50 people there; they'd soon starve. For the first time in history, there wasn't enough work even for all the men in this new system. Women were pushed out almost entirely. This led to a disastrous drop in their position.

Geographically, dry plow agriculture spread from the Middle East to other areas that had deep enough soils. This included North Africa, Europe, and the northern parts of both South Asia and East Asia.[25] Meanwhile, socioeconomic inequality skyrocketed: The plow permitted permanent cultivation, which meant peasants could till the same plot for generations—and landlords with their soldiers and rent collectors could demand half the crop as rent. Since eviction meant social and sometimes physical death, peasants had no choice. Gender inequality skyrocketed too as women lost their productive role.

Archeologists and anthropologists can compare the robust, sturdy bones of male and female hunters and gatherers with the skeletons of oppressed male and female peasants in agrarian societies—weaker, shorter, and more likely to be disease-ridden. Even the skeletons of the elites (who were taller and better nourished than peasants) were less healthy than groups living solely as hunter-gatherers.

Similarly, *gendered* well-being differences can be found not only between hunter-gatherer women and agrarian women but also between males and females in dry agrarian areas. Today, both long-dead bones and the morbidity, mortality, nutrition, and height differences of living males versus females in patriarchal agrarian areas show females' inequality. What happened?

In a nutshell, in most of the dry agrarian areas, women lost the main *prerequisite* to economic power: work in key production activities. It was not just that there was insufficient work for all the male peasants but also the fact that the large, heavy plow required considerable upper-body strength to pull it or manage the animals (such as oxen) that pull it. Women have about one half less upper body strength; they were less qualified. A quite unequal "created biology of gender stratification" arose: In dry agrarian areas, women's bones and bodies were less robust and healthy than the men's, going back millennia. Aspects of a "created biology of gender stratification" (from sex-selective abortion of females to greater female malnutrition) still can be seen in today's populations in many of the dry agrarian areas that Caldwell (1982) named the "patriarchal belt": MENA, as well as most of South Asia and (pre-Revolutionary) China. Caldwell attributed women's often-abysmal status in the "patriarchal belt" to its very male-dominated kinship/property system.

Patriarchal kinship is a factor. But women's exclusion from important work seems a bigger one: It's the *prerequisite* to women's economic power (Blumberg 1978, 1984, 1988, 1991). In the "patriarchal belt," without access to production and a male-dominated kin/property system, most women had to agree to what Kandiyoti (1988) calls the "patriarchal bargain": staying mostly housebound and acting submissive and with propriety in return for male support and protection.

To this day, women in the "dry" agrarian lands of the "patriarchal belt" have the lowest levels of labor force participation on the planet. This not only lowers their status and power, but it also dramatically cuts gross domestic product (GDP) in the subregions of the patriarchal belt. In MENA, for more than 30 years, the rate of female labor force participation rose only about 0.17% a year—so that it took some 6 years to rise 1% (World Bank 2012a). According to Kim (then the president of the World Bank), MENA loses 27% of GDP because so few women are in the labor force; South Asia loses an estimated 23% (Kim 2014; see also Cuberes and Teignier 2012, 2015).[26]

What about irrigated rice or "wet" agrarian systems? In general, they're found in wetter and often warmer areas of Asia, including much of East Asia and the lowlands of Southeast Asia.[27] Except for Southeast Asia, the kin/property system is all on the male side. In Southeast Asia, it's mainly bilateral (as among most hunter-gatherers, as well as in today's Western Hemisphere, Europe, and Australia/New Zealand). It also tends to be "matrifocal," with women preferring to live near female kin and help each other with everything from childcare to small loans for each other's businesses.

Southeast Asia has traditionally been the most gender-equal region on Earth, as shown by archeological evidence going back 4,000 years or more (White 1982, 1988, 1990, 1992a, 1992b) and extending to contemporary gender and development studies (e.g., Wolf 1991; Ireson 1996). Rural women of the Southeast Asian lowlands not only work in irrigated rice, they *inherit* rice land to varying degrees; this is because the kin/property system is either bilateral with a matrifocal tilt or fully matrilineal, with few exceptions. They also trade in the market and have other entrepreneurial activities. Southeast Asia has virtually no negative "created biology of gender stratification." In East Asia (e.g., South China, South Korea, Japan, Taiwan), where women also work in the rice paddies, their work is recognized, despite the fact that the kin/property system is patrilineal, patrilocal, and with male-dominant inheritance. They're not likely to be food-deprived even if they provide only unpaid family labor. In other words, they, too, generally avoid a strongly unfavorable "created biology of gender stratification."

But as a last point about the centuries (indeed, millennia, as shown in the White citations) of gender economic and overall equality in traditionally irrigated rice-raising Southeast Asia, here is a quote about Thai people in the early 1400s from Ma Huan (probably a Muslim, based on his Ma surname).

He was an interpreter on three of the seven ocean expeditions of Chinese Admiral Zheng He in the early 1400s:

> It is their custom that all affairs are managed by their wives, both the king of the country and the common people. If they have matters which require thought and deliberation—punishments light and heavy, all trading transactions great and small—they all follow the decisions of their wives, for the mental capacity of the women certainly exceeds that of the men. (Ma 1433 cited in Thailand's National Commission on Women's Affairs 1995:4)

4. *Industrial*. Space constraints preclude discussing the rise of capitalism and the Industrial Revolution here (see, e.g., Blumberg 1978, Chapter 5). They also preclude delving deeply into the present-day global capitalist economy and the varied, often large differences—including vis-à-vis gender equality—between the countries of the Global North and those of the Global South. That said, today's world is way beyond the Industrial Revolution. We live in a globalized capitalist economy/ecology divided into Global North and Global South. Yet it's important to know that every one of today's Global North advanced industrial nations sprang from an agrarian base (Blumberg 1978). To varying degrees, this has had lingering consequences on women's economic power, image, and status (vi).[28]

First, successful development and the level of gender equality are considered for some Global North and Global South nations. Then, in the following section, fieldwork-based data are presented for some of today's most and least gender-egalitarian groups in the Global South.

Who's Most Equal in the Global North? Among the advanced industrial societies of the Global North, high proportions of the women are in the labor force, and they have equal rights despite some lingering inequalities. So far, however, today's level of female equality cannot compare to the gender equality of hunting-gathering societies or Ma's quote about the women of Thailand in the early 1400s.

Regardless, collectively, the Nordic countries lead the pack among the advanced industrial nations, as measured by the indicators of gender equality (e.g., the Gender Gap reports) that rank all contemporary nations.[29] There is one mild damper to their economic equality: Although they have very high rates of labor force participation, it is disproportionately in the lower-paid *public* sector. They don't come close to the proportion of U.S. women who are *private*-sector executives in lower to upper-middle managerial ranks (but with very few found in the C [top executive] suite). Nor do they have anything like the large numbers of Thai women creating and running their own successful enterprises (*Nation*, 2011:1). This brings us to an aspect of the Global South rarely considered in the development, and gender and development literature.

The (Relatively Neglected) Implications of Wet Rice for Both Development and Gender in the Global South. As noted, rice is a very labor-elastic crop: You eventually can get large numbers of people working in a small plot of irrigated rice as long as you add them gradually. They'll grow enough rice to feed themselves and have a surplus to sell. Hence, China and India, which long have grown irrigated rice in their densely populated southern regions, have about 1.4 billion people each. In both nations, the Industrial

Revolution began in their irrigated rice-growing south, not their dry-agrarian north. And in both, the early industries disproportionately involved low-paid *female* workers in factories producing for export.

East Asia was first to rise. It became a major industrial exporter to the world based on labor-intensive textiles/garments, electronics assembly, toys, and the like produced by cheap female labor. It has been the fastest-growing Global South region until recently. Now Southeast Asia (with 620 million, vs. 509 million for the full European Union, including Great Britain) is the fastest-growing area, also based on industrial exports largely produced by female labor. And their labor is even cheaper than in East Asia.

It's not surprising, however, that East Asia reached advanced industrial status based on cheap women's labor and Southeast Asia may be following the same path: High proportions of rural or recent urban migrant women in those places had the perfect background for the early export industries. They had toiled sunrise to sunset in the rice paddies, mostly as unpaid family labor. Being hired for money (even a pittance vs. Global North wages) made them work very hard in the new factories. As Cohn explains in his chapter in this volume, where labor costs are the biggest factor of production, factory managers and owners would want the cheapest—but most productive—labor they could get. Young women who had toiled in family rice paddies fit the bill.

Gallin (1995) describes the rise of small factories in *rural* areas of Taiwan as the "four tigers" of East Asian industrialization—South Korea, Taiwan, Singapore, and Hong Kong—began to roar. These were not the huge production lines of multinationals' factories that sprang up in Singapore. Rather, local Taiwanese opened small plants near the supply of the cheapest, most willing female labor. These were young women who had worked, unpaid, in family rice paddies, grown up in a subordinated status in the household, and believed the Confucian obligation of a female to give back (i.e., most of her pay) to the parents who raised her. They were quite unlike the Southeast Asian young female factory workers in rural Java (Wolf 1991), who were raised in a traditionally egalitarian and more gender-equal village culture and who decided for themselves just how much and how often they would contribute to their family. Taiwan and the other three "tigers" prospered and joined the ranks of industrial nations. Most recently, their growth has slowed and their fertility has crashed. Now Southeast Asia, an irrigated rice region with even cheaper female wages but, on average, far more gender equality, is the world's fastest growing.[30]

The "Created Biology of Gender Stratification" in Today's Global South: The Extremes

1. *Groups close to gender equality.* In fieldwork in 48 countries, the author encountered seven groups with local-level gender equality/near-equality, collecting various amounts of data for five of them. There's a caveat about their gender equality, however: One has to ignore any local presence of the government or a world religion; both are more patriarchal.[31] In all the cases, women controlled *half or more of key economic resources.* If these groups had a motto, it might have been the old Army recruiting slogan, "Be all that you can be."

Gender roles in all five cases (named below) were flexible, with tolerance for variations in masculinity and femininity (Blumberg 2001a, 2002b)—the opposite of the least gender-equal groups. In all five, women were seen as skilled in economic endeavors, money management, and organizing work and groups. The gender division of productive and domestic work was fairly flexible; it would not be seen as shameful for a man to wash his own shirt or for a woman to take off for a couple of weeks of long-distance trading. The three most studied cases are (1) the indigenous Quichua village of Chanchaló in Ecuador's Central Andes, (2) six villages in Northeast Thailand (the country's most gender-equal region), and (3) their Lao coethnics across the Mekong River in the Lao People's Democratic Republic. The two less studied cases are (4) the Bijagos Islanders off the coast of Guinea-Bissau, West Africa, and (5) the Yunnan Province people the Chinese government calls Mosuo (they call themselves Nazeh). Here, due to space constraints, only the Central Ecuador and Northeast Thailand cases are discussed.

Under the Volcano: Full Male–Female Partnership Near Mount Cotopaxi, Ecuador. Researchers have found the indigenous Quichua-speaking groups to be more gender-egalitarian than the *mestizo* (mixed) majority (Alberti 1986; Poeschel 1988; Blumberg and Colyer 1990; Balarezo 1992). The author's fieldwork in Ecuadorian agricultural development projects included various indigenous villages in Cotopaxi Province, near the majestic snow-capped, near-perfect cone of the Cotopaxi volcano (19,393 feet), especially Chanchaló, which had a dairying project and was building a small cheese-making factory. Sarah Hamilton (1998) was doing dissertation fieldwork there for 2 years as part of a nutrition project funded by the National Science Foundation.[32] Our findings led to many similar conclusions (i.e., "triangulation"; see Note 30). Here are some key ones:

- Both girls and boys often are given small animals (e.g., guinea pigs, *cuyes*) to raise, breed, and sell—so both genders are used to self-managed resources, frequently bringing them to their marriages.

- Equal numbers of women and men own land; quantities don't differ significantly.

- Local ideology depicts men and women as complementary and equal partners in their marriages.

- Social adulthood comes with marriage, not age; marital decisions should be joint, even about money.

- Kinship is bilateral (both mother's and father's kin count equally); under the Spanish-imposed system, males and females have equal inheritance rights, but prior to the Spanish conquest, Quichua sons inherited from their fathers, while daughters inherited from their mothers (Silverblatt 1980).

- Another traditional pre-Inca custom that survived is the lively, colorful weekly to triweekly markets in which mostly female traders sell a wide array of wares and farm products on their own account.

- Men are more likely to migrate seasonally; women maintain crops and animals and continue to trade in the markets, managing their own resources and family survival while the men are away—but decisions on allocating the men's money when they return usually are joint, as per custom.

- Eighty percent of households are nuclear, but reciprocal labor exchanges with extended kin and friends are universal; women organize the labor exchanges because both genders see them as better managers.

- Households pool productive resources (land, labor, technology, production tools, and credit) and there are no "women's crops" versus "men's crops" as in Africa (the same is true for animal production).[33]

- The gender division of labor is quite flexible, and men participate significantly in housework (e.g., washing many of their own clothes) and childcare; moreover, most men report wives' equal or greater control of income.

- Gender equality remains strong, although commercial agriculture provides fully 90% of household cash income and over half of total income.[34]

In the Land of Silk: A Matrifocal Tilt in Northeast Thailand (Isan). Joyce White's articles (1982, 1988, 1990, 1992a, 1992b) on archeological findings about the very high level of female–male equality in Ban Chiang, Northeast Thailand, reveal the following: (1) For both males and females, grave goods were of about equal amount and value, though some differed by gender (e.g., occupational tools and some types of jewelry). (2) Although Ban Chiang is one of the oldest sites of metallurgy ever found, and it went through the full sequence from copper to bronze to iron, it was in the minority that didn't make weapons as soon as its people learned to make bronze (copper is too soft to be a weapon; bronze and iron can be). (3) Most of the objects found were useful tools and jewelry (mainly bracelets).[35] Even now, this region is one of the world's most gender-equal—with traditional village-level equality being especially striking.

The author's fieldwork in Northeast Thailand (known as Isan; Blumberg 2001a, 2002b) grew out of working on a 10-country USAID project on gender and development in which participants did case studies and met to share their findings.[36] One study (Blanc-Szanton, Viveros-Long, and Supanchainat 1989) of a failing agriculture project in Northeast Thailand found the problem was that it didn't deal with the women; it ignored previous baseline research that women were the primary farmers as well as the main owners and inheritors of rice land (Palmer, Subhadhira, and Grisanaputi 1983). Both the Palmer et al. and Blanc-Szanton et al. research found remarkable gender equality in work, wealth, and well-being. Their findings inspired the author's rapid appraisal research (Blumberg 2002a) in four villages in the heart of Thailand's silk-producing region in much of December 1992 and January 1993: Ban Nong Ngong, Ban Tong Lang, Ban Fang Noi, and Ban Nong Thum; in a second round in 2001, two villages much closer to the city of Khon Kaen were studied (Blumberg 2001a, 2002b). Here are some of the findings:

- Women and men were both crucially important in rice farming and other economic activities; however, as in Ecuador, the gender division of labor was not rigid.

- More important (given Blumberg's general theory of gender stratification), in all four villages, women earned more than men in the off season after the rice harvest. Moreover, in each village, the women did so by means of a *different* specialized activity: growing Chinese radishes, weaving and selling *mat mii* silk, weaving and selling *lai khit* cotton, and working in a cigarette factory.

- Matrilocal residence—where the young couple goes to live with/ near the *bride's* parents—remained the strongly favored pattern in the 1992–1993 research. Such a system gives the woman the advantage of remaining on her home turf, surrounded by close kin.

- At that time, there still was an expectation that, if possible, the youngest daughter should care for the parents in their old age; in turn she would inherit the house and a double share of rice land.

- Women, in fact, owned more of the land than men.

- However, echoing the findings of Palmer et al. (1983), the author and her research assistant also found that the traditional Isan inheritance system of rice land was changing. In the past, a man would generally not take any share of rice land because he could expect to marry a woman who would have her own (especially if she was a youngest daughter, who was considered an especially good catch). But a variety of factors were beginning to result in more families dividing rice lands among both daughters *and* sons:

  o Good rice land was growing scarce in many places. Western death control (e.g., vaccinations, DDT, antibiotics) preceded Western birth control by about a generation or two, leading to a period of population explosion. Although this now has ended—Northeast Thailand has had one of the world's most successful family planning efforts, as discussed below—the consequences linger.

  o Moreover, the semi-arid Northeast, with its poor soils and history of periodic drought, began to be deforested during the Vietnam War (originally, it was promoted by generals as a way to counter Lao insurgency, so large stands of trees were cut down and sold). The deforestation has caused environmental degradation and an intensification of drought.

  o Increasingly, parents are promoting education for their children, realizing that few of them will have good prospects cultivating irrigated rice; this leads to dividing rice land equally among all children, male and female (i.e., switching to an equal inheritance system).

- Women were widely viewed as better at handling and saving money and were characterized by both men and women as the principal managers of household income, regardless of who had earned it.

- Every person interviewed said that men and women are equal and that women tend to have greater clout in household decisions.

- Both men and women said that women have the final say in fertility and birth control decisions (as one man farmer said, "She has the last word—it's her body!").[37]

- Finally, because traditional spirits are associated with the house, and women traditionally inherit the house, they also are in charge of spirit offerings—which seems to provide women with an additional resource underlying their high status at the micro level (except in matters associated with Buddhism and the government, where males have the advantage).

The main difference between the 2001 research and the 1992–1993 research was that the 2001 villages were closer to the city of Khon Kaen and involved better-educated young people. More of the young couples chose to live closer to work than to the wives' mothers. But the level of gender equality among middle-aged people was still rather remarkable. In Ban Non Reang, a couple was asked who had the bigger voice in family decisions. The man pointed to his wife; she pointed to herself. Both laughed. Another woman who was present nodded and pointed to herself. In Ban Lao Nok Chung, at a housewarming celebration, a 63-year-old woman danced and sang while her 66-year-old husband played the traditional *khaen* and two young men played modern drums. The woman decided when the men should play and when they should stop but with good humor and a spirit of give-and-take. Still, it's likely few of the village young people will be rice farmers.

2. *Groups farthest from gender equality: Afghanistan and some general patterns.* The most extreme case of gender inequality the author has ever encountered was in Afghanistan. The findings of a gender analysis (undertaken over and above two final evaluations of large-scale non-gender-related UNDP projects; Blumberg 2011a, 2011b) included the following findings (Blumberg 2016b).

Women control—or have use rights—to less than 2% of the land in a country that's about three fourths rural; they run only about 6% of businesses, and 88% of women over 26 are illiterate (Blumberg 2016b). The men of the dominant ethnic group, the Pashtun, have a code, *Pashtunwali*, which considers women as property. And the No. 3 person in the Ministry of Women's Affairs told the author and a UNDP colleague that "most men don't consider women to be quite human beings."

* * *

More generally, what are the broader patterns in the most gender-unequal nations and regions? Strong gender inequality affects *both genders*, resulting in a highly negative "created biology of gender stratification."

First, where girls aren't sent to school, they're likely to rear *less healthy sons as well as daughters*. Second, where women control almost no economic resources, as in the (non-irrigated agrarian) "patriarchal belt" that encompasses the Middle East/North Africa (MENA), South Asia, and (pre-revolutionary) China, where most women are economically dependent and many are in seclusion (Caldwell 1982), they are likely to be deprived nutritionally. Blumberg and Cohn (this volume) present recent research on the "South Asian enigma" (by Blumberg, Dewhurst, and Sen 2013a, 2013b). The enigma or puzzle is *why* it has the world's highest level of child malnutrition (42%) although it is *not* the world's poorest region, whereas the *actual* poorest region, Central and West Africa, has roughly *half* that level (23%). The answer turned out to be the high level of female economic dependency (South Asia has the second lowest female labor force participation [FLFP] rates after MENA even though some South Asian nations include unpaid family labor in agriculture in their calculations of FLFP).

It's known that nutrition deficiency, especially protein deficiency, before age 2 has lifelong impact: It lops off the right tail of the IQ distribution—the brightest—skewing the curve leftward to lower IQ levels. And where females are kept in seclusion, often behind four walls nearly 24/7, especially in rural areas with no electricity or TV, they live in what ecologists call an "impoverished niche." They know little about topics or places beyond their narrow horizons. Is it little wonder that the men are likely to consider them airheads who gossip about trivial family matters? What else might they talk about?

These females' constrained knowledge and horizons negatively affect not only their children's health but also their nutrition and education. Even now, in patriarchal areas where young girls are not viewed as economically productive, they often are married as soon as feasible after puberty, before there can be any danger to family honor from even the merest suspicion of female misconduct. Since marital residence is patrilocal in these groups, they live with or near the husband's parents. If they don't earn income, they're seen as economic liabilities, not assets, and their husband and in-laws expect them to have a baby within a year.[38]

Furthermore, especially in the "patriarchal belt" delineated geographically by Caldwell (1982), women rarely control economic resources, they have less say in their own fertility and less ability to obtain family-planning services on their own, since they lack both money and freedom of movement. Fertility is generally higher where women are economically disempowered. And as demographers have long demonstrated (Hess 1988; Das Gupta, Bongaarts, and Cleland 2011), high fertility is linked to lower economic growth. Again, economically disempowered women not only suffer individually, but they also don't contribute to developmental progress in their nations.

3. *Two "historical horror stories" and two contemporary ones.* The impact of women's economic disempowerment can be seen in very harmful "created biology" customs. Here are two historical cases.

Foot-binding. This was practiced for a thousand years—from the 900s into the 1900s—in the non-irrigated agrarian north of China. All the toes except for the big toe were broken, and the bindings were tightened over time. The smallest feet were found at the top of the pyramid: wives and consorts of emperors and nobility. Frequently, this produced a long-term, low-grade infection, necessitating the small white socks women wore to cover their bound feet and the perfume they applied to hide the smell of the infection. The custom extended down to the upper peasantry in Northern China, where women did not have duties that took them out of the household compound, and a lightly bound foot did not prevent those women from laboring long and hard in their invisible domestic tasks. (It is relevant that in the irrigated rice south of China, despite the same male-dominated kinship/property system, the feet of women who worked in "wet" rice never were bound. To fertilize the rice and have a good source of edible protein, people put fish in the paddies. The fish feces fertilized the rice. But it likely would have caused the low-grade infection of a woman with bound feet to flare up and possibly kill her.)

Sati—widow burning. This was a custom practiced for centuries by many propertied castes in another part of the "patriarchal belt," northern India. After the father's death, the sons would farm his holdings jointly before ultimately dividing up the property. Their mother, however, often was much younger than their father—young enough, in many cases, to have more children if she remarried. Those children could displace the first husband's sons as inheritors. Hence, this explains the old custom of forcing or cajoling her onto the funeral pyre, certainly an effective form of prevention of widow remarriage.[39]

Bride burning/dowry deaths. This is a modern-day, mostly urban update of killing economically powerless women by burning—also in India. It's totally illegal but still persists, mostly in northern India, where women above the lowest castes don't work in non-irrigated agriculture and urban FLFP is low, as well. The following scenario is most common: A young couple marry. The bride's family has to pay a dowry to the husband's family because she doesn't have skills that would land her a well-paid job. Soon the groom's family starts demanding *additional* dowry (money or consumer goods) from the bride's family. The bride's family resists. One evening, as the bride starts cooking dinner using propane or some other flammable material, according to what the groom's family tells the police, her sari is ignited by the flame and although they try to help, she is engulfed in flames in seconds. If the young woman lives long enough, she can make a dying declaration giving her version of what transpired. Successful prosecution is rare, though. So the young man is free to seek another wife—and another dowry.

As it happens, FLFP in northern India is *declining* (Das et al. 2015); this does not bode well for improving women's status. And sex-selective abortions, although illegal (almost 100% involve female fetuses), remain fairly common. They have distorted the country's sex ratio, with the biggest shortfall in northern India, traditionally the dry agrarian and most patriarchal region. Ultimately, this will mean not enough women for somewhat marginal men to find a wife, with potentially violent results. Already, an estimated 34 million poor Indian men can't find a bride because they are the least desirable husbands due to class status, and sex-selective abortions have sharply cut the proportion of young women versus young men. Will this also reduce the prevalence of dowries and dowry deaths? After all, these are based on women's *lack of economic resources*—which make them dependent *and* vulnerable.[40]

"Bare branches" in China, potential violence in India: men with no chance of marrying. Both nations have high numbers of sex-selective abortions. They distort the sex ratio and are illegal but still widespread.

China's big shortfall of females is due to high sex-selective abortion rates during the one-child-family-law years (1979–2015). Now there are an estimated 34 million nonaffluent men (mostly from the north) called "bare branches," because they won't be able to continue their family line. Young women are in deficit, and these men have little to offer a prospective wife. India has about the same number of surplus men, also due to sex-selective abortion, who mostly reside in the patriarchal, dry agrarian north. Consequences are unpredictable in both nations. They could range from male depression to violence. But Communist China has no dowry system, and FLFP there is more than double that of India: 61% versus 27% (World Bank 2018).

In sum, rather than "be all that you can be," high gender inequality can hinder or harm males as well as females. With low FLFP, national development suffers with respect to both GDP growth and human welfare. These are things that could be changed in a single generation, however; these human-caused distortions of biological well-being are *not* long-term destiny. If FLFP rises and gender inequality falls, it is quite likely that the "created biology of gender stratification" will shift to something healthier for girls and young women.

But where low FLFP and high gender inequality prevail, there are other consequences that reverberate beyond those immediately affected. Take, for example, the inverse correlation between FLFP and armed conflict, discussed in Blumberg and Cohn (this volume).[41]

Low-Education U.S. White Males: A New "Created Biology of Gender Stratification"?

Without question, millions of manufacturing jobs have vanished (they dropped from 17 million in the 1990s to 11.5 million at the height of the Great Recession to 12.3 million now; Kessler and Lee 2017). But it should be stressed that the percentage of GDP from manufacturing has *not* suffered a steep decline: It's been more than one third of GDP every year from 1997 to 2013 except for the recession year of 2009 (Scott 2015). Automation and robots have been more important job killers than off-shoring jobs to other nations or immigrants taking U.S.-born workers' jobs.

Yet, those white men with no more than high school diplomas are suffering biological consequences as well: the diseases—and deaths—of despair (Case and Deaton 2015, 2017) are rising. These include depression; suicide; alcoholism-related liver failure; high rates of cancer deaths and heart disease from smoking; obesity, and diabetes, heart disease, and strokes linked to obesity; and most recently, widespread abuse of prescription opioids by these men—often prescribed following a work-related injury—as well as a rise in heroin addiction because it's so much *cheaper* than opioids. Of all these "diseases and deaths of despair," the opioid crisis has been the fastest rising. Now with very cheap imported fentanyl from China (1,000 times more potent than opium or heroin; a minute amount will kill), drug addiction deaths are rising into never-before-seen territory (Case and Deaton 2015, 2017). Bleak new Centers for Disease Control data show more than 72,000 overdose deaths in 2017, a twofold increase since 2007, driven by synthetic opioids—fentanyl in particular (*Washington Post*/Ingraham 2018).

Some low-education white women also have been hit by the same trends, though their numbers are far smaller. Still, the percentages are rising even faster among low-education white women than among their male counterparts—foretelling a possible worsening of the "diseases of despair" statistics.

Already, however, the rising surge of "deaths of despair" for white men and women 25 to 64, from 1999 to 2015, and not for other groups (Case and Deaton 2017), have resulted in two successive years of declining life expectancy in the United States; this is nearly unheard of for a rich Western nation and the first such downturn in nearly 60 years (*Washington Post* 2017: A12). Many see themselves as worse off than their fathers (and sometimes grandfathers), with their sons' futures precarious and possibly worse than their own—that is, "a long-term disintegration of job prospects" (Achenbach and Keating 2017).

These trends—coupled with flat wage growth (adjusted for inflation) and rising inequality and capital concentration trends—are linked to others that have affected the biological condition of many Americans. One example is height. In much of the recent past, Americans were taller than their European counterparts.

Then the Europeans got guaranteed access to health care within a short period after World War II. The United States did not. Moreover, the U.S. rate of income inequality has climbed above that of the other rich nations. Regardless of government policy, however, households with two earners fare better in an advanced capitalist economy than households with only a sole income source.

Conclusions

Nations today have varying but often considerable levels of violence (although it has declined in recent decades), and male domination that ranges from mild (e.g., the Nordic countries) to massive (e.g., Afghanistan). It's not surprising most people think that men always have been the dominant sex and that violence always has been endemic and savage. But consider the previous pages.

The historical and cross-species comparisons lead to a few important "lessons learned":

1. Anthropological, archeological, and historical data indicate that human beings—*Homo sapiens*—have been essentially gender-equal for about 96% of the roughly 315,000 years since we emerged in Africa: Woman the Gatherer seems as important as and equal to Man the Hunter in providing subsistence. In the fast-shrinking number of contemporary hunter-gatherer groups still getting high percentages of their calories from those pursuits, she still has about equal levels of economic power, due in part to her greater say in allocating what she gathered.

2. Based on what we've learned in recent years about bonobos and chimps (both have a 98.7% DNA overlap with us), there is no empirical basis for the "nasty animal" view of humans and inherent human nature.[42] Males aren't maintaining—precariously—a thin veneer of civilization over a raging beast that's not far under the skin. To the contrary, the research on bonobos shows a female-dominated group, with minimal violence, that solves potential conflicts with sex. Also, chimp male violence is far from constant, and not all males are involved (De Waal 2005).

3. Though it sounds like science fiction, scientific evidence is accumulating that humanity had a near miss from destruction by a comet or other celestial body that hit and then fragmented across the Earth about 12,900 years ago. The date matches well with the beginnings of cultivation. This entailed planting foods that (over a few thousand years) morphed into today's basic staples. These included grains (e.g., wheat, rice, corn) and root crops (e.g., cassava, yams, potatoes) that proved very "genetically plastic." They reacted to even small changes in when and where they were planted and how they were cultivated.

4. Also, it appears that it was women gatherers, not men hunters, who began planting and manipulating food crops. What became the basic staples may not have been people's favorite foods, but they were both easily modified and hardy enough to survive difficult conditions (including, perhaps, a nearly global catastrophe—if the

comet hit/fragmentation data continue to accumulate and become fully established science).

5. The rise of patriarchy seems to have been quite recent, with clear-cut cases not emerging until around 6,000 to 7,000 years ago. But history is written by the winners. And it was the more male-dominated and warlike groups that prevailed on the Eurasian landmass who got to write those histories.

6. The beginnings of patriarchy occurred shortly before the invention of the plow in the Middle East around 5,000 to 6,000 years ago. Then came the rise of non-irrigated dry plow agriculture—the first truly *male* farming system, and one that boosted patriarchy as well. Sadly, dry agriculture also proved to have history's highest levels of socioeconomic inequality. And before mechanization, handling heavy plows and the large animals pulling them required a lot of upper-body strength; women have one third to one half less than men do. Worse, dry agriculture didn't (and doesn't) require lots of labor per unit of land area. Given those facts, women were pushed out of production, losing what Blumberg's general theory of gender stratification posits as the essential prerequisite for economic power. (Recall that economic power is posited to be the strongest factor affecting the relative equality of women and men [Blumberg 1984].) Additionally, warfare, another disproportionately male enterprise, also intensified in the last roughly 7,000 years, though in recent years, the *number* of armed conflicts has declined.

7. So are we already doomed to be victims of the most aggressive male, violence as well as the emissions of the machines and energy sources that have driven the quite recent Industrial Revolution (that rose to economic dominance in England by around 1800)? But looking at the cross-history/cross-geography "big picture"—the current mix of still-present patriarchy and violence—industrial capitalism's precariousness and rising environmental destruction are fairly recent. Looking across time and space can—potentially—be energizing. It shows us that for most of our history and in a number of places we were/are not like this. We have the potential to change, and to curb emissions of greenhouse gases (hopefully in time to avoid the worst scenario of runaway climate change). After all, violence, crime, and war frequency have gone down and patriarchy is less broadly acceptable (136 countries have inserted into their constitutions language about women and men being equal; World Bank 2012b).

Finally, what about the "created biology of gender stratification"? The previous section discussed how white U.S. men with no more than high school lost economic power, mostly because of automation. Soon an increasing number began falling victim to the "diseases of despair" (Case and Deaton 2015, 2017).

Currently, the "created biology of gender stratification" seems to have more victims than beneficiaries.

Still, looking at the bigger picture, we see that for most of humanity's existence, the "created biology of gender stratification" has involved *realizing*—not aborting—one's potential (at the extant level of society and technology). Now we have more knowledge and more organizations and people promoting positive causes: combating violence, patriarchy, racism, and many other "isms," as well as climate change. The outcome is up in the (still-breathable) air. We have the potential to rise above the bad side of the past 7,000 or so years of history. Lighting candles does diminish the darkness—if enough people join in.

NOTES

1. In biological terms, the positive side ("Be all that you can be") would be "full phenotypic expression of the genotype."

2. Women had near 100% of the economic power among the Iroquois of colonial North America (Brown 1970, 1975), and were essentially equal; conversely, men currently have near 100% of the economic power in present-day Afghanistan (Blumberg 2016b) and greatly dominate women. The Iroquois still can be found in much of their original homeland; they never were forced into a "March of Tears." Afghanistan is now in year 17 of its latest war; the country has been at war for most of the past 40 years. Indicators of well-being reflect the miserable position of women: Health and education levels are low, violence against them is high, and the male-run economy includes considerable war profiteering and the opium trade, both essentially male monopolies.

3. And some quite negative impacts of "created biology" can be triggered by especially bad economic downturns that undermine many adults' livelihoods. This is happening to low-education U.S. men, as discussed later in this chapter.

4. Two exceptions are described later in this chapter. Also it should be noted that *Homo sapiens* emerged in Africa.

5. In my general theory of gender stratification, I propose that there is a *prerequisite* to economic power: work in important subsistence/livelihood activities. "Mere work," however, is *not* enough—consider all the slaves, housewives, and even workers who have toiled untold hours but, with no control over the means and/or fruits of production, have failed to gain any substantial returns. To derive economic power from one's labors, one has to have at least some of what I term "strategic indispensability factors." These include the importance of (a) the women producers' *activities* and/or (b) the women producers *themselves*, measured by how much of the output or diet the activities and/or women generate and how easy or hard it is to replace the activities and/or women. Some additional factors include the women producers' *control of technical expertise*, ability to *organize* on their own behalf, and the extent of *competition* (by countervailing groups) for the women and/or their output (Blumberg 1984:57 discusses this in greater detail).

6. Both chimpanzees and bonobos have a mother–son incest taboo; otherwise, there seem to be no other sexual taboos in either species.

7. There were exceptions. Some hunting was communal. For example, the way the short-statured Mbuti, in the dense Ituri rainforest in the Democratic Republic of Congo, hunted elephants: Most band members helped in beating the bush and throwing the nets over the elephant; several young

men then speared the immobilized elephant (Turnbull 1961). Women in other groups hunted more (though less than men), some with dogs (O'Kelly and Carney 1987).

8. The two exceptions are most Arctic and Australian aboriginal groups. Among Arctic peoples, the women are only minor producers, given plants' short growing season there. Among most Australian aboriginal groups (Kaberry 1939; Hobhouse, Wheeler, and Ginsberg 1915), males are more likely to have complex kin-based organization than females are. And organization enhances power.

9. Astronomers use the term the "Goldilocks zone" to refer to planets orbiting their sun at a distance that permits liquid water, seen as a prerequisite for most life-forms (i.e., a "just right" situation). I say gender equality is our "just right" way of life because it permits everyone to "be all they can be," as in the old U.S. Army recruiting slogan.

10. Additionally, I suggest, gathering led to other important forms of knowledge that contributed to humans' survival success and growing store of well-being-enhancing information. For example, women's gathering fostered (a) knowledge of plants with medicinal qualities (e.g., comfrey roots for healing broken bones, willow bark for pain—its active ingredient is salicylic acid, which we call aspirin, and it is apparently used for this purpose wherever willows grow) and (b) knowledge of plants with contraceptive/abortifacient properties (e.g., mistletoe).

11. Below a certain body-fat ratio, conception is difficult to impossible, and the healthy but low-fat diet plus exercise kept women close to that level; in addition, long nursing suppresses ovulation, also delaying conception.

12. Closer spacing might have hampered their survival chances. Moving around frequently is much harder and potentially dangerous. Imagine, for example, a woman carrying an infant, her partner carrying a toddler, and both taking turns carrying the 5-year-old when she or he gets tired—while also trying to juggle their necessities for survival—when a lion or hyena catches their scent. . . .

13. Forager meta-groups are akin to the perhaps 500 people sharing the same dialect who came together yearly or more. They had feasts, rituals, fun, games, and trade; this meta-group often was the breeding unit, too, since sex was part of the fun. These get-togethers also helped humans' long-term survival: Bands usually average 25 to 40 people, which is too small a gene pool to prevent "genetic drift," where generations of inbreeding result in spreading defective recessive genes to the point that the band dies out from the bad mutations (Blumberg 1978).

14. The PGEs besides platinum are iridium, osmium, palladium, rhodium, and ruthenium.

15. Though as groups became more dependent on horticulture, men cleared new plots, gradually taking a bigger role.

16. These include the New Guinea highlands (e.g., Meggitt 1970; Strathern 1972) and jungle tribes of the Amazon basin (e.g., Wilbert 1963; Murphy and Murphy 1974). Similar patterns are found among many Southeast Asian hill tribes and even in Haiti, where women are important in hoe horticulture.

17. These basic staples weren't people's favorite foods. But they mutated easily. So those who knew a lot about plants (i.e., women gatherers) could start experimenting with making them tastier, easier to cook, and so forth. Soon they'd have a new staple they could start to plant and grow. (Horticulture specialists and women farmers' groups in Nigeria, Tanzania, and Uganda described their work with cassava and sweet potato root crops to the author, e.g., just how they created improved varieties that added to the household food supply and had good commercial value as well.)

18. Both genders were buried with similar *amounts/values* of grave goods, but they differed in type for each gender.

19. Some economists argue it's more efficient to steal your neighbors' animals than to raise your own from birth. But herders' fear of theft or retaliation meant they couldn't let their animals find water and pasturage during a drought. So the animals ate even the roots of the plants where they were forced to graze. This created the world's major deserts, Griffith (2001) argues (e.g., in the Sahara/Sahel, Arabian peninsula, and dry areas of Central Asia).

20. It got even worse after plow agriculture spread across the Eurasian landmass and beyond, as we'll see later in this chapter.

21. Most sub-Saharan areas with deep soils (in much of southern and eastern Africa) became "white settler colonies."

22. Something analogous is found in the math scores of 15-year-olds taking the PISA exam. In an earlier exam (Guiso et al. 2008), the greater a nation's level of gender equality, the smaller the gap between girls' and boys' scores. Girls in most Nordic nations, the most gender-egalitarian, were only several points to a handful behind the boys, and in one, Iceland, they outperformed the boys by two points. In the 2012 PISA, Southeast Asia (the world's most traditionally gender-egalitarian area) was the only *region* where girls scored higher in math. Girls in Thailand scored a full 14 points more than boys (OECD 2012).

23. When the author was a Peace Corps Volunteer in Venezuela (teaching research methods to sociology majors at Andrés Bello University), she led a student expedition to the jungle headwaters of the Orinoco to study a Padamo River Yanomamo village and a thriving matrilineal Maquiritare village on the Cunucanuma River. The differences between the well-fed, more egalitarian Maquiritare and the more precariously situated Yanomamo village were huge. The confident Maquiritare women were a huge contrast to the timid, often-beaten Yanomamo women. But alleged chronic protein shortage among Amazonian jungle horticulturalists ended up in anthropology textbooks because of the popularity of Chagnon's writings on the Yanomamo. The well-nourished Maquiritare the author encountered would have laughed.

24. Agriculture comes from the Latin word for *field*.

25. After the European discovery, conquest, and colonization of the Western Hemisphere and Australia/New Zealand, they found that much of the land was suitable for dry plow agriculture. Large landowners and/or small-scale settlers soon pushed the indigenous, mostly horticultural populations off the land, sometimes commandeering their labor.

26. Blumberg et al. (2013a, 2013b) found that two by-products of low female economic power in South Asia (few earned and controlled income) are malnutrition and ill health—and not just for the women and girls.

27. The southernmost, wetter parts of South Asia also grow irrigated rice but with a different, more unequal system. Rather than males and females of the farmer's family all working in rice production, the only women out in the rice paddies have been from the lowest castes or otherwise marginalized groups. So in South Asia, even rice farmers of moderate means kept their wives in seclusion. The wives could, *within their household compounds,* do all the threshing and post-harvest processing of the paddy rice to prepare it for sale by the men. This meant that the husbands saw the women's productive labor as just another (uncompensated) aspect of female housework.

28. The first European countries to industrialize were England, Germany, and France, all emerging from a "dry," non-irrigated agrarian system. All had a bilateral kin/property system, recognizing both father's and mother's side relatives, though often giving somewhat more weight to the father's male kin. The only Asian country among the early industrial nations was Japan. It also was the only one with a "wet," irrigated

rice agrarian system and a patrilineal/patrilocal kin/property system in the early period of industrialization. Even today, the relative position of women in the early European industrializer countries is better than that of women in Japan, despite their history as unpaid labor in the family rice paddy. During early industrialization, European women could inherit property; Japanese women generally could not. In other words, "mere work" is not enough. Control of economic resources, however, enhances women's power and position. Additionally, it helps protect them from male violence. Consider Randall Collins's 1971 theory of gender stratification, which focuses on violence as the primary variable. In most agrarian societies, violence was endemic and women without economic resources of their own would have an increased likelihood of becoming victims of violence (Levinson 1989). Conversely, women with some long-recognized economic power are less likely to be beaten by their husbands (Blumberg 1978, based on a 61-society sample).

29. Women there kept much of their access to economic resources due to long male absence in the Viking era (800s to about 1100) and the late arrival of Christianity (about 1000 A.D.), a more patriarchal religion than their traditional beliefs. This is not to attribute the current level of gender equality in present-day Norway, Sweden, Denmark and Greenland to what transpired in the Viking era. But some of those long traditions of greater female autonomy may have helped lay the groundwork for their very near equal position today.

30. Not all Southeast Asian countries are at the same level of female economic autonomy or local-level gender equality. Vietnam was ruled by China for a millennium, ending in the 900s, and some of the patriarchy of Confucianism and a conservative Catholic Church have rubbed off. Nevertheless, Hoang's (2015) study of young Vietnamese women, often fresh from rural villages, who work as bar girls—and sometimes turn tricks, but when and with whom they decide—shows a strong sense of autonomy. Very recently, a more conservative version of Islam is translating into headscarves on young Muslim women in Malaysia and Indonesia. But so far, they remain far more autonomous and economically empowered than Muslim women from MENA and South Asia.

31. A personal methodological note: In most of the 48 countries where I've worked in development, I've used my own version of rapid appraisal (Blumberg 2002a) for field research. This entails "triangulation" to achieve validity. (Validity refers to the accuracy of one's research results. "Triangulation" is using at least two different research techniques to collect the data in exploratory research, and then comparing their findings. This "triangulation" results in greater validity [i.e., more accurate results.]) It also works best with a tightly honed list of variables and multiple methods. These can include key informant interviews, focus groups (I've found that five is the ideal number of participants), content analysis of documents, reanalysis of existing data sets to explore new angles (e.g., disaggregating a data set by gender and reanalyzing), and, possibly, a "last-step survey" to back up important findings with more quantitative methods.

32. She published it as *The Two-Headed Household: Gender and Rural Development in the Ecuadorian Andes* (1998).

33. These Quichua women and their *mestiza* neighbors across the valley both work in cultivation, animal husbandry, and market trade, but their gender ideology differs: *Mestizos* accept the Hispanic custom that "the woman is for the house" (Stolen 1987) versus the equal partnership Quichua ideology. So income brought in by *mestizas* is subject to a big ideological "discount" (Blumberg 1991) that reduces the clout it should have given them, since "they really shouldn't have been out of the house earning it in the first place." Quichua women have no such constraint.

34. This finding differs from much of the gender and development literature, beginning with Boserup's (1970) path-breaking work. She found that commercialization of agriculture tends to undermine women's economic autonomy and status. Here, however, Hamilton's statistics show that women's control of land, income, and technology—and their status—is not related to the degree of agricultural commercialization.

35. This was the same pattern as Ecuador's: 1,000+ years of using metal for jewelry and tools before starting to make lethal war weapons (Gartelmann 1986; Echeverría and Muñoz 1988; Netherly 1992; Cordero 1992; and my impressions in national and regional museums).

36. Our research was presented at the 1985 World Conference on Women in Nairobi; the author's case studies were on Guatemala and the Dominican Republic.

37. Women who fear there will be insufficient land increasingly stop after two children, regardless of their gender. This conforms to the propositions of my theory that with greater economic power, women have more control over their own fertility, which therefore more closely reflects their own pattern of utilities. So the great power of women in fertility decisions and the perceived need to limit family size may account for the greater effectiveness of family planning in Isan than any other rural region in the country—a country that has had one of the most successful programs in the world (Tipprapa 1993).

38. At this point, readers might want to go back to the "Power of the Purse" introductory chapter to see the chain of negative outcomes that accompany economically dependent, malnourished teenage wives getting pregnant in households in which they're the lowest person on the totem pole (Blumberg et al. 2013a, 2013b). Here's a summary: The first consequence is intensified malnutrition and insufficient weight gain in pregnancy—averaging only 5 kilos (11 pounds)—just half of what the World Health Organization deems the minimum (Blumberg et al. 2013a). This leads to both higher maternal mortality (200%–500% higher than mothers who are not teenagers, according to Sethuraman and Duvvury 2007), as well as South Asia having the world's highest proportion of low birth weight (LBW) babies (25%–50%; Sethuraman and Duvvury 2007). LBW boys and girls are likely to have lifelong cognitive and/or health problems.

39. There still are occasional reports about widow burning in northern India (e.g., a notorious case in 1987, when a young woman was forcibly put on the funeral pyre, and not as clear-cut cases in 2002 and 2006; BBC 2006).

40. Sadly, dowries have been spreading south of the traditionally patriarchal northern region and to less wealthy castes.

41. Here is a recap: *Every one of the bottom seven nations for FLFP is presently engaged in armed conflict.* Alphabetically, the lowest FLFP countries, averaging around 16%, compared with a world average of 53%, are Algeria, Afghanistan, Iran, Iraq, Jordan, Saudi Arabia, and Syria. Caprioli (2000, 2005) found that a 5% drop in FLFP is linked to an almost 500% increase in armed conflict. So these seven countries have a nearly 3,500% higher probability of conflict than nations with 53% FLFP, the world mean (author's calculation, 2017 data, World Bank 2018). The consequences extend far beyond the seven's borders: Some have the highest flows of refugees, a flow that is changing election outcomes in some European Union nations and possibly affecting elections elsewhere, including the United States.

42. In the 1960s to early 1970s, this became a popular view advocated by, for example, Ardrey (1961, 1966), Lorenz (1966), Morris (1968, 1969), Tiger (1969), and Tiger and Fox (1972). Despite periodic resurgences by others, the data haven't held up.

Development, the State, and Gender

A Comparative Analysis of Iran and Tunisia

Valentine M. Moghadam

Abstract. Modernization and economic development in both Iran and Tunisia have led to the growth of an educated female middle class with aspirations for greater participation and rights, but women's economic and political empowerment varies significantly, and the capacity of women's rights organizations for the achievement of legal and policy reforms has been far more limited in Iran than in Tunisia. The paper argues that the different outcomes result from (a) the nature of the development strategies in place and the role of the respective countries in the world-economy, (b) the different political systems, and (c) the different gender regimes. Drawing on world-system, world polity, and feminist conceptual frameworks, and using available data, the paper examines and contrasts the evolution of development, social transformation, and gender relations in the two countries.

Introduction

Contrary to conventional wisdom that sees the Middle East and North Africa (MENA) as a largely undifferentiated region characterized by low female labor force participation (FLFP), marginal political representation of women, and patriarchal family laws, women's social, economic, and political participation and rights are quite varied across the region. In previous work, I have identified development strategies in general, and the oil economy in particular, as key to understanding female labor supply and demand, and compared countries such as oil-rich Algeria, Iran, and Saudi Arabia with the more diversified economies of Morocco and Tunisia (Moghadam 1993, 1995, 1998, 2005). More women worked in general, and in manufacturing in particular, in the non-oil and mixed economies than in the countries with large oil and gas industries.[1] Since my early analyses, female educational attainment has increased across the region, fertility rates have declined, and women's political representation has grown, especially in Algeria, Morocco, and Tunisia, where quotas have been established (Moghadam 2013; Karshenas, Moghadam, and Chamlou 2016; Shalaby and Moghadam 2016). And yet the overall rate of FLFP, along with the female share of paid employment, remain lowest for the MENA region, when compared with other regions in the world-economy. Explanations for why the region remains behind other regions have been offered in the literature and will be summarized in a subsequent section of this chapter. The focus here, however, is a comparative analysis of Iran and Tunisia, which highlights the salience of structural and institutional features in the variations that exist in women's economic and political empowerment across the MENA region.

Iran and Tunisia are both Muslim-majority countries that experienced revolutions (Iran in 1979 Tunisia in 2011), but there the similarities end. Most interesting are the differences between the two countries. One key difference pertains to historical development: Tunisia experienced both Ottoman and French colonial rule, while Iran was never colonized. Another lies in geography, resource endowments, and place in the international system: Tunisia is a small non-oil economy that did not figure in geopolitical rivalries, while Iran is a large country with an abundance of oil and was a crucial U.S. ally from 1953 until the 1979 revolution. Iran's modernization began earlier—in the 1930s under Reza Shah, at a time when Tunisia was still under French rule. And yet, the institutional legacy of French colonialism in post-independence Tunisia includes a republican polity, French-style judicial and education systems, and a large and influential trade union, the Union Générale des Travailleurs Tunisiens (UGTT). In the 1950s in Iran, following the coup d'état against Premier Mossadegh and the return of a highly personalist monarchy, the trade unions were repressed. During the Cold War, both countries were in effect part of the camp of the West, but Tunisia did experiment with a version of socialism in the 1960s. Thereafter, the countries pursued very different development strategies: Iran's was led and indeed financed by oil revenues, while Tunisia sought to develop its manufacturing and tourism sectors. In addition, since Iran's 1979 revolution, the polities in the two countries have diverged even more; in Iran's case, a theocratic republic was established, while in Tunisia a secular republic prevailed and became democratic after the January 2011 political revolution. In 1990, the female labor force share in Iran was just 10.9% compared with 21.6% in Tunisia; in 2010, the figures were 17.9% and 26.9%, respectively.[2]

Both Iran and Tunisia have seen significant progress in women's educational attainment, age at first marriage, fertility rates, and political activism. Modernization and economic development in both countries have led to the growth of an educated female middle class with aspirations for greater participation and rights, but the capacity for women's mobilizations for legal and policy reforms has been far more limited in Iran than in Tunisia. I argue that the reasons for the differences in women's economic and political empowerment across the two countries lie in (a) the nature of the development strategies that the countries have pursued across the decades and (b) the divergent political systems, which in turn have generated (c) different gender regimes.

This chapter begins with an overview of the theoretical frameworks that inform the subsequent analysis of the structural and institutional features that help explain why FLFP is so much lower in MENA than in other world regions. I then describe the evolution of development strategies pursued in Iran and Tunisia, after which I discuss the different political systems and gender regimes. Quantitative information on Iran and Tunisia highlights the contrast in outcomes for women of the differing development strategies pursued and institutions adopted.

Orienting Theory

Proponents of world polity theory—also known as world society or world culture theory—emphasize the global circulation of legal, normative, and policy frameworks via multilateral organizations and international nongovernmental organizations, and advocacy by domestic human rights organizations (e.g., Meyer et al. 1997; Swiss 2012). States participate in international organizations, sign and ratify international laws, conventions, standards, and norms, and adopt and adapt them domestically (albeit with varying degrees of commitment and enforcement). Such adoption of international conventions, as well as the establishment of bureaucracies, practices, and procedures that are similar across countries and world regions, are said to be indicative not only of a certain institutional isomorphism but also of a kind of shared modernity (Boli 2005). Consider the United Nations' Convention on the Elimination of All Forms of Discrimination Against Women (CEDAW), adopted in 1979 and in force since 1981, and the Beijing Platform for Action, agreed on at the United Nations' Fourth World Conference on Women, in Beijing in 1995. These international conventions and norms establish women's equality, call on states to eliminate discriminatory practices and laws, and require periodic monitoring and reporting by member states, as well as shadow reports by nongovernmental organizations (NGOs). Nearly all UN member states have signed on to these treaties.

Some states, however, have chosen not to sign or ratify the conventions, while others have entered such sweeping "reservations" as to render the treaties essentially meaningless. The United States and the Islamic Republic of Iran have yet to ratify CEDAW, while Saudi Arabia's sweeping reservation—declaring that the state may ignore any article contradicting Sharia law—shows that certain states may use their standing in the world-system to ignore, circumvent, or even defy international standards and norms. That is, in the contemporary world-system, states that command significant resources or revenues, or are part of powerful alliances, enjoy more leverage than do others. In contrast, countries that are poor in economic resources and power or have experienced some form of conflict may be unable (or unwilling) to mobilize the necessary resources to implement the new institutions for women's participation and rights. The different options available to states are indicative of inequalities and hierarchies that operate across the capitalist world-system's economic zones of core, periphery, and semiperiphery. Such inequalities and hierarchies also operate subnationally, as class, ethnic, and gender inequalities.

Feminist scholars have operationalized the concept of gender at micro, meso, and macro levels of analysis. In particular, the macro-level concept of the *gender regime* (sometimes also known as the gender order or the gender system) distinguishes private and public patriarchy, and within the advanced capitalist Western context, Walby (2009) identifies neoliberal and social democratic gender regimes. For MENA countries, Moghadam (2016) has hypothesized that a transition from a "neopatriarchal" to a "modern" type of public gender regime is underway in Morocco and Tunisia (and to a lesser extent Algeria), as a result of the activities of women's rights organizations and in tandem with economic and political changes there. The gender regime is the product of different development strategies and political systems, and can be observed through the legal and institutional frameworks in place; through women's formal civil, political, and social rights of citizenship; and through indicators of women's socioeconomic and political participation. Both Iran and Tunisia are subject to norm and institutional diffusion within world society, as well as to the periodic crises of the world-system, but state and civil society responses have differed, with implications for the stability or change of the gender regime.

These theoretical insights help explain why women have more rights in Tunisia than in Iran, even though Iran is richer and more powerful. It is worth noting that the comparison in this chapter is at an aggregate and cross-country level: differences in women's economic and political participation and rights in Iran compared with Tunisia. I am not comparing "horizontal inequalities" per se—that is, differences between men and women in each country—although previous research has very much focused on those differences and some references will be made in this chapter. Nor am I comparing "vertical inequalities" within the female population, although I am fully cognizant of the salience of class and the extent to which social class determines access to economic and political resources; I have discussed class differences in previous work and make some references to them in this chapter. Comparing Iran and Tunisia achieves the goal of underscoring the way that control over substantial economic resources by a patriarchal state, which in turn entrenches a neopatriarchal gender regime, allows the ruling elite to bypass certain global standards and norms, and limits women's access to paid employment and political power.

The Regional Oil Economy 1960s to 1990s: Implications for Female Labor

The MENA region is a late industrializer. Unlike the longer history and concerted industrialization of much of Latin America, or the early turn to export-led manufacturing in East and Southeast Asia, the industrialization drive in MENA gained momentum when revolutionary regimes took over in Algeria, Egypt, Iraq, Libya, and Syria in the 1960s, and when oil prices increased dramatically in the early 1970s. In Iran, the shah decided to divert oil revenues to finance industrialization, and followed a classic pattern of import-substitution industrialization, or ISI (Karshenas 1990). In non-oil Tunisia, the economy benefited from labor flows to oil-rich Libya and from the remittances sent back (Richards and Waterbury 1990; Harik 1992). At the time, all MENA countries were part of the periphery of the world-system. Oil-rich countries provided oil (and some supplied gas) for core-based oil corporations and used petrodollars to purchase weapons and heavy machinery from the United States and Europe (a pattern that continues to this day). The poorer MENA countries sent labor abroad and relied on remittances and foreign aid.

Iran followed the typical Third World ISI industrialization pattern while remaining dependent on oil revenues for foreign exchange and to finance imports and development projects. ISI in Iran, however, did not evolve into manufacturing for export. Because of oil revenues, governments like Iran's chose to extend the import-substitution process, moving into capital-intensive sectors. Oil revenues certainly were used for domestic investment purposes, and Iran saw the emergence of an industrial labor force. The modern manufacturing sector did grow with all manner of appliances and food products, auto assembly plants, and foreign investments in iron and steel production. Nevertheless, foreign exchange from oil sales constituted the accumulation of capital, and the contribution of petroleum to the national income made the share of other sectors appear insignificant.

There is a longstanding body of literature on the economic and political effects of the "rentier state," but less has been written about its gender dynamics.[3] When a state depends on "rents" (state-owned oil, minerals, tourism, or waterways), it accrues wealth without needing to rely on income taxes. The implications are both economic, in that diversification is forestalled, and political, in that the state is less accountable to its citizenry. In addition, oil wealth enables governments to provide relatively high wages to their workers. Analyzing wage trends in the manufacturing sector, Karshenas (2001) showed that workers' wages were higher in most MENA countries than they were in Asian countries such as Indonesia, Korea, and Malaysia. Karshenas (1990) found that oil wealth had financed Iran's economic development, including infrastructural development and state-owned industries, and helped modernize agriculture, refuting the earlier argument by Katouzian (1981) that oil revenues had resulted in a "pseudo-modernization." More recently, Mohaddes and Pesaran (2013:1) demonstrate that "oil income has been both a blessing and curse."[4]

How does the preceding discussion relate to female employment? The regional labor and capital flows of the 1960s and 1970s and into the 1980s, and the presence of relatively high wages for men (Karshenas 2001) worked to the benefit of economies and a male working class but not to the formation of a female working class. During the heyday of intra-regional migration, workers and professionals moved from the non-oil countries such as Egypt, Jordan, Lebanon, Tunisia, and Yemen to labor-poor oil economies such as Iraq, Kuwait, Libya, and Saudi Arabia. Labor migration and remittances certainly improved household well-being, especially in the urban areas, but they also served to limit female labor supply and demand. Across the region, states did rely on women to serve as teachers and health workers, to occupy some positions in public administration, and to work in certain factories. But the growth of female employment proved slower in MENA countries than in other regions. The regional oil economy therefore reinforced what I called *the patriarchal gender contract*—the implicit and often explicit agreement that men are the breadwinners responsible for financially maintaining wives, children, and elderly parents, and that women are wives, homemakers, mothers, and caregivers. Codified in the region's Muslim family laws, the patriarchal gender contract justified men's domination within the public sphere of markets and the state, and women's relegation to the private sphere of the family (Moghadam 1998, Chapter 1; Karshenas and Moghadam 2001).

The MENA model of state-led industrialization and growth was swept aside in the 1990s with the global transition to the neoliberal economic policy model. Studies showed how ill-prepared MENA countries were for such a transition, whether in terms of the size and strength of the private sector and key economic institutions, or in terms of the quality and gender composition of its labor force (Karshenas 2001; Karshenas and Moghadam 2001). The large-scale entry of women into certain economic sectors that had been observed for East and Southeast Asia and parts of Latin America and the Caribbean, and theorized by Standing (1989) and others, were not replicated in MENA. Moreover, male unemployment ensuing from the end of the oil boom era in the 1980s, the return of labor

Table 5.1 Female Labour Force Participation Rates Across Regions (in %), 1980 and 2009		
	1980	2009
World	50	52
High-income countries	45	52
East Asia and Pacific	67	64
Europe and Central Asia	58	51
Sub-Saharan Africa	57	61
Latin America and the Caribbean	36	52
South Asia	33	35
Middle East and North Africa	21	26

Source: Adapted from World Bank, *World Development Review 2012,* Box 5.1, p. 200.

migrants, conflicts within the region, international sanctions (on Iraq and Iran), and the small volume of foreign direct investment during the 1990s and into the new century served to limit demand for female labor.

Table 5.1 shows how the MENA region fares in FLFP compared with other world regions. Women's economic activity rates have been growing in most regions (the decline in Europe and Central Asia is largely attributed to women's job losses after the collapse of socialist economies) and most dramatically in Latin America and the Caribbean. Fewer women participate in the labor force in MENA; data not shown indicate that FLFP rates are higher in North Africa (within which Tunisia resides) than they are in the Middle East (within which Iran resides).

If oil-led development could entrench the patriarchal gender contract, the growth of Islamist movements and governments also reinforced women's subordinate position within the family and society. In early writings, I identified the MENA state as *neopatriarchal*—that is, engaged in both economic modernization and the preservation of the traditional family. The modernizing and traditionalist tendencies of states were variable across the region, but the patriarchal elements were strengthened after the Iranian Revolution and the spread of Islamist movements in the 1980s. For example, whereas the 1960s and 1970s saw the creation of job opportunities for working-class and middle-class women in Iran, along with a modernist family law introduced in 1973 (Afkhami 1984), the trend was reversed after the Islamic Revolution, especially for working-class women (Moghadam 1988, 2013; Nomani and Behdad 2006).[5] A principal demand of Islamist movements has been the strengthening of Muslim family law, which is a key institutional barrier to enhanced female economic participation—to women's autonomy, mobility, and financial independence.

Socioeconomic Implications of Muslim Family Law

The patriarchal gender contract is by no means unique to MENA; it prevailed in Western countries in an earlier era but was slowly undermined and then superseded by the imperatives of capitalist industrialization as well as the aspirations of women's movements, which led to legal changes and policy reforms to counter discrimination and encourage women's labor force participation.[6] There have been reforms to family law in MENA but regressions as well, such as occurred in Iran after the 1979 revolution, Egypt in 1985 and again after its 2011 political revolution, and socialist southern Yemen following unification with the north in 1990. Only Tunisia's personal status code—adopted in 1956, 3 years before the newly independent country adopted its constitution—was relatively liberal from the start and was improved on in the early part of the new century.

By codifying male responsibility for the maintenance of wives, female kin, and children, Muslim family law (MFL) reinforces female financial dependence in the household. Some of the associated practices are the *mahr* (dower, or bride-price) and in the Islamic Republic of Iran, the *ujrat-ol-mesl,* or the concept of wages for housework and childcare in the event of divorce.[7] Under MFL, women are required to obtain the permission of their fathers, husbands, or other male guardians to undertake travel, including business travel. Although wives—at least those who are educated and politically aware—may stipulate in their marriage contracts the condition that they are allowed to work, many wives make no such stipulations, and courts have been known to side with the husband when the issue is contested, as Sonbol (2003:89–99) found for Jordan. Traditional gender norms codified in MFL may discourage the adoption of policies and arrangements favorable to broad-based maternal employment, such as paid maternity leaves, childcare centers, and preschool facilities. Although much research has uncovered the gap between the law and the lived reality, there does seem to be a connection between the prevalence of MFL and the persistence of low FLFP and limited involvement in paid employment in MENA.

Muslim family law has other economic implications, which derive in part from its class bias (see Spectorsky 2009). The unequal inheritance aspect—whereby sons inherit twice as much as daughters—compromises women's financial independence and, inter alia, has implications for women's ability to set up a business (Moghadam 2006). But it is a sensitive issue; it is seen on one level as a divine imperative revealed in the Qur'an and on another level as an important part of the patriarchal gender contract whereby women are provided for by their fathers, husbands, or brothers. Polygamy is not practiced widely in MENA, but it does occur (especially in the oil-rich Gulf countries), along with divorce. A deceased man's inheritance and his pension are divided among his widows, his children, and any other relatives that he may have been supporting. As a result, many widows receive insignificant pensions. Even though Islamic norms and some laws require that fathers and husbands financially support their daughters and wives, it is also the case that divorced, widowed, or abandoned women without access to jobs or a steady source of income, especially among the low-income social groups, are often left in a state of impoverishment. Indeed, for low-income women, being divorced can mean loss of children and home and a life of destitution.[8] Around the world, many countries have instituted laws that recognize marital property and a wife's right to half of the marital assets in case of divorce, but this has yet to be adopted in MENA countries with MFL. In this way, MFL both reflects and reinforces the patriarchal gender contract and women's economic dependence on husbands. Patriarchal Muslim family law remains in effect in Iran but not in Tunisia.

Contrasting Iran and Tunisia: Development Strategies and Women's Employment

Before delving into the Iranian case, it is useful to examine comparative indicators that reveal the extent to which women's economic and political empowerment has diverged in the two countries. As seen in Tables 5.2 and 5.3, Iran is a larger and far wealthier country, and yet Tunisia's women fare considerably better across a range of social, economic, and political indicators.

Table 5.2 Socioeconomic Indicators, Iran and Tunisia, 1995, 2015	Iran		Tunisia	
	1995	2015	1995	2015
Population (millions)	60.57	77.45	9.1	10.9
GDP (billions USD)	$90.8	$231.43	$18	$43.32
GDP per capita	$1,506	$15,573	$2,013	$10,768
Military spending % GDP	2.4	2.3	1.9	1.6
Education and health spending % GDP	8.2	10.4	12.3	13.3
Oil exports as % total exports	86% (1997)	70% (2011)	8%	15% (2013)
Non-oil manufacturing as % total exports	14%	30%	92%	85%
Tourism as % foreign exchange revenue	NA	NA	NA	13.0%
Female labor force participation rate	11.8	18.3 (2013)	23.5	26.9 (2013)
Female non-agricultural paid labor force (% total labor force)		15%		28%
Female unemployment rate	18.7%	20.1%	19.0%	15.5%
Youth unemployment rate, F, M		F 41.7% M 26.4%		F 29.3% M 32.0%
Estimated earned income, F, M		F $4,787 M $27,744		F $4,771 M $17,596
Estimated earned income (F/M ratio)		0.17		0.27

Sources: World Bank (2018); World Economic Forum, Global Gender Gap Report 2015, 2013, 2011, http://reports .weforum.org/global-gender-gap-report-2015/rankings/; 2002 Tunisia CEDAW Report, http://www.un.org/women-watch/daw/cedaw/cedaw27/tun3-4.pdf; International Labour Organization, http://www.ilo.org/global/statistics-and-databases/lang--en/index.htm, http://www.ilo.org/ilostat/faces/home/statisticaldata/ContryProfileId?_afrLoop=7790 11335250152#%40%3F_afrLoop%3D779011335250152%26_adf.ctrl-state%3D3hmnb459l_158; http://labo rsta.ilo.org/STP/guest.

Table 5.3 Comparative Features of the Gender Regime, Iran and Tunisia, 2017

	Iran	Tunisia
Percent married by age 18*	17%	2%
Female share of non-agricultural paid labor force	15%	28%
Female unemployment rate	20%	15%
Paid maternity leave provisions	270 days; 67% of wages; government-provided	30 days; 67% of wages; government-provided
Female share of parliamentary seats	6%	31%
Proportion female judges	0%	29%
Percentage female PhD graduates	35%	54%
Percentage female professors	20%	42%
Abortion legal?	No	Yes
CEDAW ratification	No	Yes, 1986; reservations removed in 2014*
Constitutional guarantees of gender equality?	No	Yes
Open feminist advocacy?	No	Yes
Patriarchal family law?	Yes	No

* The general declaration was maintained: Tunisia reserved the right to refuse "any organizational or legislative decision . . . [in] conflict with the provisions of Chapter 1 of the Tunisian Constitution."

Sources: World Economic Forum, *Global Gender Gap Report 2015*; Author; *UNICEF https://data.unicef.org/topic/child-protection/child-marriage/; other sources.

In the 1970s, and under the rule of Shah Mohammad Reza Pahlavi, Iran had ambitious plans for economic growth and regional military power (Amuzegar 1992). Most foreign direct investment (FDI) went into oil and gas, but the growing capitalist class did invest in the production of clothing, shoes, appliances, and food processing. Sociocultural modernization occurred primarily in the capital city Tehran. At a time when Iran was importing South Korean skilled workers for some of its industrial projects, the Shah declared in the mid-1970s that Iran would catch up to Europe in a decade's time (Zonis 1991:221). That possibility was halted with the Islamic Revolution and the 8-year war with Iraq (1980–1988). Iran did continue to develop internally, even in the face of international sanctions, but negative growth ensued, followed by stagnation. Meanwhile, South Korea, which had been at roughly the same level of economic and social development as Iran in the 1960s, surpassed Iran economically in the 1980s, experienced a democratic transition, and eventually joined the OECD.

In the 1990s, Iran managed to use its oil wealth to finance its own manufacturing sectors, develop its physical and social infrastructure, educate its population, and produce a formidable military along with nuclear capacity. Women's educational attainment steadily increased such that the gender gap in secondary schooling closed and women's university enrollments in academic year 2000–2001 exceeded those of men for the first time. The economy grew and the government developed new institutions that boosted opportunities for the expansion of modern services—education, medicine, finance, law, engineering, and the like. Although subsidies and other mechanisms were in place to prevent or alleviate poverty, income inequality increased by the end of the decade, private-sector wage earners suffered the highest poverty rates, and the majority of Iranian households contained just one income earner (World Bank 2003:20, 24, 32). According to the 2006 census, women made up just under 15% of the formal labor force.

In 2007 Iran's service sector (including government) contributed 56% to GDP, followed by the hydrocarbon sector with 25%, and agriculture with 10%. Iran ranked second in the world in natural gas reserves and third in oil reserves. It was the second largest OPEC oil producer, with output averaging about four million barrels per day; unsurprisingly, its chief source of foreign exchange derived from oil and gas. Although Iran pursued what the World Bank in 2010 called "prudent macroeconomic policies," it faced difficulties from the strict economic and banking sanctions and embargoes imposed by the United States and Europe, boom and bust cycles, and private-sector uncertainty, all of which impeded investment and job creation. Meanwhile, the state sector continued to invest in the capital-intensive, almost exclusively male-dominated sectors of oil, gas, and nuclear power.

The Iranian state's inability to attract foreign direct investment of the type that might be labor-intensive and employment-generating for women has contributed to the persistence of a small female labor force and an even smaller female working class. The sanctions regime, of course, has had an adverse effect, but Iran's free trade zones in the south did not become the "back doors to the international economy" that the authorities had hoped for. Hakimian (2011:865, 871) showed that while the zones had a modest workforce to begin with (at some 45,000), "female employment creation . . . is very weak." He concluded that "Iran's experience of free zones in the past one and a half decades has failed to achieve its principal objectives of attracting FDI, diversifying non-oil exports and generating new jobs."

In 2011, Iran's economy, at a GDP of US$400 billion, was the second largest in MENA (after Saudi Arabia), and its population, at 76 million people, second to that of Egypt.[9] It was still characterized by a large hydrocarbon sector, small-scale private agriculture and services, and a noticeable state presence in manufacturing and finance. While Iran's economy had shifted toward a market-based economy, the financial sector was largely dominated by public banks, and the state still played a key role in the economy, owning large public and quasi-public manufacturing and commercial enterprises. More than 60% of the manufacturing sector's output was produced by state-owned enterprises. The government's 2010–2015 five-year plan aimed to privatize some 20% of state-owned enterprises (SOEs) each year, although it appeared that assets of SOEs were largely purchased by the Iranian Revolutionary Guards Corps or other semigovernmental enterprises (see Harris 2013).

The presence of state-owned or parastatal monopolies, combined with a strategy in the first two decades after the Revolution that favored self-employment and the expansion of the informal sector (Nomani and Behdad 2006), created an economic and labor market environment that was not conducive to female labor incorporation. Iran's small-scale manufacturing sector continued to produce handicrafts, carpets, and rugs, and women could be found in that sector. Yet according to official statistics, such women workers were typically unpaid or contributing family members rather than paid manufacturing workers. In 1996, only a quarter of the female manufacturing workforce was salaried (Moghadam 2003:212).[10] The 2006 Iranian census showed that women's share of manufacturing was 18.7%, down from 38.2% in 1976 (largely concentrated in rural areas). Disruptions in trade and production following the Islamic revolution (see Moghadam 1988, 1998:159–160; Amuzegar 1992), including the decline in carpet exports due to the war and later because of competition from China, may explain the steep drop in the proportion of female manufacturing. Young rural women might also have been withdrawing from traditional manufacturing because of a newfound tendency to complete schooling. In contrast to the trend in rural women's economic activity, urban women's largest share—at 50%—was of jobs in the education, health, and social services sector.

Meanwhile, female educational attainment increased, as between 1999 and 2011, secondary- and tertiary-level enrollments doubled. At the tertiary level, the female share of master's degree enrollments for the academic year 2006–2007 was more than half in medicine and basic sciences, and only in engineering were female graduate students underrepresented, at 25.5% (Khosrokhavar and Ghaneird 2010:227, Table 2). Studies by UNESCO (2011) and the World Bank (2012) confirmed that by 2010, gender parity had been achieved at the secondary level, the majority of students in higher education were female, and fully 68% of science students were women.

Women's employment correlates with educational attainment; those with just elementary education are less likely to join the labor force, whereas having higher degrees tends to raise women's participation sharply. Married women are less likely to enter the labor force, although highly educated women in the professions, married or not, tend to remain at their jobs for longer periods (Salehi-Esfahani and Shajari 2012).[11] By 2012, the 20% female share of manufacturing included educated women found in managerial or technical positions in the larger industrial firms as well as in the oil and gas industry. Iran's 1395/2016 labor force survey showed that the private sector was the largest employer, employing 76.2% of the female labor force (and 85.6% of male workers), more than half of which was concentrated in public and private services (Islamic Republic of Iran 2016:38, Table 3.1).

And yet women's share of the total workforce remained small, a consequence of their near absence from many public-sector occupations as well as the private sector. According to the 2016 labor force survey, out of a total female population of 39.4 million, of which perhaps half could be considered to be of working age, and out of a total labor force of 21.3 million, just 3 million Iranian women are employed (compared with 18.2 million men). To make matters worse, the female unemployment rate has been high: In 2004, some 43% of young women with university education were unemployed, compared with 22.5% of university-educated men.[12] The 2006 census showed that women's total unemployment rate was 23.3%, more than twice that of men. A decade later this had barely changed; according to the 2016 labor force survey, women's unemployment was nearly 22%, compared with 10.4% for men (Islamic Republic of Iran 2016:19, Table 1.3).

Given high unemployment and inflation in Iran, it is likely that a majority of nonemployed women engage in home-based economic activities, both high-end and low-end. During fieldwork in Iran in 1994, I observed the presence of home-based beauty and dressmaking enterprises discreetly located within neighborhoods. Bahramitash and Kazemipour (2008) and F. Moghadam (2009) found that the upper middle-class women missing from the official labor force statistics are actually engaged in home-based income-generating activities.[13] Such women—whose activities may include making and selling jewelry or special jams; providing catering services; tutoring or counseling; desktop publishing; and directing Pilates or yoga classes—may prefer to undertake work at home rather than acquiesce to the strictures of the dress code and other irritants associated with formal-sector employment. Women from low-income and working-class families similarly engage in home-based informal labor—providing dressmaking, beauty, catering, counseling, childcare, or transportation services—to supplement the incomes of their spouses and otherwise contribute to the household budget, and to have the flexibility needed to attend to domestic duties. Such women work individually rather than as part of collective enterprises, and are not found in official statistics.

To summarize, structural features have militated against enhanced FLFP in Iran: a large hydrocarbon sector and the noticeable state presence in manufacturing and finance, which would be more receptive to male rather than female labor, and the absence of significant foreign direct investment in sectors that might be both labor-intensive and female-intensive. Since the 1979 revolution, the Iranian state has encouraged some women to enter the fields of education and health care, if only to teach and administer health care to women and girls, but in general prefers that women remain at home and care for their families. As a result, the traditional sexual division of labor continues to operate and is especially strong within working-class and lower-income households.

Tunisia

Postcolonial Tunisia, devoid of abundant oil wealth, followed a development strategy that favored import substitution for national development, the promotion and protection of domestic industries, and a preponderant role for the state in economic development (Harik 1992; Seddon, 1993; Richards and Waterbury 1996). In the 1960s, the country followed a quasi-socialist path when former UGTT leader Ahmad Ben Salah became secretary of state for planning and finance and emphasized centralized planning and the collectivization of agriculture and retail trade. Indeed, the ruling party was known as the Destourian Socialist Party until 1988. Opposition from farmers and President Bourguiba's misgivings over Ben Salah's influence led to the latter's downfall and curtailment of his policies. In the early 1970s, the economy began to open up to foreign and private domestic investment, and exports to Europe increased. Another shift occurred in the mid-1980s, when public-sector wage increases were stemmed and union power was curbed in an effort to stimulate investment and employment. Investments increased substantially, and in the second half of the 1980s, the fastest growing sectors were textiles, leather, and agro-industries. A substantial drop in the real wages of skilled workers as well as price increases, austerity measures, and cutbacks in public expenditures led to demonstrations and riots. Throughout this period, Tunisia's large and influential trade union, the UGTT, played a prominent role not only in organizing workers but also in challenging government. For example, in 1978 union-led strikes over the rising cost of living forced the government to enter into a new "social contract" with workers that provided for a 33% increase in the minimum wage (Harik 1992). The UGTT includes a women workers' section, as well as health and education sectors in which women officials are found. A key difference with Iran, therefore, lies in the development of labor market institutions, including an active trade union movement.[14]

In 1986, a poor harvest, a bad tourist season (due to the Israeli bombing of the Palestine Liberation Organization headquarters in Tunis), the oil price collapse, mounting debts, and the return of some 30,000 workers who had been expelled from Libya obliged Tunisia's government to seek the assistance of the International Monetary Fund and the World Bank. The Structural Adjustment Program lasted until 1990. Subsequently, private and foreign investments were encouraged by the introduction of a new industrial investment code that relaxed existing regulations, instituted tax holidays, and lowered interest rates. Industrial training schemes and industrial zones (similar to export-processing zones) were set up, and a number of state-owned industrial firms, including a textile and garment conglomerate, were privatized (Harik 1992). The country's export-oriented growth strategy in manufacturing favored textiles, garments, and processed food, welcoming FDI in that sector as well as in tourism, especially from Europe.[15] By 1990 the tourism sector employed more than 40,000 people (*Financial Times* 1990:11), while textiles and garments—a highly feminized sector—constituted nearly 39% of manufacturing. By the end of the decade, the privatization of state-owned hotels was completed (see Moghadam 1998:53).

The Tunisian state also concentrated on investing in human capital, promoting school completion, higher education, and skills upgrading (Ben Romdhane 2006). A fairly generous social policy regime and growing access to schooling provided women not only with educational attainment but also with access to an array of jobs in manufacturing and public and private services. Indeed, structural change in the Tunisian economy away from agriculture offered wage employment opportunities for women, who accounted for just 6% of the labor force in 1970, rising to 15% of all employees in 1980 and 23% in 1994 (Moghadam 2003, Table 2.3). By 2014 the female share of employees was 28.6% (République Tunisienne 2014:14). In terms of employment status, ILO data show that in 2012, of Tunisia's 796,000 working women, 80% were wage earners and salaried workers. Despite these positive trends, unemployment persisted and indeed grew, along with an expanding urban informal sector and changes to employment contracts.

FDI may correlate with greater female economic participation, but as world-system scholars have shown, it also exacerbates dependency and vulnerability of developing countries (Chase-Dunn 1998; Esteva, Babones, and Babcicky 2013). Involvement in international trade is important for jobs in Tunisia. Firms that export end products and import inputs (or both) account for more than 55% of total wage employment. Offshore firms, which produce entirely for export and are exempt from import duties, represented only 6% of all firms but accounted for 33% of wage employment in 2010. About 45% of offshore firms were foreign-owned (Jaud and Freund 2015:2).[16] In 2007, the three major manufacturing subsectors attracted more than 60% of FDI and created more than 80% of new private-sector jobs. The major trading partners and foreign investors in these industries were from France, Spain, Italy, and to a lesser degree, Germany. However, overconcentration of exports on European Union markets, especially southern ones, exposed Tunisia to recessions in those markets from 2009 onward (Jaud and Freund 2015:11–12), resulting in job losses and even higher unemployment rates.

Women in the Professions and in Manufacturing

In contrast to Iran, and despite its changing economic fortunes, Tunisia seems to rely heavily on its female population for various economic activities, both working class and professional. In particular, the country's educational strategy produced a stratum of women available to fill jobs in academia, the judiciary, medicine, and other domains. The proportion of women with higher education qualifications nearly quadrupled between 1994 and 2014, reaching 22% of the female labor force in 2014. Employed women with secondary schooling constituted 38.4%, while those who had completed just primary schooling were 29.6% of Tunisia's female labor force (République Tunisienne 2014:14).[17] Women with university education were especially prominent in the professions, working as lawyers, judges, medical doctors and pharmacists, and university professors. According to Ben Salem (2010:501), women made up 39% of the staff in the civil service. In 2010, they were 42% of university teaching staff (see World Economic Forum's *Global Gender Gap Report* 2010), although a smaller proportion of full professors. Within the health field, women made up 42% of doctors, 72% of pharmacists, and 57% of dental surgeons. These figures suggest the extent to which Tunisia's public and private services depend on women. Besides manufacturing, the sectors of education and of health and social services are quite feminized (57.7% and 67% female, respectively). Other sectors where women make up a significant proportion are recycling, telecommunications, postal services, insurance, and IT (Boughzala 2013, citing INS, *Enquete Micro Entreprises* 2007).

Fully 43% of Tunisia's female labor force is involved in the manufacturing sector, mostly in production, and this figure is indicative of the size of Tunisia's female working class. Feminized manufacturing industries are textiles and clothing and fur, with more than a 60% female share. Women make up a significant proportion of the workforce in "production of medical, precision, and optical instruments and watches" (Boughzala 2013:16). The textiles and garments sector is relatively labor-intensive and heavily feminized (Jaud and Freund 2015:2, Fig. B1.1.1). Women working in the private sector are concentrated in low-skill employment (Ayadi and Mattoussi 2014:5).

As a peripheral country dependent on exports, tourism, and foreign investment, Tunisia has been vulnerable to the vagaries of the world-economy and to the changing fortunes of its European partners. In the new century, the effects of the adoption of neoliberal policies began to be felt. Job losses occurred in the textiles and garments sector as a result of new trade rules that opened up European markets to Chinese and East European products and ended quotas for Tunisian imports (World Bank 2006). To remain competitive, "flexible" employment contracts expanded in Tunisia's private sector, which meant lower wages, the growth of temporary work, and job insecurity for workers. Flexible forms of employment—such as job rotation, short-term contracts, part-time work, flexible work hours, weekend work, night work, and overtime work—became widespread. Apart from the fact that these features may be prohibitive for women given their family obligations and nighttime mobility constraints, a study found that workers involved in flexible work practices faced a higher risk of work injuries and more mental strain than workers involved in a more traditional work organization (Haouas and Yagoubi 2008). This problem and low wages were behind the 2008 strikes in the industrial region of Gafsa. In 2012, 44.6% of the working population had no contract at all, workers benefiting from indeterminate-length contracts constituted 43% of the working population, and those on fixed contracts composed 12.3% (CREDIF 2017:47). Young women did better than young men in terms of type of work contract, but then their unemployment rates were much higher.

In the new century, declining government expenditure entailed a contraction of the public-sector wage bill, and public-sector employment as a percentage of total employment in Tunisia continued to fall.[18] Financialization also affected Tunisia, with increases in the price of food and other commodities. As noted, the Great Recession hit Tunisia especially hard, as the country had become reliant on the Eurozone for much of its trade and investment. These developments, along with increasing unemployment and widening income inequality, were the structural drivers of the widespread dissatisfaction that led to the protests of December 2010 and the political revolution of 2011. When a street vendor who was ordered to stop his trade resorted to self-immolation in December 2010 after being denied justice, his act seemed to symbolize a protest against the collective loss of dignity. The tragedy led to massive street protests the following January, with slogans such as *"Ben Ali, d'égage"* ("Ben Ali, get out") and *"Emploi, notre droit"* ("Employment is our right").[19]

The overview of the development strategies pursued by Iran and Tunisia over several decades reveals the stark differences: Iran has remained reliant on oil revenues for foreign exchange and to fund services and various development projects, while Tunisia has sought to enhance its export manufacturing base and its tourism sector for foreign exchange and to generate employment. Iran added to its investments in its oil and gas sector with another capital-intensive and male-intensive sector: nuclear power. In both countries, female economic activity rates remained small in comparison with rates elsewhere in the world-economy, but Iran's (16%) was much lower than Tunisia's (27%). Tunisia provided more jobs for low-income women—in factories and in low-wage services—than seemed to be the case in

Iran, where a female proletariat appeared to be missing. Women working in Iran's manufacturing sector tend to be highly educated and occupy engineering and managerial positions. In both countries, women's unemployment rates have been much higher than men's, though Iran's rates are higher than Tunisia's (see Table 5.2).

Different Political Systems, Different Gender Regimes

Patriarchy has been a longstanding feature of MENA social structures, though it has been fraying in recent decades as a result of women's educational attainment and employment, the effects of the world polity, and women-friendly legislation. Using Walby's terminology, the 1960s to 1970s saw a transition from private to public patriarchy, in that women received the right to vote, benefited from fairly liberal family codes in Tunisia (1956) and Iran (1973), experienced inroads into modern employment, and saw the appointment of the first women's affairs minister (Iran 1973) and the first woman judge (Tunisia 1967; Iran 1975). Iran's 1979 Islamic revolution, however, halted the transition in the gender regime and substituted Islamization for modernization of gender relations.

In the 1970s, Iranian women occupied about 12% of the labor force, but this declined to about 10% after the Islamic revolution of 1979, as a result of purges of ideologically nonconforming women professionals, exile, the closure of factories, and—as noted earlier—the decline of work for rural women following the loss of the carpet export markets. The first decade of the Islamic Republic was characterized by intense ideological contention between the ruling Islamists and leftists and liberals, the U.S. Embassy hostage crisis, a war economy, and violent repression. The new Islamic state instituted a number of laws that affected women's legal status and social positions. The abrogation of the 1973 Family Protection Act was followed by the reintroduction of polygamy into the Civil Code, the Shia practice of *muta'a*, or temporary marriage, and male unilateral divorce (Tohidi 2010). Quotas for women on fields of study were implemented, and women were banned from being judges, although they could serve as lawyers. A male guardian—father, brother, or husband—was needed for many transactions by women, veiling was made compulsory, and women's political representation was almost insignificant. The patriarchal gender contract became even more entrenched in the 1980s.

At the close of the decade, new developments affected the legal status and social positions of women. The end of the Iran–Iraq war, the death of Ayatollah Khomeini, and the presidential term of Ali Akbar Hashemi Rafsanjani saw the easing of social restrictions along with the end of the war economy and initiation of privatization and liberalization. A reform movement—rooted in both the incipient civil society and in political society—began to blossom in the early 1990s, culminating in the presidential election of Mohamad Khatami in 1997. New movements of feminists, students, journalists, and human rights advocates constituted an incipient civil society supported by political allies in two reformist parliaments (the fifth and sixth parliaments) and the Khatami government (Tohidi 2010; Moghadam 2013, Chapter 6). In the 1990s, the government instituted a widespread and very effective family planning program, which was embraced by most Iranian women. In concert with increases in women's educational attainment and age at first marriage, the government's program led to fertility declines that eventually fell to replacement level (Roudi-Fahimi 2002). Along with the flourishing of civil society, the phenomenon of Islamic feminism developed, along with secular feminist NGOs and a feminist press. Some legal reforms for women's rights also took place in the areas of education, divorce, and travel, legislation that occurred during the fifth parliament and the reformist sixth parliament (1996–2004).

This period ended with the coming of the very conservative Mahmoud Ahmadinejad government, which closed down the independent NGOs, including a burgeoning independent workers' union. The highly contested results of the 2009 presidential election, which saw the reelection of Ahmadinejad, generated the Green Protests, in which women were a strong presence. After several days, the protests were brutally put down. To entrench the patriarchal gender regime even further, Ahmadinejad called Iranian feminism an "alien ideology" and "a threat to national security," harassing the women's NGOs, arresting a number of feminist activists, and leading to the exile of several others. Some of the most prominent names in the Iranian feminist movement—Shirin Ebadi, Parvin Ardalan, Mahboubeh Abbas-Gholizadeh, Nargess Mohammadi, and Nasrin Sotoudeh—were questioned, arrested, imprisoned, or had their offices raided and computers removed (Ebadi 2016).

Female members of parliament make up an insignificant proportion of the Majles, and the senior women in government, such as the various vice presidents, seem not to have any influence on key economic, foreign policy, political, cultural, or social matters. Although women are important political constituents in elections, their participation and representation in the formal political structure is among the lowest in the world: 3% female parliamentary representation and 3% female share of ministerial positions in 2012, increasing to 6% following the 2016 parliamentary elections. The reality of Iranian women's exclusion makes the Iranian political system among the most masculinist in the world. Unlike Tunisia and many other countries, Iran has not instituted gender quotas to enhance women's political participation and has yet to ratify CEDAW, which was ratified by Tunisia in 1985 (see Table 5.3). The Iranian state's legal and policy frameworks, and especially its family laws, reinforce conservative social norms regarding male and female roles. Such norms are internalized by many women themselves, as well as by employers, thus reinforcing the patriarchal gender contract and limiting female labor supply and demand.

Throughout its 40-year history, the Islamic Republic's gender regime has been steadfastly patriarchal, a product of the political system, of the country's pattern of economic development and growth, and of the repression of independent and dissident civil society organizations (Moghadam and Haghighatjoo 2016). Iran's gender regime reflects the political and institutional setup.

The Islamic Republic of Iran bases its political system on a rather novel Shia Islam–influenced republican model devoid of conventional political parties. Although Iran is governed by an elected president and a 290-member parliament, two key institutions are both unelected and very powerful. The supreme leader (*rahbar*)—originally Ayatollah Rouhollah Khomeini, and after his death Ayatollah Ali Khamene'i—is meant to be the nation's spiritual guide but in fact is "the country's most powerful political figure" (Boroujerdi 2014:485). The 12-man Guardian Council—tasked with ensuring that laws, policies, and elections adhere to both the constitution and Islamic norms—frequently has clashed with parliament over legislative bills and its veto of candidates for presidential elections. As for the judiciary, "in practice it has tended to be very conservative (much like the Guardian Council itself) and opposed to reform initiatives" (487). The 1987 ban on political parties was lifted in 1998, but Boroujerdi regards many of them as little more than "professional groupings engaged in political ventures rather than full-fledged groups of full-time activities" (493). As such, Iran's political system lacks the features identified in the literature as favorable to women's "descriptive" representation—a proportional representation system with the presence of left-wing parties, along with quota adoption.[20] Moreover, as a constitutional body that vets candidates and must approve parliamentary bills, the Guardian Council prevents those it deems not sufficiently loyal from accessing political power and often blocks progressive legislation.

On the positive side, women are a strong presence in public spaces and sex segregation is not nearly as strict as it is in Saudi Arabia, though more restricted than in Tunisia. To be sure, Iranian women's presence in public spaces takes the form not only of women walking, driving, shopping, and working but also of women taking part in public protests (where possible) and petition campaigns, and their involvement in the public sphere includes the growth of women's websites and blogs as well as national debates and discussions about women's rights and legal reform. A youth subculture includes holding parties, playing music, dancing, and defying the dress code. Indeed, there have been consistent female challenges to hejab strictures, most recently with the "My Stealthy Freedom" Facebook campaign, which began in 2015 with much male support. In another pendulum swing, the reformist cleric Hassan Rouhani was elected president in 2013 and again in 2017, and promised to appoint more women to government posts.[21] An ongoing national debate on ending compulsory hejab is indicative of the power of women's public presence.

Tunisia

Unlike Iran, the women's rights movement in Tunisia is institutionalized, in part because a history of "state feminism" has enabled decades of research, advocacy, and activism on the part of the feminist organizations, which were formed by academics, artists, journalists, lawyers, and other professionals. Women in Tunisia, therefore, enjoy not only an array of rights first enshrined in the 1956 *Code du Statut Personnel* (CSP) and later in the 2014 constitution but also—as we have seen in the section on women's employment—presence across occupations and professions.

Until 2011 Tunisia had an authoritarian polity, albeit one that defined itself as modern and republican with a moderate Arab-Islamic culture. Under the country's first president, the French-educated lawyer Habib Bourguiba, Tunisia's CSP and its 1959 constitution were ahead of their time. The constitution guaranteed the equality of male and female citizens alike, and the CSP raised the age of first marriage and gave Tunisian women the right to divorce and to seek child custody. This legal framework enabled the transition from domestic to public patriarchy in the postcolonial period. Thereafter, the transition was accelerated by women's educational attainment and involvement in an array of occupations and professions, by increasing urbanization, by the advocacy work of feminist organizations, and by continued government support for women's participation and rights. Throughout, Tunisia has maintained an independent foreign policy stance that has favored integration into the world polity and good relations with its Arab neighbors.

Bourguiba ruled (somewhat erratically) until he was forced out in 1988 and was succeeded by Zein al-Abedin Ben Ali in 1989, who called himself a champion of women's rights. Ben Ali promised political liberalization and a transition to democracy. His early reforms attempted to restore a national consensus; one of these, the National Pact signed in 1989, drew together the ruling party (the Democratic Constitutional Rally, known by its French acronym RCD), the legal opposition, the Islamists, and all the national organizations. Many political parties were legalized, with the exception of the Mouvement de la Tendance Islamique (renamed Ennahda [Renaissance] Party in 1988), but the 1989 national elections failed to introduce a multiparty competition. The president gained 99% of the vote, and the RCD won all 141 seats in the legislature. Local elections in 1990, boycotted by opposition parties, were also swept by the ruling party. Following early local electoral victories by Algerian Islamists in 1990, the government began to crack down on Tunisia's Islamist political activity. In 1993, and in a post–Cold War context, it legalized the former Communist Party, now renamed Tadjdid, or Renewal. During those early promising years, the ministry of education was led by Mohamed Charfi, who sought to (re)institute a modernist outlook into the curriculum, to complement religious studies with historical studies, and to upgrade courses on geography and civic education (Charfi 2015, esp. 219–222).[22]

Progress for women continued with the formation of women's policy agencies. In 1990 the government established the Centre de Recherches, d'Etudes, de Documentation, et de l'Information sur la Femme (CREDIF), with the well-known legal scholar Soukeina Bouraoui as its first director. It was tasked with carrying out studies on various aspects of women's economic conditions and reporting these to the planning ministry. This was followed by the Ministry of Women and Family Affairs.[23] Tunisia then hosted the Center of Arab Women for Training and Research (CAWTAR), which received funding from various international development agencies (see, e.g., Gribaa 2008–2009). Both CAWTAR and CREDIF continue to produce substantive studies on women's economic, political, and social conditions.

Tunisia's women's rights advocates emerged in the 1970s, and as products of both postcolonial modernization efforts and left-wing movements, they developed a vision of expanded *citoyenneté,* or women's full and legal citizenship. Especially active in this regard were the country's two vibrant and long-standing feminist organizations formed in 1989: l'Association Tunisienne des Femmes Démocrates (Tunisian Association of Democratic Women, ATFD) and l'Association des Femmes Tunisiennes pour la Recherche et le Développement (Association of Tunisian Women for Research on Development, or AFTURD).[24] Besides setting up the first domestic violence hotline and counseling center, feminist activities included research on women's status and the production of advocacy documents that criticized the shift in the 1990s to structural adjustment and neoliberalism. In both the late 1980s and after the 2011 revolution, Tunisian feminists decried the growing Islamist movements in the region, which they saw as a threat to the progress they had achieved since the CSP.

Tunisian feminists have long been preoccupied with women's experience of both physical and structural violence. Within the framework of a Spanish-funded project on economic repercussions of violence against young women in greater Tunis, AFTURD commissioned a study, carried out in 2008–2009 by two activist researchers, that noted how women's concentration in low-wage and precarious "feminized" occupations such as domestic work or garments and textiles—and especially domestic work carried out by teenage girls from low-income families who should otherwise be in school—could make women and girls vulnerable to various forms of violence. The final report (AFTURD 2010) stressed that inconsistent social rights and economic citizenship for women constituted a structural foundation for violence. In addition to their work on violence, feminists advocated for women's equality in all areas, including inheritance, full implementation of CEDAW, and permitting women to marry non-Muslim men. These priorities continued after the 2011 revolution, and more advances were made:

- 2011—Transitional government declares gender parity in elections and lifts remaining reservations on CEDAW.

- 2012—Protests by feminist groups and supporters defeat attempt by the Ennahda-dominated Constituent Assembly to replace "equality" between women and men with "complementarity."

- 2012 (November)—State-funded women's shelter formed in Ben Arous.[25]

- 2014 (January)—The new constitution enshrines gender parity and bans violence against women.

- 2012 to 2014—ATFD and AFTURD extend networks to Sfax, Sousse, Bizerte, Kairouan; members join coalitions.

- 2014 (fall)—Women candidates win 31% of seats in the parliamentary elections.

- 2017 (July 26): Passage of the strongest anti–violence against women law to date. Also, abrogation of the 1973 decree prohibiting a Muslim Tunisian woman from marrying a non-Muslim man, and introduction of a bill for equal inheritance.

Tunisia's secular republican polity and multiparty system provides a legal and normative environment favorable to women's empowerment, and compared with other Arab countries as well as Iran, Tunisia boasts a more women-friendly normative environment, albeit one that is contested by conservative Islamists. As described in the section on women and work, many Tunisian women work as lawyers and judges: 28% of lawyers are women, while in 2010, nearly half of all constitutional judges were women (World Bank 2014). These achievements placed Tunisia at the top of the region in terms of the UNDP's 2013 Gender Inequality Index; at 46, Tunisia ranked just below the much richer United Arab Emirates, ranked 40, but much higher than other MENA countries (United Nations Development Programme [UNDP] 2013:156–157, Table 4). As this chapter has suggested, women's progress in the early decades of post-independence Tunisia was generated by the state's favorable stance toward women's participation and rights. In more recent years, however, the most enabling factor is the presence of visible and vocal women's rights organizations and women's policy agencies that conduct research and advocacy on various aspects of women's lives. They helped win the debates within the National Constituent Assembly in 2012 and 2013 to produce a constitution with the now-famous Article 46:

> The state commits to protect women's accrued rights and work to strengthen and develop those rights. The state guarantees the equality of opportunities between women and men to have access to all levels of responsibility in all domains. The state works to attain parity between women and men in elected Assemblies. The state shall take all necessary measures in order to eradicate violence against women.

The modernization of gender relations in Tunisia is not yet complete, and here the class factor is most salient. The labor law differentiates between the public and private sectors, and this can disadvantage many low-income and working-class women. In the public sector, social insurance is provided, and women are entitled to a paid maternity leave of 2 months (Ben Salem 2010:502) and on-site childcare facilities at workplaces with more than 50 workers. There are also special provisions for mothers of small or handicapped children. Private-sector employers are not required to provide paid maternity leave, although the law stipulates a leave of 30 days and the right of new mothers to leave work daily to breastfeed, for a year after the birth of their child. Small enterprises are exempted from these requirements. Although there is no gender distinction in social security provisions, the mandatory requirements apply only to civil servants (Bernard-Maugiron 2015:8), which may explain why 86% of those in health and public administration are covered.

Besides work contracts typical of the neoliberal era, Tunisian women face two other problems. One is that the female unemployment rate (22%) is twice that of males, concentrated among young and university-educated women. The highest female unemployment rates are found in the country's interior, reaching 40% to 46% in Kebili, Gafsa, and Tataouine—rates that are two to three times higher than men's (République Tunisienne 2014:16). The second pertains to the universal problem of working women's double shift. Ben Salem (2010:501) notes studies showing that many employed women find it difficult to balance work and family life. Surveys conducted by the women's policy agencies and the National Democratic Institute (2015) and interviews I have conducted since 2012 with Tunisian women's rights advocates all point to the following needs: development plans and budgets that focus on the economic conditions of marginalized women in the interior of the country, incentives to allow women to establish their own enterprises, longer paid maternity leaves, and affirmative action plans to enhance women's employment.[26]

Discussion and Conclusions

This chapter has compared two MENA countries located at the interstices of the periphery and semiperiphery of the world-system that are both majority Muslim, to highlight the role of structural and institutional factors in the achievement of women's economic and political empowerment. Iran is a larger, wealthier, and militarily stronger country than is Tunisia, and yet Tunisia's female population is more involved in the economy, more present in the formal political process, and more (legally and socially) active in civil society. In both countries, women have been beneficiaries of, and contributors to, economic and social development, but their roles have been far more visible and more widely acknowledged in Tunisia than in Iran, certainly since the 1980s. Iran's oil-based economy reduced female labor supply and demand, while Tunisia's non-oil, export-led economic development strategy favored a larger female labor force. In the 1990s and into the new century, Tunisian women's labor force participation showed a wider occupational distribution than was the case in Iran. Although Iran is ahead of Tunisia in secondary and tertiary enrollments—81% and 64%, respectively, compared with Tunisia's 50% and 43%—Tunisia has proportionately more women PhDs and more lawyers, judges, university professors, and parliamentarians than does Iran. More women are involved in manufacturing in Tunisia than in Iran, and women's rights organizations are far more vocal and visible in Tunisia than in Iran.

This study confirms research and advocacy regarding the economic basis of women's empowerment and its association with an array of positive outcomes. Women's economic participation and income control—and especially access to remunerative work in the formal sector of the economy—is key to their equality and empowerment. Employment and income earning provide women with voice, agency, and resources to make decisions within the household and community, join associations and unions, avoid domestic violence or leave an abusive domicile, join political parties and run for office, and contribute to overall economic growth and development. Employed women tend to have greater control over decision making within the family; households also benefit when women control income and spending, and the well-being of children is increasingly linked to female education and income (Blumberg 1984, 1989, 1995, 2016; Chafetz 1990; Moghadam 1998). Studies show that employed women tend to vote leftward (Iversen and Rosenbluth 2006), and Walby (2009) has argued that increased female employment could raise support for social democracy. Reviewing World Values Survey results for Morocco, Benstead (2016) finds that men who hold egalitarian values tend to be married to employed wives. Conversely, studies have found that non-employed women are less likely to hold egalitarian or emancipatory attitudes and more likely to support fundamentalist movements or ideologies (Ilkkaracan 2012; Iversen and Rosenbluth 2006, 2008; Blaydes and Linzer 2008).

Over the past four decades, neoliberal capitalist globalization has drawn on the large pool of surplus labor in peripheral and semiperipheral countries to create a feminized workforce in garment factories. From Turkey and Morocco to Bangladesh and Sri Lanka, these factories are a source of female formal-sector employment. But unsafe working conditions, long hours with no or reduced overtime, lack of childcare facilities, minimal if any maternity benefits, the presence of sexual harassment, and stagnant if not decreasing wages in real terms combine to make such employment uncertain and precarious for women. Such work environments are a deterrent to increased female labor participation, and in some MENA countries, they may have worked to limit female labor supply. Even so, more women have been available for work in Tunisia than in Iran.

Differences in political systems also have affected women's economic and political empowerment through the divergent gender regimes in the two countries. Iran's 1979 Islamic revolution interrupted a secular trend toward greater female involvement in professions and occupations, and its clerical authoritarianism precluded the growth of an autonomous feminist movement. In contrast, in Tunisia, an autonomous feminist movement was able to emerge in the late 1980s, grow in the 1990s, and expand after the 2011 revolution. Thus, whereas Tunisia shows evidence of a transition from a patriarchal to a modern gender regime, with laws and policies that grant women an array of citizenship rights, Iran's gender regime remains steadfastly patriarchal. Oil wealth at the disposal of the Iranian state allowed it to pursue gender policies (and other policies) without serious challenges; in non-oil Tunisia, the result has been compromises and negotiations with various social actors and civil society groups, including feminist groups. Women's economic and political empowerment may be influenced by trends in world society and the capitalist world-system, but as our two cases show, it is also subject to dynamics of national histories, development strategies, and political systems.

NOTES

1. This reality seems not to have changed significantly. A recent study found that "MENA's manufacturing firms engaged in exporting activities have higher proportions of female workers by an average of 3.2 percentage points compared to non-exporting firms" (Fakih and Ghazalian 2015:4).

2. See https://data.worldbank.org/indicator/ SL.TLF.TOTL.FE.ZS?view=chart, accessed October 2018.

3. The early writings on the rentier state were Mahdavi (1972), Katouzian (1981), and Beblawi and Luciano (1987). On the gender dynamics, see Moghadam (1995) and Ross (2008).

4. A similar argument has been made for Algeria, in a paper examining the relationship between oil and economic growth over time (Chekouri and Chibi 2016). The issue is less the presence of oil than its management during times of price volatility and in the absence of economic diversification. The present version of the "rentier state" argument, it should be noted, is not the same as the so-called resource curse argument (Ross 2001, 2008; Sachs and Warner 2001; Collier and Hoeffler 2004). That is, oil wealth does not necessarily result in either conflict or distorted development; how oil revenues are used for development depends considerably on the nature of governance. A comparison of socioeconomic indicators in Algeria and Nigeria, two postcolonial oil-rich states on the African continent, would be instructive in this regard. When managed appropriately, oil wealth can benefit economies, but excessive dependence of government finances on oil revenues can backfire due to oil price volatility.

5. In Egypt, the growing influence of Islamism resulted not only in women's re-veiling but also in the strengthening of conservative social norms regarding women, work, and family (Hatem 1994).

6. For a comparative study with a focus on Western countries, see Glendon (1989).

7. At first glance the idea of wages for housework may appear progressive and indeed reminiscent of 1970s Marxist-feminist arguments. However, although the initiative was urged by Islamist women as a way to make divorce more costly for men, I am not aware of any study of its implementation and efficacy. Moreover, it is premised on the idea of women as homemakers and may also help reproduce and reinforce the patriarchal gender contract.

8. For a recent discussion in the Palestinian context, see Rahsa Abou Jalal, "Palestinian Widows Lose Rights" (www.al-monitor .com/pulse/originals/2014/10/widows-gaza-increase-confiscation-rights.html), which points out that many Palestinian women are unaware of their inheritance rights but also that a widow is entitled to just one quarter of her deceased husband's wealth. She is also entitled to half the deceased husband's pension but forfeits it if she remarries.

9. The discussion in this section draws from the World Bank's country analysis on Iran, available at https://www.worldbank.org/en/ country/iran.

10. In 1994, I visited a textiles and garment factory in Tehran that had a large female labor force and an on-site nursery (see Moghadam 1998:171). Such factories and facilities for women workers were in the minority.

11. Similar findings on the effect of marriage on FLFP are reported in two recent studies on the Arab Middle East (Chamlou, Muzi, and Ahmed 2016; Moghadam, Guiahi, and Naguib 2016).

12. Egel and Salehi-Isfahani (2010), Table 6-1, p. 24, and Table 6-2, p. 25.

13. See V. Moghadam (1998, Chapter 7), Bahramitash and Kazemipour (2008), and F. Moghadam (2009).

14. Iran had a strong trade union movement, with heavy influence by the Tudeh Party (Iran's Communist Party), but it was repressed following the 1953 coup d'état against the constitutional government of Premier Mossadegh and the restoration of absolutist monarchy. (For details see Abrahamian 1982.) Oil workers played an

important role in toppling the shah during the revolutionary protests of late 1978 and early 1979, and various leftist groups helped organize workers' councils (*shoraye kargari*), but these, too, were repressed or taken over by the Islamic regime between 1979 and 1981. For details see Azad [Moghadam] (1981) and Bayat (1987).

15. Data from UNDP, *Human Development Report 2002*, tab. 14, pp. 198–201.

16. Under Ben Ali, importing-only firms did well in terms of growth and employment generation, in part because of cronyism (Jaud and Freund 2015:3). The revolution broke the stranglehold of Ben Ali and his wife's family on the country's economy, including real estate and the hotel/tourism industry (53–54).

17. In contrast, Iran's 2006 census showed that 60% of the female labor force had completed secondary schooling while 40% had higher education degrees. Put another way, 66.4% of Iranian women with higher education degrees held jobs in 2006.

18. By 2013, public-sector employment as a percentage of total employment in Tunisia had fallen to about 22%, just above the OECD average and considerably lower than the oil-rich economies (*The Economist* 2015:47). Since then, the government has increased public sector employment and wages, in response to protests and strikes.

19. Mahmoud Ben Romdhane, from my notes at a seminar on the Arab Spring, organized by UNESCO, Paris, June 21, 2011.

20. Feminist scholars distinguish women's "descriptive representation," or the numbers and proportions, from "substantive representation," which pertains to the extent to which women parliamentary members promote feminist issues or women's concerns more broadly.

21. As of January 2018, Rouhani had not carried out his promise to women. His inability to improve the economic situation, including unemployment and ever-widening income inequality, may have generated the nationwide protests between December 28, 2017, and January 5, 2018.

22. Charfi's reforms were contested by the Islamist movement and its student group, but he prevailed, though he eventually resigned his position. See especially Chapter VII of his memoir.

23. Interview with Dalenda Largueche, Directrice Générale du CREDIF, Tunis, June 22, 2017.

24. Among the founders of AFTURD was Maya Jribi, who earlier had been an activist in the student organization l'Union Générale des Etudiants de Tunisie, or UGET, and in the League of Human Rights. In 1983 she was among the founders of the Progressive Democratic Party (most recently renamed the Republican Party), which she later came to colead. In the new century, she was only one of two Arab women in a political party leadership role, the other being Louisa Hanoune of the Workers Party in Algeria.

25. This was a joint effort of the National Office of Family and Population and the Spanish international development agency (see Mahfoudh Draoui 2016:13).

26. Tunisia's inability to attract foreign investment or otherwise create jobs for its many unemployed and low-income citizens compelled it to seek a $2.9 billion loan from the International Monetary Fund, along with certain austerity measures that led to nationwide protests in early January 2018. This may affect realization of its development plans, which include the nationwide expansion of preschools, a move that could generate more employment for women (see République Tunisienne 2016).

CHAPTER

6

Poverty, Water, Sanitation Insecurities, and the Challenges of Maintaining Menstrual Hygiene

Rita Jalali

We take bath in the open outside. No bathroom, no toilets so it takes one hour for coming and going. If there is some man around we have to wait till he goes, so sometimes there is stomach pain because of this. If we have diarrhea we have to sit there. When we are menstruating we face more difficulty.

— Open-ended survey response, Kutch district woman

Menstrual cloth washing is . . . very problematic because we are having water only for 1 hour in a day. . . . Since we lack water facility at home we have to take all our clothes including our menstrual cloth with us outside for washing which is very embarrassing for us.

— Diary entry 3 of Gandhinagar Woman 1

Introduction

It is estimated that more than 2.1 billion people (30%) worldwide lack access to safe, readily available water at home[1] and 4.5 billion (60%) lack safely managed sanitation.[2] It is also known that 892 million people still practice open defecation (WHO/UNICEF JMP 2017). In addition, between nearly half a billion to 1 billion women do not have access to menstrual hygiene facilities (WHO/UNICEF JMP 2017).[3] A large proportion of those facing such insecurities are the poor and the marginalized. How do poor rural women and girls cope with menstruation or with postpartum bleeding when they lack access to not only water but money to buy sanitary napkins and a private place to manage menstrual hygiene? This paper attempts to understand the management and practice of menstrual hygiene and postpartum bleeding among poor rural women in water-scarce regions of India.

Within the field of development, menstrual hygiene is embedded in the sector on water, sanitation, and hygiene (WASH). Within the WASH sector, much of the focus globally has been on tracking health benefits of water and sanitation. Hygiene tends to be neglected. When issues of hygiene are addressed, the focus is on handwashing behavior (see WHO/UNICEF JMP 2017). Less attention has been paid to the menstrual hygiene needs

119

of women and girls in policy and practice in WASH. This neglect can be viewed at the global level in the *World Development Report, 2012* on gender equity and development (World Bank 2011) or in the water and sanitation reports of the World Bank and WHO/UNICEF, and even in the Millennium Development Goals (MDGs). In the MDGs, the mechanisms outlined for women's empowerment focused primarily on improving access to education, employment, and political representation but not to water, sanitation, and menstrual hygiene facilities, which in any case remained buried under the seventh goal on environment.

Only more recently have the global development community (United Nations, bilateral donors, nongovernmental organizations) and national governments recognized menstrual hygiene as a significant development issue and necessary for achieving gender equality (World Bank 2017).[4] Yet in the post-2015 Sustainable Development Goals (SDGs) for 2030, while WASH finally has a dedicated goal, menstrual hygiene is never explicitly mentioned. Neither are there any global data available on number of women and girls lacking access to menstrual hygiene facilities (see WHO/UNICEF JMP 2017),[5] although measurement targets for post-2015 were proposed in 2012 by the Global Monitoring Working group on hygiene (JMP 2012).

Comfortable management of menstruation[6] is a fundamental need for all women of reproductive age and its absence a denial of their basic rights. Yet women and girls in many parts of the world (Africa, Asia, the Middle East) are known to engage in unhygienic menstrual practices—from reusing menstrual absorbents to washing and drying under unsanitary conditions (Sumpter and Torondel 2013; Vaughn 2013; Hennegan and Montgomery 2016; van Eijk et al. 2016; Kuhlmann, Henry, and Wall 2017) because they lack access to basic menstrual hygiene management (MHM) facilities.

Almost three quarters of the extreme poor (< US $1.25/day) live in rural areas. Yet studies on menstrual hygiene practices of rural women are rare (Hennegan and Montgomery 2016), as are studies on poor women's management of postpartum bleeding. Nearly all studies about menstrual hygiene practices from resource-poor countries focus on rural and urban girls, especially school girls and a few on urban slum women (Garg, Sharma, and Sahay 2001; Singh et al. 2001; Das and Shah 2007; Dasgupta and Sarkar 2008; Sommer 2010; McMahon et al. 2011; Thakre et al. 2011; Crofts and Fisher 2012; Crichton et al. 2013; Shah, Nair, and Shah 2013; Yasmin et al. 2013). The few studies on rural women include Zhang, Parkin, and Yu (1986), Singh (2006), Umeora and Egwuatu (2008), Srivastava (2010), Bukar and Jauro (2013), Misra et al. (2013), Mani (2014), Das et al. (2015), Routray et al. (2015), and Sahoo et al. (2015), with many focusing primarily on gynecological morbidities.[7]

My study attempts to fill this research gap. It focuses on the poor segments of Indian society—women who work as agricultural wage earners, many of whom belong to the lower castes and tribal communities and live in poorer areas of the state. Access to water is also essential to maintain menstrual hygiene, especially when disposable napkins are not affordable. This study focuses on poor rural women who live in areas with inadequate access to water. Of the nine districts selected for this study, seven districts are listed as water-scarce by the Gujarat Water Supply and Sanitation Board and the other two districts have villages with high water insecurity. In addition, the study also gathers data on how women manage postpartum bleeding, an issue rarely focused on.

The paper is organized into four sections: First a conceptual framework is presented to understand the factors that affect MHM and its implications on health, education, and livelihood; that is followed by methods of the study (more details are provided in a supplement at the end); the third section focuses on research findings; and finally, the discussion section compares the findings of the study to other literature in the field within the context of the conceptual framework presented earlier.

A Conceptual Framework

The paper proposes a conceptual framework (see Figure 6.1) to understand the factors influencing menstrual and postpartum management of vaginal bleeding and its implications for hygiene practices, health, livelihood, education, and well-being. The framework relies on the analyses of data collected in the field and existing empirical literature to show the factors affecting MHM and its implications. Seven broad factors—from the infrastructure environment to social, cultural, and economic—shape the management of vaginal bleeding. These affect every aspect of hygiene management. Poor hygiene practices in turn have serious consequences on health, education, and well-being, including livelihood, although the evidence on the latter is sparse.

Factors Affecting Menstrual and Postpartum Hygiene Management

Gender Roles and Inequalities

While this paper does not focus on how gender inequalities affect hygiene management, the gendered nature of WASH deprivation[8] is evident in the stressful lives women lead—the lack of basic facilities to manage a natural biological process, the water-hauling burden women bear,[9] and the rigid cultural scripts enforced on women and girls. The cultural scripts (value placed on women's modesty, the taboos surrounding menstrual blood) exact a heavy price—from the inability when bleeding to wash and change in a safe, private place when needed, to feelings of shame and threats of sexual violence. Some studies have also shown women's decision-making authority within a household affect investment in WASH facilities (Hirai, Graham, and Sandberg 2016; Routray et al. 2017). Another quantitative analysis found that latrine availability is positively related to both female labor force participation and female literacy rates in India (Gius and Subramanian 2015).

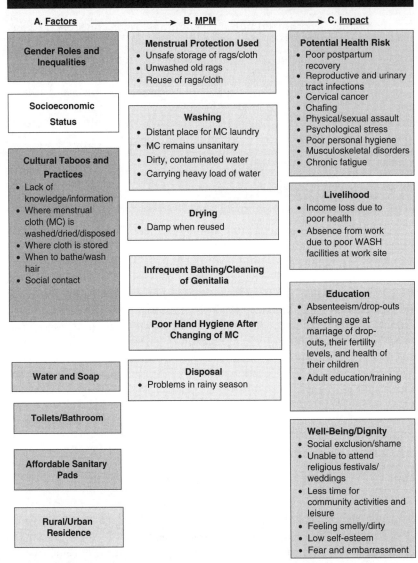

Figure 6.1 A Conceptual Framework: Factors Influencing Menstrual and Postpartum Management (MPM) and Its Implications

A. Factors → **B. MPM** → **C. Impact**

Gender Roles and Inequalities

Socioeconomic Status

Cultural Taboos and Practices
- Lack of knowledge/information
- Where menstrual cloth (MC) is washed/dried/disposed
- Where cloth is stored
- When to bathe/wash hair
- Social contact

Water and Soap

Toilets/Bathroom

Affordable Sanitary Pads

Rural/Urban Residence

Menstrual Protection Used
- Unsafe storage of rags/cloth
- Unwashed old rags
- Reuse of rags/cloth

Washing
- Distant place for MC laundry
- MC remains unsanitary
- Dirty, contaminated water
- Carrying heavy load of water

Drying
- Damp when reused

Infrequent Bathing/Cleaning of Genitalia

Poor Hand Hygiene After Changing of MC

Disposal
- Problems in rainy season

Potential Health Risk
- Poor postpartum recovery
- Reproductive and urinary tract infections
- Cervical cancer
- Chafing
- Physical/sexual assault
- Psychological stress
- Poor personal hygiene
- Musculoskeletal disorders
- Chronic fatigue

Livelihood
- Income loss due to poor health
- Absence from work due to poor WASH facilities at work site

Education
- Absenteeism/drop-outs
- Affecting age at marriage of drop-outs, their fertility levels, and health of their children
- Adult education/training

Well-Being/Dignity
- Social exclusion/shame
- Unable to attend religious festivals/weddings
- Less time for community activities and leisure
- Feeling smelly/dirty
- Low self-esteem
- Fear and embarrassment

Socioeconomic Status and Rural/Urban Residence

Women who come from poor, less educated backgrounds and live in rural areas are more likely to be deprived of access to water and sanitation facilities (WHO/UNICEF JMP 2017) and unable to afford market napkins.

Cultural Taboos

Many myths and superstitions surround menstrual blood in most parts of the world. In many countries cultural and religious beliefs prevent menstruating women from participating in worship, sex, household chores, and social activities, and affect menstrual hygiene practices, as this paper will show (Garg et al. 2001; Verdemato 2005; Thakre et al. 2011; Mason, Nyothach, and Alexander 2013; Vaughn 2013; Yasmin et al. 2013; Garg and Anand 2015; van Eijk et al. 2016; Coultas et al. 2017).

Affordable Sanitary Pads

The cost of the market napkins is one major reason why poor rural women are not able to use the product, as the evidence from this and other studies show.

Access to Water, Toilets, and Soap

The type of absorbent material used is not the only factor affecting menstrual hygiene practices. Lack of functioning toilets that have water and soap and are safe also affects the ability to maintain menstrual hygiene, as shown in Figure 6.1.

Hygiene Practices

The socioeconomic background, unequal gender norms, cultural taboos about menstrual blood, and access to WASH facilities affect the quality of the absorbent material used; where and when the soiled cloth is washed, dried, stored, and disposed; the frequency of bathing and handwashing; and genital hygiene.

Impact of Hygiene Practices

Water and sanitation insecurities have serious consequences on health (from risk of exposure to various infections to psychological stress). They also affect the education of adolescent girls and livelihood of women who miss work because of poor MHM facilities at work sites. Although this research was not designed to address these issues, the discussion section at the end will provide evidence from other studies to highlight women's burden.

Methods

The study was conducted in 2011, in the rural areas of nine districts of Gujarat, India. Women of reproductive age were enrolled if they consented to participate after being informed of the objectives of the study. Participation in the study was voluntary, and responses were kept anonymous. To increase validity, the methodology was triangulated and included focus group discussions (FGDs), surveys administered by trained enumerators, and diaries maintained by women who volunteered to write anonymously about their menstrual hygiene practices and problems (40 diary entries). A total of nine FGDs were conducted in all the districts, with an average of 17 women in each discussion group. FGDs and surveys focused on water, sanitation, and menstrual hygiene issues (taboos, hygiene practices); opinion about market napkins; and management of postpartum bleeding.

For the survey, 906 women participated from nine districts of Gujarat, with adequate representation from a variety of lower castes and tribes. Participants included only females from the reproductive age group (17–46 years), with only one female participant selected from each household (see Table 6.1). Finally, on-site field observations were made of water sources, and bathing and defecation areas in each of the nine districts based on convenience and access.

The data from survey, FGDs, diaries, and field observations were then coded into several themes: water and toilet issues (level of access and impact on daily life), management of menstrual issues (protection options; washing, drying, disposal practices; cultural taboos), management of postpartum period, and opinion on market napkins.

Results

Socioeconomic Characteristics

The ages of the survey participants range from 17 to 46; 91% are Hindus. Nearly 28% belong to the lower castes and tribes, and 53% (see Table 6.1) to the middle or "Other Backward Castes" (Indian government designation for castes between the upper and lower castes). Nearly 81% of their families work in agriculture, and of these, almost 61% are landless; 32% of the women are illiterate, and only 3% had completed 12th grade or studied beyond high school (not shown). Nearly 70% of the women work for wages, and of these, close to 79% work as agricultural laborers.

Table 6.1 Socioeconomic Characteristics of Rural Gujarati Women (N = 906)

Total	N	%
Age		
17–26 yrs.	250	27.6
27–36 yrs.	432	47.9
37–46 yrs.	221	24.4
No response	3	0.3
Education		
Illiterate	294	32.5
I–VIII >	385	42.5
IX & >	223	24.6
No response	4	0.4
Religion/caste		
High caste	89	9.8
Middle caste	480	53.0
Lower caste + tribe	258	28.5

Non-Hindu	44	4.9
No response	35	3.9
Family occupation*		
Cultivator	289	31.9
Agricultural laborer	447	49.3
Animal husbandry	114	12.6
Other	154	17.0
No response	2	0.2
Women's occupation*		
At-home women not earning any income	274	30.2
Agricultural laborer	497	54.9
Non-agriculture work (construction, road building, salt farming)	55	6.1
At-home paid work (such as incense and tobacco rolling, embroidery)	85	9.4
No response	2	0.2

*Multiple responses possible

Water, Sanitation Insecurity, and Hygiene

Nearly 59% of the Gujarat state falls under arid and semi-arid climatic zones. These arid zones are located in the north and northwestern parts of the state (Hirway 2002; Hirway and Mahadevia 2004). Seven of the nine districts selected for this study fall in this zone, with average annual rainfall in seven of the districts ranging between 300 millimeters in the west to 735 millimeters in the northern region (Hirway 2002). In other parts of the state the range is much higher (900–1800 mm). Summer temperatures in this region can rise as high as 46°C/115°F. Additionally, droughts are frequent in these parts. The Gujarat government has identified seven of these districts as water-scarce districts (Gujarat Water Supply and Sewerage Board n.d.).

Collecting and fetching water for the household is a task primarily performed by women and girls. It is an onerous task, especially in the hot summer months. Women have to stand in long queues to pump water at the bore well and then carry heavy containers of water on their heads in the long trudge back home (see Photo 6.1, a rural woman in another part of the region).

©Rita Jalali

Photo 6.1 This woman is carrying 15 to 20 liters of water. Each liter of water weighs 2.2 pounds.

Water is like ghee (clarified butter)!

— Woman from Patan district, FGD

In FGDs, severe water shortage was found to be a major concern and compared by some women to butter—that is, precious and used sparingly. Lack of an adequate water supply affects every aspect of a woman's life—from time wasted collecting water, where to bathe, and where to wash clothes and utensils to childcare, earnings, health, daughter's school attendance, the food consumed and cooked, and even their leisure time and enjoyment of festivals. Here we focus primarily on the impact of water insecurity on sanitation practices.

In the survey, Self Employed Women's Association (SEWA) members were asked about their access to water for personal and domestic purposes and the time spent (one way) walking to the water source (≤ 15 minutes; 15–30 minutes; ≥ 30 minutes). More than 50% of those surveyed report that they had inadequate water at home for all household needs. Thirty-four percent said they had to walk 15 minutes or more one way to fetch water. For many, the trip back home took 1 hour or more. During the FGD, it was learned that even in households with piped water, the supply was erratic and available for only 1 hour or less per day. In summer, piped water was available only every 3 to 4 days.

> There is a bore well provided by the Gram Panchayat (village council) and water is available for 4 hours. So women have so many difficulties to fill the water. There is difficulty to bathe and wash clothes. (Open-ended survey response, Sabarkantha woman)

The level of water service on premises and privacy issues determine the location, timing, and frequency of hygiene activity. Once water requirements for drinking and cooking are met, women are forced to compromise on water consumed for their own personal hygiene. In households with higher levels of water access, women are able to bathe at home (54%) when men are absent. The rest bathe outside at dawn in open spaces near the water source—a public bore well or pond (sometimes contaminated). In fact, most chores (even washing utensils) and personal care (other than face, hand-, and foot washing) require a trip outside the house. Nearly 60% do their laundry outside, and 56% also wash the soiled menstrual cloth outside (Table 6.2). In some areas, the nearest water source is 30 minutes away.

Given such acute shortages of water and the effort required to collect it, maintaining hygiene is a huge challenge. In fact, in the survey nearly 34% of women admit that water scarcity made it difficult to maintain personal hygiene, and 41% acknowledge problems washing menstrual cloth (Table 6.2). Even basic hand hygiene is not possible where water and soap shortages exist:

> My hands remain smelly after washing the soiled cloth. I don't feel like eating any food after that. (Gandhinagar district, FGD)

Defecation is the most challenging of the sanitation issues facing women (see Table 6.3). With no latrines at home, women are forced to walk outside at dawn, seeking a safe, relatively clean spot to relieve themselves. Only 44%

Table 6.2 Water and Sanitation Insecurities

Total	N	%
Inadequate water at home	456	50.33
≥ 15-min. walk (one way) to fetch water	308	34
Defecate outside home	649	71.63
≥ 15-min. walk (one way) to defecate	436	48.12
Urinate outside home	489	53.97
≥ 15-min. walk (one way) to urinate	101	11.15
Bathe outside home	419	46.25
≥ 15-min. walk (one way) to bathe	166	18.32
Difficult to maintain personal hygiene	305	33.66
Wash menstrual cloth outside home	506	55.85
Problem washing menstrual cloth	373	41.17
Laundry outside home	533	58.83
Wash utensils outside home	357	39.40

Table 6.3 Problems Due to Lack of Toilets*

	N	%
Lack of privacy	418	46.14
Sexual harassment	359	39.62
Nighttime access in darkness	587	64.79
Insect and snake bite	583	64.35
Control urge to defecate	353	38.96
Take a child	483	53.31
Constipation	285	31.46

*Based on input from FGDs

Diarrhea did not come up in the pilot survey or the FGDs, so was not included in the survey.

in the survey are able to urinate at home, more than two thirds defecate outside the premises, and nearly half of them (48%) walk 15 minutes or more to find a place to defecate. In summer, defecating in the open under the blazing sun and no shade, with temperatures reaching above 104°F is a hardship—as it is in the rainy season as well when rain, insects, and waterlogging also create immense difficulties.

Sexual harassment is an additional problem, so women lug a child whose duty it is to alert the mother if a man passes by.

> We have to fill water for 2–3 days because of irregular water supply. We cannot get fresh water to drink. We have no bathroom so we have to take a bath in open space, go to the jungle for a bowel movement. We are afraid of insects and drunkards and unknown persons. We have to a take child with us. (Open-ended survey response, Kutch district woman)

Lack of access to a toilet also makes it difficult to manage vaginal bleeding in a hygienic manner. Not only is it difficult to change when required, but without access to water and soap, women are unable to wash themselves and the soiled material. In fact, 59% of women found menstruation very difficult to manage without access to toilets—far more than those that found menstrual pain difficult (41%; Table 6.5).

Cultural Taboos

Menstruation is an integral part of a woman's life and fundamental for human reproduction. Yet there are many negative cultural attitudes toward it, and menstruating girls and women are perceived as impure. Many myths and superstitions surround menstrual blood in most parts of the world.

Survey findings show that 76% (not shown in table) of rural women practice menstrual taboos—from taboos regarding religious activities to prohibitions against cooking. These taboos also affect where the soiled menstrual cloth is washed and dried, and how it is disposed of, as the next section will show. There are also cultural taboos against farming crops or milking cattle when menstruating, which affects women's earning opportunities (revealed in FGDs). Forty percent of women report the monthly management of menstrual taboos very burdensome (Table 6.5). This was also revealed in the FGDs and diary entries.

> In our family we have taboos regarding menstruation, so we cannot touch anybody and cannot take food or drink water by ourselves. If we wish to eat or drink we have to ask and wait for somebody, which I don't like. It feels like I am being ostracized and this is very embarrassing. (Diary entry 3 of Gandhinagar Woman 3)

Many of these taboos also apply in the postpartum period, as will be shown later.

Menstrual Protection Options

The management of menstrual bleeding in the cramped living quarters, without adequate toilet facilities, running water, and a place to wash and dry menstrual cloths, creates many difficulties. Women are unable to afford commercial sanitary napkins. In India, commercial pads cost about INR 3.12 per piece ($0.05/piece at 2013 exchange rates)—too expensive for the rural poor

Table 6.4 Menstrual Practices of Rural Women, Gujarat (N = 906)

Total	N	%
Menstrual protection option*		
Rags	595	65.7
Fulani/market cloth	357	39.4
Sanitary napkin	39	4.3
No protection	47	5.2
Postpartum period*	832**	
Rags	635	76.32
Market cloth	239	28.73
Sanitary napkins	26	3.13
No protection	75	9.01
Reuse rags and market cloth	811	89.5
Among reusers, using ≥ 3	618	76.2
Drying methods*		
In sun	582	64.2
Covered with cloth	264	29.1
Hidden from public	161	17.8
Problem drying in monsoon	615	67.9
No response	12	1.3
Disposal methods*		
Bury	105	11.6
Burn	517	57.1
Trash	226	25.0
No response	58	6.4
Discomfort with reuse of cloth*		
Chafing/skin abrasion	236	29.1
Skin abrasions affect walking	212	26.1

* Multiple Responses Possible
** All those women who had delivered a child
*** Out of those reusing cloth

to purchase. The survey revealed that only 4% of rural women use commercial sanitary napkins (Table 6.4) and most use them only when traveling (FGD). Close to 66% use rags, and 39% use cloth bought from the market (which is called *fulani*). Nearly 5% do not use any menstrual protection; their long skirt/petticoat serves as an absorbent. There was no evidence that women used husks, ash, or sand to absorb menstrual blood (Garg and Anand 2015).

The *fulani* cloth is a small piece of maroon fabric (12 inches by 18 inches). It is available for INR 10 (about $0.16) in the market. The thick, soft, flannel-like texture and maroon color make it a popular choice for menstrual protection. Because of the poverty level of the families, nearly 89% reuse the cloth, and of these 76% wash and reuse (Table 6.4) the same cloth three times or more until it wears down. Many also admit to reusing the same cloth for 6 to 8 months. For 29% of those surveyed, spending 16 cents on the market cloth was a big burden (Table 6.5). During the FGDs it was revealed that some even washed and reused commercial napkins.

Women also admit that homemade pads are a constant source of worry—the pad could slip off or stain garments and bedding—especially while walking, sitting, and even while sleeping, an embarrassment and a washing burden. Some women report sitting in a corner while menstruating till the men leave the house, worried that the tabooed bloodstains will be visible to others (FGD).

> We have a big family so I feel very shy to change my menstrual cloth and also feel very awkward to sit in the corner. (Diary entry 1 of Kutch Woman 1)

Unhygienic menstrual practices also lead to chafing.

> My sister-in-law is also having problems during her cycle. When she is using old rags during her periods it becomes hard and due to that she gets rashes. Because of this she cannot walk and sit properly. (Diary entry 2 of Vadodra Woman 7)

Twenty-nine percent of women complained about chafing with the use of rags and *fulani* cloth (Table 6.4). According to the women, washing and reusing the material makes it stiff and causes skin abrasions in the inner-thigh area. The flannel-like texture of the *fulani* cloth is really unsuitable for the hot summer season, especially since most women engage in fieldwork. Chafing is also indicative of the prolonged use of blood-soaked pads. The abrasions are severe enough to make walking difficult for more than a quarter of those surveyed (Table 6.4).

Washing/Drying/Disposal Practices

Since 89% reuse the cloth, washing the cloth in water-scarce communities is an onerous task. Forty-one percent of women report the chore to be a burden. The preference is to wash menstrual cloth on the premises, but if water is not available, the cloth is washed once to remove the blood and then carried outside with the rest of the laundry for a thorough wash,

Table 6.5	Most Burdensome Aspect of Menstrual Maintenance for Rural Women, Gujarat (N = 906)	
Total	**N**	**%**
Pain/physical discomfort	373	41.17
Lack of toilet	531	59
Managing taboos	365	40.29
Expense of buying cloth	265	29.3
Washing cloth	373	41.2
Drying cloth	308	33.9
Disposing cloth	224	24.7
Finding cloth to use	180	19.9

which may be a day later. Given that the cloth is reused several times, the dried bloodstains are not easily removed. Of all the difficulties with menstrual cloth management that were listed in the survey (Table 6.5), washing the soiled cloth was considered by more respondents to be a burden than buying, finding, drying, or disposing the cloth.

The washing and drying of menstrual cloth has to be done in secrecy, away from male eyes and women not part of the family circle, with those menstruating made to feel as though they have an infectious disease (FGD and see quote below). In tight living quarters, with large joint families and no water, bathroom, or latrine facility, menstrual hygiene is a monthly challenge.

> As we are living in a joint family, washing and drying the menstrual cloth is a problem because we have to hide it from male eyes—we have to be very conscious. . . . Thus, these 5–6 days are very difficult for all the women. (Diary entry 3 of Gandhinagar Woman 3)

Drying in the sun is recommended to reduce infections from microbes, but only 64% of them did so. Drying menstrual cloth is a problem in the rainy season for nearly 68% of those surveyed, with some using the cloth when still damp. Additionally, cultural norms dictate that if the cloth is hung outside, it should be covered with another cloth so it is not visible. Some hang it to dry in the cattle shed, others on roof rafters—unsanitary, dusty places.

In comparison, disposal issues are easier to manage; only 25% indicate disposal to be a problem. Once the cloth wears out, it is burned (nearly 57%), buried (nearly 12%), or thrown in the garbage (25%). In the rainy season, both burning and burying are a problem.

The Postpartum Period

From the difficulties managing cultural taboos to lack of WASH facilities to manage postpartum bleeding, pregnancy and childbirth are difficult to endure in poor rural households. First, cultural taboos about menstrual blood also apply to women after childbirth. A woman who is bleeding is not allowed to touch any family member or food and water that is to be consumed by others.

> I cannot get food from the kitchen myself. I have to wait for my mother-in-law to come back from work. If she is late, I remain hungry. Even the water I drink is kept aside for me in a separate container. No one is allowed to touch me in my bleeding state. It is specially hurtful since they will take the baby from me after sprinkling some water on him but will not touch me. (A mother from Sabarkantha district, FGD)

Further, without access to disposable absorbents, managing vaginal bleeding in the postpartum period is a challenge. Only 3% are able to use sanitary napkins. Seventy-six percent use old cloth to absorb postpartum bleeding, and nearly 29% use *fulani* cloth (see Table 6.4). Through the FGDs, it was learned that mother-in-laws and expectant mothers save old clothing for such occasions. Those using market napkins are given a few packages in the hospital after their delivery. Despite their preference for the disposable product, most pregnant women cannot afford to purchase it. The 9% who do not use any protection (Table 6.4) bleed in the long skirt or petticoat. These women wear two layers of skirts so the inside layer can be changed more frequently (FGDs).

Without the facility of a disposable sanitary napkin, clothes and bedding get constantly soiled. Since men do not do laundry, even after childbirth women have no option but to walk to a distant water source to do the laundry unless other women in the household can assist them with the chore. And without running water or a toilet at home, personal hygiene is even harder to maintain during pregnancy or after childbirth—a time when women have greater need for such basic services.

It must be pointed out that since all sanitation activities (defecation, urination, bathing, hygiene related to vaginal bleeding, washing and drying of soiled material) take place in open, uncovered spaces, hygiene is especially difficult to manage in the rainy season and even more so for those who are sick or pregnant. In some districts, pregnant women voiced their concern about having a miscarriage when going out to defecate or urinate in the rainy season. Since pathways get muddy, it is easy to slip and fall when you are also holding an umbrella and a water jug.

The impact of water and sanitation scarcity on the health of pregnant women or on postpartum recovery is rarely addressed in discussions on women's health.

Coping Mechanisms

The lack of water and safe, private access to bathing spaces and toilets affects women's ability to maintain hygiene in a manner that does not impact men who are equally deprived. In WASH-deprived communities, men and women develop different patterns of hygiene behavior because of cultural norms governing male and female bodily comportment and male predatory behavior. Women in our study are forced to bathe at dawn, hold the urge to urinate or defecate (39%, Table 6.3), and walk long distances to seek a safe place to do so (a problem for 46% of women, Table 6.3). To guard their "reputations," women go in a group or lug a child with them (53%, Table 6.3), or ask a family member to accompany them if it is night-time. Women also learn to control their diet—avoiding drinking water or food especially at night so they do not have to walk out of the safety of their homes in darkness (a concern for 65%) and be attacked by male predators (40%) or bitten by insects or a snake (64%, Table 6.3). Women thus learn to schedule a time for urination and defecation, but men, free from any social opprobrium, are able to urinate and defecate whenever the need arises.

> There is no facility of toilets and bathrooms so we have to take a bath early in the morning and in the afternoon. For toileting we have to go out at night or early in the morning. If we have diarrhea, we face so many difficulties. (Open-ended survey response, Kutch district woman)

> When the toilet facility is far we have to rush through housework, fieldwork and manage to find ½ hour to walk to a place to shit. Not able to eat properly due to this problem. This often creates constipation problems. (Woman from Ahmedabad district, FGD)

Given their poverty, women also had no alternative but to reuse the rags and the market cloth, even though they were afraid it may be unhygienic and cause chafing and other infections.

> Sometimes, in rainy season even though the cloth is wet we have to use it due to which we get infection. (Diary entry 3 of Gandhinagar Woman 3)

Unmet Need for Menstrual Protection

During the FGDs, each group was shown a sample of a market napkin to encourage discussion comparing the benefits and disadvantages of the material they used with the commercial-style sanitary napkin. In the survey, too, respondents were asked their opinion about market napkins.

Why do rural women not use sanitary napkins? Lack of awareness, cost, and availability are some of the major reasons preventing greater use. Only 53% know about the market product, mostly through friends and television advertisements, and many (43%) admit they do not know if commercial napkins are useful (Table 6.6). Then there are cost issues. For close to 30% of women, even purchasing the reusable *fulani* for INR 10 per piece ($0.16) is a burden (see Table 6.5). Still, nearly 71% are willing to purchase napkins, although few are willing to pay the market price. The cheapest brand sells for INR 3.12 per piece (Rs. 25 for eight) in the market. Eighty percent of

Table 6.6 Views About Commercial Sanitary Napkins (SN)

Total	N	%
	906	
Heard about SN		
Yes	478	52.76
No	427	47.13
No response	1	0.11
Good to use SN		
Yes	446	49.23
No	70	7.73
Don't know	390	43.05
Would you purchase SN		
Yes	640	70.64
No	262	28.92
No response	4	0.44
Price preference of those wanting to purchase SN package		**% out of 640**
≤ Rs. 10	176	27.5
Rs. 11–15	338	52.81
Rs. 16–20	88	13.75
Rs. 21 ≥	19	2.97
No response	23	3.59

purchasers are willing to spend only INR 15 or less for a package of 10 (i.e., nearly half the price of the market brand).

Clearly, there is an unmet need for sanitary napkins in the rural areas, and because of poverty, close to 66% of women in our survey (those who are willing to purchase but have not done so) cannot afford the price of the commercially available product.

When asked how the use of sanitary napkins would impact their lives, several themes appeared in FGDs, open-ended survey responses, and diary entries—health and hygiene benefits (mentioned most frequently); saving of precious water resources; easier to walk, stand, or sit and attend school and work; less stain worries; less washing, drying, or disposal problems; more free time; and easier to work. The disadvantages focus not only on the expense, unfamiliarity, and unavailability but also on reluctance to trust a white, thin absorbent material to perform well (close to 29% do not want to purchase the product). The quotes below reflect some of the positive sentiments.

> If we use sanitary napkins, there will be no worries about rashes and skin boils, and no difficulty walking and standing. (Open-ended survey response, Sabakantha woman)

> Our health will be maintained; no worry about infection; good for our body; can maintain hygiene of the body and no disease will be caused; saves women from many infections; maintain health and hygiene; saves water and soap. (Combined quotes from open-ended survey response to questions about how regular sanitary napkin use will impact their lives)

Discussion

This section applies the conceptual framework presented previously to the findings from this and other studies.

Socioeconomic Status and Rural/Urban Residence

As the survey findings from this study revealed, the cost of sanitary napkins makes the product unaffordable for women; only 4% are able to use commercial sanitary napkins, and 90% reuse old rags and market cloth.

Studies of poor Indian women have also reported very low rates of commercial napkin use (Varghese et al. 1999; Garg et al. 2001; Das and Shah 2007). Where higher rates of use are found among rural women, the participants tend to be more literate and/or belong to higher socioeconomic backgrounds (Yasmin and Mukherjee 2012; Mani 2014).

An all-India survey found that among unmarried women aged 15 to 24 years, napkin use varied with age (15–19 and 20–24), residence, education, and wealth, with those who are older, urban, with 10+ years of education, and in the wealthiest quintile reporting higher use (at the lowest quintile only 6.6% used sanitary napkins, but at the highest level nearly 50% did). Overall, in this age group, nearly 29% used sanitary napkins, 76% used cloth, and 9.4% used locally prepared napkins (International Institute for Population Sciences 2010). Another study also reports higher use rates among adolescent Indian girls living in urban areas (van Eijk et al. 2016).

In other low-income countries, commercial sanitary napkin use is also less common among the poor and less educated (Umeora and Egwuatu 2008; Sommer 2010; Scott et al. 2013; Tegegne and Sisay 2014; Tamiru et al. 2015; Kuhlmann et al. 2017). In Kenya, poor girls exchange sex for money to buy the product (Mason et al. 2013; Jewitt and Ryley 2014) or use soft grass to manage their menses (McMahon et al. 2011). In rural, western Kenya, single, uneducated, poorer girls depending on their family for any money were at higher odds of having sex to buy pads (Phillips-Howard et al. 2015).

During postpartum periods, 70% of mothers were found to be using old cloth in this study, but in one Nigerian study, nearly 59% of rural women were able to use sanitary pads to stanch bleeding after childbirth and only 35% were using rags (Bukar and Jauro 2013).

Cultural Taboos

In our study, 76% of rural women said that menstrual taboos were present in their culture and reported it as the most onerous aspect of menstruation.

Cultural taboos about menstrual blood also lead to washing and drying practices that may be unhygienic, as this and other studies have shown (Garg et al. 2001; Vaughn 2013; Sahoo et al. 2015). As noted, many of the same taboos apply to postpartum bleeding (in Nepal women are confined to huts after childbirth)[10] and impose an onerous burden. No other study so far has focused on this issue.

Affordable Sanitary Pads

This study has shown that the cost of the market napkins is one major reason why poor rural women are not able to use the product. Very few studies on menstrual hygiene have examined this issue, but those that have report similar findings. Women in rural Haryana, India, found napkins too expensive to use (Misra et al. 2013). Economic factors were also reported to be the main reason why Indian adolescent girls used cloth instead of market pads (van Eijk et al. 2016). In Tanzania, Ghana, and Nigeria, girls also found commercial napkins to be unaffordable (Sommer 2010; Adika et al. 2011; Scott et al. 2013).

Access to Water, Toilets, and Soap

As this study and other studies have shown, *lack of functioning toilets makes it hard to maintain menstrual hygiene*. Many studies have focused on girls' lack of access to these facilities in schools in resource-poor countries (Sommer 2010 in Tanzania; Grant, Lloyd, and Mensch 2013 in Malawi; Boosey, Prestwich, and Deave 2014 in Uganda). A few that focus on women have also found that lack of access to WASH facilities affects menstrual hygiene practices (Das et al. 2015; Sahoo et al. 2015). The study by Das et al. (2015) conducted in India found that reproductive tract infections are less likely when "women [have] a secure and comfortable place where they can change without stress and be closer to home with better proximity to water and other hygienic materials" (12). The same study also found "indirect evidence of the protective benefits of in-house water supply in the association with frequency of washing" (13).

The impact of water supply on hygiene was also found in other studies. A study from Mozambique (Cairncross and Cuff 1987) found that the distance to the water source affected hygiene practices. Another large study done in Kenya, Tanzania, and Uganda (Thompson et al. 2001) found that unpiped households suffered "from lower hygiene levels as a consequence of not having access to a regular supply of piped water.

For both bathing and washing (e.g., dishes, clothes, house, etc.), these households used less than half the amount of water as those with piped connections" (30).

Managing hygiene in WASH-deprived communities is especially difficult during pregnancy, as noted here. In another study, pregnant women reported urinating and defecating more frequently and had greater difficulties in reaching their desired sites, pumping water, and carrying heavy buckets of water (Sahoo et al. 2015).

Hygiene Practices

Similar to the findings reported here, many other studies also have found that poor women and girls engage in unhygienic practices (use of unsanitary material, and washing and drying practices) in many parts of Africa and South Asia (Garg et al. 2001; Joshi, Fawcett, and Mannan 2011; Mason et al. 2013; Boosey et al. 2014; Sommer et al. 2014; Tegegne and Sisay 2014; Sahoo et al. 2015; Coultas et al. 2017; Kuhlmann et al. 2017), including in the West (among women who are homeless or in prisons—see Ensign 2001; Weiss-Wolf 2017) because of lack of access to facilities to manage menstrual hygiene. However, with a few exceptions, most studies have focused primarily on the role of toilet access in menstrual hygiene maintenance. This study is one of the few to highlight the importance of water access within household premises in determining hygiene. Water access was also known to affect frequency of bathing in another study.

Women from central Uganda reported skin rashes and persistent itching due to water scarcity and poor hygiene, "as shortages of supply prevent them from washing clothes regularly . . . and bathing frequently" (Thompson et al. 2001:82).

Impact of Hygiene Practices

This section is primarily based on the findings of other studies that examined the impact of poor hygiene practices on health, livelihood, and education.

Health Risks

Evidence suggests that water quantities used by households are primarily dependent on access as determined by the distance to source and/or time taken to collect water (Howard and Bartram 2003). Howard and Bartram suggest that when water is not available on premise and total collection time is 30 minutes or more, there is a high level of health concern that hygiene may be at risk. In the present study, one can estimate that the health of at least 34% of households is at high risk because they do not have enough water to practice basic hygiene. The estimate may be even higher, as the survey did not ask for waiting time at water source. Women may be at greater risk than men, because in traditional rural households men's need may take priority even though women's requirements especially during menstruation, pregnancy, and childbirth are greater (see quote below).

Avotri and Walters (1999) in their study in Ghana also report similar discrimination in accessing water for bathing.

> Sometimes, especially in summer, if there is scarcity of water then we have to give a chance to male members to take a bath and after that if the water is available then only can we take a bath. So during those days if we feel like taking a bath two times then it is very difficult to wash and take a bath, especially in summer. (Diary entry 1 of Sabarkantha Woman 4)

While this study did not focus on health risks, 29% of rural women reported chafing as a result of reusing rags and market cloth, as have other studies (see Mason et al.'s 2013 study on Kenya). In another study of poor tribal girls in India, close to 50% reported skin abrasions from the use of old cloth (Shah et al. 2013).

Unhygienic practices also pose serious health risks. Das et al. (2015:12) found that women who used reusable absorbent pads were more likely to have symptoms of bacterial vaginosis and urinary tract infections, than women using disposable pads. The same study also reports that women who did not have space for personal hygiene in the household (to change their menstrual absorbent) and had to change outdoors were more prone to have bacterial vaginosis than were those who had a private room or toilet (Das et al. 2015). Baisley et al. (2009) also found a relationship between the use of reusable pads and bacterial vaginosis among Tanzanian women. The use of unhygienic material has also been identified as a risk factor for human papillomavirus (HPV) infection in several studies (Zhang et al. 1986; Peng et al. 1991; Chaouki et al. 1998; Bayo et al. 2002).[11]

Similar to the findings in this study, fear of sexual assault when practicing hygiene without the safety of private toilets has been reported elsewhere (Sheikh 2008; Amnesty International 2010; Lennon 2011; Massey 2011; Corburn and Hildebrand 2015; Sahoo et al. 2015; Winter and Barchi 2016) and induces high levels of stress especially among adolescent girls (Hulland et al. 2015; Sahoo et al. 2015; Bisung and Elliott 2017; Caruso et al. 2017). Sexual stressors include "being watched by men during sanitation activities (peeping), men exposing themselves to women (flashing), and gender-based violence, including sexual assault and rape" (Sahoo et al. 2015:86).

Studies also have found that water hauling can lead to musculoskeletal disorders, physical injuries, exhaustion, and dehydration (Page 1996; Scott, Charteris, and Bridger 1998). Pregnant women are also at risk from carrying water and from other hygiene practices. According to one study, there might be a connection between using unclean napkins during postpartum periods and secondary infertility (Ali et al. 2007). Another study (Padhi et al. 2015) found that pregnant women who practiced open defecation were significantly more likely to have adverse pregnancy outcomes and a preterm birth. While the authors did not address the biological or behavioral reasons for these findings, they speculate that one mechanism may be related to the adverse outcomes of restricting food and water intake to cope with sanitation challenges or because of psychosocial stress due to lack of sanitation—both commonly experienced by women in this study, too. In fact, 39% in this study report restricting the urge to urinate and defecate (also reported by Routray et al. 2015 and Sahoo et al. 2015), and 31% even complained of constipation[12] due to lack of sanitation access.

Livelihood

This study did not focus on livelihood issues, but substandard facilities at work can lead to women's absences during menstruation, reducing productivity and income (World Bank 2008). NextBillion (2013) estimates that lack of access to sanitary products causes low-income women to lose an average of 5 years of lifetime wages. As Sommer et al. (2016) note, the MHM challenges faced by working adolescent girls and women in lower- and middle-income countries are compounded by the nature of their work because a large number of women are employed in the informal sector—as agricultural workers and construction workers, and often self-employed as street vendors, rag pickers, and the like. Those working in the formal sector, such as in manufacturing, also have limited access to privacy and hygienic spaces to manage menstruation, so miss work. Cambodian garment workers in factories reported facing difficulties due to the limited privacy available for managing WASH needs (Sommer et al. 2016).

MHM is time-consuming in poor communities without access to water and disposable pads, and affects the earnings of those on daily wages. In FGDs, women mentioned their wages were affected when they wasted time carrying water, washing and maintaining menstrual cloth and other stained attire, or walking back home from the fields to change and wash. There are no studies of the impact of lack of menstrual hygiene facilities for women who work in the agricultural and other informal sectors.

Education

The impact of MHM on education was not the focus of this study, but numerous studies have shown that the burden associated with menstrual management also hinders menstruating girls from attending school in many low- and middle-income countries (Ali and Rizvi 2010; Sommer 2010; Jasper, Le, and Bartram 2012; Sommer and Sahin 2013; van Eijk et al. 2016; Alam et al. 2017). A UNESCO (2014) report estimates that 1 in 10 girls in sub-Saharan Africa misses school during their menstrual cycle.

Well-Being/Dignity

Lack of WASH access is a tremendous hardship to bear and the taboos surrounding it deeply humiliating, as this study has reported. Other studies also have found that women and girls experience fear, shame, and anxiety at home, school, while traveling, or at work during menstruation (Crichton et al. 2013; Vaughn 2013; Jewitt and Ryley 2014; Sahoo et al. 2015).

In one study, 77% of rural and urban respondents found sanitation management in the postnatal period to be stressful (Hulland et al. 2015). In addition, in many countries such as India menstruating females are also socially oppressed, as they are considered impure and expected to remain hidden in a "menstrual closet" (Young 2005), leading to social exclusion.

Women in this study even reported being unable to attend the weddings of their sons or daughters when menstruating (FGD). As mentioned earlier, women are also considered in an impure state and treated as pariahs after giving birth, although the child is not.

Women also feel ashamed because they are unable to maintain their own standards of hygiene and dignity (revealed above in several quotes). As the FGDs and survey responses show, unhygienic practices are most often due to constraints under which hygiene is practiced rather than due to ignorance of appropriate hygienic behavior (see Crichton et al. 2013 on similar sentiments of girls and mothers in Nairobi slums; also see Kuhlmann et al. 2017). Thus, women want to bathe regularly, change pads frequently, not reuse menstrual cloth or rags, use water and soap for washing hands and clothes, and are ashamed and worried about infections and diseases when they cannot.

Strengths and Limitations

The study has a few limitations. First, we were not able to observe the quality of the material being used or the washing and drying practices. All the data were self-reported and may have led to desirability effect, especially on hygiene issues. Second, the study was conducted in the winter season and may not reflect seasonal differences in water availability and access to other outdoor facilities. Third, this study was not able to examine the relationship between socioeconomic background and hygienic practices, because very few respondents used sanitary napkins (only 4%) and nearly all (90%) reused rags and cloth. Fourth, since it involved only SEWA members who belonged primarily to marginal or landless farming households, it may have overestimated the prevalence of unhygienic menstrual practices in these nine districts. In addition, since many participants resided in the water-scarce districts of Gujarat, the hygiene maintenance issues may not be reflective of other parts of the country with better water access.[13] However, it is more likely to have captured the condition of the deprived communities in India and elsewhere where water insecurity is high, as Gujarati women are not alone in bearing this burden. The United Nations estimates that 1.8 billion people will be living in countries or regions with water scarcity by 2025, and two thirds of the world population could be subject to water stress. Other advantages of the study included a large sample size and multiple sources of data that enabled a better understanding of the challenges women face in coping with menstrual hygiene in a resource-poor setting.

Conclusions

The findings from this survey underline the need for a comprehensive approach to address all the challenges associated with MHM. Providing sanitary napkins alone will not address the problem. In addition to the provision of affordable sanitary napkins and their safe disposal, menstrual management requires clean water, but also soap, and private toilet facilities[14] to manage the menstrual needs of women and girls (Hennegan et al. 2016). The software package is also essential and should include educational and training programs that generate behavior change and inform girls about reproductive health to dispel myths about menstruation (as in Tanzania, see Vaughn 2013).

It must also be remembered that women bleed throughout much of their life course—4 to 6 weeks after delivery or a miscarriage and due to various abnormalities and diseases such as cervical cancer, urethral prolapse, and the like (Sommer et al. 2017). Thus, the need to have access to clean water and absorbent materials plus a safe, private facility to manage hygiene is essential for the health and well-being of all women.

Finally, despite environmental concerns about the mass adoption of disposable napkins by poor women (Sebastian et al. 2013), it would be an injustice not to encourage their adoption, especially if they are biodegradable. In fact, a study in Uganda (Hennegan et al. 2016) found that the use of reusable AFRIpads was not associated with a higher prevalence of adequate MHM. They suggest that "providing disposable pads which do not require washing or drying, and is quicker to change, might have a larger impact on MHM." Where water and privacy is at a premium, poor menstruating women value disposable napkins—just as their more privileged sisters do (despite their better access to water and toilets). The survey results in this study showed that 41% of women found washing the soiled cloth most burdensome.

A few governments have attempted to address this problem by subsidizing pads or distributing them for free. Started in 2010, the Menstrual Hygiene Scheme of the Indian government provides the pads at a highly subsidized price to adolescent girls living below the poverty line. Several state governments have also adopted similar schemes. The Government of Kenya provides free sanitary napkins to schoolgirls (World Bank 2017). The challenge is to make the product affordable, easily available, and of good quality (for a critique of the Indian program, see Chandra 2013 and Shah et al. 2013).

Countries can also reduce the cost of pads by cutting taxes as Kenya did. Currently, a number of governments around the world, including in the West, tax sanitary napkins and tampons (Chandler 2017; Weiss-Wolf 2017). In India, they are treated as a luxury item and taxed at 12% (Sikarwar 2017) while condoms are subsidized and given away for free by the government (*Economic Times* 2014).

MHM should be an integral part of the global development agenda and implemented at the household and institutional levels (schools, hospitals, workplaces). Ignoring this issue hinders the achievement of several SDGs and prevents millions of women in the Global South from gaining access to education, and improving income, health, and well-being. No development agenda can expect to empower women if it does not address this basic need.

Methods: Supplement

The study was conducted in 2011 in the rural areas of nine districts of Gujarat, India. The state has a higher per capita income than the average for the rest of India (Indian Rupees INR 63,961 vs. INR 46,492 in 2009–2010). However, on several human development indicators, such as the sex ratio and female literacy, the state fares less well (India Census 2011). Seven of the nine districts selected for the study are less developed than other parts of Gujarat. In 2001, the latest districtwide data on human development showed that out of 25 districts in Gujarat, seven districts in this study had a lower Human Development Index (HDI) value (ranging from a low of 0.394 to a high of 0.479) compared with the aggregate state HDI value of 0.565. The Gender Development Index in eight of the selected districts (ranging from a low of 0.444 to a high of 0.533) was lower than the state aggregate of 0.551 (Hirway and Mahadevia 2004).

The Gujarat districts and villages selected for the study are located in areas where SEWA (a women's grassroots organization) has an active presence. These are the less developed parts of the state, with poor water availability. The objectives of the study were discussed in several group meetings with SEWA members. Participants were randomly selected from SEWA's district membership list. Women of reproductive age were enrolled if they consented to participate after being informed of the objectives of the study. Participation in the study was voluntary, and responses were kept anonymous. The author designed and conducted the study with the assistance of SEWA facilitators, and is solely responsible for the interpretation of the results.

As mentioned earlier, to increase validity, the methodology was triangulated and included FGDs, surveys administered by trained enumerators, and diaries maintained by women who volunteered to write anonymously about their menstrual hygiene practices and problems. A pilot survey was first conducted in all the nine districts. The insights from the survey were then used to refine and develop the larger survey questionnaire and the issues of importance for the FGDs.

A total of nine FGDs were conducted in all the districts, with an average of 17 SEWA members in each discussion group. The age and community background of each participant was recorded. The 155 women (aged 17–46 years) who participated belonged to 60 castes and tribes and came from 77 villages. Each FGD focused on water, sanitation, and menstrual hygiene issues (taboos, hygiene practices), opinion about market napkins, and management of postpartum bleeding. Each FGD took an average of 3 to 4 hours to conduct and was led by trained female moderators using a guidebook. At each FGD, three notetakers (including the author) were present to document the discussion, which took place in the local language. The notes were translated into English and read by several members of the data collection team for clarification and quality control. Based on these notes, key themes emerged and were later included in the larger survey questionnaire.

For the survey, 906 women participated, from nine districts of Gujarat covering 323 villages. Enumerators received intensive training prior to the survey. The objective was to select 100 SEWA members from each of the nine districts with adequate representation from a variety of lower castes and tribes. Participants included only females of reproductive age (17–46 years), with only one female participant selected from each household (see Table 6.1). Questions focused on topics similar to those discussed in the FGDs. After the raw survey data were collected, three data analysts checked them. The codebook was refined; data were entered into Excel files, and further cross-checks were conducted.

At the end of each FGD, participants were asked if they were willing to maintain personal diaries about their experience with menstrual hygiene. Eleven volunteered from seven districts. In addition to their own concerns, volunteers wrote about the experiences of friends and family members who could not write. Thus, the diaries also included separate entries from 29 other villagers. The entries were anonymous, with only age and village recorded. The volunteers were instructed to record for a month their thoughts, feelings, and problems as they experienced menses, toilet, and bathing issues. The 40 diary entries were written in the local language and translated into English. The qualitative inputs provided knowledge of women's hygiene concerns and added depth and meaning to the quantitative analysis.

Finally, on-site field observations were made of water sources and of bathing and defecation areas in each of the nine districts based on convenience and access.

The data from the survey, FGDs, diaries, and field observations were then coded into several themes: water and toilet issues (level of access and impact on daily life), management of menstrual issues (protection options; washing, drying, disposal practices; cultural taboos), management of postpartum period, and opinion on market napkins.

NOTES

1. Located on premises, available when needed, and free from fecal and priority chemical (such as fluoride, arsenic, lead) contamination—2015 data (World Health Organization [WHO]/United Nations Children's Fund [UNICEF] Joint Monitoring Program [JMP] 2017).

2. Facilities not shared with other households, excreta safely disposed of in situ or transported and treated offsite—2015 data (WHO/UNICEF JMP 2017).

3. The range is based on assuming that half of the 892 million people that defecate in the open and half of the 2.3 billion people without basic sanitation service are women and girls who may not have access to all menstrual hygiene management (MHM) facilities (WHO/UNICEF 2015 report used this method). WATERAID (2016) assumes 1.2 billion women and girls must manage

their periods without a safe, private place to go to the toilet.

4. One example is the Indian government's 2015 National Guidelines on MHM. Examples of nongovernmental organizations include Aakar Innovations in South Asia, ZanaAfrica in Africa, and the Forum for African Women Educationalists, which is known for its advocacy work regarding MHM in sub-Saharan Africa (Vaughn 2013).

5. However, data on other personal behavior—such as contraceptive use—are regularly collected by multilateral and government agencies.

6. This paper adopts the following definition of effective MHM, proposed by the JMP of WHO/UNICEF in 2012: "Women and adolescent girls using a clean menstrual management material to absorb or collect

blood that can be changed in privacy as often as necessary for the duration of the menstruation period, using soap and water for washing the body as required, and having access to facilities to dispose of used menstrual management materials" (56).

7. For example, a systematic review of all journal articles in 2015 on menstrual hygiene and menstrual practice using the online database of SCOPUS and PubMed/Medline, supplemented by hand searches, found 1,354 references (using the search terms *menstrual hygiene*, *menstrual practices*, *sanitary napkins*, *sanitary pads*, *menstrual cloth*, and *menstrual pads*). But of these, only 96 published studies on low-resource countries in the English language were found relevant. Of these 96 studies, 59 were on girls and 28 on women (8 on both groups and 1 without age specification). In total, only 14 journal articles were on rural women, and 12 of these were primarily on gynecological morbidities.

8. The health impact of the gendered nature of WASH deprivation is the subject of another conceptual paper by the author that is under review: "Water, Sanitation, Hygiene and Women's Health: The Impact of Gender Inequality."

9. Data from 45 developing countries show that in 7 out of 10 households, the physical and time burden of water hauling falls primarily on women and girls (WHO/UNICEF JMP 2015). In another study of 24 sub-Saharan countries, it was found that adult females were the primary collectors of water in households, spending more than 30 minutes collecting water. Female children were more likely to be responsible than male children (Graham, Hirai, and Kim 2016).

10. Nieves, Evelyn. 2017. "In Nepal, a Monthly Exile for Women." *New York Times*, Jan. 5, 2017. https://lens.blogs.nytimes.com/2017/01/05/in-nepal-monthly-exile-for-women/

11. While these studies suggest a link between personal hygiene practices and reproductive tract infection and HPV infection the specific exposure pathways remain as yet undefined, and neither is the evidence conclusive. Further research is required in understanding the negative health outcomes of poor menstrual and other hygiene practices under poor WASH conditions.

12. Women in FGDs attributed symptoms of constipation to the frequent need to restrict the urge to defecate.

13. India Census (2011) data show more Gujarati households have access to water and toilet facilities than the nine districts reported here. According to the census, only 36% of households in Gujarat state do not have access to drinking water within premises, and 43% do not have access to a toilet facility.

14. In October 2014, the prime minister of India launched an ambitious national sanitation program called the Swachh Bharat Mission that aims to eliminate open defecation by 2019. The government estimates that since the start of the program, the coverage of household toilets across India has increased from 39% to 72%, although data on actual use is not known. See India Ministry of Drinking Water and Sanitation. "Swachh Bharat Mission-Gramin." http://sbm.gov.in/sbm. Accessed November 2017.

CHAPTER 7

Male Preference and Women's Economic Power

How Men's Choices Open or Close Occupations for Women

Samuel Cohn

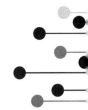

Women's economic power is heavily determined by *occupational sex-typing*, the process that divides the labor market into male occupations and female occupations. Most jobs are sex-typed as either male or female, with women facing significant barriers to entry into male sex-typed occupations. Statistical measures of occupational dissimilarity by gender continue to show marked divisions between men and women for many countries—even for data collected in the 1990s and 2000s. Furthermore, there is no tendency for indices of occupational dissimilarity to decline with increasing GDP per capita (Anker 1998; Grusky and Charles 2005). Highly developed nations and relatively poor nations show similar levels of sex-typing and similar restriction of women from both high-status, heavy manufacturing occupations and the construction trades (Anker 1998; World Bank 2011).

This division of labor has enormous implications for women's access to power. On one hand, if women cannot get jobs, women will have no economic power. They will be dependent on their fathers and husbands for economic support. If women cannot economically survive on their own, they cannot afford to leave their fathers or their husbands even if they are victims of violence. The effects of powerlessness usually show up, however, in more mundane forms. Consider the case of housework. Wives who have high income have husbands who do larger shares of the domestic chores. If women have no income, they do most of the housework and the husband does very little. Women with no income also make few routine household decisions (Blood and Wolfe 1960; Blumberg and Coleman 1989; Bianchi et al. 2000).

Not only does sex-typing affect power by determining if women can work at all, but it also determines the number of high-ranking and supervisory jobs that will be open to women. Supervisors are often drawn from the ranks of the workers they supervise. A head nurse was once a regular nurse. A school superintendent was once a teacher. While glass ceilings do exist and women are still concentrated in the lower ranks of their occupations (Grusky and Charles 2005), the more jobs that are open to women, the

Note: The author would like to thank Rae Blumberg, Val Moghadam, Christine Williams, and Christine Bose for excellent detailed comments on earlier versions of this chapter.

more upper-level jobs are open to women, allowing more women to get real economic power.

This chapter is an attempt to develop a theory of women's power through the vehicle of considering the mechanics of occupational sex-typing, which determine what jobs go to males and what jobs go to females. What determines which kinds of occupations are open or closed to women—and how does this affect women's economic power?

The study of occupational sex-typing implicitly means the study of male employers.

Employers determine who is going to be hired for what positions. Workers do not pick what jobs they get. Otherwise, everyone would pick movie star, rock musician, or CEO. People apply to companies asking for a job. Employers decide whom they will hire and what job each person will receive. If that person wants a lateral shift, or to be promoted to a higher position, the employer will decide if that move will be made. Since employers decide if a job will be filled with men or women, employers are the prime force in setting occupational sex-types.

Men make up the majority of employers in the world. Globally, women hold less than 24% of the senior jobs in large firms (Catalyst 2018). The percentage female goes up if you look at lower ranks and if you consider smaller firms and microenterprise. However, the percentage of women in management goes down if one goes back historically. In the 19th and 20th centuries, when many of the sex-types for occupations were originally set, management would have been nearly 100% male.

Given the fact that male employers control occupational sex-types, what these men want is going to make a difference. This chapter builds its theory of occupational sex-typing and women's economic power around explicit claims about what men want to achieve in their gender relations at work. The first half of this chapter uses a simple assumption that men are simple exclusionists. They want their workplaces to be all male, and they want women at home taking care of men. This simple scenario provides an immense amount of insight into the patterns of the gendered division of labor at work. This first half, with the assumption that all men want all women out of the workplace, was the basis of this author's earliest work on the subject—namely, the book *The Process of Occupational Sex-Typing* (1985; hereafter POST). The present chapter not only reviews the arguments in POST but extends them to a number of new applications and ties these arguments to women's economic power. The second half of the chapter relaxes the assumption that men are simple exclusionists. It considers a broader range of desires that men could have about women at work. These other desires lead to other predictions about women's access to jobs and female economic power. The level of empirical support provided here for the claims in the chapter will be modest. This is mostly a theoretical exercise designed to place a set of propositions before the reader. It is not usual in the literature in gender inequality to trace the differential motivations of men and show that these differences link to substantive differences in women's economic opportunities. In that regard, the approach taken here differs from those of many of the other authors in this volume.

Occupational Sex-Typing and Women's Economic Power in a World Where Men Simply Want to Exclude Women From the Labor Force

The original argument in POST argued that male employers are torn between two conflicting goals. As employers, they are looking for the cheapest possible labor. Women work more cheaply than men. In the United States in the 1960s, women earned 59 cents to the male dollar. In 2017, U.S. women earned 82 cents to the male dollar (www.infoplease.com/womens-earnings-percentage-mens-1951-2013, iwpr.org/publications/gender-wage-gap-2017-race-ethnicity). The gendered pay gap is not just an American phenomenon; it is global. Seguino (2000) reports gendered wage differences for every nation in her sample of 20 semiperipheral and peripheral nations; in her countries women earn from 48 cents to 86 cents to the male dollar. Gendered wage inequality is also reported for nations in sub-Saharan Africa, in particular for Tanzania, Ethiopia, Ghana, and the Ivory Coast (Tanzania Gender Networking Programme 1993; Appleton, Hoddinott, and Krishnan 1999). Even in early 19th century Egypt, an economy characterized by extreme poverty and large supplies of desperate male workers, women's wages were two thirds those of males (Hammam 1986). As a result, both employers in rich and poor nations who seek cost savings will tend to prefer female workers.

On the other hand, employers are men who are patriarchs. Men as sexists often wish to exclude women from the workplace. A fuller discussion of this motivation can be found in the second half of the chapter. However, for now, we put forward two prime reasons for the urge to exclude. Men like to believe that what they do at work is very difficult. They also like to believe that men do these jobs better than women would do them. So one component of the urge to exclude women is male egotism. Men are living the fantasy that they do "real men's work" women could not possibly do.

The other motivation for exclusion is to maintain the economic dependence of women on men. If women can't get jobs, they will be forced to stay home and provide domestic services for men. By excluding women from work, men are doing their part to defend "traditional family values."

So how do male employers choose among these two conflicting imperatives? The overarching proposition here is that when labor costs are not important, employers will choose to exclude women and hire men. This is because they don't need to reduce their wage bill. When labor costs are essential for organizational survival, male employers simply cannot afford to act on their patriarchal impulses. They simply have to hire women as a necessary expedient to get their costs down. POST used the technical jargon *buffering from labor costs* to refer to the condition in which employers are not dependent on reducing their wage bill and can afford the expensive luxury of hiring men. The larger propositions that are the basis of all the arguments in this first half of the chapter are as follows:

Women are more likely to be hired in settings where there is no buffering from labor costs. Because of this, settings where there is no buffering from labor costs provide greater opportunities for women to obtain economic power.

Main point: A number of propositions derive from this basic overarching principle.

1. *Labor intensity.* In some work settings, nearly all the company expenses go toward paying workers. In other settings, the expenses are divided among workers and raw material or machinery. A government office has few expenses outside of the professionals, bureaucrats, and clerical workers themselves. The office furniture does not cost much. Rent is a small percentage of total costs. Nearly the entire budget is spent on some form of labor. This kind of setting is called *labor intensive.* Offices, schools, and textile sweatshops are also labor intensive. In the case of the sweatshops, the sewing machines, the cloth, and the un-air-conditioned shed cost very little. The primary cost is that of the women doing the sewing.

The opposite of labor intensivity is *capital intensity.* In capital-intensive settings, raw material and machinery are dominant expenses. A nuclear reactor is capital intensive. The reactors themselves and all the supplemental equipment are costly. The fuel for the reactor is refined uranium, which is not cheap. Compared with that, the labor costs for the plant operators are nearly negligible.

In the office or sweatshop, if a manager wants to reduce his costs, he has to obtain cheap labor. Labor is the only expense he has. In the case of the nuclear reactor, labor savings will be barely noticeable among all the equipment and raw material charges. The labor-intensive employer has to hire women for their low wages. The capital-intensive employer can easily afford to hire the most expensive workers he can find. If he wants an all-male labor force, he can have it.

This argument has empirical support. Wallace and Kalleberg (1981) found that for the United States, the strongest predictor of the gender composition of an industry was its capital intensivity (males being in the more capital-intensive industries). Bridges replicated these findings in a more fine-scaled analysis that used a finer parsing of industries, as well as in a second analysis that considered occupations rather than industries (Bridges 1980, 1982).

Main point: Women's access to employment and economic power is likely to be greater in labor-intensive work settings.

2. *White-collar work.* The argument about labor intensity implies that women will be hired for white-collar work while men will be hired for blue-collar work. Factory work involves large amounts of machinery and raw material processing. Office work lacks such labor cost buffering. Traditional explanations of the blue-collar/white-collar split involved arguments based on the physical strength of men—arguments that are less convincing in the presence of machinery that covers most of the requirements of heavy lifting in factories. The physical strength argument is also inconsistent with the allocation of women to do extremely hard strength-related tasks such as butchering large animals in Somaliland (Hammond 2013), carrying water as they do throughout Africa (Boserup 1970), or serving as human draft

animals as they did in 19th century Egypt (Hammam 1986). Offices will not only provide employment opportunities for women but will provide supervisory opportunities with better pay.

Main point: Women's access to employment and economic power is likely to be greater in white-collar work settings.

3. *Light industry.* The capital-intensity argument also explained why men show up in heavy industry and women show up in light industry. Counterarguments have been suggested that women have greater manual dexterity for trades such as needlework. Unfortunately, greater female manual dexterity never got women into surgery or into traditional male guilds requiring hand skill, such as diamond cutting, fur trimming, or goldsmithing.

Main point: Women's access to employment and economic power are likely to be greater in light industry than in heavy industry.

4. *Petroleum and high-value minerals.* Sometimes, entire nations can be buffered from labor costs. This is the case when nations have highly valuable mineral exports, such as oil, diamonds, or gold. It is possible to make so much money from selling these high-value resources that the government does not have to engage in any other form of economic development at all. The rest of the economy can be stagnant and inefficient, but as long as the oil money comes in, the local elite will have all the cash they ever need. A government that ignores economic development in favor of just collecting resource revenues is called a "rentier state," and the inefficiency that characterizes such an economy is called the "resource curse." Not all governments with oil or valuable minerals become inefficient rentier states (Torvik 2009; Achcar 2013). But the problem is extremely common.

Countries with the resource curse are highly likely to exclude most women from employment and from positions of power. If firms don't have to be efficient for the economy to make money, they certainly do not have to use the cheapest labor possible. The government can pass laws restricting female employment or support religious institutions that restrict female employment without significantly hurting their primary resource-based sources of revenue.

The linkage of patriarchy to oil has already been made by Valentine Moghadam (1995) and Michael Ross (2008). Both Moghadam and Ross document the effect rentier states and oil have had in limiting female employment in Middle Eastern and North African countries. This is not to say that female employment is entirely absent in petro-economies. Even in Saudi Arabia, women have long been accepted as schoolteachers and nurses (El-Sahabary 2003). However, their ability to enter more contested terrains such as high-value retail occupations, manufacturing, or petroleum processing itself is highly restrained in these nations. In this volume, Moghadam shows how Middle Eastern economies that are less dependent on oil, such as Tunisia, have allowed women to obtain far more economic power than the major oil economies such as Iran.

Note that the deleterious effects of oil are less severe when oil represents only a portion of overall economic activity. In Norway with strong manufacturing and Texas with strong agriculture, manufacturing, and services, employers hire women and benefit from the cost savings involved. It is the presence of petroleum combined with the absence of other economic sectors that have to economize on labor costs that leads to relative extremes of patriarchal behavior.

> *Main point: Women's access to employment and economic power is likely to be greater in countries that do not produce oil or other valuable mineral resources.*

5. *Employees with extremely scarce skills.* Sometimes reducing labor costs is less important than simply getting labor in the first place. This is particularly the case when workers have unique irreplaceable skills. If you run a rural hospital with only one neurosurgeon in town, you will pay whatever it takes to keep that neurosurgeon on your staff. If you are a rock promoter organizing a Lady Gaga tour, Lady Gaga is probably going to get everything she wants.

Having difficult-to-replace skilled workers creates two different obstacles to the hiring of women. First, if the scarce worker is a sexist male and does not want to work with women, management is highly likely to accede to his request. Second, if retaining key workers is more important than reducing labor costs overall, management itself may not be highly motivated to recruit a cheap labor force. A good example of this process is Hollywood movie studios. Obviously, the movie stars themselves get fabulous salaries. Once the budget has been busted by the salaries at the very top, no one particularly watches expenses on the rest of the payroll. Secretaries get paid well; janitors get paid well; kitchen staff get paid well.

This process was empirically demonstrated in the 1980s in the dual-sector literature. Economic sociologists examining corporate pay structures discovered that there were whole firms that paid everyone well (rich Fortune 500 companies) and that there were also whole firms that paid everyone poorly (marginal small firms). Many factors produced these pay differentials, but one of them was worker skills (Wallace and Kalleberg 1981).

> *Main point: Women's access to employment and economic power is likely to be greater in firms that do not employ workers with irreplaceable skills.*

6. *Export orientation.* Export-oriented industries are particularly sensitive to global price competition—particularly in labor-intensive industries. Firms that produce for local markets often benefit from tariff protection, de jure legal restrictions on foreign competing products. They also benefit from de facto currency-based restrictions on foreign competing products. Inflation and low local currency valuations make it difficult for locals to buy foreign products benefiting the firms that produce for local markets. These firms sometimes also benefit from a superior understanding of local customers, allowing them in some sectors to make better-quality products than

would be available from multinationals.[1] Firms that export to global markets have to compete with cheap producers all over the world. Low wages are essential to firm survival in commodified manufacturing (Safa 1986; Gereffi 2007), and this has led to the well-known expansion of female employment in these sectors (Dunaway 2014).

Export orientation does a lot to explain the well-known high rates of female participation in East and Southeast Asia (Lie 1996; Kazeno 2004). However, export orientation is particularly helpful in explaining regional variations in women's work. Both Baslevent and Onaran (2004) and Ozler (2000) have noted that export regions and export firms in Turkey are much more likely to hire women. Female employment in the twin plant maquiladora frontier of Mexico and the United States was always much higher than was female employment in the interior of Mexico (Fernandez-Kelly 1983).

Main point: Women's access to employment and economic power is likely to be greater in firms that export to global markets.

Women's Economic Power When Men Vary in Their Hostility to Employing Women

The previous section of the chapter considered how occupational sex-typing would affect women's access to economic power in a world where men universally wished to exclude women from employment. Note that men could only control employment. They did not control all work. In some cases, self-employment was feasible. In those settings, women could "hire themselves," at least in the limited niches of the economy where male employers did not control all the jobs.

But male employers continue to control a lot of strategic sectors of the economy. In these sectors, women were *often* excluded. Note, *often* but not always. The previous discussion assumed that male employers would always exclude women. However, that is not always what men want. What happens when male employers control employment but want to use women in some way other than total exclusion?

Different men want different things. Some men are actually feminist. They are comfortable with working alongside women and having women in positions of authority.

Some men are highly sexual. They like looking at women. They enjoy the prospect of potential sexual opportunity.

Some men like gendered status displays. They want women to serve them. They want women to admire them. They want to give women orders and have these orders obeyed.

Occupational sex-typing may be heavily determined by male power and male preferences. However, if men's gendered preferences are variable, then they need to be taken into account in theories of women's economic power.

This section of the chapter considers five different empirically observable sets of male preferences, along with specification of where these particular preferences are likely to occur.

One of them is general exclusion of women, the male preference that was the focus of the first half of the chapter. Men have particular motivations for wanting to seek the complete removal of women from the workplace. Understanding the dynamics of why men sometimes want all-male workplaces helps us understand when the logic of the first half of the chapter will actually apply.

We also consider four alternative male preferences:

1. Imitative feminism, whereby men place women in visible high-status positions to show modernity, sophistication, and conformity to Western values.

2. Conformity to religious or culturally imposed patriarchal values.

3. Opportunistic wolfism, whereby men maximize their access to women's sexual and domestic services. *Wolf* here is 1940s slang for lecherous men who like to ogle and hit on women. Wolfism is my own term for men prioritizing the sexual use of women over any other economic or social considerations.

4. Geisha-ism, whereby men maintain their access to entertainment by recruiting attractive, intelligent women with social skills.

We consider each of these in turn, and their implications for women's economic power.

1. *General exclusion.* Theories of gender discrimination at work often invoke a generalized hostility of men to any employment of women. Gary Becker's (1957) famous theory of racial and gender discrimination invokes a "taste for discrimination." Men enjoy excluding women because they enjoy excluding women; they enjoy it so much, they are willing to pay for it. Heidi Hartmann's (1976) famous dual-sector theory of discrimination argued that men are vested in maintaining their position of power over the women in their lives, in their families and in their homes. If their wives and daughters cannot obtain employment, they become economically dependent on their husbands and fathers. This economic dependency will allow men to have private lives of absolute power, where they get everything they want from the women they live with. Dependence reduces women's negotiating power (Pfeffer 1981 for the general case, Hartmann 1976 for the application to women).

The exclusion of women can also be caused by an all-male workplace reinforcing men's sense of their own masculinity. The pleasure of having the value of one's own male identity reaffirmed is a benefit any employer can derive from an exclusive male labor force, regardless of the activities of other employers. In 19th century Britain and America, women were excluded from a wide variety of occupations by both workers and managers who claimed that the presence of women made the workplace "unmanly" (Lown 1990; Kessler-Harris 1993; Alexander 1995). Christine Williams (1989) has emphasized the "culture of manliness" as a critical element in her discussion of the U.S. Marines. Rituals of toughness and machismo are integral to social interaction in these settings—even if they are purely symbolic and not particularly necessary for the actual performance of military tasks themselves (Williams 2015).

There is a further economic motivation for men to exclude women from work. Workers often try to increase their bargaining power by restricting the supply of workers available to the employer. If only a limited number of candidates can work for an employer, this will raise wages through the process of supply and demand. The larger the pool of workers available to the employer, the more the employer can insist on low base salaries and simply wait until he finds someone desperate enough to accept his conditions. The smaller that pool, the more likely that the employer will find no one to fill his jobs unless he raises the pay to make the job more attractive.

Historically, most unions before the 20th century were craft unions of skilled workers who explicitly adopted the smallest possible labor force strategy. Training in the occupation was limited to the family members of people already in the union. Training in the occupation was limited to the ethnic group of the current workers. Training in the occupation was limited to men (Lane 1987; Sloane and Witney 2009). Excluding women from work was a strategy of maintaining a "decent wage for men." Many of the arguments around male resistance to women in 19th century textile factories were precisely about this economic issue (Pinchbeck 1930; Kessler-Harris 1993).

If management agrees with exclusionist workers for patriarchal reasons, then this is the situation of exclusionary male management described in the first half of the chapter. The predictions made in that section would hold.

The present discussion suggests an additional scenario where management wishes to hire women for reasons of cost and they are prevented from doing so by exclusionary male workers. Gary Becker (1957) referred to this as "employee discrimination." Usually management controls the hiring process. Only the strongest of workers are able to force their hiring policies on a resisting management. This means that the workers must have a great deal of negotiating strength, be it from scarcity, skill, or extreme deadline pressure. It may also mean that the workers are organized in either a guild or a union where they have access to a viable strike threat. This means women will have less economic power when male workers are strong and when male workers are in a union.

Main points: Women's access to employment and economic power is likely to be greater in settings where male workers are not extremely powerful.

Women's access to employment and economic power is likely to be greater in settings where male workers are not unionized.

2. *Displays of feminism to appeal to Western gatekeepers.* Winifred Poster (2013) argues that copycat feminism is an important component of business culture in many semiperipheral nations. Typically, nations in the Global North tend to be more accepting of women in positions of power than are nations in the Global South. Firms, financial institutions, state organizations, or nongovernmental organizations in the Global South that want to differentiate themselves from their "more backward" peers and appear to be as modern as organizations in the Global North will make at least some

concessions to feminist culture. These feminist or partially feminist organizations will have women in positions of power—and will have men in positions of power who will not be in favor of overtly sexist attitudes or behavior.

Corporations in the Global South that wish to appear "Western" or "modern" or "nontraditional" are likely to imitate the behavior of highly visible Western role models. This process has been described well within organizational theory by Dimaggio and Powell (1983), in their discussion of institutional isomorphism. Dependent organizations conspicuously imitate the behavior of highly visible role models—whether or not the decision makers in the dependent organization internalize the original logic of the imitated behavior. Imitation occurs because outside powerful organizations insist on compliance with the role model's norms, because fields of professionals encourage their members to engage in the "most up-to-date" practice, and because of the halo effect that all the practices of successful organizations must somehow lead to their success. Dimaggio and Powell refer to this process of imitation as "institutional isomorphism."

This means that corporations in the Global South that wish to impress gatekeepers, either in their own society or in the West, are likely to make conspicuous public displays of following "best" Western practice. This means putting high-status women in positions of high visibility to the outside world—to show that the organization in question is in compliance with the highest American and European standards. Poster (2013) notes that multinationals in southern India often place women in "showcase" positions dealing with foreign customers, suppliers, and vendors—while maintaining traditional gender roles and preferential male access to positions of authority in backroom offices that have little external exposure. Western isomorphism produces an inside/outside split in gender policy that would not be predicted from Becker/Hartmann models of patriarchal exclusion.

Ironically, Poster-style opening of external show jobs to women can have beneficial effects in promoting the access of women to positions of power and status over the long term. Formal organizational theorists of power such as Dill (1958) or Pfeffer (1981) argue that managers in corporate positions that involve dealing with strategic external actors tend to accrue more power status and personal autonomy than do those who narrowly work within the firm. Agents who bargain with the outside tend to become what Ronald Burt (1992) calls "structural holes." They obtain knowledge about the outside world that more internal managers do not have; they also have knowledge about their own firm that outside customers, vendors, and regulators don't have. All three authors argue that managers in these boundary-spanning positions use the information advantages available to them to gain arbitrage and strategic advantages. They can set agendas and structure the interactions between the firm and the environment to their personal advantage. The "show" feminism of isomorphic display can turn into genuine bona fide feminism if women use their advantages as external brokers to bargain for better positions and policies in the firm both for themselves and for their female allies.

Main points: Women's access to employment and economic power is likely to be greater in settings in the Global South that need to appear modern and nontraditional to Western gatekeepers.

Women's access to economic power is likely to be greater in settings where they are put in positions of external visibility where they negotiate and interact with important outsiders.

3. *Conformity to religious or culturally imposed patriarchal values.* Religion and traditional culture are often the basis for legitimating the exclusion of women from work. This is most often invoked in the case of Islamic societies (Moghadam 1993). However, conservative religious values are relevant to gender relations and keeping women at home in many settings, including Christian southeastern Europe and Hindu South Asia.

The most historically important incidence of an external religious agenda affecting women's access to work may have occurred in Britain in the early 19th century. Female labor force participation was widespread in Britain before the Industrial Revolution. This was a function of the widespread participation of women in certain farm tasks and in spinning and weaving, in which workers manufactured goods at home that were sold on the market (Pinchbeck 1930). The Industrial Revolution initially increased female labor force participation with the well-known rise of mechanized female spinners and weavers in factories. Increasingly, there was a movement against female factory women, and women came to be excluded from many forms of paid employment (Honeyman 2000).

A key cause of the defeminization of the British industrial structure was a religious revival that placed renewed emphasis on female domesticity. Leonore Davidoff and Catherine Hall (1989) argue that the Industrial Revolution produced a religious split between England's aristocratic and capitalist classes, with the aristocracy favoring the Church of England while the new industrial entrepreneurs favored Methodism. Nineteenth century Methodism reconfigured Christianity to emphasize entrepreneurial values such as thrift, hard work, and self-denial. Methodist gender teaching emphasized the "cult of domesticity" (Welter 1966), in which respectable women stayed home and raised their families while unrespectable women went out on the street. Removing women from the corrupting aspects of professional life and returning them to a life of piety and domesticity became increasingly important to religious men in the managerial classes of Britain and the United States. Methodist employers were active in the movements to pass protective legislation limiting female employment and acted as social models by firing women from the enterprises they controlled. Kessler-Harris (1993) notes that the early 19th century produced a catastrophic decline in economic opportunity for women and jobs only began to reopen in significant numbers for women workers after 1870. The Victorian exclusion of women had enormous repercussions throughout the Global North because other industrializing nations used British policy as the example around which they organized their own gendered hiring regimes.

Clearly, where women are being removed from the labor force, they are also being removed from positions of power in the workplace.

Main point: Women's access to employment and economic power is likely to be greater in settings where there are no strong antifeminist social or religious movements.

4. *Opportunistic Wolfism.* Frontier towns have their own distinctive gender dynamics, which can be called opportunistic wolfism. Wolfism is the confinement of women to hyper-female jobs, generally those involving sexuality. Because traditional female sex roles are being exaggerated, side opportunities, such as they are, can be opened in domestic service. The dominant theme of opportunistic wolfism is newly enriched males celebrating their wealth and power through the conspicuous consumption of female resources. Men as men are celebrating their increased access to women as women. In the Global South, frontier towns in commodity booms represent good examples of this phenomenon.

Frontier towns have extremely distinctive social structures. They are disproportionately or nearly totally male. Social control over these males is relatively weak. Most male employees have migrated away from family and former associates—leading to an attenuation of social network ties; the issue of weak ties is exacerbated by the selective recruitment of loners and drifters to isolated frontier locations in the first place. Usually, the first wave of work in these towns is extremely lucrative. The new mine or the new crop was developed in response to world shortages and favorable price trends. So as a result, there is a full-fledged boom in progress, and both profits and wages are extremely favorable.

The result is what Durkheim might argue to be a perfect environment for widespread deviance. The town is disproportionately male. Everyone has lots of money. This is all new money, so everyone has experienced a dramatic upswing in their economic fortunes. Social network ties to figures of responsibility are weak. The result is substantial conspicuous consumption and high levels of celebratory deviance. Rex Lucas's *Minetown, Milltown, Railtown* (1971) discusses the general evolution of single-industry frontier towns in extensive detail. These communities settle down over time as women migrate into the town, the gender balance stabilizes, and the initial boom winds down, returning profits and wages to normal levels. However, the opening decades of frontier towns can be pretty wild.

The gender relations of frontier towns are highly patriarchal. However, the logic of patriarchy is different from that of Becker and Hartmann. There is very little need to exclude women from work either to protect a threatened male economic monopoly or to force a local female population into docility. There *are* no other women, and male domination of the environment is complete. The active principle of gender domination in frontier towns is more akin to the dynamics of heightened boundary maintenance that Rosabeth Moss Kanter discusses in *Men and Women of the Corporation* (1977). Kanter argues that when two groups are present in the same setting in extremely unequal numbers, the visibility of the minority group becomes conspicuous. There is a tendency for the majority to exclude the minority from nearly every form of professional and social interaction, for the minority to be stereotyped with the extremely standard characteristics associated with the group, and for majority members to act more like the stereotypes of majority members when they are around members of the minority. In the case of gender in highly male environments, women become stereotyped into hyper-female roles—generally those involving either sexuality or domestic work—and men act in super-macho, super-sexual ways when around small, outnumbered groups of women.

A good empirical illustration of these principles is the early history of gender relations in Singapore.[2] Singapore was originally a center of rubber plantations. Since the southern Malay Peninsula was sparsely settled and the plantations needed substantial numbers of rubber workers, these had to be imported from elsewhere in Malaya, China, and southern India. The sex ratio was about 15 men to 1 woman. Early Singapore was a fairly rowdy place, with secret societies, a great deal of crime, and substantial labor militancy. Women were intentionally brought in by the plantation authorities from southern China.

Essentially, the only jobs that were available to women on arrival were prostitution and domestic labor. Brothels were widespread throughout the colony—and even by the 1880s, well after the founding of the rubber plantations, the brothels employed more than a third of Singapore's women. Female house servants were also in demand. Very young girls would be bought from their parents in China and taken to Singapore to work either in the brothels or as domestic labor. Older women generally graduated to domestic labor. Later on, women would marry rubber workers and become integrated into the rubber economy. However, the early jobs open to women were extremely female stereotyped.

The early years of frontier towns put women into an extreme state of vulnerability. It is difficult to attain meaningful economic power from a position as a domestic servant or a sex worker.

Main points: Women's access to employment and economic power is likely to be low in frontier settings where a Wild West culture prevails.

Women's access to employment and economic power is likely to be low in geographic settings of gender imbalance where women are greatly outnumbered by men.

5. *Geisha-ism.* Geisha-ism is the hiring of intelligent, attractive workers with high social skills for their entertainment value for management. Employers are not hiring workers; they are hiring playmates. This process can operate for workers of both genders. An athletic male may be hired because he would be a good racquetball partner. An attractive, witty woman might be hired for her value during coffee breaks or at business dinners. Geisha-ism of course refers to Japanese courtesans who were recruited primarily for their conversational, artistic, and entertainment skills. The operation of Geisha-ism in the American setting has been documented by a series of articles by Lauren Rivera on the hiring practices of elite New York law firms and management consultancies (Rivera 2012, 2015; Rivera, Owens, and Gan 2014).

Geisha-ism is most likely to occur in the most elite and prestigious of firms, such as Wall Street banks. There are several features of such elite settings that promote geisha-ism as a hiring principle.

a. *Hiring can be random, because all the candidates are exceptionally qualified.* The recruitment pool consists exclusively of students from the most prestigious and highly regarded schools, such as Wharton or Harvard. All of them have top GPAs, dazzling records of extracurricular activities, and sterling letters. The extraordinary quality of the candidate pool means that the firm can make its hires virtually randomly and be assured of obtaining outstanding candidates.

b. *Hiring can be random, because it is impossible to predict performance in the firm from any indicator of past behavior.* The jobs that will be given to new recruits to the firm are substantively different from what they were doing as undergraduates or in professional school. Doing well in law school classes or working on a law review is not the same as generating new business for the firm, filing motions, or dealing with the actual legal questions facing the firm's clients. Doing mergers and acquisitions is completely different from taking finance courses.

The distinctiveness of the actual work of elite firms means that interviewers have very little guidance from the files on their candidates that would allow them to tell who will be good or who will be bad. The problems that corporate recruiters face are analogous to those professional sports teams trying to draft rookies from the college pool. They may have access to the full statistical record of a student athlete's college performance on the field, along with game tapes and medical records. These pre-screening devices are of little use in predicting how college players will perform in a professional setting.

c. *Hiring can emphasize social attractiveness and entertainment potential, because work processes are social and collaborative.* Work in investment banks, elite law firms, and management consultancies is highly social. All projects are team projects. Workers are in constant contact with each other via live meetings, e-mails, texts, or phone calls. Furthermore, there is extensive contact with clients. Social attractiveness and entertainment potential both increase the pleasure of joint interaction and facilitate building goodwill with clients.

d. *Long hours and ambiguous criteria for the evaluation of personal performance increase the need for managers to fulfill their emotional needs during the workday.* A professional split between job-related duties and personal life is easier to maintain when the workday is sufficiently short to give people time to fulfill their individual needs outside of working hours. This becomes less practical when managers and employees are working 70-hour weeks.

This puts a premium on managers surrounding themselves with fun, entertaining colleagues with whom they can relax and speak casually. Kanter (1977) argues that this leads to *homophily* in hiring, in which managers hire workers like themselves to facilitate easy social interaction. This is a reasonable point. But a further implication of social needs and performance stress is that managers will hire people with high social skills regardless of similarity simply to find someone with whom they can talk and unburden. Furthermore, under conditions of ambiguity in the quality of performance, managers will surround themselves with people they consider to be vital and interesting—simply to obtain the reflected glory of being on a team that is vital and interesting.

Rivera found that elite corporate interviews consist of almost no substantive questions concerning professional capacities, qualifications, or performance records. Interviews overwhelmingly consisted of social questions. The likelihood of being hired was based on the interviewer's emotional response to the candidate's answer to social questions—and whether the interviewer was "excited" about working with the candidate in the future. The key to getting hired was being "interesting" and getting the interviewer to anticipate fun social interaction with that candidate if he or she were to get the job. Candidates were expected to entertain the interviewer with sparkling conversation and interesting anecdotes; if they succeeded, they received some of the highest-paying jobs in the country. In many ways, they were "chatting for profit," leading to the present characterization of this hiring dynamic as geisha-ism.

Rivera's professional findings can be validated from the actual life of one of the editors of this volume, Rae Blumberg. Before she was a famous sociologist, she was a struggling young college student seeking summer jobs in the Chicago labor market. She got a job as a secretary at a food company in Chicago. She was hired by a senior male executive. Her getting the job was based on her looks as well as her brains. She was not given a serious evaluation of her skills for the job at hand—which in this case meant shorthand and typing. Once she was on the job, she found her social responsibilities to be at least as important as her professional ones. She was expected to join the male managers at lunch for group eating and drinking. She was expected to make entertaining conversation at the table. She also had meaningful responsibilities at the office; objectively, she was a productive worker. Geisha-ism involves hiring workers for both professional and social capacities. Blumberg had to fill this double role.

What are the gender implications of geisha-ism? Job candidates of both sexes are expected to be entertaining. However, female job candidates are also expected to be beautiful. In Rivera's study, female physical beauty was not correlated with being hired when a female candidate was interviewed by a woman. However, beauty was strongly correlated with being hired when the candidate was interviewed by a male. Future hires, like geishas, were expected to be good-looking—even if no physical intimacy was anticipated by the hirer/consumer.

What are the implications for women's access to power? The good news is that geisha-ism provides a limited route for women to obtain positions in some of the most lucrative and powerful organizations in the country. The social networking that creates access to these positions is not that different from the operation of the "old boys' network" that put elite WASPs into these positions in an earlier era.

The bad news is that it is not known whether geisha-ism leads to enduring careers, promotions, and access to top management positions. Are the women treated as decorative second-class citizens in elite settings, or do they have the same probability of promotion as comparably qualified males? Note also that the mere existence of highly prestigious firms with equal prestigious candidate pools has not historically guaranteed female hiring. The geisha-ism of the 2000s occurs in the same settings as the closed all-male elite networks of the 1940s and '50s.

Main point: Women's access to employment and economic power can increase in elite settings where all candidates are highly qualified and evaluations are based on social compatibility. Access to top jobs within these settings may be limited.

Men's Gendered Desires and Women's Economic Power

This chapter has argued that women's economic power is dependent on the gender preferences of male employers. The intermediating mechanism between these two is occupational sex-typing. There is enormous variability in what male employers want from women—which in turn affects the occupations that will be open or closed to females. This determines their access to employment and their access to superior jobs within these occupations.

Probably the most common male utility is simple exclusion. There are many men who value the contributions of men more than they value the contributions of women. They associate all-male workplaces with "hiring the best candidates." This has led to the exclusion of women from occupations that are buffered from labor costs, are capital intensive, are blue-collar, and have men with irreplaceable skills, and from workplaces in nations whose economies are exclusively based on valuable mineral resources. There is a broad swathe of occupations in which women have limited access to both employment and positions of power.

Many men, however, are feminist and do not want to exclude women. Other men want to look feminist so that they are respected by external feminist gatekeepers. Other men are more worried about being respected by authorities that are relatively patriarchal. Yet another population of men is not so feminist—but wants to have women around for sexual or social reasons. These alternative logics lead to predictions that are different from those expected from a model of simple exclusion. Women will be in public, highly visible jobs if men are trying to look feminist. Women will be in invisible jobs or no jobs if men are trying to look traditional. Women will be in sexualized or domestic work if men are trying to maximize their consumption of access to women's services. Women will be in high-status jobs with high sociability if they are being hired as corporate geishas. The complexities of women's power stem in part from the simultaneous coexistence of these different motivations among different male employers. What powerful men want from women may vary; however, the powerful men are going to get what they want.

Sometimes these male scripts benefit women. Often they don't. A woman who is hired as "an interesting person" by a geisha-oriented elite firm benefits from the high pay and status linked to being associated with an elite firm. A woman whose scientific career is crushed by exclusionary male superiors who think women don't do good science receives no benefits at all.

There are three strategies for overcoming exclusionary male preference:

a. One can try to change men's minds. Women have tried this unsuccessfully for thousands of years, but progress may be made in the present era.

b. One can make gender discrimination illegal. This is a practical and effective solution . . . so long as the law is enforced. Weak enforcement has been the Achilles' heel of affirmative action.

c. Women can create their own opportunities through self-employment and women hiring other women. Women have had their own farming operations or have been independent traders in many parts of sub-Saharan Africa, Southeast Asia, and Latin America. Not every economy has space for a viable self-employment niche. Not every society gives women easy access to self-employment. When women control their own economic operations, they obtain a degree of autonomy from patriarchal men. They may have to deal with male creditors, legal authorities, and customers, but they don't have to ask a male employer for a job.

However, many of the best economic opportunities will continue to be those in large bureaucratic firms. Large firms have employers and employees; if the employers are male, they will exercise male preferences in whom they hire. The only enduring solution to gender inequality in large firms will be women obtaining enough positions in the upper ranks that they are doing the hiring rather than men.

NOTES

1. This is most typically the situation with local foodstuffs, but it can also apply to other consumer goods, where locally based production knowledge and a deep understanding of local tastes are important.

2. The empirical material for this section is drawn from Kazeno (2004), Heyzer (1986), and Lee, Campbell, and Chia (1999).

Women on the Fast Track?

Coloniality of Citizenship and Embodied Social Mobility

Manuela Boatcă and Julia Roth

The most recent Oxfam report, titled "Reward Work, Not Wealth," alerted the world to the fact that the year 2017 had seen the biggest increase of billionaires in history—at the incredible pace of one more every 2 days (Oxfam 2018). In 1 year, the very wealthy saw their fortunes grow by $762 billion. This amount itself—how much richer the very rich became in the past 12 months—is seven times higher than the one needed to end extreme poverty worldwide. The current gap between the rich and the poor at the global level—maybe more appropriately termed an abyss—makes today's world more unequal than it has been at any previous time in history (Reid-Henry 2015).

At the same time, wealth is disproportionately gendered (i.e., overwhelmingly male). Although the number of women on the Forbes World's Billionaires list reached an all-time high in 2018 and their collective net worth outpaced the total gains of men and women for the past year, only 1 out of 10 billionaires worldwide are women and only 1.4% of them are first-generation billionaires (Pendleton and Cannon 2018; Wang 2018). In turn, women own less than 2% of the world's land, represent the majority of the world's poorest, and provide $10 trillion in unpaid care annually (Oxfam 2018). At both ends of the world wealth and income distribution, gender disparities explain a large part of the currently rising global economic inequalities.

The same is true for the possibilities of counteracting inequality and poverty. As the gaps in average incomes between countries have been increasing alongside the global gap between the rich and the poor, international migration has become one of the most effective strategies of upward mobility (Korzeniewicz and Moran 2009; Shachar 2009; Reid-Henry 2015; Milanovic 2016). Although more people migrate internationally within the Global South, rather than from the Global South to the Global North, accessing the territory and resources of a country relatively better-off than one's country of birth or residence awards immediate economic benefits to people in most parts of the world. To explain that being born in a very rich country equates being better-off than someone born in a very poor country at any point of the income distribution, Branko Milanovic (2016) has recently coined the term *citizenship premium*. Just by being born in the United States rather than in the Congo, a person would multiply their income 93 times (Milanovic 2016). Depending on where they are located and where they can migrate to, citizens of poor countries can thus double, triple, or even increase their real incomes tenfold by moving to a rich country. As Korzeniewicz and Moran (2009) have shown, anyone in the poorest seven to eight income deciles of Bolivia or Guatemala could move up several global income deciles by migrating to Argentina or Mexico, respectively. Even more strikingly, anyone but people in the top decile in both Argentina and Mexico could "skip" several global income deciles by entering Spain or the United States' second-poorest decile through migration (Korzeniewicz and Moran 2009:108f).[1] In all these cases, the upward economic mobility of migrants is considerably higher than the income gains that either a further education, better pay at home, or their country's economic growth would have allowed them during a lifetime.

Yet access to international migration to a richer country is itself unequally distributed. Knowledge about possible travel routes and better economic prospects, transportation costs (whether legal or unauthorized), and travel expenses require considerable physical mobility as well as material and immaterial resources. Such resources are much less available to the poorest strata, the lower-skilled, racialized people, and women (especially when accompanied by children), than to the middle and upper classes, the educated, the racially unmarked, and men able to travel alone. In addition, the limitation of women's rights, mobility, and access to capital, which has historically made them more vulnerable to physical and sexual violence in Western societies (and all the more so in the context of colonialism and enslavement), continues to do so today. Currently, non-Western women—and other marginalized persons of nonconforming gender performance—still are the most vulnerable migrants.

Hence, while it is true that "as a global redistribution tool, migration fails to reach those at the bottom of the distributional matrix" (Shachar 2009:84), fast tracks are open to those higher up the income ladder. This is particularly visible in the commodification of citizenship rights for non-Western investors throughout the Western world in recent years. So-called "investor citizenship" or "investor residence" programs allow a wealthy, overwhelmingly male, non-Western minority to acquire a residence permit or a second citizenship in a rising number of European Union and Commonwealth member states in exchange for a sizable investment in real estate or government bonds (Boatcă 2015, 2016). Such programs were either revamped or implemented in independent Caribbean countries as well as Southern and Eastern European Union member states in the wake of the global 2008 recession. They provide male, non-Western investors with the right of visa-free travel to core countries, the citizenship of a Commonwealth or European Union state, the right to reside and work anywhere in the European Union (in the case of the European programs), or exemption from personal income tax (in the case of some Caribbean programs). Their main beneficiaries have been Chinese, Russian, but also Lebanese, Egyptian, and Syrian investors (Arton Capital 2017)—evidence of the fact that the number of billionaires in middle-income countries tripled in just 6 years despite the 2008 recession. Brazil, Hong Kong, and India registered a twofold, Russia almost a threefold, and China a staggering twelvefold increase in their respective number of billionaires from 2006 to 2012 (Albrecht and Korzeniewicz 2018:103). At the same time, China and India are expected to contribute disproportionately to the prospected growth of the billionaire population by nearly 80% before 2020, an increase of 1,700 billionaires (Arton Capital 2017). Unlike older residence and green card programs in the United States, Canada, or Australia, investor residence and citizenship programs do not require their beneficiaries to move to the national territory or spend regular amounts of time there. Investors thus often sidestep the actual migration process altogether. Instead, they use the "citizenship premium" they purchased for business and travel purposes as well as to send their children to European schools, especially in the United Kingdom.

It is important to note that, while any state's citizenship could theoretically be commodified by becoming the object of investor programs, it is the citizenship of only a few states that lends itself to being commodified by virtue of being a scarce good awarding (relatively) rare benefits. From this point of view, states whose citizenship includes the advantage of visa-free travel to core countries or even the right to legal employment in them— those that Milanovic sees as having a "citizenship premium"—can thus in turn offer "premium citizenships" that are attractive to investors. States that are not part of the core may use the residual benefits of former colonies that today share, among other things, a visa-free travel area, as in the case of the British Commonwealth. This, however, hardly compares to the rights accruing from EU citizenship, which include free movement, residence and non-discrimination within the European Union, the right to vote for and stand as a candidate in European Parliament and municipal elections, diplomatic protection outside the European Union, and so forth. Citizenship for sale is not only unavailable to the majority of the world's population but would not prove a viable economic strategy in any but "premium citizenship" states, among which EU member states rank highest.

For wealthy individuals of non-Western countries, investment citizenship clearly represents a means of global social mobility that eludes both ascription and migration, and at the same time trumps race. In this regard, it is a globalized instance of what, in the context of racial inequalities in Brazil, has been referred to as "whitening with money" (Hasenbalg 2005)—a capital-facilitated symbolic move up the racial ladder (Boatcă 2017). Such monetary—and momentary—disconnect from the racialized body through possession of a Western passport is however no reason for celebrating a postracial order. On the one hand, it belies the experience of the great majority of transnational labor migrants, for whom border crossing awarding upward economic mobility simultaneously entails the opposite risk—being reclassified as nonwhite and thus experiencing downward racial mobility.[2] On the other hand, disconnecting from the racialized and gendered body is an option unavailable to most women, who have significantly less access to both capital and existential resources worldwide. As Ayelet Shachar (2009) has argued, for a girl born in 2001 in Mali, one of the poorest countries in the world, the chances of surviving to age 5, having access to clean water, or getting an education were incomparably lower than for a baby born at the same time in the United States, where chances for boys and girls on all these counts are nearly identically high. Contrary to the tenets of an entire Western tradition of citizenship theory (from Max Weber to T. H. Marshall and Talcott Parsons to Bryan Turner), citizenship and gender, two ascribed statuses, are the most decisive factors accounting for these extreme inequalities between individuals in poor and rich countries in the 21st century.

Women therefore often rely on strategies of social mobility anchored in the body. What we call the *embodied social mobility* of women and feminized Others can thus be said to represent the counterpart of the *monetized social mobility* disproportionately available to wealthy men.

In this chapter, we therefore argue that, unlike predominantly male, wealthy investors, who can achieve almost instant global mobility[3] in exchange for a check, women and feminized Others, particularly LGBTIQ and racialized individuals, exchange their gendered bodies in lengthy arrangements eventually resulting in upward mobility through residence or citizenship. Thus, women's and feminized Others' access to social mobility as mediated through economic capital both involves more precarious means (their own bodies) and yields more precarious results than in the case of men and unmarked individuals. We contend that women's economic power partially counters the coloniality of power that has systematically relegated them to more precarious positions in the global mobility structure, yet in the process creates ambivalent fast tracks that change the content but reproduce the terms of the same coloniality.

We accordingly want to zoom in on the structural distribution of such unequal means of access to fast tracks to mobility in the case of women and feminized Others, who consciously employ their gendered bodies as alternative means of bettering their economic prospects. In the following, we explore how the colonial legacy embedded in current citizenship arrangements that we have termed the coloniality of citizenship is complicated by gendered strategies of embodied social mobility. By discussing women's and feminized Others' strategies of accessing citizenship rights as forms of "embodied social mobility," we examine the gender dividend enforced by the coloniality of citizenship and the way it is currently destabilized by women and feminized Others with limited or considerable economic power.

Coloniality of Citizenship and the Colonial Traffic in Women

From a global perspective, the institutionalization of citizenship rights in Western nation states coincided with the legal (and physical) exclusion of non-European, nonwhite, and non-Western populations from social and cultural rights. The Western construction of gender in the course of the European colonial expansion (McClintock 1995; Oyewumi 1997; Stoler and Cooper 1997; Lugones 2007) has shaped the modern/colonial institution of citizenship since it came into existence. Inside and outside the West, citizenship rights were granted to women only gradually, while men and women of other regions were en-gendered along colonial lines. In line with the literature on coloniality (Mignolo 2000; Quijano 2000; Lugones 2007, 2008) we view the structural distribution of unequal and en-gendered citizenship rights as a crucial component of coloniality/modernity (see Boatcǎ and Roth 2016; Roth and Boatcǎ 2016). Not only the naturalization of women but also

that of peasants and slaves in the colonies occurred temporally and (ideo)
logically parallel to the process of housewifization of bourgeois women and
to that of the proletarianization of male non-wage workers in the industrial centers. Both were conceived as dimensions of the larger civilizing process (von Werlhof, Mies, and Bennholdt-Thomsen 1983; Mies 1996). Pnina
Werbner and Nira Yuval-Davis (1999) accordingly describe the exclusion
of women from citizenship rights as "intrinsic sign of their naturalization
and as embodiment of the private, the family and the emotional" and thus
as "crucial for the construction of the public space as masculine, rational,
responsible and respectable" (6, our translation). By relegating women,
children, and foreigners to the (however recent) past of the civilizing process that adult men had presumably accomplished, the implementation of
seemingly universal principles of citizenship created constantly racialized
and en-gendered particularisms. The corresponding exclusions historically
ranged "from colonial subjects to women, particular classes and racialized
minorities, up to people with different sexualities and abilities" (Dobrowolsky and Tastsoglou 2006:10). Gender positions have been racialized and
ethnicized along colonial patterns, creating the image of the white virtuous
woman and "mother" of the race/nation—and later housewife—to be monitored and protected from black male aggression, or of the sexually threatening, eroticized, and permanently available black female body, accordingly
deprived of (the right to) protection and motherhood. It is at this juncture
of gender, race, and ethnicity as products of the colonial crucible that the
institution of citizenship is revealed to be a key element in the maintenance
of the coloniality of power of the modern/colonial world system (Mignolo
2000). It is to the specific mechanisms of its functioning throughout the history of the system that we refer as the coloniality of citizenship.

By targeting the racialized and eroticized body, the coloniality of citizenship has made the circulation of the female body as a commodity a central part of the colonial order of gender relations ever since its emergence.
In her 1975 essay "The Traffic in Women," Gayle Rubin (1975) described
the "sex/gender system" as a "set of arrangements" through which sex is
translated into gender and which serves as a prototype of all social and economic relations. In this system, men exchange women among themselves
on a continuum ranging from prostitution to marriage. In turn, Jean Franco
maintained that particular forms of the "exchange" of colonized women—
such as enslaved indigenous women given as a gift to the Spanish conquerors or exchanged between Aztecs and Spanish men—were already part and
parcel of the conquest (Franco 1999:71ff). Gender has thus informed the
modern/colonial institution of citizenship from its emergence, while gender
and citizenship have been entangled in complex ways with other dimensions
of stratification and inequality such as racialization and enslavement that
placed cisgender men, cisgender women, and transgender persons at very
different positions in racialized colonial hierarchies.

Such stratification patterns went hand in hand with distinct forms of
embodiment. Vice versa, differently positioned actors have applied different
practices and strategies of embodiment to counter and/or gain agency within
these hierarchized positions. The subjection of bodies to normalizing practices (Butler 1990, 1993, 2004) becomes not only a way in which already

male and female bodies seek to approximate an ideal but the very process whereby sexed and gendered subjects come into existence.[4] Femininity and masculinity become, broadly, bodily styles that bodies incorporate to yield a gendered subjectivity. The Others created in the process—women, homosexuals, LGBTIQ persons, those with differently abled bodies—are treated socially as outsiders, "the abject," and subject to social punishments. Embodied practices are therefore always already also marked by—and produce—not only en-gendered but simultaneously sexualized, racialized, and classed subjectivities (see Fanon 1963; Lorde 1984; hooks 1990; Ahmed 2000).

Women on the Fast Track and Embodied Social Mobility

It is precisely such strategies of "embodied social mobility" based on the gender dividend enforced by the coloniality of citizenship that we are interested in. As we argue, women and feminized Others, particularly LGBTIQ and racialized individuals, exchange their gendered bodies for upward mobility through residence or citizenship—unlike predominantly male wealthy investors, who can "buy into" global mobility and whiteness. Their strategies provide fast-track access to citizenship and/or upward social mobility and economic power for those who cannot exchange such privileges for a check. In the process, they challenge and sometimes revert the content of the coloniality of citizenship, but not its terms. In other words, they bend the rules in the favor of women and racialized Others but cement them by following their logic. In the following, we examine marriage to the owner of a Western passport, (sex) tourism, and childbirth as ways of anchoring social mobility in unequally gendered bodies and thus as distinct forms of the "body-politics of knowledge" that put their respective colonially en-gendered epistemologies to use (Mignolo and Tlostanova 2006; Tlostanova 2010).

Fast Track 1: Marriage— The International Market Option

For middle-class women from many parts of the Americas, the range of options for getting on a fast track to advantageous citizenship is much broader than for lower-class, undocumented women, yet it is narrow compared with the options of the wealthy elites. Unlike lower-class migrants of any gender, middle-class women can count on the social and financial capital to make it to a richer country as well as capitalize on positive exoticized stereotypes ascribed to their bodies to actively embody social mobility.

A telling recent example comes from the work of Katharine Braun (2016), who has examined everyday practices of middle-class Bolivian migrant women from Santa Cruz de la Sierra in Geneva, Switzerland. Since the 1980s, the former Bolivian middle class has lost its relatively privileged position. The modernization programs initiated in the Santa Cruz de la Sierra region by the U.S. development ministry in the early 1950s focused on investments in the industrialization of the agrarian sector through credits.

The resulting formation of a new agro bourgeoisie and the accompanying land reform, however, did not break with the agro bourgeoisie's clientelist land concentration (Braun 2016:212; cf. Prado et al. 2007). The region's economic boom and the implementation of a neoliberal order also saw the rise of a new "narco bourgeoisie" and new forms of social mobility (Braun 2016:212). Against this background, women striving for education and for entering the labor market become the protagonists of the necessary break with the formerly rigid class structures, particularly when it comes to mobility and the transformation of gender relations. Their family's loss of privilege in the new economic context forced former middle-class Bolivian women into small entrepreneurship and migration and led to the unemployment of the men—the previous breadwinners. Their privileged class status, European heritage, and light—"golden"—skin gained these Bolivian women the label *chicas de oro* ("golden" girls). The first of their class to migrate internationally, they describe themselves as "pioneers" who, unlike labor migrants, have not migrated to Europe primarily for economic reasons but in search of marriage to an EU citizen. Legal residence in Europe as a result of such a marriage earns them a better social position and enables them to care for the families they left behind in Bolivia. To this end, the *chicas de oro* particularly target men from Southern Europe, who up to the 1990s had made up the largest number of migrants to Western Europe. Having since regularized their residence status, the men now possess the legal papers and the employment opportunities that make them attractive as marriage partners for middle-class Latin American women. The exoticized erotic capital the *chicas de oro* apply to attract Southern European men—a strategy they refer to as "fishing *bacalaos*"—draws from the repertoire of colonial hierarchies to re-create an exchange economy in the migration context. In line with feminist scholar Gayle Rubin's concept of the "traffic in women," the circulation of the female body as a commodity can be viewed as continuing a long tradition as part of a colonial order of gender relations in Bolivia, where entering sexual relationships with men of higher social strata led to the upward social mobility of entire families and therefore became an organizing principle of social relations in rural areas. Following Braun, this hierarchy has also been crucial for the organization of gender relations: "the lighter the (skin) pigmentation, the higher the esteem and the chance to 'conquer' an economically well-situated man. Following this paradigm, the *chicas de oro*'s largest resource as *mestizas* of European origin is their 'golden' skin" (215), resulting in the sexualization and economization of their bodies. As Braun concludes, the "logic of their depictions is closely entangled with the forms of en-gendering and the meaning of the body in transforming economies of survival in Bolivia" (Braun 2016:214). An attractive appearance and related "techniques of the body" play a crucial role for that matter. In line with the logic of the coloniality of power (Quijano 2000), "beauty" has been identified with "being white" as dominating paradigm of femininity in Santa Cruz de la Sierra, expressing a racialized hierarchy of population groups (215).

Similar eroticized and exoticized colonial ascriptions apply also to women of lower social strata. However, due to their lower economic power and physical mobility, they are more likely bound to their country or region of origin to look for partners with a privileged passport as a fast track to social mobility. To many destinations, possible candidates (first) travel as tourists.

Fast Track 2: Sex (and) Tourism— Mobility Through Erotic Capital

Given the rise in business mobility, North–South tourism, and communication technologies, which facilitate the maintenance of far-distance relationships, tourist encounters in many spaces provide the only means to fast access to social mobility or even a privileged citizenship status for those who lack the economic power to travel to the respective destinations. Aaron Kamugisha (2007) defines the "coloniality of citizenship" as the "complex amalgam of elite domination, neoliberalism and the legacy of colonial authoritarianism" (21) that continue to limit the aspirations of Caribbean citizens and their access to full citizenship rights. Following this notion, citizenship encompasses a broad range of practices and "tropes of belonging and identity" experienced by Caribbean people and their institutions, for which Caribbean actors have developed numerous strategies to undermine persistent colonial structures (Kamugisha 2007:21). We are particularly interested in these concrete (embodied) practices as material means for gaining access—or even a fast track—to upward social mobility beyond "tropes of belonging and identity." As Kamugisha points out, the "tourism economy" in (Anglophone) Caribbean states follows a colonial pattern, given that in many destinations the number of tourists outnumbers the number of citizens, which—in combination with the high dependency on tourism—blurs the line of who is a (legitimate) citizen. Tourists enjoy a sort of "extra-territorial citizenship," since they provide a decisive part of the national income.

As shown above, marriage to the owner of a Western passport provides one of the few legal and comparatively easy means of access to social mobility and privileged citizenship status as opposed to life-threatening illegalized border crossings. In some regions, tourism serves as a platform of options for all parties. Yet North–South tourism—and sex or "romance" tourism in particular (Pruit and LaFont 1995)—is based on deeply unequal power structures. Who can be a tourist and where, and by whom she or he is served, is related to highly asymmetrical and colonial axes of stratification, deeply marked by racial and gendered dimensions. Owners of a Western passport (with a medium or high income) can use their citizenship privilege to travel to racially eroticized "fantasy islands," for example, to the Caribbean (O'Connell Davidson and Sánchez Taylor, 1999; see also O'Connell Davidson, 2001). In most formerly colonized regions, highly dependent on the tourism industry, romance and/or sex are often part and parcel of the package dream holiday of Western tourists of all genders and sexualities. Against the backdrop of a long tradition of exoticizing and sexualizing the colonial "Other" (McClintock 1995; Tlostanova 2010), Western men's and women's disadvantageous age, gender, and/or class positions are crisscrossed with the "cultural/racial capital of whiteness" (Stam and Shohat 2012:191) derived from their class and citizenship privilege as sex tourists to a poorer country. Sex workers in tourist destinations such as the Caribbean, in turn, can transform their class and citizenship disadvantage into erotic capital rooted in colonial and racialized erotic imaginations of the black body and thereby gain financial advantage in a structurally unequal encounter (Roth 2013). In many places, tourism provides one of the few ways of access to hard currency, consumer goods, or luxury products. In some cases, encounters with tourists even result in such global mobility prospects—or fast tracks—as a holiday abroad through a tourist visa, permanent residence, up to marriage and a Western passport. However, the non-Western partners are highly dependent on their privileged passport partners, and women are, again, particularly vulnerable to physical, psychological, or sexual violence.

A number of studies on sex tourism illustrate how much such encounters are based on colonial structures that persist in unequally distributed economic power and the racialization and sexualization of colonized bodies. Julia O'Connell Davidson's (2001) research on hard-core sex tourists who exchange information on their travel destinations in Internet blogs provides an illustrative example. Numerous heterosexual male sex tourists on the one hand naturalize their partners' racialized bodies and veil the inequalities and economic dimension of their encounter by maintaining that sex "comes naturally" to them. On the other hand, a number of interviewed males state that longer-term relationships with (one or several) much younger women in the Caribbean enable them to outdo the ageism they face in their home countries, where they would be reduced to dating same-age women. Moreover, many Western hard-core sex tourists see their fantasy island romances as a way out from feminist gains in Western countries, where women (can) sue their partners for violent behavior.

Films such as *Paradies: Liebe* (2012), *Heading South* (2006), and *Sand Dollars* (2015) show that, since women in Western countries have been integrated in large numbers into the labor market and enjoy economic power, independence, and mobility, neo-colonial tourism encounters are no longer restricted to males (or heterosexual desires),[5] even though studies of such phenomena often refer to female sexualized tourism as "romance tourism" (thereby masking the structural similarities to male sex tourism). Their example points to the colonial dimension of gender relations and the coloniality of citizenship, which positions intersectionally differently en-gendered men and women at very distinct social locations on a global scale. The single rituals might differ, but like their male counterparts, female (sex) tourists take advantage of their economic power, privileged citizenship status, and racial capital to counteract the age (and often gender and class) disadvantage they face at home, where their options on the marital market are limited. Vice versa, the sex workers in tourist destinations make use of embodied practices based on stereotypical ascriptions and expectations and their (exoticized) erotic capital to make up for their highly disadvantageous economic power and reduced mobility. However, their situation is often precarious, since, unlike in the case of "classical" sex work encounters, the mostly veiled character of the economic dimension also often makes the receivers entirely dependent on the tourists' (or expats') benevolence. This might vary and range from providing food, drinks, sometimes clothes or expensive gifts, and accommodation in a luxury hotel during the stay; regular payments; or even a ticket and a visa to a Schengen destination. For some, what started as tourism encounters even result in long-term relationships or matrimonies.[6]

The case of (sex) tourism in the context of the increasing economic power and social and physical mobility of a small elite provides an insightful example of the revival of intersectional inequalities based on colonial power and knowledge structures on a global scale. In their study on male and female sex tourism to the Caribbean, Julia O'Connell Davidson and Jacqueline Sanchez Taylor (1999) maintain:

> The demand for sex tourism is inextricably linked to discourses that naturalize and celebrate inequalities structured along lines of class, gender and race/Otherness; in other words, discourses that reflect and help to reproduce a profoundly hierarchical model of human society. . . . That the Western sex tourist's pocket can contain sufficient power to transform others into Others, mere players on a pornographic stage, is a testament to the enormity of the imbalance of economic, social, and political power between rich and poor nations. (52, 53)

The sexualized and racialized coding and exploitation in an unequal world-system becomes even more apparent in our next example, in which childbirth as the ultimate path to embodied social mobility provides a strategy of ensuring citizenship rights for the next generation.

Fast Track 3: Childbirth— Deferring Mobility to the Next Generation

One roundabout way of accessing U.S. citizenship is giving birth on U.S. soil. Since being born in the country's territory ensures citizenship rights, any child born on U.S. soil becomes a U.S. citizen and can extend U.S. citizenship to his or her parents at the age of 21. This right goes back to the 14th Amendment to the U.S. Constitution granting citizenship to "all persons born or naturalized in the United States, and subject to the jurisdiction thereof." Adopted in 1868, the amendment was a repudiation of the Supreme Court's 1857 ruling, in *Dred Scott v. Sandford*, that people of African descent could never be American citizens. In 1898, the Supreme Court, in *United States v. Wong Kim Ark*, interpreted the citizenship provision as applying to a child born in the United States to a Chinese immigrant couple (Lacey 2011). The 14th Amendment denied citizenship to Native Americans, even though they obviously were "born" in the United States, because they were subject to the jurisdiction of their tribal governments. Congress did not grant citizenship to Native Americans on reservations until 1924, 56 years later. Babies born in the United States to foreigners are clearly citizens of their mothers' country, so granting U.S. citizenship creates the possibility of dual citizenship, which the United States has never recognized as valid.

Although a waiting period of 21 years can easily be described as the opposite of a fast track to social mobility and has rightfully been deemed a poor immigration strategy, it provides instant social mobility to the next generation. For non-Western women of the upper class, such legal loopholes to an otherwise rigid regime of citizenship ascription systematically provide the basis for a fast track to U.S. citizenship. Paradoxically, for wealthy Russian investors, it is in the Florida Trump properties that they take advantage of this option. So-called birth-tourism companies offer Trump apartments as part of packages costing upwards of $75,000. The privately owned condos are investment properties for Russia's hyper-wealthy, a safe place to store savings in U.S. dollars (Blakely and Parfitt 2018). The Miami-based company Status-Med offers a Trump Royale penthouse apartment for $7,000 a month alongside full access to the Sunny Medical Centre, which organizes get-togethers, beach yoga, and medical care for expectant mothers. Sunny Medical Center openly advertises citizenship as one of the primary benefits its clients receive, and the women using its services openly tell U.S. officials that the aim of their travel is giving birth on U.S. soil in order to obtain citizenship for their babies (Pavey 2017).

For the growing middle and upper classes in Russia and China, U.S. citizenship secures their children financial aid at U.S. schools, easier access to jobs in the United States, and the possibility to gain Green Cards for their offspring and family. In Los Angeles, birth-tourism agencies cater to largely Chinese clients. In New York, the Manhattan hotel Marmara offers mothers from Turkey an all-inclusive package for delivering their babies on U.S. soil: $17,000 for 2 months in a hotel suite, including a cradle and a gift set for the newborn. The hotel directory estimates that its 12 clients in the year 2009 paid up to an additional $30,000 for their hospital bills. When rich women make use of the 14th Amendment and check into a luxury hotel to deliver, President Donald Trump's immigration policies are seemingly suspended. Lower-class migrants' children and the recipients of the DACA program that shields children of immigrants (the so-called Dreamers) are instead in constant threat of deportation. Such politics point to the 14th Amendment's persistent racial-colonial bias as part of the coloniality of citizenship.

The described strategy of giving birth on U.S. soil is currently subject to sanctions and criminalized through ethnic and racial profiling when practiced by poor and/or illegal immigrants who are accused of having abused the right of soil. Several Republican attempts at amending the U.S. Constitution since 2010 have mobilized terms such as *anchor babies*, *birth tourism*, and *accidental citizens* to end the automatic granting of citizenship to poor migrants, arguing that the provision attracts high numbers of unauthorized migrants (Feere 2010; *Huffington Post* 2013). For lower-class immigrants arriving to give birth in the United States, U.S. citizenship for their newborns is, however, by far not the reason for migrating. The overwhelming majority of expecting mothers are frequent border crossers with valid visas who travel legally to take advantage of better medical care—one of the main advantages of the citizenship of a wealthy state.[7] Also, many poor women crossing the Mexican border from Honduras eventually abandon their initial plan to continue all the way to the United States along highly insecure paths and therefore are increasingly exposed to sex crimes and enforced prostitution. A number of women stuck in a migrant shelter in this border region get pregnant, as a baby born on Mexican soil promises permanent residency for the mother (and the father), as well as access to health care and education (Guevara González n.d., 2015). Moreover, although the total U.S. immigration population continues to grow, unauthorized immigration has slowed in the past decade (Pew Research Center 2013). Nor do children born on U.S. soil to undocumented parents represent a guarantee against their parents' deportation. In 2014, the state of Texas stopped issuing birth certificates to children born on its territory to undocumented migrants and bearers of a Mexican passport without a valid U.S. visa, making it impossible for parents to authorize medical treatment for their children or enroll them in day care or school (*Texas Observer* 2015).

For poor women and women with the "wrong"—that is, non-Western— passport, giving birth to a child on U.S. soil thus provides no fast track to citizenship and the corresponding upward social mobility. Their pregnant bodies are not pampered in luxury condos, in spas and yoga sessions, but exposed to exhaustive travels, precarious housing, hygiene, and health conditions, and sexualized violence. Non-Western women who travel to the United States on a business or first-class ticket to give birth do not face the criminalization and sanctions to which poor migrant women are exposed. Nor are they affected by the same sort of restrictions, violence, and vulnerability that poor migrant women or (expectant) mothers face who cross the borders by foot, on the backs of trucks, or with the help of *coyotes*. Nevertheless, both make use of the same strategy of embodied social mobility for themselves and their children, with widely different prospects of success.

As in the case of non-Western male investors with access to disembodied monetized social mobility, women's embodied social mobility works for only a select few—those who already are members of the upper class or have economic power and access to upper-class conditions at the global level. In this case, wealthy non-Western women use the terms of the coloniality of citizenship to their advantage; they literally embody social mobility for the next generation by securing Western citizenship rights for their children. They thus *trump* (pun intended) their gender and racial disadvantage. The gender and racial hierarchy underlying the coloniality of citizenship is, however, only momentarily—and monetarily—suspended and is left unquestioned for the next contenders to the same rights.

Outlook: Fast Track to What Mobility?

The boom in the number of non-Western capitalists seeking the advantages of residence and citizenship in the United States and Europe points to the paramount role that race continues to play for a global stratification. The "premium citizenships" of core Western states highly correlate with whiteness; only very wealthy non-whites have recently gained access to them through the commodification of rights in semiperipheral states that share a visa-free travel zone with core Western states. For wealthy non-Westerners, investment residence and citizenship of Western states constitute global social mobility as well as a means of "buying into" whiteness.

All three embodied strategies for fast tracks to privileged citizenship and upward social mobility—marriage to the owner of an EU passport, sexualized encounters with Westerners in tourist destinations, and giving birth on U.S. soil—are crisscrossed and counteracted by colonially stratified axes of inequality that mark economic power and mobility on a global scale. Embodied practices of citizenship are thus highly ambiguous since they offer completely distinct options and also bear very different risks to en-gendered actors of different socioeconomic classes and forms of racialization.

Our three exemplary attempts to create "fast tracks" to citizenship and social mobility attest to the en-gendered dimension of global inequalities. Unlike male wealthy investors, women and feminized Others are often forced to exchange their bodies in search of a visa or passport. They apply embodied practices that revive colonial racialized gender hierarchies and the respective exoticized, eroticized images and imaginations ascribed to nonwhite bodies (of all genders). Their break with the coloniality of citizenship is therefore a limited one: While their strategic use of their own bodies reverses and momentarily overcomes both gender hierarchies and colonial power relations, it does not change the systemic logic of operation that their actions target. It does not become a transformative project grounded in the body politics of knowledge, but, as a form of "everyday politics" (Braun 2016:223), makes embodied social mobility a systematic option.

NOTES

1. The data refer to the average incomes of the mentioned countries before the 2008 economic recession and would thus have to be adjusted to reflect the impact of the recession. Incomes of European countries were thus considerably lower after 2008, but still award considerable economic mobility to migrants from outside of Europe.

2. The fact that such racial reclassification poses very different degrees of difficulty depending on the colonial and imperial history of the context where one's racial identity is being negotiated only reinforces the hierarchies underlying the constructed racial continuum.

3. Citizenship rights through investment in state bonds or real estate can be purchased in as little as 4 weeks (Arton Capital 2017)

4. See also, for example, de Beauvoir (1953), Rich (1979, 1980), Foucault (1979), Bartky (1990), Fausto-Sterling (1992, 2000), as well as Halberstam (1998).

5. Studies on same-sex tourist encounters in Brazil or Cuba (Stout 2014) or heterosexual male sex workers (many of whom are family fathers) in the Dominican Republic who cater to male clients for lack

of a heterosexual female "clientele" show the complexities and ambiguities of sex tourism encounters, which also vary from context to context (see Padilla 2007).

6. In numerous European states—among them Germany, Greece, Denmark, Estonia, Lithuania, and Latvia—the legal residence permit of both partners is the precondition for marriage or same-sex partnership in case one partner is an EU citizen and the other is not. However, in most Western countries, binational couples have to face permanent suspicion, control, and illegalization for years after marriage—measures that patently violate international human rights standards, especially the right to family life and privacy (Messinger 2013:377).

7. Likewise, great numbers of U.S. citizens cross over to Mexico for cheaper medical treatment, and numerous dental clinics catering in English to U.S. clients can be found in the Mexican region to the United States (a trend that can also be observed in Europe, where Western Europeans escape to a rapidly growing market of medical services in Eastern European countries that, due to the immense income discrepancies, offer services at costs much lower than in the rich countries).

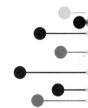

CHAPTER 9

Gender Through the Looking Glass

The Role of Low-Status Men in the Production of Global Gender Violence and Racial and Ethnic Bigotry

Kevin T. Leicht and Phyllis L. Baker

Introduction

Regardless of where one looks, relationships between men and women are changing on a global scale. Whether one points to the global crisis of patriarchy (Castells 1997, 1998), male overcompensation (Willer et al. 2013), the upending of local patriarchal bargains (Kandiyoti 1988), or the growing voluntary nature of gender and family relationships (Giddens 1991), most of the world's people are seeing and experiencing serious changes in gender norms and roles.

But these changes have not been passively accepted, especially by men. Changes in gender-based norms and roles have been driven by or accompanied major changes in economic opportunities produced by globalization and the incessant competition globalization has produced. The very real losses of economic roles and opportunities for men have (in many cases) been accompanied by increased opportunities for women and accompanying cultural messages in favor of greater gender equality.

In prior analysis (Baker and Leicht 2017), we explained one manifestation of this dynamic in less developed and rapidly developing societies. A major consequence of globalization and widespread shifts in economic opportunities has been a rise in public gender-based violence—public gang rapes, acid burning, domestic violence, and honor killings. These drastic actions reflect an attempt to reassert traditional gender roles in highly patriarchal societies by reclaiming public and cultural space for men. We argue that these actions are chosen because they are culturally available and the repertoires for gender control are culturally available as well.

In this chapter we suggest that the public, culturally available responses to patriarchal threats are not limited to less developed and rapidly developing societies. We trace the rise of global gender-based violence in developed societies through three examples: (1) the problem of sexual violence in the U.S. military, (2) the growth of militias and hate groups in the United States and other Western nations, and (3) the rise of "global populism" that seeks to reassert local prerogatives over and above regional or global standards for the defense of human rights, refugees, and immigrants. These manifestations of and responses to cultural and economic change represent the responses of "left behind" men to losses in cultural and economic status.

In our previous analysis (Baker and Leicht 2017), we explained the apparent rise in publicly based gender violence as culturally specific attempts to reassert patriarchal authority over public space in rapidly developing societies. While systematic international and national statistics are hard to come by, our fragmented evidence suggested that there have been increases in public displays of gender-based violence in India, Pakistan, and other parts of the developing world. Our argument is that these seemingly contradictory developments involving the slow empowerment of women and growing public displays of gender-based violence are tied together. We contend that the economic and cultural effects of globalization (1) drastically increase class-based inequality among men, (2) increase cultural and economic opportunities for women, and (3) introduce new cosmopolitan cultural ideas and images that disrupt local patriarchal bargains (Kandiyoti 1988; Castells 1997).

These contradictory developments produce cultural and geographic locations where men from traditional patriarchal societies are "left behind"— situations where the only claim to social status available is a gender-based claim of dominance over women. Theoretically, we meld the male overcompensation thesis (Willer et al. 2013) and observations on the global crisis of patriarchy and resistance politics (Castells 1997, 1998) to explain why these violent, gender-based, very collective public responses to globalized social change happen. Then we suggest that collective, public, violent responses persist because of the sunk, asset-specific investments in existing cultural arrangements and the transaction costs, uncertainty, and ambiguity associated with changes to gendered cultural institutions and norms (Williamson 1975, 1985).

We think the most volatility occurs in situations where economic change increases opportunities for women in new industries and markets while limiting or destroying traditional industries and markets dominated by men. If these economic changes are accompanied by shifts in or exposure to cultural cosmopolitan repertoires that differ considerably from traditional practices, then there is a recipe for expressions of "gender fundamentalism" (Giddens 1991). We argue that these dynamics increase the number of low-status men in an absolute sense (where traditional social and economic status claims are destroyed) and in a relative sense (situations where the existing economic and social status of men declines as women's opportunities expand and change). The creation of low-status men leads to different forms of resistance, as we discuss later in this chapter.

Why Do These Expressions of Resistance Happen? The Male Overcompensation Thesis and the Global Crisis of Patriarchy

Gender scholars point to a variety of institutional and interpersonal mechanisms that make up the gender system (cf. Epstein 2007; Ridgeway 2014).

Researchers also point to situations where threats to social status are likely to lead to attempts to reestablish gender hierarchies. Willer et al. (2013) define the male overcompensation thesis as "men react[ing] to masculine insecurity by enacting extreme demonstrations of their masculinity" (981). They argue that "extreme masculine behaviors may in fact serve as telltale signs of threats and insecurity . . . and conceal underlying concerns that they lack exactly those qualities they strive to project" (1016).

Castells's (1997) work on the global crisis of patriarchy helps bridge the gap between micro-level male overcompensation (research embedded in a Western context) and the global diffusion of new gender norms and ideas that ferment new forms of male violence and cultural resistance. Specifically, Castells (1997:134–242) argues that the decline of global patriarchy fosters widespread interpersonal violence and anger because men are losing power. Missing from both the interactional and the institutional analyses is a discussion of why this pattern endures even when the disadvantages of persistence and the benefits of change seem obvious to outside observers.

Why Do These Expressions of Resistance Endure? Asset-Specific Investments, Discounting New Information, and Political Opportunism

There is considerable evidence that violence against women, as a form of this resistance, is associated with other forms of social pathology, including poorer overall health, higher infant mortality, shorter life spans for women, lower educational attainment for women and men, child neglect and abuse, widespread alcohol and substance abuse (by perpetrators and victims), and millions of dollars in lost productivity (see Cohen 1998; Heise 1998; Benson and Fox 2002; Watts and Zimmerman 2002; Vandello and Cohen 2003; Vandello et al. 2008; Haegerich et al. 2014). Violence against women, in a broader context, is also associated with continued obstacles to development in multinational contexts, and the perpetuation of larger subcultures of violence and honor that maintain social inequality (see Cohen 1998).

In spite of the growing evidence that violence against women harms victims, perpetrators, their families, and the wider community, gender-based violence globally and nationally seems to persist if not increase. Our analysis here seeks to explain why this problem persists in spite of growing efforts to intervene and growing recognition that gender-based violence produces enduring harms not just for those involved but the wider society and social institutions. Why are these patterns so persistent in spite of this evidence?

The reason elaborate institutional structures (such as gender roles and patriarchal cultural practices) are so hard to change has to do with the biases against new information, making choices, and then monitoring the agreements that are a consequence of those choices. We suggest that these problems are due to asset-specific investments resulting in sunk costs and path dependence, the discounting of new information due to confirmation bias, reinforcement from subcultural groups, and political opportunism.

Asset-Specific Investments Resulting in Sunk Costs and Path Dependence

Existing cultural commitments often require investments in actions and resources that are specific to the relationship. These investments will be lost if a different course of action is chosen. Worse still, even contemplating a different course of action requires openness to new information and the search for potential social reinforcement for promoting change. Investments in specific relationships constitute a "sunk cost" that is lost if changes are made. This gives decision making a path-dependent quality. The decision to go down a specific path is a decision that cannot be easily changed once the asset-specific commitment has been made.

An example of gender in interaction would be that for men generally, and for low-status men in particular, adherence to local patriarchy is an asset-specific investment. In many cases given the changing economic and cultural landscape, it is the only investment they have left and it is more or less completely lost if women's empowerment is promoted. The costs associated with a different course of action appear very high and the payoffs in the future uncertain at best.

Discounting New Information: Confirmation Bias and Subcultural Reinforcement

While a standard economic treatment of transaction costs would talk about the high costs of information (or "information impactedness," as Williamson [1985] describes), information is widely available in Western contexts and there is plenty of it suggesting that violence against women (and patriarchy in general) is harmful in numerous ways. "Information impactedness" happens when the costs associated with searching for new information and assessing the relative quality of that information are considerable, deterring attempts to try something new. In the Western context, most cultural information is cheap and easily available. The more likely scenario here involves the combination of confirmation bias (see Nickerson 1998; Jonas et al. 2001) and social disorganization that promotes the creation of distinctive subcultures (cf. Burgess and Akers 1966; Sampson and Groves 1989; Dobrow 2016).

In the classic social psychology literature on confirmation bias, we tend to accept messages that conform to our preestablished opinions and discount or ignore information that would suggest we're wrong (see Nickerson 1998; Jonas et al. 2001). In a context filled with social media, where cultural fragmentation leads to general distrust of media sources generally and "mainstream" media sources in particular, it is very easy to stick with what you know and find the information you need to defend your position. If we have extensive ego investments in that position, accepting new information will be more difficult. If the new or contrary information is difficult and threatening to the status quo, the chances of acceptance will be harder still. To do so from a position of seeming powerlessness is even more risky. If we add to that the very real social disorganization that has occurred in many communities experiencing the brunt of the effects of globalization and economic change (cf. Cherlin, 2014; Vance 2014; Hochschild 2016; Eberstadt 2017) and the subcultural groups that are created by cultural fragmentation and social disorganization (Dobrow 2016), the motivation to continue on the present path is considerable and socially reinforcing.

There is quite a bit of evidence that communities in different parts of the developed world have experienced considerable economic decline and that this decline has led to increases in what criminologists term *social disorganization* (see Sampson and Groves 1989). There is also ample evidence online and elsewhere that this social disorganization has fueled a male-supremacist subculture on Facebook, blogs, and news websites, and a rise of virtual hate groups of various kinds (cf. Simi et al. 2017). The tendency toward confirmation bias combines with the cultural reinforcement of subcultural groups to keep prevailing cultural practices (and beliefs in them) alive and well even if change seems to be in the air.

Political Opportunism

In addition to confirmation bias and reinforcement by subcultures (and on top of the general confusion that fragmented social media create under the best of circumstances), the situation now isn't the best for discerning truth from falsehood; media actors desire to withhold or provide misleading information for their own benefit. This increases the costs of finding reliable information and may influence actors' choices. In the context of gender interactions, low-status men have considerable interest in information that claims they have been victims of amorphous conspiracies, used, and exploited. There are loads of social media outlets that are more than ready to prey on these fears and stoke them. These same outlets will spend a great deal of time discrediting media outlets that promote alternative views, complete with a set of labels designed to elicit negative emotions in vulnerable readers ("feminists," "secular humanists," "antiwhite," "politically correct," "clueless elite," and so on). Confirmation biases and subcultural bonding provide low-status men with a bevy of opportunities to limit access to or distort information that threatens their dominant position.

But this argument leads to the question of who, exactly, the opportunists are and whether those opportunists actually promote gender violence or a more amorphous dread of social change that leads to lashing out at anything that is different. One distinct possibility is that political actors are using social disorganization and fragmentation to build a political base to enhance their own power. In this scenario, online portals and other venues are used to mobilize culturally disenchanted people to support economically retrograde programs designed to bring power back to "real people" even though the politicians and media elites involved are not of their number. The crowded field of media outlets also has incentives to promote their distinctiveness and brands and take advantage of cultural fragmentation to form their own market niches ("Fair and Balanced" in the Fox News parlance is a classic example, as is MSN's "Moving Forward"). Individual actors may be opportunistic or not, but there are an array of media and political figures eager to exploit their unhappiness to stoke grievances and political support.

The concept of male overcompensation explains why and in what situations male gender identity becomes most salient and for whom (low-status men). The transaction cost perspective, combined with confirmation bias and the creation of fragmented subcultures, helps explain why cultural investments are so path dependent, why change is so difficult, and why collective violence and backlash will be resorted to in order to preserve existing cultural arrangements. Regardless of the abundance of information, the costs associated with change and the uncertain benefits resulting from change lead to path-dependent resistance to new social arrangements that empower women and other disadvantaged groups. The benefits of new gender roles and other cultural arrangements may be too vague and the costs of change too high to promote anything except redoubled efforts to maintain the current system.

The Cultural Manifestations of Public, Gender-Based Violence in the West

Our analysis to date has focused on the development of collective, gender-based violence in rapidly developing societies that are experiencing the simultaneous shocks of economic and cultural globalization. These effects produce a volatile mix of local cultures and global cosmopolitanism that come right to the household door, upending traditional cultural assumptions and improving the economic and cultural standing of some people while reducing or eliminating the cultural and economic standing of others. Most important for our analysis, these cultural and economic forces upend traditional gender hierarchies without providing a coherent cultural or economic narrative for those "left behind." The net result is downward social and cultural mobility for small but significant pockets of men and economic and cultural opportunities and perils for small but growing numbers of women.

But we don't think that our argument is limited to less developed countries experiencing rapid cultural and economic change. We believe that the same general mechanisms are becoming pervasive in Western nations as well, but the specific cultural manifestations and mechanisms of revolt and violence differ. We offer three Western examples in support of our argument: sexual assault in the U.S. military, militia groups, and growing global populism in developed democracies.

Sexual Assault in the American Military

Gender-based violence is not limited to distant places grappling with rapid globalization and economic change. The same dynamic can be seen in the crisis of sexual assault within the U.S. military. A 2012 confidential survey by the U.S. military estimates that some 26,000 women and men in the military have been sexually assaulted. Of those, 3,374 cases were reported. In 2014, 5,061 cases were reported (see Department of Defense 2014).

While it is difficult to tell if the number of assaults is increasing or whether reporting has improved, the accounts of sexual assault (see, e.g., www.mydutytospeak.com) are harrowing. Here are just two examples:

I was at Sather AB, Iraq in November 2009, this was my third tour to the region. I was having trouble with a co-worker and one night I went into to the bathroom as I came out of the stall he was standing there and threw me up against the wall and raped me and then told me "that is how you fuck a whore". He left me there and when I finally left I went to my Commander who told that it is a "he said she said". 12yrs of service went down the drain that night. From that point on the Air Force saw me as damaged goods and they told me I had PTSD and medically discharged me just a year before I was a rising star doing what I love and now I spend my days at the VA, taking pills, and trying to find a reason to live!

It was in June 5th 1982, I was 18, and at my first duty station in Roosevelt Roads, Puerto Rico. I lived in the Bundy Barracks and worked for the Navy Exchange, (I ran a mini store at the main barracks). One night a friend named Sara asked me to go to the Seabee Club with her so I went one Saturday night, I remember we were talking to a couple of guys who had bought us a couple of cokes, I believe my coke was drugged because the next thing I remember was being at the bus stop alone the next morning waiting for a bus to be taken back to the Bundy Barracks. I do not remember what happened to Sara. As I was sitting there waiting for the bus I was having vivid memories of different men having sex with me, I did not know who they were or that they even knew me. I do not remember faces; all I could see in my mind was that there were several men. I have no clue as to whom or where I even was the night before or even how I got there. The vivid memories I now have are of different men's penises in my mouth and in my vagina at different times throughout the night. I remember I was in such a daze in and out. My body was limp and I remember just lying there with no control over anything I did or was being done to me. I remember being dragged from one bed to another I was completely out of it. I remember being at work the next Monday and this guy came in and told me everything that had happened I did not realize that all that had happened. He told me that at least 25 different guys had sex with me. (These accounts and more can be found at www.mydutytospeak.com.)

The U.S. volunteer military represents an organization that is attempting to change a very deep and entrenched culture of male dominance (Turchik and Wilson 2010). But (and this is where our theory of male overcompensation and gendered transaction costs comes in) it is doing so in an environment that is dominated by low-status men who view the military as one of the few routes of legitimate socioeconomic and status advancement for themselves and their families (see Lutz 2008). The appearance (if not the reality) of competition with upwardly mobile women, many of whom are from the same social class as male recruits and officers, sets up a compressed version of the dynamic we've laid out in the confines of a single large and complex organization:

1. Male recruits are almost uniformly of lower socioeconomic status and have few other avenues of upward mobility. The military is conventionally viewed as a male enclave that is now being "invaded" by women. The women are also recruited from the same social classes as men. The situation seems ripe for male overcompensation behaviors—attempts to marginalize women or declare them unfit for military service and especially high-prestige combat missions. The fact that many of the officers in the military are from the same circumstances only adds to the gender dynamic at play (see Abrams 1993; Turchik and Wilson 2010). This is clearly an environment where there are considerable selection effects into a distinctive subculture of male dominance and where recruits and military organizations have expended considerable resources to promote warrior culture.

2. When attempts to marginalize women within the military don't work, gender violence (both individual and collective) follows in short order. Sexual harassment is more or less assumed, but this transitions rather quickly into actual direct assertions of gender superiority through sexual assault and rape (Castro et al. 2015). Sexual assault and rape serve as the ultimate confirmation bias that female recruits are unfit for military roles.

3. In this case the selection mechanisms into voluntary military service as an avenue of upward mobility for men clashes directly with the larger culture's desire to promote gender equality. Because the men so recruited have few claims to social status beyond a claim of masculinity, this is an especially glaring collective affront to the world as they understand it. Shorn of other avenues for upward mobility and social status (because of deindustrialization, the rise of the service, high-technology economy, and globalization) military men are "stuck" with an asset-specific investment that is now being invaded by women. When they are unable to secure another avenue of upward mobility, gender-based violence is an obvious alternative for defending their path-dependent investment (see Turchik and Wilson 2010).

There is far more that could be said and written about gender, the military, and sexual assault. The current record of prosecuting sexual assaults in the military through the military system of justice is so poor that there are several bills before Congress to remove sexual assault cases from military oversight and move them to the civilian courts (cf. Cooper 2014).

In this environment, there is definite self-selection into a distinctive subculture associated with military service. This subculture historically has been very masculine oriented and has recruited individuals who are comfortable in and want to be in a hypermasculinized environment, where any and all information that women are fit to serve will be discounted. This subculture helps perpetuate the ideas and ideologies that come from male dominance even in the face of the military's attempts to change the subculture. The insertion of women from the same social and economic classes as male recruits produces the volatile environment that the military has yet to overcome.

The Rise in Militias and Hate Groups

Our second example comes from the rise in the number of American militia and hate groups. The Southern Poverty Law Center has extensively documented and tracked the waxing and waning of support for militia and extremist hate groups for years. The number and membership in such groups rose substantially through the 2000s and was spurred by the elections of Barack Obama (see Bunch 2010) and Donald Trump.

Militia groups come in a variety of styles. Almost all put forward a militant antigovernment ideology that focuses on "taking back control" of local politics and culture from "clueless elites" in distant places (New York City and Washington). Tied to these antigovernment ideologies are (in many cases) ethnic supremacist claims, conspiratorial theories of federal government takeovers of local government functions, and quasi-paranoid claims about mind control, gun control, or other issues that are fueled by web-based communications among the like-minded (cf. Zhou et al. 2005), producing a distinctive subculture and support network for the perpetuation and support of group claims. Recently, Mark Potok (2016), a senior fellow at SPLC, showed that the number of hate and antigovernment patriot groups grew the previous year, and terrorist attacks and radical plots proliferated.

> Antigovernment militiamen, white supremacists, abortion foes, domestic Islamist radicals, neo-Nazis and lovers of the Confederate battle flag targeted police, government officials, black churchgoers, Muslims, Jews, schoolchildren, abortion providers, members of Black Lives Matter protest movement, and even drug dealers.

Militia and patriot groups fit the classic profile of reactive mobilization (Van Dyke and Soule 2002) where men mobilize in response to the perceived loss of power and cultural relevance. Most research results suggest that growing demographic diversity, economic changes associated with the decline in reliable manufacturing jobs, and declines in the agricultural sector of the economy are associated with the rise of patriot/militia groups. These groups are often defined in contrast to the U.S. civil rights and feminist

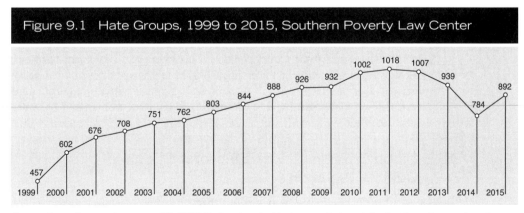

Figure 9.1 Hate Groups, 1999 to 2015, Southern Poverty Law Center

Source: https://www.splcenter.org/file/11756. Reprinted with the permission of the Southern Poverty Law Center.

movements, both of which are viewed as producing less power for white males in preference to others (see Gibson 1994; Castells 1997). As stated by Freilich and Pridemore (2005), "The perception of increased female and minority power in the *overall American culture* led to a backlash among some white American males, who responded with *subcultural* adaptations that emphasized male authority figures, white dominance, American power, and a willingness to use violence" (531; emphasis in the original). Other scholars have found hostility to feminism and acceptance of traditional notions of masculinity as popular among militia members (Kimmel and Ferber 2000). Empirically, there is the most support for the notion that militia activity is a response to job loss and accompanying social disorganization (Freilich and Pridemore 2005).

While not directly connected to militias, there is growing evidence that hate crimes are tied to perceived status threat and loss of status by men. The consensus opinion among scholars is that hate crimes are vastly underreported, and there is fragmentary evidence that the number of hate crimes has risen with the presidential candidacy and election of Donald Trump (SPLC 2017).

An especially active subset of hate crimes includes crimes against Muslims. Hate crimes against Muslim Americans have risen to their highest level since the period following the September 11 attacks, a new report tracking extremism and hate in the United States has found. The sharp increase appears to be partly fueled by a string of recent terrorist attacks, but researchers also found a disturbing spike in hate crimes after Republican presidential nominee Donald Trump proposed a Muslim ban. Hate crimes against Muslims were up 78% during the course of 2015, with a particular increase in crimes that targeted people viewed as Arab, according to a report from the Center for the Study of Hate and Extremism at California State University, San Bernardino. The *Huffington Post* received an advance copy of the report, which analyzes official hate crime data across 20 U.S. states. There were about 260 anti-Muslim hate crimes in 2015, the report notes. That's the worst total since 2001, when a record 481 anti-Muslim hate crimes occurred. Hate crimes against Muslims and people of Middle Eastern descent skyrocketed nationally in late 2001, following the September 11 attacks (Ferner and Scheller 2016).

In this case, social disorganization is tied to the creation of a distinctive, self-reinforcing subculture that perpetuates beliefs and activities associated with maintaining white male supremacy. In spite of abundant evidence to the contrary, the selection of culturally concordant messages and the reinforcement that comes from adherence to group ideologies has been described as akin to an addiction (Simi et al. 2017). Militia groups develop extensive networks of self-reinforcing followers with extensive investments in their worldviews, views that include the resubordination of women and the valorization of male roles (Simi et al. 2017).

Global Populism: The Electoral Choice of Cultural Isolation

Our next example branches out from the United States. In each of the mature electoral democracies of the post–World War II era, we are witnessing the overt development, spread, and success of populist electoral movements.

While some have stated that these populist movements defy easy political categorization (combining economic policies often associated with the left or far left with cultural policies associated with the right or far right), it is the cultural policies and the demographics of those who join such movements that interest us here.

Populist political parties of the far right have made significant electoral inroads in every Western democracy (Hawley 2017). The specific appeals vary slightly, but the overall message is the same:

1. The native citizens (and especially the men) have lost economic and cultural influence to foreigners, cosmopolitan bureaucrats, or supporters of globalization whose interests are not with local people and local issues.

2. There is more or less overt hatred of foreigners, especially Muslims and dark-skinned immigrants from Africa and the Middle East. These people are characterized as criminals, rapists, and parasites on the generous social benefits the state provides. Such groups are accused of attempting to "take over" local cultural and economic spaces with the help of clueless, cosmopolitan, or distant elites.

3. Support for these groups tends to come from less educated men and the elderly. The men involved often feel threatened by the presence of foreign, nonwhite men, the presence of their families, and the perception (if not the reality) that the fertility rates of new arrivals are surpassing those of the natives. Tied to this is a longing for a return to national sovereignty and boundaries.

4. In the more virulent fascist and neo-Nazi manifestations of populism, racial and ethnic ideologies of superiority and inferiority tie men and whites to culturally fundamentalist themes emphasizing their inherent superiority to foreign others. At minimum, such groups advocate political and cultural separation as the only remedy to growing multiculturalism. More violent groups either seek to intimidate foreigners and minorities into leaving the country or actually advocate various forms of genocide.

These groups are also known to adopt traditionally religious (Christian) or Nordic pagan themes to justify their ideologies. In each case the return to national and local sovereignty is the primary goal along with the creation of a monolithic ethnostate devoted to "blood and soil." Granted, women join populist electoral movements in developed democracies, too, but the over-riding cultural script is tied to grievances associated with male downward mobility and loss of respect.

In this case the resort to populist and xenophobic political movements is a defense against the loss of asset-specific investments associated with traditional gender and racial hierarchies.

We also see the use of social disorganization to create a distinctive sub-culture for political mobilization by opportunistic elites. The political leaders of populist movements rarely, if ever, come from the ranks of downwardly mobile men. The creation of distinctive media outlets that cater to their perspectives (for profit in addition to political expression) reinforces the message of opportunistic politicians that "the world is stacked against you" and "we are here to take our country back," and discounts alternative information as "biased," "tainted," or worse. The inability of EU- and U.S.-based populist movements to develop coherent policy themes is symptomatic of this opportunistic form of organizing that is unlikely to benefit the downwardly mobile people they have stirred up.

Two classic and recent examples of populist revolt (and the accompanying confirmation biases it portends; see Rogers 2017 and Pippenger 2017) are the UK vote in support of leaving the European Union (commonly known as BREXIT) and the U.S. election of Donald Trump as president. The nuances of each case differ, but the overall themes are the same: Globalization has produced a "democratic deficit" (Stiglitz 2013) where decisions about people's lives are surrendered to distant cities filled with people who are immigrants or otherwise viewed as "other." Many of these Others (foreign and domestic) are skilled professionals who are viewed as out of touch with the "real people" who view themselves as harmed by the prerogatives of experts and the policies they advocate. The politicians that populist voters champion are viewed as political outsiders, but more directly they are outside of the conventional corridors of information from which elected politicians and policy analysts come. In the case of BREXIT, voters seemed to be expressing exasperation with globalization and the idea that their lives needed to be tied to a group of "unknown others," many with whom they shared little culturally. In the case of Donald Trump, we saw the revolt of so-called "common people" against "inaccessible and clueless elites" promoting globalization and multiculturalism while paying no attention to the short-term havoc such changes cause. In both cases, campaigns were waged using blatant inaccuracies if not outright lies passed off as truth. The almost complete free pass granted by the public and supporters to these inaccurate claims has led many to conclude that we are entering a "post-truth" world (see Gibbs 2016; Rose 2017).

The Growing Visibility of Gender-Based Violence and Racial and Ethnic Bigotry: Application of Theory to Examples

From a theoretical standpoint these developments (and expert interpretation of them) are fairly consistent, and their creation and endurance are at least partially explained by our combination of the male overcompensation thesis, the globalization of the crisis of male social status, and our gendered theory of transaction costs with accompanying confirmation biases and subcultural fragmentation.

First, *the men involved are relatively low status and threatened.* This is most obvious in the case of the U.S. military, but it is also quite present in the other examples. Militia supporters, populist political supporters, and the trolls who continually question established experts are engaged in expressions of status resentment. Almost all this resentment is indirectly pointed at distant elites (many of them male) who are viewed as "out of touch" with the "real world." The fact that the elites of most developed democracies are becoming more gender and ethnically diverse only increases the resentment and animus (see Williams 2016).

Second, *there is an extensive set of asset-specific investments that is clearly under threat.* Men who lack the credentials and job skills to thrive in a globalized information economy are not going to instantaneously acquire those skills. Cultural assumptions about their domination of the public sphere and (more important perhaps) their own homes is not going to disappear instantaneously either, and the more amorphous threats to those assumptions appear on the doorstep, the more the assumptions are embraced and defended. These defenses are fueled by an increasingly fragmented media environment where any and all cultural biases are supported by subcultures of like-minded people who discount or attack alternative (and usually abundant) information suggesting that they are wrong.

Third, *there is a great deal of opportunism that takes advantage of subcultural fragmentation and confirmation biases.* As one communications professor lamented regarding the World Wide Web, "90 percent of the information is crap" (quoted in Nichols 2017). The selective consumption of social media increases the likelihood that low-status and status-threatened men will simply "dig in" with like-minded people to fight back and restore their rightful place in the status hierarchy. At minimum the confused media landscape makes it very unlikely that threatened men will sit down and rationally think through a set of alternatives to their changing world.

Fourth, *the distortion of information by supportive subcultures, and the sunk-cost investments and path dependence in the current system limit the ability of low-status men to see clear alternatives.* Social psychologists tell us that the response will be to discount any and all information that the world is changing in ways that disfavor one's current orientation, embrace any and all information that "elites" and distant others are wrong, and concoct conspiracies as reasons for declines in economic status and social influence (see Hochschild 2016). The modal response is simply to double down on what one knows because either the costs of change are too high, the benefits are too amorphous, or they are simply unclear and muddled.

In situations where there is growing class inequality among men, and where globalization has produced pockets of opportunity that lead to widening social roles and social ambiguity for men and women, the embrace of radical alternatives is a product of masculine overcompensation, culturally available resistance media that support biases, and asset-specific investments in patriarchal social arrangements. These actions are most likely resorted to among low-status men because they have no other master social status on which to base their claims to social position. Further, the inability to "control gender" during these times of ambiguity and change leads to attempts to reassert control using the only tools that are culturally available and consistent with the path dependence of investments by low-status men.

Conclusions

Our overall argument can be summarized very briefly. The expansion of economic and cultural globalization along with a push to empower women has co-occurred with increased public expressions of economic and cultural discontent. At the same time it has, at minimum, culturally challenged male supremacy if it has not produced outright economic displacement from dominant patriarchal and gender roles of provider and head of the household. The combination of economic dislocation and culturally cosmopolitan messages from media centers around the world has produced a volatile mix of expanding cultural and economic opportunities for women and other disadvantaged groups and reduced or eliminated cultural and economic opportunities for men. This rapid shifting of economic and cultural opportunities has produced a growth in publicly based expressions of radical, unconventional politics, bigotry, and violence. The objects of such hatred vary based on the cultural availability of potential victims, how and where blame is attributed to those victims, and the preexisting cultural repertoire of culturally permissible actions in response to status threats. Our earlier work has focused on objects of hatred in non-Western societies. In this chapter we expand our focus, looking at manifestations of radicalism and violence in developed Western democracies.

For both of these broad contexts, we draw on the concepts of male overcompensation, the global crisis of patriarchy, asset-specific investments, social disorganization, and confirmation bias to explain this seeming growth in publicly based gender violence and ethnic bigotry. Theoretically, we meld the male overcompensation thesis (Willer et al. 2013) with concepts of asset-specific investments and sunken costs from transaction cost economics (see Williamson 1975, 1985) and growing inequalities among men to explain these violent, gender-based responses to globalized social change. Left-behind men respond to status threats through displays of hypermasculinity because that is all they have left.

Our chapter points to a mechanism that not only interferes with gender equality and helps create gendered public violence but also interferes with economic development and global competitiveness. The resulting violence is likely to get worse as globalization advances. The promotion of gender equity and equity for other disadvantaged groups cannot be pursued apart from an understanding that the growing instability among men will stymy equity and grow violence at least in the short run. A comprehensive plan for promoting women's and other disadvantaged groups' rights and opportunities in the global sphere must directly address the shifting and diverging social status of men as globalization advances. This is critical for understanding the future of a global human rights regime that values and rewards women while also dealing with anxieties provoked by changing gender relations.

War, Women, and the Aftermath

Finding Resilience in Rwanda, Bosnia, and Nepal

Marie E. Berry

It is widely known that war is destructive and that women often bear the inordinate brunt of mass violence. But recent research has emphasized that this focus on women's suffering belies many examples of women's agency and resilience during war. In short, while devastating, war is also a period of rapid social change that can disrupt gender hierarchies and allow space for women to increase their participation in public, political life (see Aretxaga 1997; Sharoni 2001; Viterna 2013; Berry 2015a, 2018; Hughes and Tripp 2015; Tripp 2015).

Rwanda, Bosnia, and Nepal all serve as important examples of this phenomenon. Each country has experienced armed conflict since the early 1990s. In Rwanda, a civil war and one of the bloodiest genocides in history left an estimated 800,000 dead and 4 million displaced. In Bosnia, Serbian territorial aggression and ethnic cleansing left more than 100,000 people dead and nearly 2 million people displaced. In Nepal, Maoist rebels fought to overthrow the country's monarchy during a decade-long civil war that killed about 13,000 people and left more than 100,000 displaced. These armed conflicts—which encompass extreme, moderate, and low levels of armed violence—were clearly different in many ways. However, despite the varied levels and dynamics of violence, in each case there is evidence that violence shifted the power some women had in their households and communities and catalyzed women's leadership in their communities. Moreover, each conflict ushered in an increase in women's political participation and economic power (see Berry 2018 and UN Office of the High Commissioner for Human Rights 2012 on Nepal). In the years since, international organizations have implemented development projects that prioritized women's economic empowerment and social well-being.

This chapter explores the way war can shape gendered power relations in the aftermath. More specifically, it investigates whether and how war in each context was not only a period of destruction but also a period of transformation in women's lives. By exploring the social processes through which war can usher in new possibilities for women, this chapter lays the foundation for a deeper conversation about how humanitarian organizations and development agencies might be able to better serve women's needs in shifting political landscapes by designing interventions that more effectively capitalize on the work women are already doing.

Background

Social scientists have long investigated the causes and destructive effects of war. Yet much less research has explored war's unintended and unanticipated effects on social institutions and power relations. At its most fundamental level, war is an accelerated period of social change. Often in a period of days or weeks, the social structures in society are destroyed, institutions are dismantled, and power relations at all levels of society shift. While the actors involved may or may not achieve their stated objectives, the effects of violence can reach far beyond these goals and have unintended social effects. Violence is thus a liminal historical moment, which has both transformative and destructive potential (see Berry 2018).

The experience of living through violence can have a range of effects on an individual's life, from leaving physical scars to destroying economies and livelihoods. Recent scholarship has also explored the unanticipated effects of war. Rather than focusing on the economic deprivation and psychosocial trauma, research in development economics explores the unexpected "positive" outcomes after violence (Bellows and Miguel 2009; Blattman 2009; Annan et al. 2011; De Luca and Verpoorten 2011). For instance, Blattman (2009) discovered that Ugandans abducted into the Lord's Resistance Army are more likely to participate politically later in life than non-abductees, and that a strong positive association also exists between acts of violence witnessed and increased voting and mobilization (238). Political scientist Elisabeth Wood (2003:2) also showed that *campesinos* affected by El Salvador's civil war in the late 1970s engaged in collective action as part of an emotional response to the violence they witnessed. Without the war experience as a trigger, she argued, protests, rebellious movements, and contentious politics could not have occurred.

Scholarship focused specifically on women and war has similarly revealed war's potential to catalyze wide-ranging social shifts (Bop 2001; Sharoni 1995, 2001). Jocelyn Viterna (2013) showed how women's mobilization in the FMLN (Farabundo Martí National Liberation Front) in El Salvador ushered in political and social changes for women in the movement, which shaped the postwar era. Participating in a revolutionary struggle in any capacity allows women to become members of the dominant political organization, which grants women newfound power and political advantages (Kampwirth 2004; Viterna 2013). Simona Sharoni (2001) has also shown how war transformed women's sense of political engagement in Northern Ireland and Israel/Palestine. Building on this, recent research documents the mobilizing effects of war on women. Melanie Hughes and Aili Tripp (2015), for example, showed that countries in sub-Saharan Africa that had experienced armed conflict had higher levels of women in national legislatures. Hughes's previous work (2009) demonstrated that this trend holds globally. Work by Milli Lake (2014, 2018) has shown that conflict-affected regions can produce unexpected opportunities for seeking justice for gender-based crimes. However, these increased opportunities usually dissipate after violence has ended, as conventional ideas of masculinity and femininity and the public/private divide reemerge (Enloe 1993; Sharoni 1995, 2001;

Aretxaga 1997; Yuval-Davis 1997). In the end, violence often complicates and sets back women's struggles for gender equality.

This chapter aims to theorize the opportunities brought about by war more deeply, with the goal of identifying spaces where women's gains might be better preserved by international nongovernmental organizations (INGOs), foreign governments, humanitarian actors, and other actors involved in the postwar recovery process.

Data and Methods

This chapter stems from my work on this broader project over the past decade. Between 2009 and 2013, I conducted more than 150 semistructured interviews with women in Rwanda about their experiences during and after the war. Between 2010 and 2016, I made many trips to Bosnia as well, interviewing more than 100 women about the way the war shaped their lives, political engagement, and imagined futures. In 2016, I began conducting interviews with women in Nepal. A collaborator and I interviewed 50 Nepali women on this topic (see Berry and Rana n.d.).[1] In each case, I aimed to interview women in government, women in civil society organizations, and "ordinary," or non-elite, women directly affected by the wars in each place. I interviewed each respondent in English or in her preferred language with the help of a local research assistant; interviews were then transcribed and coded for common themes. A subset of the interviews with women directly affected by war were conducted in small groups to facilitate a more safe and comfortable environment for participants (see Berry 2018 for a full explanation of methodology). In addition to interview data, this chapter draws heavily from hundreds of informal conversations I had with local and international development personnel, as well as my analysis of organizational reports and government documents.

Case Overviews

Rwanda

The genocide and war in Rwanda left an estimated 800,000 people dead (Prunier 1995; Des Forges 1999). Rooted in decades of conflict over political power, violence initially broke out in 1990 when the Rwandan Patriotic Front (RPF), a primarily Tutsi rebel army, invaded Rwanda from Uganda. Many members of the RPF had been born in Rwanda but grew up in exile after waves of anti-Tutsi violence broke out during the country's struggle for independence. Desiring to return to their homeland with the guarantee of political rights, the rebel army's attack ignited widespread alarm among predominantly Hutu Rwandans, who feared being put back under the yoke of colonial servitude. Despite attempts at peace negotiations over the following years, violence escalated rapidly in April 1994 as unknown assailants shot down Rwandan president Habyarimana's plane as it attempted to land in Kigali. Blaming his assassination on the RPF, members of Habyarimana's government rallied the security forces and local militias to identify and kill all political opponents. Before long, they expanded their focus to all Tutsis, whom they suspected of collaborating with the RPF. The violence that unfolded over the subsequent 3 months was characterized by widespread destruction, tremendous brutality, and sexualized violence. Between genocidal violence targeting Tutsi and a war between the RPF and the Rwandan Army, perhaps half the population was displaced from their homes (Mamdni 2001; Straus 2006; Fujii 2009).

The war and genocide in Rwanda came to an end when the RPF solidified its control over the country. The former regime fled into exile, taking millions of Hutu Rwandans—and the entire net worth of the national bank—with it. Many of the displaced settled in Democratic Republic of the Congo (then Zaire), where they were subjected to continued instability and insecurity in subsequent years. To solidify its control over the country, the RPF relied heavily on the strength of its military wing. Extrajudicial killings and political repression characterized the immediate postwar years. The RPF resisted international pressure to hold democratic elections, arguing that democratic reforms were to blame for the genocide itself (see Thomson 2018 for a discussion of the post-genocide years).

Yet despite the reliance on repressive tactics to secure its political legacy, the RPF placed women at the center of many of its governance plans. Women held important roles in the Broad Based Transitional Government, and in 2003, less than 10 years after the end of violence, Rwandans elected the world's highest percentage of women to parliament (Burnet 2008). Today, Rwanda is widely recognized as one of the world's most gender-progressive governments, although many scholars have questioned the extent to which the elevation of women matters against the backdrop of the regime's authoritarian practices (Berry 2015b). Nevertheless, Rwandan women's political successes complicate the dominant narrative of women as *only* victims of war, and instead suggest that violence can upset traditionally male-dominated political space and open opportunities for women to participate in new social and political roles.

Bosnia

The war in Bosnia between 1992 and 1995 left more than 100,000 people dead, 2 million people displaced from their homes, and the entire population reeling from the violence that divided cities, families, and the country as a whole. The conflict had its roots in the disintegration of Yugoslavia, as Slovenia and Croatia declared their independence in 1991. In 1992, Bosnia followed suit. Days after its declaration, the Yugoslav People's Army (JNA), controlled from Belgrade, Serbia, launched an attack on Bosnian soil. For the next 3 years, the country was engulfed in a complicated and bloody war that pitted a host of Serbian irregular forces, the JNA, and the newly formed Serbian Army of Bosnia-Herzegovina against Bosnian civilians and the newly formed Army of Bosnia-Herzegovina and the Croatian Defense Council. The violence varied widely across the country; Sarajevo was subjected to the longest siege of a capital city in modern history while non-Serb citizens in other parts of the country were targeted for murder, widespread abuse, detention, rape, and other forms of sexual torture (Malcolm 1996; Silber and Little 1997).

The war came to an end as a result of the internationally brokered Dayton Peace Agreement, which divided the country into two consociational entities (the Federation of Bosnia and Herzegovina and the Republika Srpska) and allowed the political parties most responsible for the war to remain in politics. Women were completely shut out of the peace negotiations; they were neither present at Dayton nor reflected in the terms of the agreement (Björkdahl 2012). Peace-building efforts in Bosnia after the war followed an orthodox "liberal peace" logic, emphasizing democracy and market sovereignty. Under the guidance of international actors—with the United Nations at the helm—reforms focused on police and security sector reform, assessing the function of the judicial system, establishing a human rights office, facilitating freedom of movement, and so forth (see UN Mission in Bosnia and Herzegovina). The International Criminal Tribunal for the former Yugoslavia, based in The Hague, took the lead in criminal prosecutions and indicted 161 people responsible for war crimes and crimes against humanity. The remainder of the judicial process was left to the Bosnian state courts to sort out. However, these cases have been fraught with delays, corruption, and accusations of judicial dysfunction. As a result, many war-period crimes have gone unpunished.

More than two decades after the end of the war, peace in Bosnia remains fragile. Cities across Bosnia remain ethnically divided; schools have infamously adopted the "two schools one roof" policy, where children from different ethnic groups are taught different curricula in ethnically segregated classrooms (Halilovic-Pastuovic 2018). Many Bosnians lament that Dayton may have ended the shooting but it did not end the war. Unemployment in the country has hovered around 50% for the past decade, leading many young Bosnians to migrate to the European Union when the opportunity arises. Many Bosniaks and Croats who returned to their hometowns that now fall within the Republika Srpska feel the constant presence of war from their Serb neighbors; likewise, many Serbs who once lived in mixed neighborhoods now find it uncomfortable to live in the Federation (Berry 2018).

Nepal

Nepal's "People's War" lasted from 1996 until 2006, leaving more than 13,000 dead and about 1,300 disappeared in its wake. The violent, leftist uprising led by the Communist Party of Nepal (Maoists) had its roots in historical inequalities, including widespread caste-based discrimination, marginalization of the indigenous communities, unequal land distribution, and a complete disconnect of the urban political elite from their rural constituencies. Moreover, a democracy movement that began in 1990, and the subsequent rise in political consciousness among the population, set the stage for revolution.

In this political context, thousands of disaffected youth from the rural far west picked up arms against the state in 1996. Their primary goal was to overthrow the monarchy and implement a system of government led by the people. The People's Army attacked government outposts such as police stations, military compounds, public transportation, and schools. Government security forces then pushed back, engaging in arrests, beatings, and assassinations of suspected Maoists. After multiple rounds of stalled negotiations, the mobilization of the national army, and two instances of state of emergency, in 2006 the Maoist rebels finally signed a comprehensive peace accord (CPA) with the seven-party alliance, bringing the decade-long civil war to a formal end (Adhikari 2014).

Since then, Nepal has ticked off most items on the international donors' postconflict checklist: DDR (disarmament, demobilization, and reintegration), elections, democratic governance, and transitional justice mechanisms. There were free and fair elections for a Constituent Assembly in 2008, which saw the meteoric rise of the once warring Communist Party into mainstream politics. In 2013, Nepal successfully integrated a little more than 1,400 former guerrillas into the national army (Bohara 2015). After an aborted attempt, the country finally promulgated its new constitution in 2015 and in the same year set up two bodies to investigate war crimes and punish perpetrators: the Truth and Reconciliation Commission and the Commission of Investigation on Enforced Disappeared Persons. There has been no major resurgence of violence.

On the surface, Nepal is a success story in postwar rebuilding and rehabilitation where international donors and development partners have played a substantial yet contested role since the end of conflict. There also has been a concerted push to promote gender-friendly norms and policies. However, women were completely missing from the multiple rounds of peace negotiations between 2001 and 2006. Neither the state nor the Maoist party made efforts to include women in their delegation as "mediators, participants, observers or signatories" (Falch 2010:22). While the Truth and Reconciliation Commission has received 65,000 complaints, there has been weak accountability and ongoing concerns about the effectiveness of these transitional justice mechanisms (Human Rights Watch 2017).

Political stability and economic prosperity, too, have evaded Nepal thus far. Ongoing unrest in the southern Terai region has led to recent clashes between protestors and police. While the postwar economy never quite picked up, the earthquakes and subsequent blockade of the border in 2015 led to major setbacks. Nepal is still largely dependent on remittance and foreign aid. At least 2 million Nepalis—about 10% of the population—work abroad, largely in India and Gulf nations; money sent home by these workers makes up more than 30% of the country's GDP (Human Rights Watch 2017).

Analysis

How did wars in each case open space for women to engage in their households, communities, and national political sphere in previously infeasible ways?

Household Level

In each case, demographic shifts—including massive population displacement and the disproportionate conscription, incarceration, and death of men—led to shifts in the way women exercised power in their homes. For many women, the absence of their male relatives, husbands, and sons meant that they needed to take control over household decision making. These demographic shifts catalyzed sweeping changes in women's roles and the organizational structure of caregiving at the local level.

In Rwanda, women who lost their husbands and families to violence, exile, or prison found themselves shouldering massive new responsibilities, regardless of ethnicity and their role during the genocide. Men made up 56% of the dead in Rwanda (Republic of Rwanda 2004). Before the violence, women's activities were typically confined to the household sphere and centered on childcare and the production of food. After, many had to replant land, make bricks to rebuild their houses, and sell anything they could to generate an income—all activities that had been done primarily by men before the genocide (Newbury and Baldwin 2000). As one member of parliament (MP) put it,

> In my region . . . there were some activities that were done by men, and others done by women. Like cutting down a bush; women were not supposed to do that. Or hard stone farming; the men had to go do that. But for a widow, since she had no husband, she would have to go do that for herself. (Interview, July 2012)

These new responsibilities deepened the poverty and isolation of many women. Jacqueline, a 46-year-old genocide widow and mother of four, described her frustration with this new division of labor:

> Even just survival at home is also another hassle. It is like you become a father and a mother, so you get all of the man's responsibilities as well as the woman's responsibilities. . . . My agreement with my husband was him taking care of me and my kids—buying food, knowing that the kids have all of the materials that they need to go to school. This is not what we agreed on. It's not me. If the roof is off, because it was blown off by the wind, that should not have been me, it should be him. You can imagine. Now it is all my responsibility. (Interview, February 2013)

As Jacqueline described, widows faced tremendous challenges assuming these new roles. Imyaka, a 55-year-old genocide widow, recounted how the death of her husband and many other family members left her struggling to take care of her disabled son:

> There are responsibilities that should have been taken over by our husbands that we are doing. For example, my kid has a mental problem. For him it should have been like—even other family members, if they were here, they would be helping take care of him, but it is all me. It is all my responsibility. (Interview, February 2013)

In many cases, the overwhelming burden of these new activities forced many rural women to seek basic economic, emotional, and legal support from others in their communities, catalyzing the formation of community organizations focused on women's needs discussed below (Berry 2015a).

Women in Bosnia also suffered greatly from the loss of their family members—and since 90% of those killed during the war were men, especially their sons, husbands, brothers, and fathers. A vast amount of research has been dedicated to this topic (see Stiglmayer 1994; Mertus 2000; Skjelsbæk 2006). Many women also experienced temporary separation from male relatives, as many were incarcerated or displaced in various regional armies. This reflected a shift from before the war when, as NGO founder Beba Hadzic put it, "women were kind of protected by their husbands. If they wanted something to happen they would tell them" (interview, April 2013). This demographic displacement caused a shift at the household level, as women were forced to "take all of the roles that men had" to adjust for the absence of their partners (interview, June 2013). This included dealing in cash after being displaced into internationally displaced people camps where they could no longer grow their own food; interacting with international humanitarian organizations; and petitioning government representatives for various documents, services, and benefits.

Merima exemplifies these shifts. A housewife before the war, as the violence intensified in the area around Sanski Most, Merima fled with her family to Travnik. Serb militias had killed many people in the region and raped many women, so many of the refugees Merima met in Travnik were in desperate need of basic goods and psychological aid. While many of the men who arrived left immediately to join the Bosnian Army, Merima described how the "women had to take on all the responsibilities from kids to food . . . they had to live with fear because they were throwing grenades at them still. They had to take care of both the whole family and other things" (interview, May 2013). Merima and other women in Travnik formed a small organization dedicated to helping the most vulnerable displaced women. As the war ended, Merima and others returned to their village, where they found animals in the streets, no electricity, no water, and their homes destroyed—so they continued to work. Soon, with some funding and training from a Swiss NGO, Merima's organization began to organize women for human rights advocacy, income-generating projects, and psychosocial support. While she noted that she has always been an ambitious person, she had no idea that the war would push her to become involved with work on social issues and women's rights. Today, she describes how the war led women to "have power, more than people would expect."

The war in Nepal also uprooted families and led to many changes in the way women affected by the war exhibited power within their own homes. Women composed about 40% of the Maoist forces. Those who joined left their family homes and became accustomed to a new, grueling life operating out of military camps. Others who were married to members of the police or army faced a protracted separation from their husbands, who were often deployed to suppress the uprising in the western regions of the country. Others still moved out of the areas in the pathway of the insurgency; some families sent their daughters to India to secure their safety, while others moved away from unstable rural highlands and into the security of cities.

According to the 2011 census, there are almost 500,000 widows in Nepal—a number partly the result of the civil war and partly the result of HIV, hard overseas labor, and other forms of gender inequalities. For many women, the death or disappearance of their husband during the war resulted in the sudden uprooting of a life they once knew. Because Nepali women marry into their husband's families, widows lose control over their choice of clothes and ornaments, their mobility, their finances, and sometimes even their children. Hindu customs dictate that they lead isolated and austere lives at least for the first year after the death.

Wives of the disappeared face an added layer of burden, as they are pressured to carry out last rites without knowing with certainty about their husband's death. As such, they find themselves excluded from religious and social functions. Women who dare to step outside their homes in search of justice put themselves at even greater risk because families no longer trust them. For instance, Babita Basnet, the director of a media advocacy group, described a woman she had met who did not yet know if her husband was dead or simply missing:

> What she said was that she still puts on bangles, red sari, or red tika on her forehead. But every time she looks into the mirror, she thinks of if her husband has passed away and she should not be wearing all these things that symbolize their marriage. Then she told me that she takes them off. But then again, she feels like she is not a widow yet and there is no reason to look like she is mourning. (Interview, August 2016)

This sense of unknowing permeates women's identities, situating them in a liminal status between marriage and widowhood and thereby preventing them from having a clear role within Nepali society.

These shifts in women's roles as a result of demographic shifts led to a rise in women's political consciousness. According to a member of Nepal's Truth and Reconciliation Commission, "Earlier, women were confined to the four walls of the home; now they are outside. Women who could not do politics are now involved in open politics. Women in the villages and at the grassroots have gotten a taste of politics." This increased political agency of women created an opening for women to engage in new roles outside of the home, ultimately catalyzing women's leadership in civil society, discussed below.

Community Level

Many of the changes that affected women in the household also shaped the way women engaged in their communities. In each of the three cases, the impact of war—including displacement, homelessness, trauma, financial scarcity, and physical damage—pushed women to seek economic resources and care outside the home. This led to the emergence of community organizations, which were encouraged and formalized by INGOs engaged in humanitarian relief and women's economic advancement.

By destroying infrastructure, displacing millions, and collapsing the economy, the violence in Rwanda indirectly forced women to join together with neighbors, friends, and strangers to secure food and shelter and retain control of their land. In addition to the household shifts discussed above, in the aftermath of the violence, women joined with other women to form thousands of small, informal groups to address these urgent material needs. By 1997, an astonishing 15,400 new women's associations had emerged across the country (see Newbury and Baldwin 2000). Most, if not all, of these organizations were *feminine*, not *feminist* in nature; in other words, they did not explicitly aim to challenge traditional patriarchal society and instead often essentialized women's roles as "mothers" or as "peaceful" (Stephen 1997; Viterna, Fallon, and Beckfield 2008). However, the existence of these organizations provided a foundation for women's coordinated action and participation in the public sphere and, as such, upset gendered expectations that had long existed in the country. They also provided a space for the social ties and relationships that had been torn apart by the war to be regenerated.

Community-based organizations that formed after the genocide were generally focused on one of two initiatives. First, many groups were formed informally to provide solidarity and financial support to anyone affected by the genocide, particularly to support widows and orphans. These groups were geared toward self-help activities and frequently evolved into income-generating cooperatives. The second type of initiative focused on advocacy for women's issues at the local, regional, or national level (Gervais 2003). These groups directed their efforts toward local land-rights disputes, health care initiatives, and other critical issues facing their communities, which led to coordinated claims against the state.

Within 5 years of the violence, women's collective efforts at obtaining legal rights to land and basic social support institutionalized a network of organizations interacting directly with the government. Like other civil society entities, these organizations needed leadership, rules and regulations, and a system to communicate with their members. This led to a process of institutional isomorphism, as women reproduced the formal structure of the organizations they sought funding from in their own nascent organizations (DiMaggio and Powell 1983). The women (and men) who came to lead these organizations became well-known in their communities; one study found that 50% of the members of two large widows associations held leadership positions in their communities (Zraly and Nyirazinyoye 2010). Women's participation in these organizations thus disrupted traditional understandings of what the gendering of public spaces should look like. In 2011, the International Center for Not-for-Profit Law estimated that 37,000 organizations exist in Rwanda, many of which are led by women. A leadership role in a grassroots organization qualifies individual women for more prominent roles in larger organizations and local, regional, or national government. These organizations became the locus of women's collective mobilization.

As in Rwanda, the volatile and threatening environment during and immediately after the war in Bosnia led to the rapid formation of community organizations to respond to "the twin crises of destitution and trauma" (Cockburn 2001:87). Women faced enormous pressure to assume new responsibilities and secure basic material supplies, leading many to collaborate with friends, neighbors, and strangers to help each other in their time of collective need. Women gradually collectivized into informal groups as the urgent need for food, clothing, and shelter pushed them together. With the arrival of INGOs and actors, many of these grassroots efforts became well-funded and formalized, and led to women's control over household economic decision making for the first time.

Widows and mothers of those killed, in particular, began to mobilize to protest the international community's failure to protect them and, eventually, the Bosnian government's failure to prosecute those who were guilty of killing their family members. Kada Hotić, a founding member of the NGO Mothers of Srebrenica, exemplified this process. A factory employee before the war, she lost her husband, son, and many other family members during the massacre. She described how women's lives transformed after the loss of their family members:

> [Serbs] began genocide. . . . In my family, it was my son, my husband, his brother, and later on I realized that 56 of my family members had been killed. We had questions. Where are the people we love? Are they imprisoned? Are they alive? What was their destiny? We did not have a lot of answers. (Interview, May 2013)

In the aftermath, she joined with other women from the Srebrenica region to find the bodies of their loved ones and to pressure the government for aid. While Rwandan women joined grassroots organizations to gain official documentation of their land rights, Bosnian women joined together to pressure the government to find missing persons. For example, believing that "protests were the only way to be heard," Kada described how the loss of men sent thousands of women into the streets to demand rights, a search for their loved ones' bodies, and reparations. Hajra Catic, another NGO leader, shared a similar story. After describing how "the bulk of [her] family was killed during the war," she explained how she worked with other women to search for her husband and son, who she hoped were alive in concentration camps:

> We went from one institution to another. For 2 or 3 years we were trying to find them. And then we found some mass graves, and then we realized that all of them were killed. Then we started looking for their remains, and of course, we put pressure to arrest the people who did this genocide, and that is why we protest on every July 11. (Interview, April 2013)

As Kada and Hajra's experiences reveal, the death of close (predominantly male) family members initiated new processes of mobilization as women searched for their loved ones' bodies, pressured local leaders to arrest perpetrators of the violence, and publicly protested the injustice surrounding their deaths. As in Rwanda, the demographic shifts in Bosnia catalyzed a shift in women's public engagement, and new organizations began to form to support these campaigns.

Alongside widows and mothers' organizations, many women were involved with other service-providing organizations during and after the war. In the context of widespread state dysfunction, these organizations soon emerged as a parallel power structure to that of the state. Organizations such as Medica Zenica and BOSFAM became the primary service providers in the country, offering medical services, psychosocial support, preschool, income-generating initiatives, and so forth (Mertus 2000; Bagić 2006). Many of these organizations became implementing partners of the UN High Commissioner for Refugees, connecting them to the resources and bureaucratic network of the United Nations (Walsh 2000). While women were far removed from the formal peace process in Bosnia, they took the lead as providers of food, health care, psychosocial support, and employment training for women and men in their communities (Walsh 2000; Helms 2002, 2013). As such, once established, organizations helped institutionalize women's leadership at the local level.

In Nepal, the war led to a massive influx of international actors who implemented peace-building initiatives, DDR programs, and other initiatives aimed at rebuilding after war. Many of these programs prioritized women and girls, especially since UN 1325 and 1820 were invoked to structure the international community's involvement in Nepal (Goswami 2015). This led to the emergence of women-run organizations, which have created spaces where women from different sides of the conflict can come together and appreciate their shared experiences (Berry and Rana n.d.). Men in Nepali society generally have easier access to public spaces and the ability to socialize outside their homes. Women, conversely, face social stigma and even challenges to their reputation when they socialize outside of their familial homes. Thus, when women need space to heal from their experiences during war, women-run community organizations serve a vital role.

For example, Manika, a young woman whose father was killed during the war, described how a training series put on by a women-led organization, Nagarik Aawaz, gave her an easy environment in which to interact with people who had been on different sides of the conflict. As she put it:

> We got to know about the grievances of a lot of other people. I never really wanted to keep links with people because of how my father passed away. But then seeing that there are others who were victim to the conflict as well eased the process of interaction. Now I do not really feel like a victim anymore. (Interview, August 2016)

Sanju, another young woman, described how being in a group helped her overcome her fears about interacting with people from different sides. She said:

> At first, I was scared. [I] did not really know what we should say. Every time I thought of my family's story, I almost cried. I was even too scared to speak about what happened. Once everyone started talking, it got better. Everyone was tearing up during our introductions. In the sessions later on, we felt like we were part of a family. (Interview, August 2016)

Saujanya, another woman who had attended this program, described making strong friendships through it. She described how "in the trainings, we began to understand that this did not happen to just us. We began to understand how we were connected." This led her and her newfound friends to release some of the anger they shared with her toward Maoists, who had killed her father, a police officer. She described how they began to realize that it was all happening in the situation of the war, allowing them to understand that "it is not about revenge but about resolution. . . Yes, the criminals should be punished and brought to justice. But trying to go through a broken process of trying to get justice for my dad only angered me more." In Saujanya's experience, this space for sharing was more effective at bringing her resolution and peace than the "broken" justice process was, affirming the importance of women's participation in community organizations after the war. Many of these organizations ultimately transformed and adopted new priorities after the earthquake in 2015, which again created a tremendous need for housing, medical care, and other basic services among the population.

National Politics

Finally, war shaped the way women were integrated into the national political space, both informally and formally. As recent scholarship has shown, war can create space for building new institutions, which are often designed with international normative frameworks in mind (Tripp 2015). This happened in part because of the arrival of international actors (e.g., NGOs, journalists, and policy specialists) who brought with them a new vocabulary for speaking about women's rights and advanced international priorities focused on women. These international actors convened dozens of trainings and workshops for emerging female leaders, offering guidance on how to "be confident" and "take charge" at this time. As each country implemented new constitutions or laws; saw new political actors come to power; and created new ministries, initiatives, and priorities, they often explicitly included women or principles of gender equality. International norms, codified in conventions like Convention on the Elimination of All Forms of Discrimination Against Women (CEDAW) or the Beijing Platform for Action and, after 2000, UNSC Resolution 1325, provided the formal language and international validation for many of these reforms.

Rwanda experienced total regime change after violence. There was a complete dismantling of the old political system and an overhaul of existing laws and institutions. This created both personnel and policy vacancies at all levels of power, which ushered new political actors into formal political offices. Before long, the regime was looking to leaders in communities across the country to fill vacant offices at all levels. Anglophone Tutsis who had grown up in Uganda dominated the RPF; as such, the party needed a non-ethnic political constituency it could mobilize in its ranks. Women were well positioned to serve in this role as they were often seen as less complicit in the genocide, and therefore both Hutu and Tutsi women could be appointed to leadership roles. While this orientation was part of a broader strategy of consolidating political control (see Longman 2006; Straus and Waldorf 2011; Thomson 2013), it also reflects the valued place women had held in the movement since its origins in the mid-1980s in Uganda (interviews, Rose

Kabuye, February 2013; Aloesia Inyumba, July 2009). President Kagame in particular has been a vocal champion of women's rights, describing how "the politics of women's empowerment is part of the politics of liberation more generally" (Kagame 2014).

For these reasons, many Rwandan women had opportunities to participate in local politics that were previously infeasible. For example, a current MP described how she was motivated by the horrible suffering she had witnessed:

> After seeing how many people have died, how many innocent people had died because of the bad politics. How my family was also [killed], most of my family died. There were only two children left. Me and my big sister . . . and I was like, this can't happen! I really need to do something with politics. . . . So I felt like I should do something for my country and really drag it in a good way with the good politics. (Interview, July 2009)

This MP attended several trainings hosted by Pro Femmes, a large, foreign-funded umbrella organization for grassroots women's initiatives. These trainings taught her how to run for office, how to be confident, and how "to know that you are able and you can do whatever you want to do, when you want to do it, as a woman." She soon ran for a position at the local government level, but described how "when I reached that position I was like I need to go higher up, to where I am now." Vacancies at the top administrative level of the country also allowed women who had close ties to the RPF to assume positions of power; for example, Lt. General Rose Kabuye became the mayor of Kigali City and Aloesia Inyumba became the minister of gender. Both women had held prominent roles in the military and fundraising arm of the RPF during its early days and served as highly visible examples of women's legitimate presence in politics. Combined with the trainings and legal instruments provided by international actors, these widespread vacancies allowed women to run for local, regional, and national political offices.

In Bosnia, the Dayton Accords completely excluded women at every stage of decision making or policymaking in the aftermath (Cockburn 1998; Björkdahl 2012). In the first postwar elections, women were elected to merely 2.4% of the seats in the federal Bosnia-Herzegovina House of Representatives, and no woman was elected mayor of a municipality (Cockburn 2001:23). Therefore, this peace settlement did not upend gender norms at the national political level but, rather, cemented gender hierarchies that had defined the nationalist, patriarchal politics of the past.

There was, however, a swell of advocacy among women's activists and organizations to increase women's legal rights and political representation after the war. With support from organizations like the Organization for Security and Co-operation in Europe and the National Democratic Institute, women's organizations spearheaded a series of national campaigns. For example, Norwegian People's Aid trained more than 1,000 Bosnian women through their "Women Can Do It" initiative that aims to help women reach positions of decision-making power in professional fields such as academia, media, and business (Kleiman 2007). As a result of these efforts, the Provisional Election Commission introduced a 30% quota for women on electoral lists in 1998. In the following elections, women were elected to 21% of the seats in the federal House of Representatives. While there was a perception that many women who gained seats were pawns of powerful male elites, many of the women I interviewed instead described being motivated to engage in politics because of their war experience.

Besima Borić, for example, is a former member of the Federation parliament and a high-ranking member of the Social Democratic Party. While she was politically active before the war, she described how her "serious" political life began after, as the tragedy compelled her to do something. Besima was raised secular in a partisan family and identified as Yugoslav before the war, although her ethnic heritage is Bosniak (Muslim). With children from two different mixed-ethnicity marriages, her family represented all the ethno-national groups within Bosnia. As ethnic nationalism intensified during the war, Besima felt motivated "to make some positive change. I believe if I do good, I do good for my kids, and then I do good for my country, then it is good for everyone" (interview, April 2013). She described the war as an awakening, since she began to think about what it meant to kill other human beings on the basis of an ethnicity that she had never seriously considered before. She emphasized that women who came from mixed families, like her own, had an easier time crossing ethnic lines after the war.

In Nepal, the egalitarian focus of the Maoists drew awareness to the need for conversations about women's political inclusion—and the inclusion of other previously marginalized groups, such as those from low castes, the Madhesi, or Janajati—in the postwar period. This has created a groundswell of female candidates for political offices. According to a member of Nepal's Truth and Reconciliation Commission:

> War impacted women positively. Currently, the president, the speaker of the house, and the chief justice are all women. . . . The conflict made us focus on inclusion. The People's Movement of 2006 gave encouragement to Madhesi, Janajati, and Women's Movement. The Janandolan gave a big push to marginalized groups. The first Constituent Assembly had 33% women. (Interview, July 2016)

This prioritization of women in formal political spaces was an explicit goal of many within the Maoists. According to Hasila Yami, the former first lady of Nepal and a leading figure during the insurgency, from the beginning of the conflict, "We said women has to be part of this. Even during the war, we said, women are the main element which prevents counterrevolution. We are for the continuous revolution. [Women] have to keep pushing. That's why the women's issue became very consistent, strong issue throughout" (interview, August 2016).

Of course, the increasing level of women in Nepal's political system does not negate the pervasive patriarchy that persists in that country or the fact that women from marginalized ethnic and caste backgrounds are often at a profound disadvantage in gaining leadership positions. Moreover, many of the women I interviewed expressed concern that many men are not willing to accept women's leadership and would prefer that women remain within the home. Nevertheless, the People's War catalyzed a shift in the way Nepali women featured into political discussions. According to Babita Basnet, "One of the best achievements [of the war] is that women have been able to be vocal and fight for their rights and empowerment. There is a sense of empowerment" (interview, September 2016).

Discussion and Conclusions

In all three cases, war caused tremendous suffering, destruction, and loss. Yet it also transformed the way women were able to exert power in their households, communities, and national politics. War forced women to provide for their families in the absence of male relatives; it led to tremendous needs that mobilized women to join together with others in their communities; and it opened institutional space for international norms and legal frameworks to be domesticated, securing women's inclusion in formal political spaces.

In the years since the wars in each case, however, there is evidence that many of the shifts women experienced, and the gains they made, were set back. This was in part because of the way patriarchal norms reemerged, often as men returned to the home and reasserted their position in the community. But as I've shown elsewhere (see Berry 2017, 2018), it was also because humanitarian and development efforts in each case arrived on scene with priorities established at the international level, rather than in local communities. Funding priorities changed on a whim, and many of the issues women identified as critical needs in their communities were ultimately set aside by initiatives prioritizing democracy promotion, justice, and psychosocial care.

Exploring war's transformative impact on women should encourage us to look for possibility and even opportunity amid destruction. Women's subordination to men in the majority of societies around the world is not easily disrupted; war may be one of the few comprehensive social disjunctures that can catalyze rapid shifts in women's political agency and power. International organizations engaged in humanitarian relief and development efforts after war should be attuned to the way gender hierarchies can be thrown into flux during periods of upheaval. Interventions that more effectively harness such change and place funding decisions into local hands, rather than divert agency and control away from local, bottom-up, women-led efforts, hold potential to further women's rights and political gains in the future.

NOTES

1. Special thanks to Trishna Rana (Korbel MA 2017) for collecting the interviews in Nepal with me. All discussions of Nepal in this chapter stem from our collaboration.

CHAPTER 11

No Way Out

Women in Nepal Trapped in Cycles of Poverty, Gender Inequality, and Economic Disenfranchisement

Jennifer Rothchild and Priti Shrestha

My name is Sabita Sunuwar. I think (I am) 29 years.

In my childhood, I wanted to study and be a great person but then my marriage happened. That old time . . . (laughs) After marriage, we need to go to husband's house and he didn't allow me to study. After giving birth to children my aim also got lost. . . .

I studied up to class 5. My school was nearly 2 hours walk from home. Early morning we used to work at home and come to school and study. When I passed from class 5 to class 6, people came to ask for my hand and my family accepted one marriage proposal. I left school. I got married at age 15/16.

He (husband) is 5 years older than me. He used to do farming. I said it's worthless to do such things and he went for foreign employment. . . . I wake up early in the morning. Release goats and feed the hens and pigs. I wake up at 4:30 a.m./5 a.m. usually. Cook food, feed kids to send to school on time. Then I clean the dishes, clean the rooms and prepare "raksi" and "chyaang" (a local spirit and beer prepared in rural villages). In this way my day goes on. I can't sit freely for a single minute. I wish to do a lot in life, but what to do? Imagination only doesn't work.

I have two sons. Younger one was born at home. I myself went alone for (medical) checkup. My husband was in Malaysia for foreign employment. It's been only 5 months. He just went some months ago. *Did he send money?* No, he didn't after he went. *How do you earn your livelihood?* Just doing here and there, getting busy in shop and help in education of son and not much. There are also goats, pigs.

There are some types of trainings provided in the village. Did you attend any? Yes, I did. Financial management with the organization named xxxx. I was issued (loaned) 1 lakh (about $1,000 USD) from that organization. Later I left it (the organization) when I couldn't mobilize that money. I had to pay interest on it. I had brought (borrowed) 1 lakh from that organization and couldn't pay (back) at the time.

Yes, (weeping) there is suffering. What to expect more than this? I just want to earn more money and live happily. We couldn't study at our time. So, I wish my children to get their better study and move them in the right path.

Introduction

Gender and development scholars conceptualize gender as a socially constructed identity and role, reinforced by social interactions and social institutions, which maintain traditional attitudes and distinctions about gender. In this light, gender is not what we are but, instead, things we do, and each social interaction serves to create, reinforce, or contest this idea. Social constructions of gender have long been used to legitimize inequality between girls and boys and women and men in societies throughout the world. Consequently, gender negatively impacts both girls' and boys' potential to access opportunities and improve standards of living. The family is a particular arena in which social constructs of gender play a discriminatory role: The gendered division of labor assigns the lion's share of household and care work in the family to women and girls. Education is another gendered institution, where gender socialization processes therein construct and reinforce gender in a way that shapes and determines who goes to school, who stays in school, and who excels in school.

Our goal in this chapter is to illuminate previously overlooked dynamics within the social constructions of gender and pathways to economic power as these dynamics play out among the understudied population of women living in Nepal. With gender stratification maintained in the home, and with little to no education, women like Sabita Sunuwar,[1] face diminished possibilities for better life opportunities. Lacking economic power and access to opportunity continually traps women in an endless cycle of persistent poverty, early marriage, high fertility rates, and diminished overall health. To fully grasp this cycle, we must closely examine both the macro- and micro-level influences as well as the micro-level outcomes. Specifically, we contend that individual women experience gender in more complex ways than perhaps considered in the conceptualization and broad-stroke implementation of development programs, particularly those geared toward gender equality and social inclusion (GESI). Whether a nongovernmental organization (NGO) offering small loans to women or a donor-driven handicraft initiative or a remittance company advertising jobs overseas, many programs that seek to mainstream women into market activities are developed as top-down and one size fits all, and often end up maintaining the status quo. We argue that these options for women may be well intended but are macro-level designed and gendered in their implementation and ultimately do not enable women to gain economic power. Many women then continue to be trapped in cycles of poverty and economic disenfranchisement.

Nepal's legal, political, economic, and family institutions reflect strict and consistent gender inequality. These institutions are founded on cultural and religious beliefs that reinforce the constructed gendered order that maintains and benefits the status quo. For example, the extensive work Nepali women do on both the farm and in the household is not regarded as an economic contribution at all. On an average day, women in Nepal spend three times more than men on unpaid work; specifically, women spend an average of 6 hours doing unpaid work as compared with the 1.5 hours per day spent by men (GESI Working Group 2017). Being marginalized from earning any cash directly compromises women's autonomy, both economically and socially. With subsequently diminished self-esteem, women are less likely to push for equal treatment or their own independence. As Acharya and Bennett (1985) assert, women's participation in the market economy increases their status, while confinement to nonmarket subsistence production and domestic work diminishes it. Thus, bringing women into the market economy is both an effective step toward a more efficient use of local resources and a means of improving women's status and economic security in Nepal. Women's involvement in market activities gives them much greater power within the household in terms of their input in all aspects of household decision making. At the same time, confining women's work to the domestic and subsistence sectors reduces their power vis-à-vis men in the household.[2] Given the propensity for assigning women's contributions as supplementary or complementary service, Nepal becomes an interesting site to study how this invisibility of women's unpaid contributions begins at the household level and gradually translates into women's exclusion from the market economy at large.

In addition, Nepal's ongoing political instability, corruption, and skyrocketing out-migration for remittance work have displaced thousands of families. The *Nepal Demographic and Health Survey 2016* reports the proportion of female-headed households has almost doubled over the past 15 years, from 16% in 2001 to 31% in 2016 (Ministry of Health, New ERA, and ICF 2017). On top of these challenging social dynamics, Nepal endured two major earthquakes (and many powerful aftershocks) within three weeks of each other in spring 2015. These macro-level forces of natural disasters, political economic instability, and social institutions that reinforce structural inequality all shape women's lives and heavily determine their economic status. Further, the rapid economic, social, and political transition of present-day Nepal creates a particularly remarkable set of social circumstances for examining development through a gender lens. Nepal has made progress in social indicators such as education, health, and life expectancy in recent years, but the country continues to have one of the lowest-ranked levels of human development according to UNDP (United Nations Development Programme) standards: The UNDP (2016) ranked Nepal 144th of 188 countries.[3]

The challenge for promoting women's individual economic empowerment is to address directly the root cause of gender inequality and examine the gender socialization taking place at the micro level. Women's (re) negotiations of their own gender contribute to our understandings of how gender is constructed in broader society. The focus—on these understudied women themselves and their individual experiences—is an important way of expanding our epistemology and consideration of so-called legitimate knowledge vis-à-vis Dorothy Smith's (1987) "everyday world" and Patricia Hill Collins's (1990) "everyday knowledge."

Listening to Women's Voices

Over a period of 5 months, beginning in July 2016, we collected 84 life history narratives in five districts of Nepal: Kathmandu, Dolkha, Gorkha, Nuwakot, and Sindhupalchok. These districts were selected based on the impact of the 2015 earthquakes, road accessibility, availability of Nepali language speakers, and participant availability per the agricultural calendar. Within each of these five districts, we implemented a combination of purposive and quota (nonprobability) sampling, or what Wendy Luttrell (1993) describes as a "stratified, selective sampling" (509). We selected interviewees with the intention of having a sample varied by caste, age, income, and educational level.

The UNDP HDI (Human Development Index) of 2016 illustrates greater discrepancies when the data are disaggregated by ethnicity: Newars have the highest HDI value (0.565); followed by the Brahman-Chhetris (0.538); followed by Janajatis,[4] excluding Newars (0.482); Dalits (0.434); and Muslims (0.422). We see the greatest inequalities in education, with pronounced long-lasting effects on capabilities (UNDP 2016). Thus, given this variation in HDI among ethnic groups, it becomes imperative to study the economic status of women with the perspective of the gender processes within their respective ethnic or social groups.

We treat Nepali women in this study as a singular entity based on their commonly shared experiences, but we use two categories of women for analysis:

1. One category is high-caste Hindus of Indo-Aryan descent. This includes women from Brahmin and Chhetri (high Hindu castes) families, as well as Newar women, who have Tibeto-Burman origins but have mixed cultural and religious practices with Indo-Aryans.[5]

2. Our other category of women includes Dalit (low-caste Hindu) women, Janajati women, and women of Tibeto-Burman origin. We also include in this group Indo-Aryan Brahmin women who converted to Christianity and thereby have altered or changed their familial sociocultural practices.

These divisions are made on the basis of the prevalence of dominant patriarchal values in women's life experiences as revealed in our study. We assert that the focus here is not on a particular religious or ethnic background but, rather, on the ideology of patriarchy that is adhered to within the various groups or cultures. In addition to caste and ethnicity, a group's sociocultural practices are also influenced by geography and proximity to the culture of the dominant group in a particular place. Thus, we envision identity as a fluid concept, and our focus is on how sociocultural ideologies shape gender socialization and, in turn, how those gendered practices determine economic autonomy.

Collecting the life history narratives took between 1 and 5 hours, with the average interview lasting 3 hours. Because of the length of these interviews, we tried to be as accommodating as possible with scheduling the time and location. The life history narrators often chose to be interviewed at their homes or in the fields where they worked. We placed emphasis on locations with minimal distractions and high levels of comfort so that each of the life history narrators would feel at ease. However, it was almost guaranteed that there would be at least one interruption of some kind during the interview. Further complicating matters were the rugged terrain, remoteness, and sparse populations in some areas of the districts in our sample. Finding willing and able participants, especially during the harvest season as well as the rainy season, often proved difficult. The reproductive and productive demands placed on women—the same socially constructed gendered obstacles that diminished women's economic status—also constrained participants' ability to sit and talk with us for an extended period of time.

We conducted the interviews and audio-recorded them in Nepali. We subsequently transcribed and translated the life history interviews into English. These taped transcriptions would later "become the basis for the written narrative account—the life history" (Davison 1996:16). Each member of the research team analyzed the data, and the team collectively identified and discussed themes and patterns as they emerged in the data.

By centering on the distinct life experiences of individual women living in Nepal, this project develops a focused analysis that brings the applied field of gender and development together with the established ideological frameworks on the social constructions of gender. Specifically, our life history interviews with individual women reveal a consistent theme: Rural women in Nepal experience gender discrimination and persistent poverty throughout their lives. To best understand this, we need to take a micro-level approach. We need to examine the entirety of individual women's lives, as the cycle of poverty and dearth of education and life opportunities, consistently inherited from one's mother, continues on to the next generation.

However, we do see a shift at the micro level: Our interviewees were educating their daughters, which will ideally offer the next generation better life chances and greater access to economic power. Researching gender at the micro level reveals important dynamics about gender formation, the perpetuation of power (particularly economic power and who has it and who does not), access to education and other opportunities, and the resistance to gendered constructions that can be extrapolated beyond the context of Nepal and across international borders to new spaces.

Gender Constraints Experienced Across the Lifespan

To best understand women's relative economic power, we need to look at the cumulative effect of gender discrimination and persistent poverty throughout women's lives. A culture governed by patriarchy and rigid gendered norms enforced (and reinforced) in all social structures shapes and determines women's lived experiences in Nepal. Drawing from life histories collected from Nepali women, we organize our findings into three broad parts: (1) a dearth of economic opportunity in early life, (2) lack of economic agency after marriage, and (3) dead-end pathways to economic empowerment.

Women in this study experienced treatment first as a daughter and later as a daughter-in-law, and we found that this treatment varied greatly across castes, ethnicities, and religions. In fact, the way women were treated in their families actually placed these women (as a specific group) at different levels of economic power or control. Meaning, women from high-caste Hindu groups[6] reported greater dependency and lack of economic autonomy compared with women belonging to non-Hindu, Tibeto-Burman, or low Hindu caste groups. Needless to say, as a whole, women still lag behind their male counterparts in terms of economic power or control. While the gendered division of labor in all rural households was almost identical, how women were placed in their respective groups created difference in their economic agency and autonomy.

A Dearth of Economic Opportunity in Early Life

In this section we focus on the lived experiences of our study participants as children and adolescent girls. From an early age, these women experienced gender discrimination at the micro level from within their families and at the macro level by such institutions as the state. In the study, the early lives of rural women were often characterized by persistent hardship, poverty, and gender discrimination. Women in all the districts reported heavy domestic chores (including cleaning, washing, working in the kitchen, tending livestock, and looking after siblings). Not only did these situations shape and determine their chances for education and life skill opportunities, but these situations also further rendered them vulnerable to gender discrimination and even exploitation.

Economic Hardship and Constructs of Gender

Women of rural Nepal experience persistent hardship and poverty throughout their lives. Early childhood memories of the rural women from our sample included undertaking domestic chores, collecting fodder for animals, grazing animals, and working as domestic servants. Because of the gendered division of labor, contribution to the household by girls at a young age was both expected and to some extent accepted. This division of labor also restricted mobility and independence. Interviewees reported being discouraged from walking around, especially after they reached adolescence and began to menstruate. In most cases, not abiding by these gendered restrictions often resulted in social sanctions and punishments. In contrast, some respondents belonging to non-Hindu groups shared they had more liberty regarding their mobility, even after their first menstruation. But generally, daughters faced far more restrictions in terms of mobility compared with sons. Due to a pervasive patrilineal structure of families and kinship in all ethnic groups, daughters were seen more as a liability in the sense that they were members of the family who would have to be married off. This gendered restriction on mobility, largely socially constructed to control young women's sexuality, hindered their seeking economic opportunities outside their homes. And even when they were able to seek out economic opportunities, women often were made to feel (and felt themselves) that these pursuits would call their character into question and that they would not be considered ideal homemakers.

With much sadness in their voices, women interviewees, particularly rural women, also shared how they lived amid great scarcity of basic needs. Many women shared how rice was considered a luxury, and they would eagerly anticipate festivals to have "good food." Ramkumari Lamichhane, a 43-year-old Brahmin Hindu, recalled,

> I had to collect grass, firewood, keep away the monkeys. . . . Although I had feared tigers and foxes, I had to look after the goats in the jungle. There wouldn't be cooked and delicious food when I arrived (home) from work. I had to eat the same left over food in the evening that I had left in the morning.

Women's families' poverty, compounded with their lower status as daughters, meant a diminished quality of life and limited nutrition. The *Nepal Demographic and Health Survey 2016* reported 41% of all Nepali women and 46% of pregnant or breastfeeding women were anemic. Anemia in children and young adults is a serious health concern as it can impair cognitive development and is associated with long-term health and economic effects as well.

Most women interviewees said they had virtually no memories of recreation or play in their childhoods. Subsistence living required much hard work, and the gendered expectations of work did not leave time for play or any leisure activities. Life was especially difficult if a girl was the oldest daughter. Tripti Shrestha, a 45-year-old Newari interviewee, recalled,

> Since I was the eldest, I had to do a lot of things, from helping my siblings to lending a hand to my parents as well. . . . I had to go to school after working and basically had to go to work from a young age.

This unequal division of labor socially constructed as natural and inevitable would continue throughout women's lifetimes. And these experiences of economic hardship and gender expectations would be passed from one generation to the next.

Gender and Social Discrimination From Generation to Generation

Most of the women interviewees recounted the hardships faced by their mothers, too, which largely dictated the kinds of lives they had. In many cases, mothers of respondents faced even worse discrimination and hardship than their daughters would eventually face. Many interviewees' mothers died during childbirth or died early without medical treatment. With the previous generation (the mothers of our interviewees) belonging to a subsistence economy, the present generation found themselves caught in the transition between a subsistence economy and a cash economy.

The condition was even worse for rural women from marginalized caste groups. Rekha Sunuwar, a 20-year-old Janajati woman, recalled how in her mother's village, "my mother used to go to a common water tap (which she was not allowed to touch) and then others used to take the water first before my mother." Rekha's mother was not educated and faced much hardship and discrimination as a low-caste member of society. Rekha also shared with us that her mother would have preferred to have had a son.

Lack of Education

Because of gender bias in their own families and communities, many of the women in our sample had not been sent to school, which not only left them vulnerable but also greatly diminished their potential economic opportunities. Of our total sample (N = 84), both urban and rural respondents combined, only 30% of our interviewees attained secondary or higher education. An even smaller percentage (16%) of the rural women we interviewed (N = 66) had completed SLC (School Leaving Certificate after 10th grade). Not having their SLC sharply limited their chances of participating in the formal economy. The women in our sample compared similarly, if not worse, to Nepali women at the national level: Among the 15–49 age group of women, 3.3% reported having no education, 42.4% reported having reached below secondary education, and only 24.4% attained secondary and higher education (Ministry of Health, New ERA, and ICF 2017).

Mingma Sherpa, a 47-year-old Tibeto-Burman woman, told us, "These days schools are opened everywhere, but at that time there were no schools and also we couldn't study due to poverty." Most women shared that they could not attend school because of lack of awareness, long distances to school, and poverty. The latter often resulted in parents' deciding to prioritize educating their sons.

Compared with the younger women in our study, older women reported being discouraged from attending school, as their parents saw no future in girls' education and believed it to be a waste of time and money. As Acharya and Bennett (1985) and others have noted, unless the time women and adolescent girls spent away from the house would bring some concrete contribution to the household, the families could not justify the time or expense. Older women interviewees reported that their families believed girls' education would only benefit another household after the daughters' marriage. Ranju Maya Basnet, a 48-year-old Chhetri Hindu woman, shared:

> We were six daughters altogether. Both brothers went to school and are educated now, but none of us (girls). . . . My father would say, "Daughter will go to other's house. She must learn to take care of house, clean dishes and girls should not study." He used to say, "A daughter is worthless like a husk which flies away with wind, useful to fill in someone's wall."

This refusal of older generations to educate girls, while maintaining a subsistence mode of living, confined women to agricultural and domestic work after marriage. The pervasive structure of families as patrilineal, offering no or limited inheritance for daughters, further increased women's dependency on their husbands after marriage. A preference for sons, gendered discriminatory practices, and an overall lack of opportunity in their early lives would continue (and intensify) once women married.

Lack of Economic Agency After Marriage

Women's early life, rife with gendered expectations and constraints, continued to determine their agency after marriage. As girls, they were expected to carry out most of the domestic chores in their parental home, and these expectations followed them to their new home after marriage. The livelihood for Nepali women after marriage generally was the worst of their lives, as revealed by their experiences of early marriage, early pregnancy, persistent poverty, abuse from husbands and other family members, an unequal gendered division of labor within both the private and public spheres, and virtually no recognition of women's unpaid care work.

Early Marriage and Early Pregnancy

Amid gender disparity and other discriminatory social norms within the context of Nepali society, Nepali women and girls face a complex set of challenges related to puberty and sexuality. Early marriage, early sexual activity, and early childbearing continue to be common, culturally entrenched practices.

Child marriage (marriage below 18 years of age) is still widely practiced in Nepal, although it is legally prohibited. The *Nepal Demographic and Health Survey 2016* reported that 13% of Nepali women were married by the age of 15, while 17% of teenagers reported bearing a child (Ministry of Health et al. 2017). Importantly, early marriage and early pregnancy often diminish opportunities to engage in economic activities, as women are consumed by family care work, domestic chores, and subsistence farming responsibilities. Reflecting national trends, women from our sample generally married early: Most of the women married before the age of 20. And marrying early often meant discontinuing one's educational pursuits. Laxmi Maharjan, a 30-year-old Newari woman, shared that she dropped out of her bachelor's program soon after her marriage. She enrolled again later only to drop out due to pregnancy. Likewise, Kesar Jirel, a 41-year-old Janajati/non-Hindu woman, married at 17 and had a child by 19. Having a baby compelled her to work in a carpet factory under exploitative circumstances to support her family. Goma Rai, a 23-year-old Janajati woman, shared,

> We got married before we were able to stand up on our own feet. We regret this. . . . If I was able to study properly then it could have been different . . . but there was work in my maternal home and after being married we got a child after one year.

Similarly, Pooja Rana, a 42-year-old high-caste Hindu, studied until she got married. After marriage, she could not pass and then stopped studying altogether. There is a clear association between median age of marriage and level of education: The *Nepal Demographic and Health Survey 2016* (Ministry of Health et al. 2017) reported that women with an SLC (10th grade) pass level of education or higher marry almost 5 years later (at an average of 21.4 years) than women with no education (at an average of 16.8 years old).

In some cases, even women working prior to marriage discontinued this paid work after marriage to look after the household. For instance, Shweta Basnet, a 25-year-old Chhetri Hindu interviewee, used to work as a primary school teacher. After eloping with her husband, she had to leave the job, as she moved to a new place. She expressed regret as far as being dependent on her husband. When asked about resuming her job, she said,

Who will come to offer job at home? . . . I have to look after home and have many responsibilities. . . . Once I get up, I have to cook food, give grass and feed the goat. . . . I have to take my daughter to school . . . again after returning (home), I do work at home, and in the evening, I have to go to receive her in her school. And so on.

Furthermore, the number of children in a family affected the overall quality of life for women interviewees. The *Nepal Demographic and Health Report* (2016) reported that on average, women in the lowest wealth quintile had twice as many children as women in the highest quintile (3.2 versus 1.6 children). Thus, rural Nepali women who experienced early marriage, early pregnancy, and bore more than one or two children inevitably had diminished possibilities for pursuing economic opportunities during their reproductive adult age. And high-caste Hindu women reported marrying earlier than their non-Hindu counterparts. In almost all the interviewees' experiences, child-rearing was assumed to be a natural responsibility for women and for women only. With little or no help from their families, in addition to a general lack of access and proximity to public services and day care, women felt they did not have the capacity to venture into income-generation activities.

Once a woman moves away from her family and community of birth to her married home, a patrilocal residence, which is typically an altogether new place, she becomes more vulnerable, dependent, and without a choice but to comply with the demands of her husband's household. Thus, the mobility and activities of a woman after marriage are sharply curtailed by domestic chores and other expected gender roles. The *Nepal Demographic and Health Survey 2016* reports that 28% of Nepali women did not have decision-making power in terms of accessing health care, purchasing land or a house, or visiting relatives (Ministry of Health et al. 2017).

No Way Out: Dead-End Pathways to "Economic Empowerment"

Involvement With NGOs

Since the 1990s, there has been a significant increase in the number of NGOs and community organizations working to support women entering the public sphere and participating in the local economy. As most rural areas in Nepal lack modern banking facilities, these cooperatives, especially those providing microeconomic project loans, have the intention of ensuring access to economic opportunities as well as savings. In our study, 63% of women reported their affiliation with savings and credit cooperatives or a training institution, yet affiliation with a group had not necessarily elevated their status in their families or communities; rather, the focus of these organizations centered on accessing resources. Kesar Maya Jirel (Janajati and non-Hindu) was able to start up her restaurant business with the loan from such a group with little interest. In other cases, less educated women fell victim to high interest rates.

Women's participation in these organizations was not readily accepted by some men, as it reduced their control over their wives. Shanta Lamicchane, a 45-year-old Brahmin Hindu, shared,

> XXXX organization had opened an office and my mother-in-law was engaged with them. . . . They made (water) taps and did silk worm farming. . . . Our mother-in-law often went for the training too and would walk along with them. Our father-in-law scolded her because of that. My father-in-law and his brother went to fight with them (the organization).

And while some women shared with us how they ventured into their own businesses with the help of local cooperatives and NGOs, many of these women's husbands controlled their earnings.[7] Ranju Maya Basnet (Chhetri Hindu) told us,

> I wanted to buy a house . . . we had taken 2 Lakh rupees (about $2,000 USD) loan from a cooperative . . . (my) husband did all the documentation without letting me know (and she ended up paying a considerable interest rate). He didn't put the house in my name. Also there is a piece of land I bought but he also didn't let me have the property in my name . . . and we had a quarrel regarding this.

This type of patriarchal or gendered control is commonplace in Nepal. According to the *Nepal Demographics and Health Survey* (2016), 24% of ever-married women said that their husbands got jealous or angry if they talked with other men; 15% said that their husbands insisted on knowing where they were at all times; 12% said that their husbands did not allow them to meet their female friends; and 9% reported that their husbands tried to limit their contact with their families. Again, our findings showed that such control of a woman's household activities, mobility, and income generation was more prominent among women from high-caste Hindu groups in comparison with non-Hindu, Janajati, or Tibeto-Burman groups of women.

Sometimes women would try to generate income in other ways. For example, Sarita, a 24-year-old Dalit woman, not only worked on her family's farm but also worked on others' farms as a tenant for Rs 40 per day (about $0.40 USD). She also made alcohol at home to sell. She was able to sell her two buffaloes and a large pile of firewood, which she had worked hard to collect. She later migrated to Kathmandu to work as a domestic helper washing clothes and dishes for just Rs 3000 (about $30 USD) per month, which was not enough to pay her rent.

Even while trying to earn outside the home, women reported that household chores and child-rearing remained their primary duty. Ghosh, Singh, and Chigateri (2017) found that access and proximity to public services such as water taps, electricity, roads, and the like not only affected how unpaid care work was organized in the household but also determined the intensity and drudgery of the tasks performed. Work such as fetching firewood and water and cutting grass was particularly arduous in nature and burdensome in terms of the time involved.

For the most part, women in our study relied on their husbands and other male family members to bring in income. NGOs, community organizations, cooperatives, and other development programs that are designed to help women raise their economic status but do not frame their initiatives around women's specific contexts (specifically, the gendered division of labor within most Nepali households and women's general lack of access to public services) inevitably fail to reach their intended goals.

Migrating to Urban Areas for Work Opportunities

Women, especially in rural societies, are more likely to lack important life options and be physically and politically oppressed when they lack economic power relative to men (Blumberg 2015, 2016). Women interviewees, particularly those born into poor families, indicated that physical violence was commonplace. The everyday hardships women endured sometimes led them to take drastic steps, such as running away from home. Inevitably, things turned worse for them rather than better as a consequence and rendered them vulnerable to sex traffickers and further abuse. Sangita (age 41) from Jiri said,

> My aunt had been working in a carpet factory and I had heard from them talking about it. They would say that life is better in Kathmandu. You can earn money, so I ran away with them . . . that is how we got the job. It was very difficult work . . . you cannot earn money working in the carpet factory . . . you just survive but it's very difficult work . . . you cannot take leave.

Rather than earning wages and subsequently becoming more economically empowered, these women were further exploited in gendered ways.

Migrating Overseas for Job Opportunities

Women in our study revealed that despite sharing the economic burden, none of the male members of the family shared the workload inside the home, which would diminish feelings of drudgery and double burden and even open up the possibility of women pursuing economic opportunities. The double burden, instead, meant some of the care work would be most often transferred to girl children. Perhaps in response to persistent poverty and gender discrimination, many of our younger respondents expressed that they were either planning or hoping to go abroad for earning opportunities. However, women's access to and participation in foreign employment has been highly regulated by the Nepali government. For example, the 1985 Foreign Employment Act prohibited women from leaving the country without the consent of their guardians; the second amendment of the act in 1998 maintained its restrictive position and added a clause requiring permission from the government in addition to their guardians'. From 1998 to 2003, the Nepali government imposed a complete ban on the migration of Nepali female workers to Gulf Cooperation Council countries following the death of a Nepali domestic worker in Kuwait. The ban was partially lifted in 2003 to allow women to migrate for work but only in the formal sector, so domestic work was still banned. The ban was lifted in 2010 after protective mechanisms were introduced for outgoing workers but then was reinstated in 2012 to prevent any women younger than 30 from traveling to the Middle East for domestic work. The government claimed that the bans and restrictions were to protect women from risks, including long working hours, sexual violence, physical abuse, and economic exploitation. Young women continued to migrate for domestic work to Middle East countries but did so through irregular channels. In response to this, the government reviewed the policy and issued the Directive on the Management of Sending Domestic Workers for Foreign Employment 2015, which reduced the minimum age criteria to 24 years for women wanting to work in the domestic sector in Bahrain, Kuwait, Lebanon, Malaysia, Qatar, Saudi Arabia, and the United Arab Emirates (Ministry of Labour and Employment, Government of Nepal 2015:58). The *Nepal Demographic and Health Survey 2016* estimates that only about 7% of women have migrated to the Middle East and to other countries (Ministry of Health et al. 2017). While this means of pursuing economic opportunities is more regulated and monitored than the examples of young women running away to Kathmandu for job opportunities, the Nepali government, with its paternalistic approach and gender-specific restrictions, reinforces the patriarchal culture and the state as another gendered institution.

Men's Migration and Control of Remittance

Nepali women find themselves having to assume more responsibility for agricultural and community work at home at the same time as outmigration of men to urban centers and international locales has increased. *Nepal Demographic and Health Survey 2016* reports that the proportion of female-headed households has almost doubled over the past 15 years, from 16% in 2001 to 31% in 2016 (Ministry of Health et al. 2017). This increase in responsibility, however, is not commensurately met with an increase in authority and participation in decision making (Maharjan, Bauer, and Knerr 2012). Most of the women we interviewed (especially the rural women in our sample) had husbands or sons who had left Nepal for jobs overseas, and these women relied on those male family members to send back remittance. As Til Maya (age 41) from Jiri explained, "We have to pay so much money to do farming and we don't get much return on our investment. So many people are leaving farming nowadays . . . many people are abroad earning and their families move to the city." However, this was not without a cost: The remittance process regularly begins with a heavy loan that carries a high interest rate. While some succeeded in providing for the family with money earned overseas, others failed and were forced to return home to Nepal, particularly after their health deteriorated. Sarita, a Dalit woman, shared that her family took out a loan of 90,000 NPR (about $900 USD) at an interest rate of 36% that would normally take three years to pay back. But her husband had to return after 2 years due to deteriorating health. Similarly, Til Maya also expressed that her husband's work abroad was

> very difficult and the salary is very low and we have taken a loan before he flew. . . . He could save only 10,000 NPR (about $100 USD) per month, which he used to send to me and the money

was spent on the education of our children. So many years, like 10 years, were spent like that.

As our study reveals, while local cooperatives and NGOs have attempted to support women entering the market economy and women themselves have attempted to take advantage of direct and indirect job opportunities abroad, a shift in women's economic status and power will not take place amid existing gendered social structures, particularly the gendered division of labor and gendered expectations at the household level. As discussed above, rural women, particularly from high-caste Hindu families, were more rigidly bound by gendered norms. These socially constructed norms then prevented them from pursuing economic empowerment despite educational and earning opportunities. A conducive and supportive environment for them to do so simply does not yet exist. At the same time, although Janajati and non-Hindu women have had more social liberties and a somewhat more equitable division of labor in the home compared with their high-caste Hindu counterparts, this potential has not been captured by the market or the state, both of which remain inherently patriarchal and maintaining of the status quo.

Conclusions and Implications
....

Every individual is a complex set of intersecting identities, and all those intersecting identities shape and determine everyday experiences. Thus, it is essential that we look at individual women in their particular sociocultural contexts when examining economic power. In the context of Nepal, the majority of women in this study, especially those living in rural areas, faced a dearth of education, persistent poverty, and gender discrimination throughout their lives.

Women's relative economic power varies at both micro and macro levels, from the household to the state (Blumberg 1984). We found that women belonging to dominant high-caste Hindu groups were more confined to their households than were their non-Hindu or low Hindu caste counterparts. High-caste Hindus lacked the social conditions, not opportunity—as they had more access to education and information—needed to enter the market. And even in situations where these women could take advantage of those opportunities, their income ended up in the hands of their husbands and/or male family members. Conversely, women belonging to subordinate castes or groups and non-Hindu (Janajati) groups typically had better social conditions; they were not as restricted in terms of making their own decisions. Yet these groups often lacked the necessary opportunities to take advantage of their cultural liberties. Meanwhile, the market itself has remained male dominated, with the state failing to put forth and regulate policies that would be conducive to women, as the state has also remained male dominated. Similarly, NGOs, cooperatives, and development initiatives have failed to conceptualize their programs around the specific contexts of women's lived experiences: the gendered division of labor in most rural Nepali households that thwarts women's ability to take advantage of economic opportunities, as well as the lack of infrastructure, day care, and other public services and resources necessary for women's economic success and empowerment. All this has resulted in the maintenance of the status quo: The predominately high-caste and patriarchal system, woven into all the social structures in Nepal, has continued to reinforce the inferior status of all women at the household, state, and market levels.

We did, however, observe micro-level shifts in our interviews. Among our respondents who had daughters, each one ensured that their daughters were educated, and all our interviewees believed girls should be educated. We saw a shift in gender dynamics within the family, such as for Dil Maya Bajagain, a 26-year-old Brahmin Hindu, who had been educated, earned an income, and was on equal footing with her husband in regard to household work and decision making. Dil Maya was one of the very few women in our study who had completed her secondary (high school) education. Like others, she had also lost her home in the earthquake. Soon after the earthquake struck her village, she started working in a community-based development project. Her work focused primarily on social problems and conflicts faced by women. For her own life, she shared,

> I found it difficult to manage my working schedule at first because my child was too young . . . but after my husband arrived (from abroad), he helped me to do household work so that I can do my job. . . . I used it (earned income) for household expenses, and I save a little amount in micro finance. . . . We also save it (husband's income) in micro finance. . . . We both discuss about all the things and make a decision. He never himself took any decision regarding anything. We both make decisions. . . . My husband's (salary) and my salary are the source of our family income. And we get 3 to 4 thousand per month by selling milk, which helps to maintain household . . . we had plans to build new house after this *Dashain* (Hindu holiday season).

Advocating for girls' education, such as the education Dil Maya received, is a step in the right direction but is not enough. Comprehensive education, with sensitization on gendered roles for both girls and boys, has tremendous potential to bring about social change. Education that develops and reinforces critical thinking skills (inside and outside the classroom) facilitates awareness of power structures and existing inequalities.

Further, initiatives and programs hoping to redress poverty and support girls' and women's economic empowerment must also work to foster and encourage men's understanding and addressing of the gendered division of labor and power relations. The program in which Dil Maya became involved was based in her own community and centered on social problems faced by local women. Whether offering women a loan or promoting job opportunities in Kathmandu or Dubai, development agencies and organizations must first ground their programs in the lived experiences and contexts of women themselves.

To do gender and development work, and to do it well, we need to look at the complexities of poverty and gender inequality at the individual and local level. We need to move beyond demographics and survey data most often implemented in "women's empowerment" or gender and social inclusion assessment reports and programs, and instead ground our analyses in the specific sociocultural contexts and lives of women *themselves*. This will enable us to develop local and national policies and programs that support women's empowerment, autonomy, and economic power in that particular context. Individuals' lived experiences and "everyday knowledge" should be at the forefront of every development initiative.

NOTES

1. To ensure confidentiality, all interviewees have been given a pseudonym.

2. This study intentionally builds on the important work of Meena Acharya and Lynn Bennett. See Acharya and Bennett (1981).

3. In the past, Nepal held the distinction of being one of the very few countries in the world where women had a lower life expectancy than men. However, the life expectancy trends are showing improved life expectancy for women, with a decrease in maternal deaths and greater access to health services. See Gaha Magar and Kumar (2015).

4. The National Foundation for Development of Indigenous Nationalities has defined "Janajati" as a community that has its own mother tongue and traditional culture and yet does not fall under the conventional fourfold Varna of Hindu or Hindu hierarchical caste structure (Central Bureau of Statistics, 2014).

5. Although Newars are counted among Janajati groups, they are similar in their practice of Hinduism that subsequently determines their gender values, norms, and practices, which in turn influence their economic autonomy. Therefore, in this study, we group Newar women with their high-caste Hindu (specifically, Brahmin and Chhetri) contemporaries.

6. Again, by "high-caste Hindu women," we are referring to Brahmin, Chhetri, and some high-caste Newar Hindu women.

7. Thus, there remains ample space to collectivize women to assert more power and redistribute power through these groups and organizations.

12

Authentic Activism

Domestic Workers as Global Development Agents

Jennifer N. Fish and Justin Sprague

If they could pay us what they owe us from our girlhood, the entire economy would be in debt.

— Juana Flores, International Domestic Workers Federation

Domestic Development: Anchoring a Movement Through the International Labour Organization

Domestic workers have most often featured in development discourse as the iconic oppressed—poor women from the Global South whose lives are largely determined by a transnational economy that forces life migration trajectories. Relegated to household labor outside of the protections of the state, development has dealt with domestic work through the lens of globalization's failures. Among the least paid and most severely exploited, domestic workers present one of the largest obstacles to gender and development theories and practice. The particular struggles of this sector took center stage at the 2010–2011 International Labour Organization (ILO) meetings at the United Nations, when governments, workers, and employers debated a proposed global convention on "Decent Work for Domestic Workers." In this first consideration of policy protections for paid household work, the terms of representation turned, as domestic workers themselves gained access to the ILO through international nongovernmental organizations, global unions, and policy institutes. Bolstered by new strategies of activism and a transnational public presence, the International Domestic Workers Network (IDWN) embodied this sector as "decent," worthy of human rights, and deserving of global policy protections.

This chapter centers on domestic workers as activists, policymakers, and protagonists in UN rights making, rather than the "victims" of development's failures. The achievement of this global policy came about through an unprecedented presence of domestic workers themselves, advocating for their own economic rights and social protections within the United Nations. When representatives of this global sector literally and symbolically demanded that the global elite power structures and policymakers "think of their mothers" when voting on the world's first set of international standards for household labor, new forms of activism emerged within the iconic international governance system. As embodiments of the social, economic, and political injustices of the existing world order, domestic workers brought a new possibility to the larger production of development discourse as actors within the UN policymaking system.

We explore these new avenues of international policy change through the persuasive influence of those who suffer most directly from globalization's sharp divides. Our reflections draw from ethnographic data collected from within the ILO policy process and fieldwork alongside the world's only international domestic workers' organization for the past 8 years. This chapter explores how women domestic workers reframed their own representation, thereby contesting their former place as the victims of globalization in development discourse. Our analyses introduce a theory of *authenticity as activism* that emerges directly from this original policymaking process and is transferable to related human rights struggles worldwide. From this symbolic policy victory, we examine implications for gender and development and the economies of influence that structure domestic workers' lives and access to global protections.

Domestic work grounds the global economy. As a central source of informal labor, the private household space has become an emblematic site of globalization. The ILO estimates about 100 million domestic workers worldwide, 75% to 90% of whom are women and girls. Migrant women leave their own children to care for the families of their employers, often in countries far from their communities and languages of origin. As a global gendered commodity, paid household labor has become the largest occupation for young women worldwide (International Labour Office 2013). Dependence on this form of transnational exchange has fueled geopolitical relations around the trade of care work between sending and receiving countries.[1] Scholar Cinzia Solari asserts, "Nothing signals 'Third World' in the international arena like the mass emigration of women to do domestic labor abroad."[2] Yet human rights and labor protections have not traveled with domestic workers.

The complexities of setting standards for household work stem from core ideological assumptions about the devalued nature of domestic labor, which takes place in the private household sphere and is quintessentially feminized, racialized, and rooted in deep histories of slavery and colonialism.[3] Women of color, 90% of whom are from the developing world, compose this sector, making it a conduit for the reproduction of sharp divides between "maids and madams."[4] In many senses, domestic workers present one of the greatest challenges to development's reach. Isolated in private households, often without citizenship benefits, domestic workers have struggled to access education, economic empowerment, and basic human rights protections. These structural barriers have virtually cemented domestic work as an icon of migrant labor exploitation and the failures of globalization. While local governments often overlook and afford domestic workers minimal rights and protections, the UN governing body sets standards with aspirations of a global reach in both policy and practice. Subsequently, the domestic workers who took center stage in these global policy debates enabled a rethinking of the role of activists, "actual workers" and "grassroots women" as policy change makers themselves. With the interlocking systems of exploitation solidly entrenched across national histories, the symbolic and empirical macro scale of the UN international governance institution provided the first crack in the pavement for changes in protections, recognition, and rights.

"Movements matter."[5] Domestic workers' transnational activism around ILO Convention 189 became the largest coordinated social–political movement to address the global economic gender disparity contained in paid household labor. With "one foot in the labor movement and one foot in the women's movement,"[6] the "decent work for domestic workers" campaign mobilized dual concerns for economic and gender equity through the prominence of UN-level attention (Chen 2011). The ILO served as a meeting ground to bring national domestic worker movements together around a common plight for global human rights and decent work. This international governance institution played a community house role, to a certain extent, as the tangible gathering space, and common purpose galvanized activists' cause at a particularly ripe moment in UN development discourse. Just as the IDWN set up its structure and solidified its cause, the ILO announced that the negotiations for Convention 189 would take place in the 2010–2011 International Labor Conferences. The possibility of gaining global rights centered the mission of the IDWN on a very tangible common claim to rights. By putting their voices on the table, in an organized activist form, the IDWN infiltrated the world's largest labor institution and demanded a space for the experiences of those most directly impacted by the existing migrant informal economy.

Over the course of 2 years, this international network of domestic workers joined the tripartite negotiations, officially as observers yet in practice as active policy change agents. They gained access through two ally organizations—Women in Informal Employment: Globalizing and Organizing (WIEGO), a global policy-research institute, and the International Union of Food, Agricultural, Hotel, Restaurant, Catering, Tobacco and Allied Workers' Association (IUF), the only global union to take on the cause of domestic work as part of its own mission.[7] These organizations got domestic worker representatives "into" the International Labour Conference. While tripartite negotiations are reserved for government delegates and one representative of the worker and employer group, the presence of so many women who literally and symbolically represented the cause of those most seriously marginalized by the global economy made voluminous statements throughout the negotiations. Domestic workers fed their experiences into government delegates and the chair of the worker group to humanize policymaking and ensure that those most directly impacted by the discussions carried a tangible and prominent place in the negotiation room. With the backing of several international nongovernmental organizations and the WIEGO–IUF bookends, domestic workers succeeded in ensuring that the "Decent Work for Domestic Workers" negotiations carved new spaces for activists within global policymaking while setting in place a revolutionary moment in the making of human rights. On June 16, 2011, government, employer, and labor delegates to the International Labor Conference (ILC) of the ILO voted nearly unanimously to adopt Convention 189, "Decent Work for Domestic Workers." The UN-level negotiations on these formative policy protections connected national domestic workers' organizations to a global campaign, with a common appeal for the "same rights to 'decent work' as any other workers" (International Domestic Workers' Network 2010:3). For development, the lessons of this acclaimed moment for women in the informal migrant economy stem from the shaking up of a very traditional global power center by the first coordinated international movement of domestic workers. As president of the IDWN, Myrtle Witbooi proclaimed, "This is something that the ILO has *never* seen before."[8] From this encounter of forces, the terms of domestic workers' activism and the ILO institution changed while the negotiation process became a symbol for larger gender and development struggles worldwide.

Drawing From Development Discourse: Decency and Human Rights Appeals

They [domestic workers] are challenging the tripartite sectors in the ILO, who are considered instruments of change, to prove our value for freedom and human rights.

— Florencia P. Cabatingan, executive board member of the Trade Union Congress of the Philippines

The notion of deeming domestic work worthy of international policy protections reflected an attempt to install "floor" protections for this sector, so often constructed as women workers who represent the "poorest of the poor" in the global economy. Just as "Black Lives Matter" reflects a "minimal kind of plea,"[9] the notion of "decent work for domestic workers" echoed less of an aspirational and more of a baseline request for recognition in the sphere of UN protections. To be *seen*, indeed, composed much of domestic workers' demands. Yet without any formal recognition in international protections, a policy that would bring domestic workers under an umbrella of rights "just like any other worker" represented a symbolic victory in the struggle for recognition among domestic workers themselves. The achievement of Convention 189 on "Decent Work for Domestic Workers" brought this formerly invisible and excluded category of workers and so many migrants into the mix of international protections.

The IDWN leaders saw strategic opportunities to leverage the ILO policy debates as a means to build a movement from the public relations and global recognition such a forum provided. Their capacity to use the "tools of the house" through the discourse of UN development speak became a central strategic maneuver in how domestic workers showed up and embodied their claim for basic rights and protections. Even though the resistance and revolutionary foundations of the national movements that composed this international network held more radical notions of labor justice, socialist feminist struggles, and Marxist underpinnings, in UN speak, domestic workers asked for "decent human rights" as a fore into a global system that would legitimize their existence as central contributors to the international global economy. From here, once recognized, domestic workers could revisit their radical movement origins in the context of international coalition building. Thus, drawing on development speak served as one of the most persuasive strategies for the IDWN to claim a transnational state social contract where recognition materialized through tangible rights.

Domestic workers' claim to decent work and rights drew strength from their simultaneous capacity to point to the ethical obligations of the ILO as a global standard-setting entity with the widest capacity to develop policy on the transnational flow of human beings. They used moral considerations, personal stories, emotional content, and historical conditions of injustice as compelling evidence to build central frameworks that linked domestic labor to three larger values: human rights, gender equity, and economic justice. By placing domestic work in a much wider context of shared priorities and ethical commitments within the international community, domestic work became a conduit for the ILO to demonstrate its emphasis on human rights, as well as the promises of gender equity and economic opportunities central to development discourse.

Domestic workers staked their claim as human beings with "universal and inalienable rights" to social and legal protections.[10] According to the UN doctrine, adopted in 2003, human rights must be indivisible, interrelated, equality-based, inclusive, and accountable to the rule of law. The domestic worker front pierced these principles by showing the existing divisibility of rights to social and labor protections because of the distinct nature of work within the private household, as well as the complexities of migrant, gender, and class-based location. Marcelina Bautista, IDWN's Latin American regional coordinator, contended, "As domestic workers, human rights in the workplace are particularly important, as they are the least respected."[11] While they spoke of the discrimination they faced in their everyday work contexts, domestic workers called the ILO to uphold its commitment to the UN Common Understanding of Rights. Just as the ILO Conventions require states to uphold labor policy agreements, within the negotiations domestic workers held the ILO itself accountable to aspirational UN standards, where human rights are esteemed in the highest light. Their statements interrogated the ILO on its inability to ensure human rights for all. Again and again, domestic workers, who carried the visible and symbolic bodies of struggle, proclaimed that in the ever-increasing exploitation of the economic terms of globalization, their own human rights were "right, just and long-overdue." When asked about the purpose of domestic workers' participation in the negotiations, Mexican leader Bautista surmised, "Like all people, we're reclaiming our human rights."[12]

By using the very human rights and decency-centered discourse of the ILO in a framework in their activist appeals, domestic workers held a trump card in their ability to demand that the ILO honor UN standards and ensure congruency between such lauded aspirations and actual practice. This capacity bolstered domestic workers' credibility while rendering the denial of their rights unethical through the use of UN values as a litmus test of allegiance to international standards.

Affective Authenticity: Speaking to the Heart

In addition to the activist strategy of learning UN development language, domestic workers occupy the rare position of being able to, in a way, "embody affect," through speaking on their personal experiences in the field.

Being able to simultaneously code switch between the rhetorical strategies of policymakers while maintaining an air of "authenticity" in the deployment of their own personal narratives, domestic workers have crafted a rare position in which they are both experts in the subject *and* symbols of the struggle for basic human rights. When these embodied "actual workers" entered the discourse of policy debate, their narrative positions carried legacies of struggle, social justice movements across the world, and the lived experiences of women in this invisible economy—making Convention 189 unlike any other policy process. By centralizing authenticity, affect, and emotion as vehicles for analysis, the discursive power of domestic workers speaking from their own lived experiences brings a new lens into the crafting of UN development policies. We engage with an affective framework that positions standpoint as the center of both rhetorical and organizational power for domestic workers and the organizations representing them.

While this study is specifically examining the narrative power of domestic workers, it should be noted that domestic workers' rights organizations are not *entirely* facilitated and headed by domestic workers themselves. Professional advocates are critical components of these organizations as well. In fact, of the original network at the 2010 ILC, only 28% worked full-time as domestic workers. The others had made their careers advocating for this underrepresented sector. In the case of the IDWN, for example, while the organizational message and mission spoke as a united front of domestic workers at the ILO policy debates, its actual leaders varied according to the level of their direct dependence on the field for survival, as well as their levels of education.

Likewise, it cannot be ignored that while organizations like the IDWN are fundamentally invested in the human rights of *all* domestic workers globally, the composition of an organization such as the IDWN is also lacking in regional diversity. No domestic workers from the Middle East were able to join the organization; in some cases, workers could not physically get to the ILO, and very importantly, the state political landscape in some places prohibited the movement of domestic workers into this highly politicized space. In some instances, Switzerland denied the visas of domestic workers, and at the most pragmatic level, the actual costs of travel were too burdensome for some. On a different note, for those that were there, language barriers and the lack of translators also created major issues of representation on the debate floor, burdening the ability for a *truly* global representation of domestic workers in the physical space. These realities complicated the ability of the IDWN to physically embody a truly transnational standpoint, despite having one in mission and construction. Some of these constraints also showed themselves in the organizational process, where certain hierarchies between professional domestic worker advocates had privileged positions due to their abilities to maintain a full-time investment in this cause. Given the unfortunate reality of attaining truly diverse representation in all forms of organization, it is always wise to be wary of essentializing the goals of any organization as adequately representing every constituent it acts on behalf of; however, as our investments are in the rhetorical strategies and ability of organizations like the IDWN to craft a narrative of *authenticity* on behalf of all domestic workers for the purpose of justice and liberation, we are invested in the potential global impacts of these political strategies.

Nonetheless, the message of this united front prioritized the individual narratives of domestic workers themselves to enable these experiences to become beacons for conscious organization and advocacy. Despite internally recognizing the potential pitfalls of using "one voice" to address all the unique issues that domestic workers in different regions and political climates face, the core epistemological standpoint of organizations like the IDWN is to put the voices of domestic workers first, and within that structure, a theory of authenticity *as* activism emerges. Thus, while the numbers indicate that not all advocates were domestic workers themselves, the employment of affect and authenticity *by* the domestic workers in these organizations was positioned in critical spaces to most effectively create change. Much like a professional degree held by an organizational advocate, authenticity becomes another factor that is critical for the members who were/are domestic workers and for the larger organizations themselves to embody.

In his 2010 ILC opening remarks, chair of the overarching ILO workers' group Sir Leroy Trotman stated that because domestic workers were "present in the room" the deliberations would assuredly reflect a certain "reality on the ground." The underlying message here is one recognizing that in many instances, policymaking decisions are often carried out in scenarios *on behalf* of the constituents they most affect. Domestic workers being present in policy deliberations has palpable impacts not just on the decision-making process but on the dynamics of the negotiations themselves. More than just spectral murmurs on the UN floor, power exists in physical presence. Thus, the domestic workers themselves act as a kind of "boundary objects" (i.e., objects that are meant to maintain certain meanings in different spaces, places, or times) between the lived experiences of women in this global profession and the institutions that determine the laws and protections they receive. In this case, domestic workers enable a form of translation to occur, where their lived experiences become credible and critical forms of evidence and data to support the development of self-protective legislation. More than simply being employed as passive symbols to tug at heartstrings, these women become active agents in the process of building policy to promote the promise of liberation.

The "authenticity" of their narratives becomes a speaker box for the diverse standpoints of domestic workers worldwide. While each experience with the domestic service sector is unique, and in many ways determined by a number of extenuating local factors depending on who and where the labor takes place, the narratives of those heard at the global stage become markers for the conditions that the women have endured and continue to endure. Authenticity as a defining characteristic cannot be learned or earned, which is a critical factor in the power these narratives possess on the negotiation floor. Traditionally, authenticity as a theory has been one attributed to the modern convention of individualism, where one articulates a sense of originality for self-fulfillment (Taylor 1992:29). Interestingly, in the case of domestic workers and the IDWN, their narratives are all unique and informed by their social locations and the circumstances of their employment; however, authenticity moves from these traditional modes into ones where authentic individual experiences are employable to speak on behalf of a very large and diverse community of women. By aligning affective appeals with the persuasive capacity of grounded evidence, the IDWN crafted new strategies that build a social movement around these authentic activist voices.

Hence, it is important to narrate certain *trends* that become indicators of an "authentic" experience despite individual nuances—at least an experience that is authentic enough to be useful on the negotiation floor. Authenticity becomes an interesting space where individuality and community meet to enact positive change. Be it in the kind of work, feelings of subjugation, issues of housing, or even violence, there exist narrative threads of synchronicity that link the experiences of domestic workers together in ways that are intentional and multipronged, contributing to a larger, "authentic," and *global* narrative of the conditions that domestic workers face. What are the elements of these narratives that imply a kind of "collective identity"? While the experiences of domestic workers are inevitably individual in nature and determined by local conditions, there is a *political* attempt to link the narratives together in a way that discusses a similar "origin," or in the case of domestic workers, similar working conditions, linked invariably through dominant concepts of gender and labor. Likewise, with a similar political *destination*, which is to generate legislative protections with a shared goal of liberation, a homologous social identity is scripted, creating parameters of an authentic and cogent community despite unique individual living conditions (Ferrara 1998:111). Linking data about the material conditions of domestic work, along with narrative heartbeats that span continents, domestic workers themselves, and organizations like the IDWN can create complex and nuanced arguments for legal protections that actively engage policymakers and domestic workers alike, in equitable ways.

The continual injection of "real-life" experiences of domestic workers infused a repeated human connection to the formation of global labor policy. When delegates heard of the story of Shirley Pryce, for example, who was forced to sleep in a doghouse for years while caring for her employer's home, the need for global standards sharpened in scope, application, and urgency. Furthermore, the presence of workers who had lived through the struggles of unregulated household labor rendered opposition to the convention a cold denial of human rights. In essence, domestic workers like Shirley became living symbolic representations of the costs accrued in the historical failure to provide standards for this group of workers. While her situation may not have been the norm, by presenting her experience through the lens of collective struggle or as an enunciation of general working *conditions,* Shirley's narrative contributes to the larger structure of collective authenticity. Interestingly, while unique experiences have traditionally been theorized as a threat to collective identity and collective authenticity (Ferrara 1998:117), in the case of the narratives of domestic workers and the larger function of the IDWN as a unifying body for women in this occupation worldwide, the uniqueness of their experiences actually serves as a binding agent in the collective identity. By sharing distinct *experiences* but similar *sentiments*, the efficacy of these narratives in the realm of advocacy and policymaking is strengthened, rather than weakened. All the while, the experiences of the domestic workers themselves are not subject to flattening for a collective voice; rather, the individual experiences create a (disparate) community that is fundamentally rendered genuine by nature of the "authentic" voices that are used in public forums, echoing through the collective sentiments of domestic workers everywhere.

Recognizing the political efficacy of domestic workers having agency in speaking on their own behalf, ILO Director-General Juan Somavía endorsed domestic workers' inclusion in the convention negotiations by stating, "I'm also happy that in different ways, domestic workers' activities are in fact present here in the room, which I think gives it an important capacity to come down to the reality of what you are discussing today."[13] This notion of "reality" or "realness" is a powerful political tool, and it is something that cannot be bought or traded, offering organizations like the IDWN, and the domestic workers that speak out individually, a great amount of social and political influence. An experience being rendered as authentic, then, also implies recognition by outsiders. Authenticity is as much a concept that is self-invested as it is one that is read onto bodies. Its definition and the parameters of such change depend on who is articulating it, how many people agree on that definition, the relationships that people have to an object or place, and even the time period or region in which a particular object or idea exists. In all cases, in a given object, authenticity is assumed to be inherently objective and measurable (Jones 2010:182). People are also objects of authenticity, boundary objects of sorts, that fluctuate between read as authentic in the physical state and as symbols of authenticity in the ideological state. Rendering people as authentic operates on two different levels. Authenticity implies a form of honesty, or *truth*. This directly influences the second form of authenticity we read onto people. It is read on the bodies themselves. Authentic people are "real."

The injection of lived experience into the political debates of domestic workers implies an understanding that not only are these women very much "real" but their experiences with gendered and oppressive labor conditions is in some capacity universally understood. The nuances in experiences, like Shirley Pryce's, for example, work to humanize the conditions of an international labor trade that a diverse and globally reaching network of women are experiencing in some form or another. Thus, by asserting that global gendered labor inequality and oppression are indeed "real" (as backed by legitimate data and via organizations like the IDWN), the individual narratives of domestic workers on the debate floor become that much more powerful. "Authenticity," then, is a tool for political advocacy. This tool takes a particularly persuasive form in international policymaking spaces, where identities vary by location and language, yet congeal around shared authenticity of representation.

In a telling example, Ernestina Ochoa, IDWN vice chair from Peru, expressed in her report to the media immediately following the Convention 189 vote:

> I am a domestic worker. I *work*. Up to this day, I have worked. I am here because I want to be re-vindicated of all of the mistreatment of our ancestors. We are asking you governments. We do not want nice speeches; we want *actions*. We want you to hear us. We need your support. . . . We don't want you to say, "this is what we have done for women." We want you to open the doors, sit down with us and listen to our voices. (Fish, Crockett, and Ormiston, 2012)

In her conviction, Ochoa references historical suffering to gain universal rights that go beyond gender-sensitive rhetoric alone. As she later proclaimed in her reflections on the convention victory, "it is not free, it is what society owed to us." Just as domestic workers asked for democratic relations of respect with employers, on a larger scale, the IDWN demanded that the ILO recognize domestic workers through global rights. Ochoa's call to action at once referenced her individual position and experiences while also using inclusive language that further solidifies domestic workers globally, as a community. She embraces the political efficacy of individualism for inspiring sentiments of empathy and compassion in her personal narrative while also engaging in the political strategy of collective effort that many social justice–oriented political movements have employed historically.

The physical embodiment of struggle brought centuries of suffering to the contemporary debates. When domestic workers referred to both their ancestors and the hundreds of thousands of "poor migrant women" who have been excluded from protections, they drew on an imagined body of workers to strengthen their demands for institutional reparations. In her opening public statement at the 2010 ILC, IDWN president Myrtle Witbooi professed:

> We want to say to you the ILO delegates: We have been waiting for *65 years* for this to happen and we cannot lose this opportunity to appeal to you to please secure the minimum labor standards for the millions of domestic workers that are still unprotected in their respective countries, in order to create an international instrument that will not only protect domestic workers, but will also give us back our dignity and allow us to walk tall as workers, just as any other worker in the world![14]

The repeated use of historical struggles to attain "dignity" and "respect" in the household became an extremely effective tool of moral and collective persuasion. At the same time, by asking the ILO to "set right a historic record of injustice" at the 100th meeting of the ILO, activists placed a great deal of confidence in the potential for international policy to set right centuries of historical marginalization. For domestic workers, this use of story was one of the most important tactics to ensure that the lives of their sisters earned a central stage in the debates around the terms of their very protections.

Affect as Power: Employing Emotion

We ask you to bear with us when we became emotional the first day of the conference. But, as you all say, this was a historical moment for the ILO as well as for domestic workers worldwide.

— Myrtle Witbooi, 2010 opening speech

The IDWN repeatedly posed direct emotional appeals to advocate for policy protections. As they brought affect into their claims, domestic workers asked delegates to *see* the women who "face abuse every day" and "are left alone in the backyards of their employers." Their representative voice,

Halimah Yacob, now the first woman president of Singapore, encouraged delegates to listen to the stories of domestic workers and look "deep in your heart and your conscience" when voting on the convention. This strategy of affect continually asked the tripartite body to integrate empathy when hearing the stories of domestic workers and considering their daily experiences. More than simply a rhetorical strategy, what this evocation offered was a narrative of expertise facilitated through an emotional appeal. Affect becomes a space of agency. These stories were more than simply a peppering of emotion in an otherwise policy-driven debate, but more an act of employing narrative as a means of establishing urgency and credibility. As emotion entered the negotiations, like Witbooi's opening speech above, domestic worker representatives often acknowledged their bending of the usual protocol of the ILO tripartite procedure, thereby making this convention-setting process "a bit special." An organized body such as the IDWN employing this affective strategy was a way of legitimizing the use of *experience* on the debate floor. This use of emotion as a lobbying tool contributed to the distinct nature of Convention 189's negotiations; however, it would be myopic to view the use of emotion as a flash in the pan. Domestic workers simultaneously offered a rhetorical strategy for debate as key organizers and influencers within these organizations. Thus, their strategically integrated emotional appeal in their arguments built legitimacy for the long-term role of domestic workers in organized bodies like the IDWN.

Domestic workers' use of emotion is critical to the analysis of this distinct development in policy formation for myriad reasons. Our examination of emotion is twofold. First, emotion is employed as a means of establishing authenticity. Rather than a static entity that is immediately afforded outright, authenticity is a dynamic formation of a combination of expertise and ethos. Simply being a domestic worker is enough to establish credibility in one's ability to talk about domestic work; however, it is not necessarily an iteration of authenticity. By focusing a collection of narratives that have common themes, a coordinated entity like the IDWN can refocus the entire organization as an exercise of collective authenticity. There is power in numbers, sure, but in an organization where one of the pillars of foundation is advocacy, a sense of collective legitimacy is afforded to its members as experts able to speak on behalf of *all* domestic workers globally. Thus, as an organization, emotion is employed in policy debates as a means of establishing authenticity. One domestic worker's story can pluck emotional heartstrings on the debate floor, but her appeal to emotion also serves the dual purpose of authenticating the larger goals of activist organizations. The use of narrative and experience acts as a way to buttress one's existence as a domestic worker but also to link domestic workers as a group, together. As described in the previous section, authenticity is prescribed to individuals *through* synchronicity as a group.

Emotion should not be confused with affect outright, however. The second way we examine emotion is to correlate emotion as a *vehicle* for affective power. It is critical to engage with the understanding that "affect is not a personal feeling. Feelings are *personal* and *biographical,* emotions are *social,* and affects are *prepersonal*" (Shouse 2005:2). Emotion and affect work in tandem. Where the rhetorical move of employing emotion is used to inspire empathy and understanding of the struggles and injustices often encountered in domestic work, using emotions to recall and incite physical reactions is key in recognizing the actual power of emotional appeal. Affect becomes an abstract symptom of the empathy evoked from an appeal to emotions. In essence, "affect plays an important role in determining the relationship between our bodies, our environment, and others, and the subjective experience that we feel/think as affect dissolves into experience" (11). Emotion is used to manipulate the air in the room in a way that inspires empathy but, more importantly, necessitates *action*. Take, for instance, Myrtle Witbooi's ILC closing statement in 2011. She appeals:

> If somebody would have said to me 45 years ago that I would have sat here today and really get to the end of slavery, I would not have believed them. But 45 years ago, I was sitting in my employer's garage and I was organizing domestic workers. Today I'm here. And I'm here because of the cause of so many domestic workers. And if you did not believe in us, if you were not so passionate, we would not have been able to win this fight. But because all of you believe, you believe there's a better life for domestic workers, you believe that the time of repayment has come now for all of us. We want to be free. We don't want to be called slaves anymore. We want to get what every other worker has in this world.

Witbooi is not simply recalling her experience organizing domestic workers. By evoking physical reactions and historical trauma through her use of the metaphor of slavery, Myrtle is appealing to emotions as a means of *creating* affect. She is directly appealing to one's (individual) understanding of the concept of slavery while suturing it into a narrative about her role as a key organizer of domestic workers. Similarly, she directly engages the audience by indirectly indicting their actions as being supportive. She is establishing a relationship between the various "bodies" at the convention, domestic worker and otherwise, into a collective struggle by employing emotion as a rhetorical vehicle and by having been established beforehand as authentic, and therefore credible.

Throughout the debates, domestic workers' strong affective claims took form by emphasizing three key dimensions of domestic work. First, by centering the historic exclusion of domestic workers, a legacy of human suffering heightened the onus of responsibility for the ILO to redress past circumstances that separated families, normalized servitude, and enslaved people of color throughout the world. Second, domestic workers emphasized their high vulnerability to abuse, using extreme cases to highlight the potential for severe exploitation and all forms of trauma. By drawing on the sharp power imbalances between employers and domestic workers, IDWN representatives often referenced cases of extreme abuse central to the nature of unregulated labor in the private household. In their statements and input in the process, they demonstrated how such abuse takes physical, emotional, and sexual forms. By highlighting the bodily and emotional layers of oppression in their own experience, domestic workers repeatedly evidenced the painful realities of abuse to sensitize delegates' understandings of the impact of protections.

Affect in these instances is a means of capitalizing on the tension between trauma, storytelling, and its effects in a debate space. For instance, domestic worker statements often referenced severe psychological suffering as a result of the frequent familial separation required to perform domestic work, sharpened by the demands for migration embedded in the work. As one domestic worker activist from Guatemala asserted, "Our children are left at our grandmothers' houses." As they drew on the power differentials between employers and domestic workers, representatives highlighted the emotional hardship of facing the sharp inequalities between their own lives and those of the families they served. For instance, daily tasks like walking employers' dogs—while leaving their own children to the care of aunts and grandmothers who often reside far away in the most basic living standards—caused extreme psychological hardship for women. As president of the South African domestic workers' union Hester Stephens recollected, "There is a gap between you and your children." Thus, affective claims making took form through compelling stories and examples of extreme suffering that placed exclamation points on domestic workers' rhetorical stances. Their cris de coeur created a social dialogue process that demanded a certain level of respect and empathy for the workers in the room, who had lived through experiences of severe suffering and emerged as activist leaders. This affective rhetoric ultimately played a central role in tipping the favor to convention support for domestic workers.

Employing affect is not without its drawbacks, however. The use of emotion as a means of facilitating affective power is a method of creating visibility. Recalling harrowing and triggering instances of trauma is a project in ethos building, and domestic workers are becoming hypervisible; for a population that has historically been rendered all but invisible and silent, the process of *being seen* is incredibly powerful and politically advantageous. Hypervisibility, however, can lead to the undesirable effect of surveillance, which is critical to acknowledge (Ahmed and Stacey 2000:16). For domestic workers who are still actively in the profession, there runs the possibility that their words or their recounting of experiences, particularly triggering or traumatic experiences, on the debate floor could have potentially harmful impacts on them in their respective spaces of employment. That said, from a feminist standpoint, the benefits of visibility outweigh the possible disadvantages, given that it is domestic workers themselves who are the gatekeepers of the narrative. As they are spokespeople for all domestic workers (at least within the confines of the ILO debate floor), their agency and expertise on the matter is of utmost importance. Therefore, the projects of authenticity and affect serve as a means of differentiating domestic workers from other politicians and advocates by positioning the domestic worker (in a plural sense) as the only entity truly capable of appealing to emotion and using the power of affect, as they are the only actual "authentic" agents in the larger debate about human and domestic workers' rights.

By using emotional appeals, domestic workers developed a very particular policy-activist strategy. In their arguments and public statements, IDWN leaders aspired to "reach the hearts of employers." The technical training sessions that prepared domestic workers for their public delivery emphasized that speeches should "leave the audience in tears." In doing so, to a certain extent, leaders of the IDWN drew on traditional constructions of gender by enacting an emotional "women's story" within the predominantly masculine space of the ILO. This approach feminized the wider appeal for domestic worker rights, which held a particular moral power within the heavily masculinized organization. In many ways, the quest for authenticity contributes to this gendered dichotomy. By positioning authenticity as a means of establishing credibility, affective arguments become ensconced in reproducing the notion of "emotion" as oppositional to "reason." By making the image of domestic work concrete through strong affective appeals, domestic workers notably increased the legitimacy and impact of their claims. As domestic workers asked for the "hearts" and "tears" of delegates, they positioned the predominantly male representatives of employer and government bodies as their protectors—able to ensure rights through their power locations. Their plea to bring emotion into the negotiations recognized the normalized value of the rational, male-centered global governance institution. IDWN leaders often represented delegates' own use of domestic workers, and at times played on this in their interpersonal encounters with governments and employer representatives. "How would you feel if your domestic workers were not protected?" they would ask. Through these exchanges, delegates in each of the tripartite bodies had to look at their own lives when confronted with the affective appeals of domestic workers. In many ways, the IDWN's affective strategy served to use guilt as persuasion by making it look as if policymakers were heartless (as well as immoral) if they ignored domestic workers.

Ultimately, affective strategies have deeply subversive potential. From a feminist standpoint, the use of affect through the vehicle of authenticity and emotion normalizes and validates the shared struggles of being a domestic worker, and its presence on a debate floor is inherently transgressive. Where masculinized spaces like the UN debate floor are supposed to be the arena of ration and reason, by injecting the "outlaw" of emotion in a manner that creates power (affect), the space is "feminized" through an act of rhetorical subversion (Jaggar 1989). Forcibly engaging affect in a space where emotion and affect are rendered suspect, and doing so in a way that lends credibility and legitimacy to larger claims about human rights, domestic workers' narratives are simultaneously empowering their right to literally occupy said space and to metaphorically challenge hegemonic masculinity. To recall Myrtle Witbooi's ILC statement, strategically employing her "authentic" experience through an emotional appeal to human rights and the historical correlation with slavery, opposing her position indirectly suggests an acceptance of slavery. Therefore, while potentially upholding historically nefarious gendered dichotomies, it is within the application of these very dichotomies that domestic workers are able to exercise a "right" over their occupancy in this masculine space of debate, or "reason."

Nowhere is this more palpable than in the direct indictment of ILO delegates for their direct roles in systems of oppression by the domestic workers in attendance. By directly exposing the intimate labor of the private worlds of those seated in the negotiations, their subsequent responses and actions in the debate become deeply personal. The IDWN's approach refused to allow the debate to dissolve into esoteric or impersonal terms. Therefore, delegates became directly accountable for their position within this global system of labor. In her 2010 address to the entire ILC, Vicky Kanyoka exemplified this embedded accountability when she asked delegates to look at the core contributions of domestic workers, and the women in that very chamber who performed that work each day. "It is us who take care of your precious children and your sick and elderly; we cook your food to keep you healthy and we look after your property when you are away." Through her use of the second-person *you*, Kanyoka made delegates' own lives material for the negotiations. Similarly, Myrtle Witbooi, in an assertion to government officials, plainly states, "You would not be here today if it were not for the domestic worker in your household." She went on to ask, "Who ironed your shirt?" to point to the inherent contradiction in delegates who opposed standard setting yet benefited extensively from domestic service in their everyday lives. By directly engaging with the delegates and the participants themselves, domestic worker leaders forced those in the room to take the issue seriously, making decent work protections not just a policy issue but a moral and ethical one. The indictments paired with the physical presence of domestic workers in the room put pressure on delegates to take their votes as ones steeped in personal accountability. Support for Convention 189, particularly among employers, became a means of showing how "compassionate capitalism" may operate to protect the world's caretakers. In essence, colonial notions of employers' benevolence merged with the transnational informal economy realities to carve new spaces for development policies to protect those deemed "most vulnerable."

Likewise, this integration of domestic workers' stories, and the emphasis on the moral obligation of those in power to redress the experiences of suffering on the floor, functioned in two ironic ways. On the one hand, it ensured that domestic workers' narratives remained central considerations in policymaking—a maneuver that played a key role in the overall negotiations. At the same time, this collapsing of women's emotional stories with domestic work reproduced vulnerable gendered subjects—placed in visual and narrative forms as poor migrant women of color from the Global South, dependent on the state and transnational institutions to protect their rights. In essence, the IDWN played with this dialectic of dependency as a pragmatic feminist activist maneuver through the use of emotion. This affective rhetoric became a vital strength in domestic workers' strategy; however, it also rendered a benevolent state that holds the power to protect disempowered women. To a certain extent, domestic workers recognized and played on this evident mutual dependency. In doing so, they both reinforced the power of traditional male institutions and subverted it by performing as *well-behaved activists*.

To further exemplify their operation in this liminal space between upholding gendered conventions and challenging them, the domestic workers' narratives often unapologetically problematized the very gender roles they were upholding in their political strategy of appealing to emotion. Hester Stephens brought memories of her childhood experience to the public forum to show how women and girls suffer in the gendered family constructions that send them into domestic work at a very early age:

> While we are here, it just runs through my mind, where did I come from and where am I today. I mean if you really think about the domestic workers as a whole, because we don't have proper education, there was no time for us to go to school, because we had to leave school and to try to provide and help our fathers put bread on the table.

This positioning of emotion through shared historical suffering across diverse geographic divides widened the legitimacy that domestic workers brought to the negotiations. Their shared suffering recalls our earlier investments in establishing authenticity as a collective effort as much as an individual one, and subsequently allows for the individual narrations of experience as credible evidence for the larger argument of domestic workers' rights. As other social movements for justice reveal, the demonstration of bodily harm and collective pain strengthens the use of story as a symbolic political tactic for transnational activist networks. Within the ILO policymaking landscape, no other group could offer the depth and rhetorical influence of real-life stories as domestic workers themselves can. Their testimonials of prolonged hardship imposed serious challenges to decision makers' abilities to ignore these public statements of private trauma.

These narratives of domestic workers interwove emotional, psychological, and economic hardships to embody suffering in policymaking. Marissa Begonia, a Filipina domestic worker activist in the United Kingdom, exemplified this use of persuasion tactic when she wove her experience of mothering into her public ILO speech:

> Years ago I took a decision to leave my children behind. It is my responsibility to keep my children alive. Through domestic work, that is how my children grew up, it is how I educated my children. This has made me strong. It has given me the courage to continue.

Begonia's experience locates her as both a victim of the harsh requirements of physical separation central to domestic work and a strong advocate who became a labor activist as a result of her circumstances. This dual positioning of domestic workers as both victims of suffering and resourceful international activist survivors set up a persuasive standpoint throughout the policy negotiations. As they called on emotional appeals to recognize their history of suffering, domestic workers simultaneously demanded that they be taken seriously as central stakeholders in the policy process. U.S. activist Juana Flores captures this sufferer-survivor stance in an interview with the Latin news agency Agencia Efe during the 2011 conference:

> Honestly, there are those of us who have gone through those types of abuses, and we've remained silent. Or if we've talked, we've had the experience of what happens at those times when we say: "That's enough for me. No. Enough already. Today, today, it's enough. I'm going to risk it."

Flores's capacity to "risk it" placed her on the official U.S. labor delegation as one of the most prominent experts on domestic labor in the country.

This technique brought power and legitimacy to domestic workers as they took the public ILO stage. Yet this use of affective capital also links women to the emotional domain while reconstructing domestic labor as feminized through the "heartstrings" these stories intended to pull. Even though this technique worked as a distinct strategy in the case of this policy, these narratives of struggle also fed into a subtext of domestic workers in need of charity, which allows the ILO to come in as a paternalistic rescuer to the "millions of abused women out there in this field." Thus, this strategy teaches us that the trade-offs between "selling suffering" for a greater good and risking further essentialized constructions of "vulnerable" domestic workers is constantly negotiated in the larger purpose of a movement and its immediate goals. In this case, constructing vulnerability and suffering more often won over the risks of reconstructing traditional associations to race, national status, gender, class/caste, sexuality, and religion in the process of presenting a collective transnational domestic worker story.

By suturing the concept of authenticity and emotion into the political strategies of affective employment, it is possible to see that while engaging in acts that reproduce this notion of gendered pain as a method for seeking liberation, the very women who are being strategically employed as symbols of oppression are very much *active* agents in the formation of public policy. It is myopic to assume that the domestic workers' use of their experiences renders them different than "experts" in any other field. Authenticity as a theoretical framework is a useful tool for recognizing the critical importance that these personal narratives have in engaging and contributing to a larger social movement dedicated to the ending of prohibitive and oppressive working conditions for domestic workers worldwide. Emotion and affect, then, serve as the evidence to the ethos established by authenticity. This process implies realness, a realness that is understood both by the individual and those outside a given community, and simply by acknowledging these very real experiences (whether they wish to or not), policymakers are validating the gravity of the situation of domestic work globally. They are forced to react. They are reached at an emotional level, and physically and psychologically compelled to act from an affective level. Despite the gendered nature of emotion, domestic workers and their accompanying advocacy organizations are using affect as a way to promote their visibility in traditionally male-dominated and masculine-oriented spaces. Regardless of the outcome, there is no denying that the approach is inherently transgressive and subversive. Affect is power.

Conclusions

This policy victory marks a new form of economic and political agency for domestic workers. Formerly coded as the "failures" of development's reach, domestic work centered ILO dialogue as a symbolic recognition of the informal economy and migrant workers. At the heart of this historic moment, the transnational organization of domestic workers carved a new space for activists to take part in the formation of policy. Through the use of affective narratives, domestic workers became key agents in creating changes in global policy to protect the interests of their own group. By using a framework of "authenticity," domestic workers strategically held this global governance house accountable to the workers who would be most impacted by its policies. In fact, the use of affective claims held new ground within the UN policymaking system by challenging the power structure to listen to the voices of "actual workers" within the policymaking process. These narratives of "authenticity" operate as a framework of evidence and a key argument in liberation strategies at the policy level. We suggest that this strategy broke new ground through its particular persuasion. When those who are the sources of development discourse speak out, within the international institutions responsible for development policy, collective agency takes form in both altering the system and gaining ground in the realm of policy protections.

As the slogan that carried this global movement proclaimed, "women won't be free until domestic workers are free." The Convention 189 policy victory led domestic worker activists to contend, "Now we are on the map!" As a public relations tool, the recognition this movement gained through the ILO is unprecedented. Yet the "real work" of development is in the application of these protective policies at the state level. To date, 26 countries have ratified Convention 189, ensuring that its protections are mirrored in national laws. Domestic worker organizations continue to advocate for change at the national level through the use of affective strategies as a means to insist on empathy in policymaking. In the larger development scheme, we suggest that this embodied use of authenticity paints new landscapes of possibility to empower those impacted most directly by policy change. Juan Somavía, then director general of the ILO, proclaimed that unlike any other moment, when "domestic workers and diplomats" sat together to construct policy, the UN systems shifted to respond to "grassroots organizations." We suggest that the integration of grassroots representation in global governance inscribed a new language of affective authenticity. Beyond imagery of women in development—picture a pair of girls in rural Africa adorned with water buckets on their path walk—domestic workers embodied the *actual recipients* of the labor policies that would directly impact their sector. Rather than the affect of association to such essentialized images, as an organized transnational movement, domestic workers spoke to policymakers directly, claiming, "We know you have a heart." The real test of empowerment will be seen as these affective strategies influence the daily practices of private households, where women continue to face exploitation, abuse, and economic injustice. In the eyes of the domestic worker representatives with the transnational movement, now is the time to translate affect to economic action. As policy becomes practice, these "heart votes" will hold meaning only in the translation to economic empowerment and everyday agency— as domestic workers' compensation recognizes their place as "cogs in the wheel" of the global economy.

NOTES

1. For a comprehensive analysis of the state's participation in the export of domestic workers, see Christine Chin's (1998) account of the relationship between the Philippines and Malaysia in her formative book *In Service and Servitude: Foreign Female Domestic Workers and the Malaysian "Modernity" Project.*

2. Drawn from the Fourth Conference of the Sociology of Development Section in reference to earlier work. See Solari (2010).

3. For in-depth analyses of the institution of domestic labor and its embedded race, class, gender, and geographic divides, see Rollins (1985); Chaney, Garcia Castro, and

Smith (1989); Romero (1992); Gill (1994); Heyzer, Lycklama à Nijehold, and Weerakoon (1994); Bakan and Stasiulis (1997); Chin (1998); Anderson (2000); Gumburd (2000); Chang (2001); Hondagneu-Sotelo (2001); Parreñas (2001); Fish (2006); and Ally (2010).

4. See Cock (1989) for a full analysis of these terms under apartheid South Africa.

5. This insight is drawn from a personal conversation with Ai-Jen Poo at the 2011 ILC meetings in Geneva.

6. Marty Chen, founder of WIEGO, originally made this statement at the 2010 ILC meetings among domestic worker representatives.

7. Dan Gallin spearheaded this movement as the leader of the IUF. For a more comprehensive history of these leaders' roles, see Fish (2017).

8. Public speech at the ILC, 2010.

9. Cornelius Edy, Association of Writers and Professionals Conference, Tampa, Florida, March 2017.

10. For further reference, see "The Human Rights Based Approach to Development Cooperation: Towards a Common Understanding Among UN Agencies," HRBA Portal, http://hrbaportal.org/the-human-rights-based-approach-to-development-cooperation-towards-a-common-understanding-among-un-agencies.

11. CONLACTRAHO (Confederación Latinomericana y del Caribe Trabajadoras del Hogar) interview conducted by WIEGO.

12. Marcelina Bautista, personal interview conducted by Sofia Trevino, WIEGO.

13. Juan Somavía, statement to the ILC Committee on Domestic Workers, June 3, 2010.

14. ILC field notes, 2011.

References

Chapter 1

Adams, D. W. 1984. "Are the Arguments for Cheap Rural Credit Sound?" Pp. 65–77 in D. W. Adams, D. Graham and J. D. Von Perschke (Eds.), *Undermining Rural Development With Cheap Credit?* Boulder, CO: Westview Press.

Asian Pacific Infoserve. 2018. *International Directory of Women's Organizations.* Sydney, Australia: Asian Pacific Infoserve.

Bashaw, Zenebe. 2005. "Trajectories of Women, Environmental Degradation and Scarcity: Examining Access to and Conflicts Over Resources in Ethiopia." Pp. 67–86 in *Council for the Development of Social Science Research in Africa, Gender, Economies and Entitlements in Africa.* Dakar, Senegal: Council for the Development of Social Science Research in Africa.

Behrman, Julia, Ruth Meinzen-Dick and Agnes Quisumbing. 2012. "Gender Implications of Large Land Deals." *Journal of Peasant Studies* 39:49–79.

Blumberg, Rae Lesser. 2016a. "Magic Potion/Poison Potion: The Impact of Women's Economic Empowerment vs. Disempowerment for Development in a Globalized World." Pp. 153–189 in Gregory Hooks (Ed.), *Handbook of the Sociology of Development.* Berkeley, CA: University of California Press.

_____. 2016b. "A Walk on the Wild Side of Gender, War and Development in Afghanistan and Northern Uganda." Pp. 134–154 in Rae Lesser Blumberg and Samuel Cohn (Eds.), *Development in Crisis: Threats to Human Well-Being in the Global South and Global North.*

_____. 2015. "'Dry' vs. 'Wet' Development and Women in Three World Regions." *Sociology of Development* 1(1):91–122.

_____. 2009. "Mothers of Invention? The Myth-Breaking History and Planetary Promise of Women's Key Roles in Subsistence Technology." Pp. 227–259 in Yair Amichai-Hamburger (Ed.), *Techno-Well: Impact of Technology on Psychological Well-Being.* London, UK: Cambridge University Press.

_____. 2008. "Gender, Environment and Environmental Ethics: Exploring the Critical Role of Economic Power in Thailand, Ecuador and Malawi." Presented at the UNESCO Conference on Ethics of Energy Technologies: Ethical Views of Nature, held in conjunction with the World Congress of Philosophy, Seoul, South Korea, August.

_____. 2004a. "Doing Well by Doing Good: Promoting Increased Income for Men and Women Through Conservation of Malawi's Natural Resources." Blantyre, Malawi and Bethesda, MD: USAID/DAI COMPASS II Community-Based Natural Resources Management Project.

_____. 2004b. "Extending Lenski's Schema to Hold Up Both Halves of the Sky: A Theory-Guided Way of Conceptualizing Agrarian Societies That Illuminates a Puzzle About Gender Stratification." *Sociological Theory* 22(2):278–291.

_____. 2002. "Fast, Cheap and Valid? Using Rapid Appraisal for Gender Research: A Guide and Some Cases From the Global South." Paper presented at the meetings of the International Sociological Association, Brisbane, Australia, July.

_____. 2001a. "Risky Business: What Happens to Gender Equality and Women's Rights in Post-Conflict Societies? Insights from NGOs in El Salvador." *International Journal of Politics, Culture and Society* 15:161–173.

_____. 2001b. "'We Are Family': Gender, Microenterprise, Family Work and Well-Being in Ecuador and the Dominican Republic—With Comparative Data From Guatemala, Swaziland and Guinea-Bissau." *History of the Family: An International Quarterly* 6:271–299.

_____. 1998. "Enterprise and Gender Among Six Ethnic Groups in Guinea-Bissau." Bissau, Guinea-Bissau and Washington, DC: USAID/Labat-Anderson Trade & Investment Project: Technical Report.

_____. 1991a. "Gender and Microenterprise in Ecuador." Pp. 61–91 in John Magill et al. (Ed.), *Ecuador Micro-Enterprise Sector Assessment: Key Characteristics of the Micro-Enterprise Sector.* Washington, DC: GEMINI. GEMINI Technical Report No. 12.

_____. 1991b. "Introduction: The 'Triple Overlap' of Gender Stratification, Economy and the Family." Pp. 7–34 in Rae Lesser Blumberg (Ed.), *Gender, Family, and Economy: The Triple Overlap.* Newbury Park, CA: SAGE.

_____. 1989. *Making the Case for the Gender Variable: Women and the Wealth and Well-Being of Nations.* Washington, DC: Agency for International Development, Office of Women in Development. PN-ABC-454.

_____. 1988. "Income Under Female vs. Male Control: Hypotheses From a Theory of Gender Stratification and Data From the Third World." *Journal of Family Issues* 9(1):51–84.

_____. 1987. "The Half-Hidden Economic Roles of Rural Nigerian Women and National Development." Washington, DC: Research monograph prepared for the World Bank, October.

_____. 1984. "A General Theory of Gender Stratification." *Sociological Theory* 2:23–101.

_____. 1978. *Stratification: Socioeconomic and Sexual Stratification*. Dubuque, IA: Wm. C. Brown.

Blumberg, Rae Lesser, Kara Dewhurst, and Soham Sen. 2013a. *Gender-Inclusive Nutrition Activities in South Asia, Volume II: Lessons From Global Experiences*. Washington, DC: World Bank. http://documents.worldbank.org/curated/en/2013/04/18123770/gender-inclusive-nutrition-activities-south-asia-vol-2-2-lessons-global-experience

_____. 2013b. "Gender-Inclusive Nutrition Interventions: Lessons From Global Experiences for South Asia." *Dissemination Note No. 4, South Asia Social Development Unit*. Washington, DC: World Bank.

Blumberg, Rae Lesser, and Joyce Malaba. 2016. *Women Cross-Border Traders in Southern Africa*. Washington, DC: USAID Southern Africa Trade Hub/AECOM International Development.

Blumstein, Phillip, and Pepper Schwartz. 1991. "Money and Ideology: Their Impact on Power and the Division of Household Labor." Pp. 245–260 in Rae Lesser Blumberg (Ed.), *Gender, Family, and Economy: The Triple Overlap*. Newbury Park, CA: SAGE.

Boserup, Ester. 1970. *Woman's Role in Economic Development*. New York, NY: St. Martin's Press.

Brown, Judith. 1975. "Iroquois Women: An Ethnohistoric Note." Pp. 235–251 in *Toward an Anthropology of Women*, edited by Rayna R. Reiter. New York: Monthly Review Press.

_____. 1970. "Economic Organization and the Position of Women Among the Iroquois." *Ethnohistory* 17:151–167.

Caldwell, John. 1982. *Theory of Fertility Decline*. London, UK: Academic Press.

Caprioli, Mary. 2005. "Primed for Violence: The Role of Gender Inequality in Predicting Internal Conflict." *International Studies Quarterly* 49:161–178.

_____. 2000. "Gendered Conflict." *Journal of Peace Research* 37(1):51–68.

Cavalluzzo, Kenneth, Linda Cavalluzzo and John Wolken. 2002. "Competition, Small Business Financing and Discrimination: Evidence From a New Survey." *Journal of Business* 75:641–679.

Central Intelligence Agency. 2018. *The World Factbook: Singapore*. https://www.cia.gov/library/publications/the-world-factbook/geos/sn.html

Chapkis, Wendy, and Cynthia Enloe. 1983. *Of Common Cloth: Women in the Global Textile Industry*. Amsterdam, the Netherlands: Transnational Institute.

Cochrane, Willard. 1979. *Development of American Agriculture: Historical Analysis*. St. Paul, MN: University of Minnesota Press.

Cohn, Samuel. 1999. *Race, Gender and Discrimination at Work*. New York, NY: Routledge.

_____. 1985. *Process of Occupational Sex-Typing: Feminization of Clerical Labor in Great Britain*. Philadelphia, PA: Temple.

Das Gupta, Monica, John Bongaarts, and John Cleland. 2011. "Population, Poverty and Sustainable Development: A Review of the Evidence." Policy Research Working Paper 5719. Washington, DC: World Bank, Development Research Group, June.

Denison, Edward F. 1962. *The Sources of Economic Growth and the Alternatives Before Us*. New York, NY: Committee for Economic Development.

Diamond, Jared. 1997. *Guns, Germs, and Steel*. New York, NY: Norton.

Doering, Laura, and Christopher Liu. Forthcoming. "From the Ground Up: Gender, Self-Employment, and Space in a Colombian Housing Project." To appear in *Sociology of Development*.

Economist, The. 2006. "Forget China, India and the Internet: Economic Growth Is Driven by Women." (Special Report: The Importance of Sex) April 12:16.

Eisler, Riane. 1987. *The Chalice and the Blade*. New York, NY: Harper & Row.

Elondou-Enyegye, Parfait M., and Anne Emmanuele Calves. 2006. "Till Marriage Do Us Part: Education and Remittances From Married Women in Africa." *Comparative Education Review* 50(1):1–20.

El-Sahabary, Nagat. 2003. "Women and the Nursing Profession in Saudi Arabia." Pp. 71–83 in Suha Sabbagh (Ed.), *Arab Women: Between Defiance and Restraint*. New York, NY: Olive Branch.

Engels, Friedrich. 1884. *The Origin of the Family, Private Property and the State*. Hottingen-Zürich, Switzerland.

England, Paula. 1992. *Comparable Worth: Theories and Evidence*. New York, NY: de Gruyter.

Fishlow, Albert. 1966. "Levels of Nineteenth Century American Investment in Education." *Journal of Economic History* 16(December):418–436.

Folbre, Nancy. 1988. "Patriarchal Social Formations in Zimbabwe." Pp. 61–80 in Sharon Stichter and Jane Parpart (Eds.), *Patriarchy and Class: African Women in the Home and Workforce*. Boulder, CO: Westview Press.

Gamble, William K., Rae Lesser Blumberg, Vernon C. Johnson, and Ned S. Raun. 1988. *Three Nigerian Universities and Their Role in Agricultural Development*. Washington, DC: U.S. Agency for International Development A.I.D. Project Impact Evaluation Report No. 66.

Gimbutas, Marija. 1982. *The Goddesses and Gods of Old Europe, 7000–3500 BC*. Berkeley, CA: University of California Press.

_____. 1980. *The Early Civilization of Europe*. University of California at Los Angeles: Monograph for Indo-European Studies 131.

Goldin, Claudia. 1986. "The Female Labor Force and American Economic Growth." In Stanley Engerman and Robert Gallman., *Long Term Factors in American Economic Growth*. Chicago, IL: University of Chicago Press.

Grace, Jo. 2005. "Who Owns the Farm? Rural Women's Access to Land and Livestock." Working paper. Kabul: Afghanistan Research and Evaluation Unit.

Hammam, Mona. 1986. "Capitalist Development, Family Division of Labor and Migration in the Middle East." Pp. 158–173 in Eleanor Leacock and Helen Safa (Eds.), *Women's Work*. South Hadley, MA: Bergen and Gervey.

Henn, Jeanne. 1995. "Women in the Rural Economy: Past, Present and Future." Pp. 1–18 in Margaret Jean Hay and Sharon Stichter (Eds.), *African Women South of the Sahara*. New York, NY: Longmans.

Heyzer, Noeleen. 1986. *Working Women in Southeast Asia: Development, Subordination and Emancipation*. Philadelphia, PA: Open University.

Hijab, Nadia. 2003. "Women and Work in the Arab World." Pp. 43–53 in Suha Sabbagh (Ed.), *Arab Women: Between Defiance and Restraint*. New York, NY: Olive Branch.

Hill, Polly. 1969. "Hidden Trade in Hausaland." *Man* 4(3):392–409.

Hirschman, Albert. 1970. *Exit, Voice and Loyalty: Responses to Decline in Firms, Organizations and States*. Cambridge, MA: Harvard.

Howe, Gary. 1985. *The Present and Potential Contribution of Women to Economic Development: Elements of Methodology and Analysis of the Yemen Arab Republic*. Washington, DC: Report prepared for the Agency for International Development, Office of Women in Development.

Huber, Joan. 1991. "A Theory of Family, Economy, and Gender." Pp. 35–51 in Rae Lesser Blumberg (Ed.), *Gender, Family, and Economy: The Triple Overlap*. Newbury Park, CA: SAGE.

Hublin, Jacques-Jean, et al. 2017. "New Fossils From Jebel Irhoud, Morocco, and the Pan-African Origin of *Homo Sapiens*." *Nature* 546(June):289–306.

Hudson, Valerie M., Mary Caprioli, Bonnie Ballif-Spanvill, Rose McDermott and Chad F. Emmett. 2009. "The Security of Women and the Security of States." *International Security* 33(3):7–45.

Hurstwic. n.d. *The Role of Women in Viking Society*. Hurstwic LLC/William R. Short, Southborough, MA. http://hurstwic.org/history/articles/society/text/women.htm

Inter-Parliamentary Union. 2018. "Women in National Parliaments: Situation as of 1st June 2018." www.ipu.org/wmn-e/classif.htm

Ireson, Carol J. 1996. *Field, Forest, and Family: Women's Work and Power in Rural Laos*. Boulder, CO: Westview Press.

Ishengoma, Christine. 2005. "Accessibility of Resources by Gender: Case of Morogoro Region in Tanzania." Pp. 53–66 in Council for the Development of Social Science Research in Africa, *Gender, Economies and Entitlements in Africa*. Dakar, Senegal: Council for the Development of Social Science Research in Africa.

Jesch, Judith. 2011. "Viking Women." BBC. http://www.bbc.co.uk/history/ancient/vikings/women_01.shtml

_____. 1991. *Women in the Viking Age*. Suffolk, UK: Boydell.

Kandiyoti, Deniz. 1988. "Bargaining With Patriarchy." *Gender and Society* 2(3):274–290.

Kapteijns, Lidwien. 1993. "Women and the Crisis of Communal Identity: Cultural Construction of Gender in Somali History." *Working Papers in African Studies* 173, African Studies Center, Boston University.

Kazeno, Sumiko. 2004. *Role of Women in Singapore: Collaboration and Conflict Between Capitalism and Asian Values*. Nagoya, Japan: Privately Published.

Kessler-Harris, Alice. 1993. *Women Have Always Worked: An Historical Overview*. New York, NY: Feminist Press.

Khan, Ahmed. 2012. "Women & Gender in Afghanistan." Kabul: Civil-Military Fusion Centre (CFC) /Afghanistan Resource Desk.

Lee, Jean, Kathleen Campbell, and Audrey Chia. 1999. *Three Paradoxes: Working Women in Singapore*. Singapore, Malaysia: Association for Action and Research.

Lee, Richard B. 1969. "!Kung Bushmen Subsistence: An Input-Output Analysis." In Andrew P. Vayda (Ed.), *Environment and Cultural Behavior*. Garden City, NY: Natural History Press.

_____. 1968. "What Hunters Do for a Living, or How to Make Out on Scarce Resources." Pp. 30–48 in Richard B. Lee and Irven DeVore (Eds.), *Man the Hunter*. Chicago, IL: Aldine.

Lenski, Gerhard E. 1966. *Power and Privilege: A Theory of Social Stratification*. New York, NY: McGraw-Hill.

Levinson, David. 1989. *Violence in Cross-Cultural Perspective*. Newbury Park, CA: SAGE.

Lewis, Barbara. 1984. "Impact of Development Policies on Women." Pp. 170–187 in Margaret Jean Hay and Sharon Stichter (Eds.), *African Women South of the Sahara*. New York, NY: Longmans.

Leyser, Henrietta. 2002. *Medieval Women: Social History of Women in England 450–1500*. New York, NY: Weidenfeld and Nicholson.

MacGaffey, Janet. 1988. "Evading Male Control: Women in the Second Economy in Zaire." Pp. 161–176 in Sharon Stichter and Jane Parpart (Eds.), *Patriarchy and Class: African Women in the Home and Workforce*. Boulder, CO: Westview Press.

Magill, John, et al. 1991. *Ecuador Micro-Enterprise Sector Assessment: Key Characteristics of the Micro-Enterprise Sector*. Washington, DC: GEMINI. GEMINI Technical Report No. 12.

Mann, Michael. 1986. *Sources of Social Power Volume I: A History of Power From the Beginning to AD 1760*. New York, NY: Cambridge University Press.

McCarthy, John, and Mayer Zald. 1977. "Resource Mobilization and Social Movements: A Partial Theory." *American Journal of Sociology* 82:1212–1241.

Melish, Jacob. 2015. "Power of Wives: Managing Money and Men in the Family Businesses of Old Regime Paris." Pp. 77–90 in Daryl Haftner and Nina Kusher (Eds.), *Women and Work in Eighteenth Century France*. Baton Rouge: Louisiana State Press.

Microcredit Summit Campaign. 2015. *Mapping Pathways Out of Poverty: The State of the Microcredit Summit Campaign Report 2015*. Washington, DC: Microcredit Summit Campaign.

Mierswa, Emily. 2017. "Women Traders of the Viking Age: An Analysis of Grave Goods." Department of Anthropology, University of New Hampshire, May. https://cola.unh.edu/anthropology/women-traders-viking

Mies, Maria. 1982. *The Lace Makers of Narsapur*. New York, NY: Springer.

Mijid, Naranchimeg. 2014. "Why Are Female Small Business Owners in the United States Less Likely to Apply for Bank Loans Than Their Male Counterparts?" *Journal of Small Business and Entrepreneurship* 27:229–249.

Moghadam, Valentine. 2010. *Modernizing Women: Gender and Social Change in the Middle East*. Boulder, CO: Lynne Reiner.

Ogena, Steven, and Alexander Popov. 2015. "Gender Bias and Credit Access." *European Central Bank Working Paper* 1822.

Ogilvie, Sheilagh. 2003. *Bitter Living: Women, Markets and Social Capital in Early Modern Germany*. New York, NY: Oxford University Press.

Orser, Barbara, Allan Riding and Kathryn Manley. 2006. "Women Entrepreneurs and Financial Capital." *Entrepreneurship Theory and Practice* 30:643–665.

Pfeffer, Jeffrey. 1981. *Power in Organizations*. New York, NY: Pitman.

Pinchbeck, Ivy. 1981. *Women Workers and the Industrial Revolution 1750–1850*. London, UK: Virago.

Pruitt, Sarah. 2016. "What Was Life Like for Women in the Viking Age?" History/History Stories. https://www.history.com/news/what-was-life-like-for-women-in-the-viking-age

Roth, Louise. 2004. "Bringing Clients Back In: Homophily Preferences and Inequality on Wall Street." *Sociological Quarterly* 45:613–635.

Schlegel, Alice. 1972. *Male Dominance and Female Autonomy: Domestic Authority in Matrilineal Societies*. New Haven, CT: HRAF Press.

Schweitzer, Mary M. 1980. "World War II and Female Labor Force Participation Rates." *Journal of Economic History* 1(1):89–95.

Seguino, Stephanie. 2000. "Gender Inequality and Economic Growth: a Cross-Country Analysis." *World Development* 28:1211–1230.

Sethuraman, Kavita, and Nata Duvvury. 2007. "The Nexus of Gender Discrimination With Malnutrition: An Introduction." *Economic & Political Weekly* November 3:49, 51–53.

Stalsberg, A. 2001. "Visible Women Made Invisible: Interpreting Varangian Women in Old Russia." Pp. 65–79 in Benitta Arnold and Nancy L. Wicker (Eds.), *Gender and the Archaeology of Death.* Walnut Creek, CA: AltaMira Press.

Stig Sorensen, Marie Louise. 2009. "Gender, Material Culture and Identity in the Viking Diaspora." *Viking and Medieval Scandinavia* 5:253–269.

Tilly, Charles. 1988. *From Mobilization to Revolution.* New York, NY: Random House.

Treas, Judith. 1991. "The Common Pot or Separate Purses? A Transaction Cost Interpretation." Pp. 211–224 in Rae Lesser Blumberg (Ed.), *Gender, Family, and Economy: The Triple Overlap.* Newbury Park, CA: SAGE.

UNIFEM. 2006. *Uncounted and Discounted: A Secondary Data Research Project on Violence Against Women in Afghanistan.* Kabul: UNIFEM Afghanistan.

United Nations Development Programme. 2017. *Gender Equality Strategy 2014–2017.* New York, NY: United Nations.

———. 2015. *Human Development Report 2015: Work for Human Development.* New York, NY: United Nations.

Viterna, Jocelyn. 2013. *Women in War: Micro-Processes of Mobilization in El Salvador.* New York, NY: Oxford University Press.

Walsh, Mary Roth. 1977. "Doctors Wanted: No Women Need Apply." *Sexual Barriers in the Medical Profession 1835–1975.* New Haven, CT: Yale University Press.

Ward, Jennifer. 2006. *Women in England in the Middle Ages.* London, UK: Bloomsbury.

White, Joyce. 1992a. Interviews at American Anthropological Association meeting, San Francisco, CA, November.

———. 1992b. "Prehistoric Roots for Heterarchy in Early Southeast Asian States." Paper prepared for the meetings of the Society for American Archeology, Pittsburgh, PA.

———. 1990. "The Environmental Context for Early Rice Cultivation in Thailand." Proceedings of the Circum-Pacific Prehistory Conference. Seattle: Washington State University.

———. 1988. "Early East Asian Metallurgy: The Southern Tradition." In Robert Maddin (Ed.), *The Beginning of the Use of Metals and Alloys.* Cambridge, MA: MIT Press.

———. 1982. "The Peaceful Bronze Age." In Joyce White (Ed.), *Discovery of a Lost Bronze Age: Ban Chiang.* Philadelphia: University of Pennsylvania, University Museum.

World Bank. 2018. *Unrealized Potential: The High Cost of Gender Inequality in Earnings.* Wodon, Quentin and Benedicte de la Briere. Washington, DC: World Bank.

———. 2015. *Gender Inequality, Poverty Reduction and Inclusive Growth.* Washington, DC: World Bank.

Chapter 3

Alsema, A. 2017. *Colombia Military Assassinated More Civilians Under Uribe Than FARC Did in 30 Years,* January 5. http://colombiareports.com/colombia-military-murdered-civilians-uribe-farc-30-years/

Alzate, M. 2007. "The Sexual and Reproductive Rights of Internally Displaced Women: The Embodiment of Colombia's Crisis." *Disasters* 31(1):131–148.

Amnesty International. 2004. *Colombia: Scarred Bodies, Hidden Crimes—Sexual Violence Against Women in the Armed Conflict,* October 13. http://web.amnesty.org/library/print/ENGAMR230402004?open&of=ENG-Col

Araghi, F. 2009. "The Invisible Hand and the Visible Foot: Peasants, Dispossession and Globalization." Pp. 111–147 in A. H. Akram-Lodhi and C. Kay (Eds.), *Peasants and Globalization: Political Economy, Rural Transformation and the Agrarian Question.* London, UK: Routledge.

Baird, A. 2012. "The Violent Gang and the Construction of Masculinity Amongst Socially Excluded Young Men." *Safer Communities* 11(4):179–190.

Barr, H. 2017. *Time to Get Serious About Child Marriage in Latin America.* Human Rights Watch, July 13. https://www.hrw.org/news/2017/07/13/time-get-serious-about-child-marriage-latin-america

BBC Mundo. 2016. "País por País: El Mapa que Muestra las Trágicas Cifras de los Feminicidios en América Latina," *Redacción BBC Mundo,* November 17. http://www.bbc.com/mundo/noticias-america-latina-37828573

Bello, W. 2009. *The Food Wars.* London, UK: Verso.

Bott, S., A. Guedes, M. Goodwin, and J. Mendoza. 2012. *Violence Against Women in Latin America and the Caribbean: A Comparative Analysis of Population-Based Data From 12 Countries.* Washington, DC: Pan American Health Organization.

Bourdieu, P. 2002. *Masculine Domination.* Malden, MA: Polity Press.

Briceno-Leon, R., and V. Zubillaga. 2002. "Violence and Globalization in Latin America." *Current Sociology* 50(1):19–57.

Bueno-Hansen, P. 2010. "Feminicidio: Making the Most of an 'Empowered Term.'" Pp. 290–301 in R. Fregoso and C. Bejarano (Eds.), *Terrorizing Women: Feminicide in the Americas.* Durham, NC: Duke University Press.

Buvinic, M., A. Morrison, and M. Shifter. 1999. *Violence in Latin America and the Caribbean: A Framework for Action.* Sustainable Development Department Inter-American Development Bank.

Carpenter, R. C. 2006. "Recognizing Gender-Based Violence Against Civilian Men and Boys in Conflict Situations." *Security Dialogue* 37(1).

Cockburn, C. 2004. "The Continuum of Violence: A Gender Perspective on War and Peace." Pp. 24–44 in W. Giles and J. Hyndman (Eds.), *Sites of Violence: Gender and Conflict Zones.* Los Angeles: University of California Press.

CODHES (Consultoría para los Derechos Humanos y el Desplazamiento). 2017. *Violencia Sexual Contra Niños, Niñas y Adolescentes en Colombia.* Retrieved from https://issuu.com/codhes/docs/doc_20codhes_2033 _20violencia_sexual

Cohn, C. 2012. "Women and Wars: Contested Histories, Uncertain Futures." Pp. 1–24 in C. Cohn (Ed.), *Women and Wars: Contested Histories, Uncertain Futures.* Cambridge, UK: Polity Press.

De Angelis, M. 2001. "Marx and Primitive Accumulation: The Continuous Character of Capital's Enclosures." *The Commoner,* September. http://www.thecommoner.org

De Medeiros, L. S. 2007. "Social Movements and the Experience of Market-Led Agrarian Reform in Brazil." *Third World Quarterly* 28(8):1501–1518.

El Colombiano. 2017. "Soldado Violó a Una Bebé de 4 Meses de Edad en el Meta," Abril 24. http://www.elcolombiano.com/colombia/soldado-abuso-de-bebe-en-el-meta-YN6384562

El Espectador. 2015. "Y a la Pobreza, ¿Cómo le Irá en 2015?" March 24. http://www.elespectador.com/noticias/economia/y-pobreza-le-ira-2015-articulo-551251

El Tiempo. 2017. "EE. UU. Condena a Hernán Giraldo a 16 Años de Prisión por Narcotráfico," March 17. http://www.eltiempo.com/justicia/conflicto-y-narcotrafico/condena-contra-paramilitar-hernan-giraldo-63948

_____. 2016. "El 61,7 por Ciento de Colombianos Solo Tiene Para lo Necesario," March 3. http://www.eltiempo.com/economia/finanzas-personales/cifras-de-la-pobreza-en-colombia/16526302

Enloe, C. 2007. *Globalization and Militarism: Feminists Make the Link.* Lanham, MD: Rowman and Littlefield.

_____. 2000. *Bananas, Beaches and Bases: Making Feminist Sense of International Politics.* Berkeley: University of California Press.

Federici, S. 2004. *Caliban and the Witch: Women, the Body and Primitive Accumulation.* Chico, CA: AK Press.

Fisk, J. 1991. "Colonization and the Decline of Women's Status: The Tsimshian Case." *Feminist Studies* 17(3):509–535.

Fox Piven, F., and R. A. Cloward. 1993. "Relief, Labour, and Civil Disorder: An Overview." Pp. 3–42 in *Regulating the Poor: the Functions of Public Welfare.* New York, NY: Random House.

Fregoso, R. L., and C. Bejarano. 2010. "Introduction: A Cartography of Feminicide in the Américas." Pp. 1–41 in R. L. Fregoso and C. Bejarano (Eds.), *Terrorizing Women: Feminicide in the Américas.* Durham, NC: Duke University Press.

Garcia-Moreno, C., A. Guedes, and W. Knerr. 2012. *Understanding and Addressing Violence Against Women: Sexual Violence.* WHO. http://apps.who.int/iris/bitstream/10665/77434/1/WHO_RHR_12.37_eng.pdf

Giles, W., and J. Hyndman. 2004. "New Directions for Feminist Research and Politics." Pp. 301–315 in W. Giles and J. Hyndman (Eds.), *Sites of Violence: Gender and Conflict Zones.* Los Angeles: University of California Press.

GRAIN. 2014. *Hungry for Land: Small Farmers Feed the World With Less Than a Quarter of All Farmland,* May. https://www.grain.org/article/entries/4929-hungry-for-land-small-farmers-feed-the-world-with-less-than-a-quarter-of-all-farmland#sdfootnote6sym

Guatemala Human Rights Commission. 2017. *For Women's Right to Live.* https://www.ghrc-usa.org/Programs/ForWomensRighttoLive/FAQs.htm

Henao, M. 2015. "Powerful Photos Capture Impact of 'Narco Aesthetic' in Medellín, Colombia," *Huffington Post,* June 19. https://www.huffingtonpost.com/manuela-henao/powerful-photos-capture-impact-of-narco-aesthetic-in-medellin-colombia_b_7623998.html

Holmes, J. S., S. A. Gutierrez de Pineres, and K. M. Curtin. 2008. *Guns, Drugs, and Development in Colombia.* Austin: University of Texas Press.

Hristov, J. 2014. *Paramilitarism and Neoliberalism: Violent Systems of Capital Accumulation in Colombia and Beyond.* London, UK: Pluto Press.

_____. 2009. *Blood and Capital: The Paramilitarization of Colombia.* Athens: Ohio University Press.

ICFTU. 2005. *Colombia: Unions Appeal to Europe and ILO*, February 25. http://www.icftu.org/displaydocument .asp?Index=991221674&Language=EN

Kay, C. 2001. "Reflections on Rural Violence in Latin America." *Third World Quarterly* 22(5):741–775.

Kerssen, T. M. 2013. *Grabbing Power: The New Struggles for Land, Food and Democracy in Honduras.* Oakland, CA: Food First Books.

Lagarde, M. 2010. "Preface: Feminist Keys for Understanding Feminicide." Pp. xi–xxiv in R. Fregoso and C. Bejarano (Eds.), *Terrorizing Women: Feminicide in the Americas.* Durham, NC: Duke University Press.

Lewontin, R. C. 2000. "The Maturing of Capitalist Agriculture: Farmer as Proletarian." Pp. 93–106 in F. Magdoff, J. B. Foster, and F. H. Buttel (Eds.), *Hungry for Profit.* New York, NY: Monthly Review Press.

Li, T. M. 2011. "Centering Labor in the Land Grab Debate." *Journal of Peasant Studies* 38(2):281–298.

———. 2009. "Exit From Agriculture: A Step Forward or a Step Backward for the Rural Poor?" *Journal of Peasant Studies* 36(3):629–636.

MacKinnon, C. 1989. *Towards a Feminist Theory of the State.* Cambridge, MA: Harvard University Press.

Marx, K. 1867/1990. *Capital I.* London, UK: Penguin Books.

McMichael, P. 2006. "Reframing Development: Global Peasant Movements and the New Agrarian Question." *Canadian Journal of Development Studies/Revue Canadienne d'études du Dévelopement* 27(4):471–483.

McMichael, P., and M. Schneider. 2011. "Food Security Politics and the Millennium Development Goals." *Third World Quarterly* 32(1):119–139.

McNally, D. 2002. *Another World Is Possible.* Winnipeg: Arbeiter Ring.

Medina, C. 1990. *Autodefensas, Paramilitares y Narcotrafico en Colombia: Origen, Desarrollo y Consolidación. El Caso de Puerto Boyaca.* Bogotá: Editorial Documentos Periodisticos.

Meertens, D. 2010. "Forced Displacement and Women's Security in Colombia." *Disasters* 34(S2):147–164.

Mohanty, C., M. Pratt, and R. Riley. 2009. "Introduction: Feminism and U.S. Wars—Mapping the Ground." Pp. 1–16 in R. Riley et al. (Eds.), *Feminism and War: Confronting US Imperialism.* London, UK: Zed Books.

Muñoz, C. B. 2007. "The Tortilla Behemoth: Sexualized Despotism and Women's Resistance in a Transnational Mexican Tortilla Factory." Pp. 127–139 in A. L. Cabezas, E. Reese, and M. Waller (Eds.), *The Wages of Empire: Neoliberal Policies, Repression, and Women's Poverty.* Boulder, CO: Paradigm.

Norwegian Refugee Council. 2018. *Global Report on Internal Displacement 2018.* http://www.internal-displace ment.org/global-report/grid2018/downloads/2018-GRID.pdf

O'Connor, D., and J. P. Bohorquez. 2010. "Neoliberal Transformation in Colombia's Goldfields: Development Strategy or Capitalist Imperialism?" *Labour, Capital, and Society* 43(2):86–118.

Olivera, M., and V. Furio. 2006. "Violencia Femicida: Violence Against Women and Mexico's Structural Crisis." *Latin American Perspectives* 33(2):104–114.

Paley, D. 2014. *Drug War Capitalism.* Oakland, CA: AK Press.

Pearce, J. 2010. "Perverse State Formation and Securitized Democracy in Latin America." *Democratization* 17(2):286–306.

———. 1990. *Colombia: Inside the Labyrinth.* London, UK: Latin America Bureau.

Perez-Rincon, M. A. 2006. "Colombian International Trade from a Physical Perspective: Towards an Ecological 'Prebisch Thesis.'" *Ecological Economics* 59(4):519–529.

Prensa Latina. 2012. "Las Alarmantes Cifras de la Pobreza Extrema en Colombia," March 5. http://matrizur.org/ index.php?option=com_content&view=article&id=20 335:las-alarman es-cifras-de-la-pobreza-extrema-en-co lombia&catid=37:patria-grande&Itemid=56

Preston, V., and M. Wong. 2004. "Geographies of Violence: Women and Conflict in Ghana." Pp. 152–169 in W. Giles and J. Hyndman (Eds.), *Sites of Violence: Gender and Conflict Zones.* Los Angeles: University of California Press.

Programa Somos Defensores. 2017. *Informe Enero: Junio 2017 Sistemas de Informacion Sobre Agresiones Contra Defensores y Defensoras de DDHH en Colombia.* https://www .somosdefensores.org/index.php/en/publicaciones/ informes-siaddhh/146-aguzate

Raven-Roberts, A. 2012. "Women and the Political Economy of War." Pp. 36–53 in C. Cohn (Ed.), *Women and Wars: Contested Histories, Uncertain Futures.* Cambridge, UK: Polity.

Richani, N. 2010. "Colombia: Predatory State and Rentier Political Economy." *Labour, Capital and Society* 43(2):120–141.

Ruiz, G. A., and P. A. Valencia. 2016. "Expresiones de la Violencia Basada en Genero en las Afectaciones por Minas Antipersonal en Colombia." *Revista de Dialectologia y Tradiciones Populares* 72(2):535–557.

Ruta Pacifica de las Mujeres. 2013. *La Verdad de las Mujeres: Victimas del Conflicto Armado en Colombia.* https://www.rutapacifica.org.co/descargue-los-libros/208-la-verdad-de-las-mujeres-victi mas-del-conflicto-armado-en-colombia

Salzinger, L. 2003. *Genders in Production.* Berkeley: University of California Press.

Sanin, F., and F. Franco. 2017. "Organizing Women for Combat: The Experience of the FARC in the Colombia War." *Journal of Agrarian Change* 17:770–778.

Scheper-Hughes, N., and P. Bourgois (Eds.). 2004. *Violence in War and Peace: An Anthology.* Oxford, UK: Blackwell.

Semana. 2017a. "Día de la Mujer: La Violencia Silenciosa Contra las que Hacen Política," March 8. http://www.semana.com/nacion/articulo/dia-de-la-mujer–violencia-politica-contra-la-muj er-en-colombia/517847

_____. 2017b. "El Aberrado Sexual que es Capo del Clan del Golfo," May 19. http://www.semana.com/nacion/articulo/alias-gavilan-el-aberrado-sexual-que-es-capo-del-clan-del-golfo/525711

_____. 2017c. "El Depredador Sexual de Uraba," May 15. http://www.semana.com/nacion/articulo/clan-del-golfo-el-depredador-sexual-de-uraba/525264

_____. 2017d. "Las Esclavas Xexuales de Otoniel." http://www.semana.com/nacion/multimedia/sexo-con-menores-de-edad-tiene-otoniel-lider-de-los-urabenos/420895-3

_____. 2013. "Cifras de la Violencia Contra la Mujer," November 25. http://www.semana.com/nacion/articulo/cifras-de-la-violencia-contra-la-mujer-en-colombia/366030-3

_____. 2012. "Violencia en Cifras." http://www.semana.com/wf_multimedia.aspx?idmlt=93

_____. 2009. "Los Usurpados del Choco," March 14. http://www.semana.com/noticias-nacion/usurpados-del-choco/121717.aspx

Shipley, T. 2017. *Ottawa and Empire: Canada and the Military Coup in Honduras.* Toronto: Between the Lines.

Simms, G. P. 1992. "Black Women of the Diaspora." Pp. 113–134 in R. Bourgeault, D. Broad, L. Brown, and L. Foster (Eds.), *Five Centuries of Imperialism and Resistance, Socialist Studies* (Vol. 8, 1492–1992). Winnipeg/Halifax: Society for Socialist Studies/Fernwood.

Sistema de Informacion Sobre Agresiones Contra Defensores de Derechos Humanos. 2016a. "El Cambio: Informe Anual SIADDHH 2015 Sobre Agresiones Contra Defensores de Derechos Humanos." http://www.comitepermanente.org/index.php/escuela-de-ddhh/informes/968-el-cambio-informe-anual-siaddhh-2015-sobre-agresiones-contra-defensores-de-derechos-humanos-en-colombia

_____. 2016b. "Este Es el Fin? Informe Enero Junio 2016." https://coeuropa.org.co/este-es-el-fin-informe-semestral-2016-i-del-programa-somos-defensores/

Solano, L. 2015. *Under Siege: Peaceful Resistance to Tahoe Resources and Militarization in Guatemala.* International Platform against Impunity in Central America. https://miningwatch.ca/sites/default/files/solano-underseigereport2015-11-10.pdf

Stevenson, M. 1992. "Columbus and the War on the Indigenous People." In R. Bourgeault, D. Broad, L. Brown, & L. Foster (Eds.), *Five Centuries of Imperialism and Resistance, Socialist Studies* (Vol. 8, 1492–1992). Winnipeg/Halifax: Society for Socialist Studies/Fernwood.

Stokes, D. 2005. *America's Other War: Terrorizing Colombia.* London, UK: Zed Books.

The Guardian. 2017. "Families of Victims of Colombia's Paramilitaries Get Their Day in US Court," March 2. https://www.theguardian.com/world/2017/mar/02/colombia-paramilitaries-victims-us-court

Thomson, F. 2011. "The Agrarian Question and Violence in Colombia: Conflict and Development." *Journal of Agrarian Change* 11(3):321–356.

Tovar-Restrepo, M., and C. Irazábal. 2014. *Latin American Perspectives* 194(41):39–58.

UN Office on Drugs and Crime. 2014. *Global Study on Homicide 2013.* https://www.unodc.org/documents/gsh/pdfs/2014_GLOBAL_HOMICIDE_BOOK_web.pdf

USAID. 2017. *Fact Sheet: Improving Women's Land Rights in Colombia.* https://land-links.org/document/fact-sheet-improving-womens-land-rights-colombia/

_____. 2010. *USAID Country Profile: Property Rights and Resource Governance Colombia.* http://www.globalprotectioncluster.org/_assets/files/aors/housng_land_property/Colombia%20HLP/Country_Profile_Land_Tenure_Colombia_2010_EN.pdf

Verdad Abierta. 2014. "Miles de Niños Abusados Sexualmente por Actores Armados," March 12. http://www.verdadabierta.com/violencia-sexual/5285-miles-de-ninos-abusados-sexualmente-por-actores-armados

_____. 2010a. "12 Porciento de los BACRIM son Desmovilizados," January 8. https://verdadabierta.com/12-por-ciento-de-las-bacrim-son-desmovilizados-policia-nacional/

_____. 2010b. "La Guerra y las 500 Mil Mujeres que Fueron Victimas de Violencia Sexual," December 16. http://www.verdadabierta.com/index.php?option=com _content&id=2929

_____. 2008. "Entre el Poder Político y el Abuso Sexual en San Onofre," October 23. http://www.verdadabierta .com/justicia-y-paz/versiones/499-entre-el-poder-polit ico-y-el-abuso-sexual-en-san-onofre

Viveros, M. 2001. "Contemporary Latin American Perspectives on Masculinity." *Men & Masculinities* 3(3):237–260.

Webster, P. C. 2012. "Colombian Gold-Mining Village Fights to Stay Put," *National Catholic Reporter*, March 2. http://ncronline.org/news/global/colombian-gold-mining-village-fights-stay-put

Wilson, T. D. 2014. "Violence Against Women in Latin America." *Latin American Perspectives* 41(1):3–18.

Wirtz, A., et al. 2014. "Gender-Based Violence in Conflict and Displacement: Qualitative Findings From Displaced Women in Colombia." *Conflict and Health* 8(10):1–14.

World Health Organization. 2014. *Global Status Report on Violence Prevention*. http://www.who.int/ violence_injury_prevention/violence/status_report /2014/en/

Yagoub, M. 2016. "Why Does Latin America Have the World's Highest Female Murder Rates?" *Open Democracy*, February 16. https://www.opendemocracy.net/democra ciaabierta/mimi-yagoub/why-does-latin-america-have-worlds-highest-female-murder-rates

Zamora, R. 2013. "About Santos' Cruel Economic Policies." FARC Peace Process. http://farc-epeace.org/index.php/ what-you-should-know/item/151-about-santos'-cruel -economic-policies.html

Chapter 4

Achenbach, Joel, and Dan Keating. 2017. "New Research Identifies a 'Sea of Despair' Among White, Working-Class Americans," *Washington Post*, March 23, https:// www.washingtonpost.com/national/health-science/ new-research-identifies-a-sea-of-despair-among-white-working-class-americans/2017/03/22/c777ab6e-0da6-11e7-9b0d-d27c98455440_story.html?noredirect=on&utm _term=.4af11adabaf1

Alberti, Amalia. 1986. *Gender, Ethnicity and Resource Control in the Andean Highlands of Ecuador*. PhD Dissertation, Stanford University.

Andronikov, A. V., A. Van Hoesel, I. E. Andronikova, and W. Z. Hoek. 2016. "Trace Element Distribution and Implications in Sediments Across the Allerod-Younger Dryas in the Netherlands and Belgium." *Geografiska Annaler: Series A, Physical Geography* 98:325–345, doi:10.1111/geoa.12140

_____. 2015. "Geochemical Evidence of the Presence of Volcanic and Meteoritic Materials in Late Pleistocene Lake Sediments of Lithuania." *Quaternary International* 386:1–12.

_____. 2014. "In Search for Fingerprints of an Extraterrestrial Event: Trace Element Characteristics of Sediments From the Lake Medvedevskoye (Karelian Isthmus, Russia)." *Doklady Earth Sciences* 457:819–823.

Ardrey, Robert. 1966. *The Territorial Imperative*. New York, NY: Atheneum.

_____. 1961. *African Genesis*. New York, NY: Atheneum.

Balarezo, Susana. 1992. Interviews concerning her research among the Quichua and Saraguro Indians of Ecuador; conducted in Quito and Cuenca, Ecuador, in August and September.

BBC/Ali, Faisal Muhammed. 2006. "Visitors Flock to 'Sati' Village." http://news.bbc.co.uk/2/hi/south_asia/ 52788989.stm

Birdsell, Joseph B. 1968. "Some Predictions for the Pleistocene Based on Equilibrium Systems Among Recent Hunter-Gatherers." Pp. 229–240 in Richard B. Lee and Irven DeVore (Eds.), *Man the Hunter*. Chicago, IL: Aldine.

Blanc-Szanton, Christina, Ana María Viveros-Long, and Nongluck Supanchainat. 1989. "The Northeast Rainfed Agricultural Development Project in Thailand." In Paula O. Goddard, *Women in Development: AID's Experience, 1973–1985, Vol. II—Case Studies*. Washington, DC: U.S. Agency for International Development (USAID).

Blumberg, Rae Lesser. 2016a. "Magic Potion/Poison Potion: The Impact of Women's Economic Empowerment vs. Disempowerment for Development in a Globalized World." Pp. 153–189 in Gregory Hooks (Ed.), *Handbook of the Sociology of Development*. Berkeley: University of California Press.

_____. 2016b. "A Walk on the Wild Side of Gender, War and Development in Afghanistan and Northern Uganda." Pp. 134–154 in Rae Lesser Blumberg and Samuel Cohn (Eds.), *Development in Crisis: Threats to Human Well-Being in the Global South and Global North*. London and New York: Routledge.

_____. 2015. "'Dry' Versus 'Wet' Development and Women in Three World Regions." *Sociology of Development* 1(1):91–122.

_____. 2011a. "Afghanistan National Development Program (ANDP) Support Project: Final Project Evaluation." Kabul: United Nations Development Program Afghanistan.

_____. 2011b. "Afghanistan National Development Strategy (ANDS) Project: Final Project Evaluation." Kabul: United Nations Development Program Afghanistan.

_____. 2009a. "Mothers of Invention? The Myth-Breaking History and Planetary Promise of Women's Key Roles in Subsistence Technology." Pp. 227–259 in Yair Amichai-Hamburger (Ed.), *Techno-Well: Impact of Technology on Psychological Well-Being*. London: Cambridge University Press.

_____. 2009b. "'The World-Historical Defeat of the Female Sex'? A Theory-Guided Revision of Engels: Five Scenarios for the Rise of Gender Inequality and One Where It Didn't Quite Happen." Colloquium presentation, University of Virginia, November.

_____. 2004. "Extending Lenski's Schema to Hold Up Both Halves of the Sky: A Theory-Guided Way of Conceptualizing Agrarian Societies That Illuminates a Puzzle About Gender Stratification." *Sociological Theory* 22(2):278–291.

_____. 2002a. "Fast, Cheap and Valid? Using Rapid Appraisal for Gender Research: A Guide and Some Cases From the Global South." Paper presented at the meetings of the International Sociological Association, Brisbane, Australia, July.

_____. 2002b. "A 'Natural Experiment' for Gender Stratification Theory? The Lao of Northeast Thailand and Laos." Paper presented at the meetings of the American Sociological Association, Chicago, August.

_____. 2001a. "Adventures Along the Gender Frontier: Encounters With Gender Equality in Ecuador and Thailand and Glimpses in Guinea-Bissau and China." Proceedings of the International Conference on Gender and Equity Issues: Humanistic Considerations for the 21st Century. Bangkok: Srinakharinwirot University Press.

_____. 2001b. "The Created Biology of Gender Stratification." Department of Sociology, University of Virginia. Unpublished paper.

_____. 1991. "Introduction: The 'Triple Overlap' of Gender Stratification, Economy and the Family." Pp. 7–34 in Rae Lesser Blumberg (Ed.), *Gender, Family and Economy: The Triple Overlap*. Newbury Park, CA: SAGE.

_____. 1988. "Income Under Female vs. Male Control: Hypotheses From a Theory of Gender Stratification and Data From the Third World." *Journal of Family Issues* 9(1):51–84.

_____. 1984. "A General Theory of Gender Stratification." *Sociological Theory* 2:23–101.

_____. 1978. *Stratification: Socioeconomic and Sexual Inequality*. Dubuque, IA. Wm. C. Brown.

Blumberg, Rae Lesser, and Dale Colyer. 1990. "Social Institutions, Gender and Rural Living Conditions." Pp. 247–266 in Morris D. Whitaker and Dale Colyer, *Agriculture and Economic Survival: The Role of Agriculture in Ecuador's Development*. Boulder, CO: Westview Press.

Blumberg, Rae Lesser, Kara Dewhurst, and Soham Sen. 2013a. *Gender-Inclusive Nutrition Activities in South Asia, Volume II: Lessons From Global Experiences*. Washington, DC: World Bank.

_____. 2013b. "Gender-Inclusive Nutrition Interventions: Lessons From Global Experiences for South Asia." Dissemination Note No. 4, South Asia Social Development Unit. Washington, DC: World Bank.

Blumberg, Rae Lesser, Alexandra Maryanski, and Kirstin Ralston-Coley. 2002. "The Voyage of the Beagle II: A Journey Across the Continuum of the 'Created Biology' of Gender Stratification." Paper presented at the annual meetings of the Southern Sociological Society, New Orleans, April.

Boserup, Ester. 1970. *Woman's Role in Economic Development*. New York, NY: St. Martin's.

_____. 1966. *The Conditions for Agricultural Growth*. London, UK: Allen & Unwin.

Boulding, Elise. 1976. *The Underside of History*. Boulder, CO: Westview Press.

Brown, Judith. 1975. "Iroquois Women: An Ethnohistoric Note." Pp. 235–251 in Rayna R. Reiter (Ed.), *Toward an Anthropology of Women*. New York, NY: Monthly Review Press.

_____. 1970. "Economic Organization and the Position of Women Among the Iroquois." *Ethnohistory* 17:151–167.

Caldwell, John. 1982. *The Theory of Fertility Decline*. London, UK: Academic Press.

Caprioli, Mary. 2005. "Primed for Violence: The Role of Gender Inequality in Predicting Internal Conflict." *International Studies Quarterly* 49:161–178.

_____. 2000. "Gendered Conflict." *Journal of Peace Research* 37(1):51–68.

Case, Anne, and Angus Deaton. 2017. "Mortality and Morbidity in the 21st Century." *Brookings Pap Econ Act* (Spring):397–476.

_____. 2015. "Rising Morbidity and Mortality in Midlife Among White Non-Hispanic Americans in the 21st Century." *Proceedings of the National Academy of Sciences* 112(49):15078–15083.

Chagnon, Napoleon. 1968. *Yanomamo: The Fierce People*. New York, NY: Holt, Rinehart, Winston.

Childe, V. Gordon. 1942. *What Happened in History*. London, UK: Penguin Books.

Clignet, Remi. 1970. *Many Wives, Many Powers*. Evanston, IL: Northwestern University Press.

Collins, Randall. 1971. "A Conflict Theory of Sexual Stratification." *Social Problems* 19:3–21.

Cordero, Juan. 1992. Interviews on prehistoric Ecuadorian metallurgy, war, ecology, and social and gender stratification, conducted in Cuenca, Ecuador, Universidad de Azuay, in August and September.

Cuberes, David, and Marc Teignier. 2015. "How Costly Are Labor Gender Gaps? Estimates for the Balkans and Turkey." Policy Research Working Paper 7319. Washington, DC: World Bank.

_____. 2012. "Gender Gaps in the Labor Market and Aggregate Productivity." Economic Research Paper 2012017, Department of Economics, University of Sheffield, June.

Das, Sonali, Sonali Jain-Chandra, Kalpana Kochlar, and Naresh Kumar. 2015. "Women Workers in India: Why So Few Among So Many?" Washington, DC: International Monetary Fund, Asia and Pacific Department.

Das Gupta, Monica, John Bongaarts, and John Cleland. 2011. *Population, Poverty and Sustainable Development: A Review of the Evidence*. Washington, DC: World Bank Working Paper.

De Waal, Frans. 2005. *Our Inner Ape*. New York, NY: Penguin/Riverhead Books.

Diamond, Jared. 1997. *Guns, Germs and Steel*. New York, NY: Norton.

Draper, Patricia. 1975. "!Kung Women: Contrasts in Sexual Egalitarianism in Foraging and Sedentary Contexts." Pp. 77–109 in Rayna R. Reiter (Ed.), *Toward an Anthropology of Women*. New York, NY: Monthly Review Press.

Dyble, M., G. D. Salali, N. Chaudhary, A. Page, D. Smith, J. Thompson, L. Vinicius, R. Mace, A. B. Migliano. 2015. "Sex Equality Can Explain the Unique Social Structure of Hunter-Gatherer Bands." *Science* 348(6236):796–798.

Echeverría, Jose A. and Christina Muñoz G. 1988. *Maiz: Regalo de los Dioses*. Instituto Otavaleño de Antropología/Foncultura, Colección Curinan.

Elondou-Enyegye, Parfait M., and Anne Emmanuele Calves. 2006. "Till Marriage Do Us Part: Education and Remittances From Married Women in Africa." *Comparative Education Review* 50(1):1–20.

Firestone, R. B., et al. 2007. "Evidence for an Extraterrestrial Impact 12,900 Years Ago That Contributed to the Megafaunal Extinctions and the Younger Dryas Cooling." *Proceedings of the National Academy of Sciences USA* 1-4:16016–16021.

Forbes. 2017. "Ancient Stone Tablet Found: Reveals Comet Impact Sparking the Rise of Civilization." April 30. https://www.forbes.com/sites/trevornace/2017/04/30/ancient-stone-tablet-found-reveals-comet

Fried, Morton H. 1967. *The Evolution of Political Society*. New York, NY: Random House.

Gallin, Rita S. 1995. "Engendered Production in Rural Taiwan: Ideological Bonding of the Public and Private." Pp. 113–134 in Rae Lesser Blumberg et al. (Eds.), *Engendering Wealth and Well-Being: Empowerment for Global Change*. Boulder, CO: Westview Press.

Gartelmann, Karl Dieter. 1986. *Digging Up Prehistory: The Archeology of Ecuador*. Quito, Ecuador: Ediciones Libri Mundi.

Gimbutas, Marija. 1982. *The Goddesses and Gods of Old Europe, 7000–3500 BC*. Berkeley: University of California Press.

_____. 1980. *The Early Civilization of Europe*. University of California at Los Angeles: Monograph for Indo-European Studies 131.

Gough, Kathleen. 1971. "The Origin of the Family." *Journal of Marriage and the Family* 33(4):750–771.

Griffith, Brian. 2001. *The Gardens of Their Dreams: Desertification and Culture in World History*. London, UK: Zed Books.

Guiso, Luigi, Ferdinando Monte, Paola Sapienza, and Luigi Zingales. 2008. "Culture, Gender and Math." *Science* 320(5880):1164–1165.

Hamilton, Sarah. 1998. *The Two-Headed Household: Gender and Rural Development in the Ecuadorean Andes*. Boulder, CO: Westview Press.

Hess, Peter. 1988. *Population Growth and Socio-Economic Progress in Less Developed Countries: Determinants of Fertility Transition*. New York, NY: Praeger.

Hill, Polly. 1969. "Hidden Trade in Hausaland." *Man* 4(3):392–409.

Hoang, Kimberly Kay. 2015. *Dealing in Desire: Asian Ascendancy, Western Decline and the Hidden Currencies of Global Sex Work.* Oakland: University of California Press.

Hobhouse, L. T., G. C. Wheeler, and M. Ginsberg. 1915. *The Material Culture and Social Institutions of the Simpler Peoples.* London, UK: Chapman and Hall.

Hoffman, Moshe, Uri Gneezy, and John A. List. 2011. "Nurture Affects Gender Differences in Spatial Abilities." *Proceedings of the National Academy of Sciences* 108(36):14786–14788.

Hublin, Jacques-Jean, et al. 2017. "New Fossils From Jebel Irhoud, Morocco and the Pan-African Origin of *Homo sapiens.*" *Nature* 546 (June): 289–306.

Ireson, Carol. 1996. *Field, Forest and Family: Women's Work and Power in Rural Laos.* Boulder, CO: Westview Press.

Kaberry, Phyllis. 1939. *Aboriginal Women.* London, UK: George Routledge.

Kandiyoti, Deniz. 1988. "Bargaining With Patriarchy." *Gender & Society* 2(3):274–290.

Kessler, Glenn and Michelle Ye Hee Lee. 2017. "Addressing Some of the Hyper-Exaggeration in Trump's Inaugural Address." *Washington Post: The Fact Checker*: A17, January 21.

Kim, Jim Young. 2014. "The True Cost of Discrimination: Blocking Productive People From Full Participation Only Hurts Countries." *Washington Post*, Feb. 28:A15.

Kolata, Gina Bari. 1974. "!Kung Hunter-Gatherers: Feminism, Diet and Birth Control." *Science* 185:932–934.

Lee, Richard B. 1969. "!Kung Bushmen Subsistence: An Input-Output Analysis." In Andrew P. Vayda (Ed.), *Environment and Cultural Behavior.* Garden City, NY: Natural History Press.

———. 1968. "What Hunters Do for a Living, or, How to Make Out on Scarce Resources." Pp. 30–48 in Richard B. Lee and Irven DeVore (Eds.), *Man the Hunter.* Chicago, IL: Aldine.

Lenski, Gerhard E. 1966. *Power and Privilege.* New York, NY: McGraw-Hill.

Levinson, David. 1989. *Violence in Cross-Cultural Perspective.* Newbury Park, CA: SAGE.

Lorenz, Konrad. 1966. *On Aggression.* New York, NY: Harcourt, Brace and World.

Ma, Huan. 1433/1995. *The Overall Survey of the Ocean's Shores.* Cited in National Commission on Women's Affairs. *Women of Thailand.* Bangkok, Thailand: National Commission on Women's Affairs.

Mann, Michael. 1986. *Sources of Social Power Volume I: A History of Power From the Beginning to 1760.* New York, NY: Cambridge University Press.

Marshall, Lorna. 1965. "The !Kung Bushmen of the Kalahari Desert." In J. Gibbs (Ed.), *Peoples of Africa.* New York, NY: Holt, Rinehart, Winston.

Martin, M. Kay, and Barbara Voorhies. 1975. *Female of the Species.* New York, NY: Columbia University Press.

Meggitt, M. J. 1970. "Male-Female Relationships in the Highlands of New Guinea." In T. Harding and W. Wallace (Eds.), *Cultures of the Pacific.* New York, NY: Free Press.

Meyers, J. T. 1971. "The Origin of Agriculture: An Evaluation of Three Hypotheses." Pp. 101–121 in Stuart Struever (Ed.), *Prehistoric Agriculture.* Garden City, NY: Natural History Press.

Moore, Christopher R., et al. 2017. "Widespread Platinum Anomaly Documented at the Younger Dryas Onset in North American Sedimentary Sequences." *Scientific Reports* 7 [Nature] Article #44031 doi.10.1038/srep44031

Morris, Desmond. 1969. *The Human Zoo.* New York, NY: McGraw-Hill.

———. 1968. *The Naked Ape.* New York, NY: Dell.

Murphy, Robert F., and Yolanda Murphy. 1974. *Women of the Forest.* New York, NY: Columbia University Press.

Nation. 2011. "Thai Women Lead World in High Business Positions." May 8:1.

Netherly, Patricia. 1992. Interviews about prehistoric Ecuadorian metallurgy, war, ecology, and social and gender stratification. Quito, Ecuador, August.

Nolan, Patrick, and Gerhard E. Lenski. 2015. *Human Societies*, 12th ed. London and New York: Oxford University Press.

OECD. 2012. PISA 2012 Data File. Interactive Selection, Variable STO4Q01, Gender. http://www.oecd/org/pisa

O'Kelly, Charlotte G., and Larry S. Carney. 1987. *Women & Men in Society: Cross-Cultural Perspectives on Gender Stratification*, 2nd ed. Belmont, CA: Wadsworth.

Palmer, Ingrid, Sukaesinee Subhadhira, and Wilaiwat Grisanaputi. 1983. "The Northeast Rainfed Development Project in Thailand: A Baseline Survey of Women's

Roles and Household Resource Allocation for a Farming Systems Approach." New York, NY: Population Council—Case Studies of the Impact of Large-Scale Development Projects on Women, Study No. 3.

Petaev, M., S. Huang, S. B. Jacobsen, and A. Zindler. 2013. "Large Pt Anomaly in the Greenland Ice Core Points to a Cataclysm at the Onset of Younger Dryas." *Proceedings of the National Academy of Science USA* 110:12917–12920.

Poeschel, Veronica. 1988. *La Mujer Salasaca*, 2nd ed. Quito, Ecuador: Ediciones Abya Yala.

Sahlins, Marshall D. 1968. "Notes on the Original Affluent Society." Pp. 85–88 in Richard B. Lee and Irven DeVore (Eds.), *Man the Hunter*. Chicago, IL: Aldine.

Saito, Katrine, and Jean Weidemann. 1990. "Agricultural Extension for Women Farmers in Africa." Washington, DC: World Bank. Women in Development Working Paper.

Scott, Robert E. 2015. "The Manufacturing Footprint and the Importance of U.S. Manufacturing Jobs." Washington, DC: Economic Policy Institute.

Sethuraman, Kavita, and Nata Duvvury. 2007. "The Nexus of Gender Discrimination With Malnutrition: An Introduction." *Economic & Political Weekly* (November 3):49, 51–53.

Silverblatt, Irene. 1980. "'The Universe Has Turned Inside Out . . . There Is No Justice for Us Here': Andean Women Under Spanish Rule." In Eleanor Leacock and Mona Etienne (Eds.), *Women and Colonialism*. New York, NY: Praeger.

Slocum, Sally. 1975. "Woman the Gatherer: Male Bias in Anthropology." Pp. 36–50 in Rayna R. Reiter (Ed.), *Toward an Anthropology of Women*. New York, NY: Monthly Review Press.

Stolen, Kristi Anne. 1987. *A Media Voz: Relaciones de Género en la Sierra Ecuatoriana*. Quito: Abya Yala.

Strathern, Marilyn. 1972. *Women in Between: Female Roles in a Male World: Mount Hagen, New Guinea*. London, UK: Academic Press.

Sweatman, Martin, and Dimitrios Tsikritsis. 2017. "Decoding Gobekli Tepe With Archeoastronomy: What Does the Fox Say?" *Mediterranean Archaeology and Archaeometry* 17(1):233–250.

Telegraph. 2017. "Ancient Stone Carvings Confirm How Comet Struck Earth in 10,950 BC, Sparking the Rise of Civilisations." www.telegraph.co.uk/science/2017/04/21/ancient-stone-carvings-confirm-comet-struck

Tiger, Lionel. 1969. *Men in Groups*. New Brunswick and London: Transaction Press.

Tiger, Lionel, and Robin Fox. 1972. *The Imperial Animal*. New Brunswick and London: Transaction Press.

Tipprapa, Somjit. 1993. (Director, Community-Based Integrated Rural Development Bureau, Population and Community Development Association (PDA)). Interview about PDA data on declining fertility in Thailand, especially the Northeast. Bangkok, January.

Treas, Judith. 1991. "The Common Pot or Separate Purses? A Transaction Cost Interpretation." Pp. 211–224 in Rae Lesser Blumberg (Ed.), *Gender, Family and Economy: The Triple Overlap*. Newbury Park, CA: SAGE.

Turnbull, Colin. 1961. *The Forest People*. New York, NY: Simon & Schuster.

Washington Post. 2017. "Opioids Are Sapping Our Life Expectancy." A12, December 2017.

Washington Post/Christopher Ingraham. 2018. "Fentanyl Use Drove Drug Overdose Deaths to a Record High in 2017, CDC Estimates." A17, Wonkblog, August 15.

White, Joyce. 1992a. Interviews at American Anthropological Association meeting, San Francisco, CA, November.

_____. 1992b. "Prehistoric Roots for Heterarchy in Early Southeast Asian States." Paper prepared for the meetings of the Society for American Archeology, Pittsburgh, PA.

_____. 1990. "The Environmental Context for Early Rice Cultivation in Thailand." Proceedings of the Circum-Pacific Prehistory Conference. Seattle, WA: Washington State University.

_____. 1988. "Early East Asian Metallurgy: The Southern Tradition." In Robert Maddin (Ed.), *The Beginning of the Use of Metals and Alloys*. Cambridge, MA: MIT Press.

_____. 1982. "The Peaceful Bronze Age." In Joyce White (Ed.), *Discovery of a Lost Bronze Age: Ban Chiang*. Philadelphia: University of Pennsylvania, University Museum.

Whiting, John M. 1968. "Pleistocene Family Planning." Pp. 248–249 in Richard B. Lee and Irven DeVore (Eds.), *Man the Hunter*. Chicago, IL: Aldine.

Wilbert, Johannes. 1963. "Indios de la Región Orinoco Ventuari." Caracas: Fundación La Salle de Ciencias Naturales.

Wolbach, Wendy S., et al. 2018a. "Extraordinary Biomass-Burning Episode and Impact Winter Triggered by the Younger Dryas Cosmic Impact ~12,800 Years Ago. 1. Ice Cores and Glaciers." *Journal of Geology* 000 DOI:10.1086/695703.

_____. 2018b. "Extraordinary Biomass-Burning Episode and Impact Winter Triggered by the Younger Dryas Cosmic Impact ~12,800 Years Ago. 2. Lake, Marine and Terrestrial Sediments." *Journal of Geology* 000 DOI:10.1086/695704.

Wolf, Diane. 1991. "Female Autonomy, the Family and Industrialization in Java." Pp. 128–148 in Rae Lesser Blumberg (Ed.), *Gender, Family and Economy: The Triple Overlap*. Newbury Park, CA: SAGE.

World Bank. 2018. "Labor Force Participation Rate, Female (% of Female Population Ages 15+) (modeled ILO estimate). World Development Indicators. http://data.worldbank.org/indicator/SL.TLF.CACT.FE.ZS

_____. 2012a. *Opening Doors: Gender Equality and Development in the Middle East and North Africa*. MENA Development Report. Washington, DC: World Bank.

_____. 2012b. *World Development Report: Gender Equality and Development*. Washington, DC: World Bank.

Wu, Y., M. Sharma, M. A. LeCompte, M. Demitroff, and J. Landis. 2013. "Origin and Provenance of Spherules and Magnetic Grains at the Younger Dryas Boundary." *Proceedings of the National Academy of Sciences USA* 110(38):E3557–3566.

Chapter 5

Abrahamian, Ervand. 1982. *Iran Between Two Revolutions*. Cambridge, UK: Cambridge University Press.

Afkhami, Mahnaz. 1984. "The Future in the Past: The 'Prerevolutionary' Women's Movement in Iran." Pp. 330–338 in Robin Morgan (Ed.), *Sisterhood is Global: The International Women's Movement Anthology*. New York, NY: Feminist Press.

Amuzegar, Jahangir. 1992. "The Iranian Economy Before and After the Revolution." *Middle East Journal* 46(3):413–425.

Association of Tunisian Women for Research on Development (AFTURD). 2010. «Les Aides Ménagères á Temps Complet: Violences Et Non Droits. Présentation Des Résultats De L'étude Dans Le Cadre Du Projet 'Répercussions économiques Des Violences Sur Les Jeunes Filles Dans Le Grand Tunis, 2008–2010.» (Elaborée par Samira Ayed et Abdessatar Sahbani.) Tunis: AFTURD Espace Tanassof.

Ayadi, Mohamed, and Wided Mattoussi. 2014. *Scoping of the Tunisian Economy*. Working Paper No. 17. Helsinki: Brookings Institution.

Azad, Shahrzad [V. M. Moghadam]. 1981. "Workers' and Peasants' Councils in Iran." *Monthly Review*.

Bahramitash, Roksana, and Shahla Kazemipour. 2008. "Economy, Informal Sector." Pp. 156–159 in Mehran Kamrava and Manochehr Dorraj (Eds.), *Iran Today: An Encyclopedia of Life in the Islamic Republic*, Vol. 1. Westport, CT: Greenwood Press.

Bayat, Asef. 1987. *Workers and Revolution in Iran: A Third World Experience of Workers' Control*. London, UK: Zed Press.

Beblawi, Hazem, and Giacomo Luciano (Eds.). 1987. *The Rentier State in the Arab World*. London, UK: Croom Helm.

Ben Romdhane, Mahmoud. 2006. "Social Policy and Development in Tunisia Since Independence: A Political Perspective." Pp. 31–77 in Massoud Karshenas and Valentine M. Moghadam (Eds.), *Social Policy in the Middle East: Economic, Political, and Gender Dynamics*. New York and Geneva: Palgrave Macmillan and UNRISD.

Ben Salem, Lilia. 2010. "Tunisia." Pp. 487–516 in Sanja Kelly and Julia Breslin (Eds.), *Women's Rights in the Middle East and North Africa: Progress amid Resistance*. Washington and Lanham: Freedom House and Rowman and Littlefield.

Benstead, Lindsey. 2016. "Explaining Egalitarian Attitudes: The Role of Interests and Exposure." Pp. 119–146 in Marwa Shalaby and Valentine M. Moghadam (Eds.), *Women's Empowerment After the Arab Spring*. London, UK: Palgrave Macmillan.

Bernard-Maugiron, Nathalie. 2015. *Impact of Legal Frameworks on Women's Economic Empowerment*. Issues paper for seminar on Supporting Women as Economic Actors in the Middle East and North Africa Region, June 15. Paris: Programme MENA-OCDE l'Investissement, Paris, Organization for Economic Cooperation and Development.

Blaydes, Lisa, and Drew Linzer. 2008. "The Political Economy of Women's Support for Fundamentalist Islam." *World Politics* 60(4):576–609.

Blumberg, Rae Lesser. 2016. "Magic Potion/Poison Potion: The Impact of Women's Economic Empowerment or Disempowerment for Development in a Globalized World." Pp. 153–189 in Gregory Hooks (Ed.), *Handbook of the Sociology of Development*. Berkeley: University of California Press.

_____. 1995. "Introduction: Engendering Wealth and Well-Being in an Era of Economic Transformation." Pp. 1–14 in Blumberg et al. (Eds.), *Engendering Wealth and Well-Being: Empowerment for Global Change*. Boulder CO: Westview Press.

_____. 1989. *Making the Case for the Gender Variable*. Washington DC: USAID.

_____. 1984. "A General Theory of Gender Stratification." *Sociological Theory* 2:23–101.

Boli, John. 2005. "Contemporary Developments in World Culture." *International Journal of Contemporary Sociology* 46(5–6):383–404.

Boroujerdi, Mehrzad. 2014. "Iran." Pp. 478–506 in Ellen Lust (Ed.), *The Middle East*, 13th ed. Los Angeles, CA: SAGE.

Boughzala, Mongi. 2013. "Youth Unemployment and Economic Transition in Tunisia." Washington, DC: Brookings Institution, Global Economy and Development Working Papers No. 57 (January).

Chafetz, Janet Saltzman. 1990. *Gender Equality: An Integrated Theory of Stability and Change.* Thousand Oaks, CA: SAGE.

Chamlou, Nadereh, S. Muzi, and H. Ahmed. 2016. "The Determinants of Female Labor Force Participation in the Middle East and North Africa Region: The Role of Education and Social Norms in Amman, Cairo, and Sana'a." Pp. 323–350 in Nadereh Chamlou and Massoud Karshenas (Eds.), *Women, Work and Welfare in the Middle East and North Africa.* London, UK: Imperial College Press.

Charfi, Mohamed. 2015. *Mon Combat Pour les Lumieres.* Tunis: Elyzad.

Chase-Dunn, Christopher. 1998. *Global Formation: Structures of the World-Economy.* Lanham, MD: Rowman and Littlefield.

Chekouri, Sidi Mohammed, and Abderrahim Chibi. 2016. *Algeria and the Natural Resource Curse: Oil Abundance and Economic Growth.* Working Paper No. 990. Cairo: Economic Research Forum.

Collier, Paul, and Anke Hoeffler. 2004. "Greed and Grievance in Civil War." *Oxford Economic Papers* 56(4):563–595.

CREDIF. 2017. "La Violence à L'Econtre Des Femmes, Une Réalité Alarmants en Attendant La Loi IntéGrale." *La Revue du CREDIF.* Tunis: Revue semestrielle éditée par le Centre de Recherches, d'études, de Documentation et d'Information sur la Femme, no. 50 (Mars).

Ebadi, Shirin. 2016. *Until We Are Free: My Fight for Human Rights in Iran.* New York, NY: Random House.

The Economist. 2015. "Arab Bureaucracies: Aiwa (yes) Minister" (Nov. 14):47.

Egel, Daniel, and Djavad Salehi-Isfahani. 2010. "Youth Transitions to Employment and Marriage in Iran: Evidence From the School-to-Work Transition Survey." *Middle East Development Journal* 2(1). https://doi.org/10.1142/S1793812010000198

Esteva, Gustavo, Salvatore Babones, and Philipp Babcicky. 2013. *The Future of Development: A Radical Manifesto.* Bristol, UK: Policy Press.

Fakih, Ali, and Pascal L. Ghazalian. 2015. "Female Employment in MENA's Manufacturing Sector: The Implications of Firm-Related and National Factors." Cairo: ERF Working Paper 917 (May).

Financial Times. 1990. "Survey: Tunisia." July 27.

Glendon, Mary Ann. 1989. *The Transformation of Family Law.* Chicago, IL: University of Chicago Press.

Gribaa, Boutheina. 2008–2009. *Mapping of the Situation of Women's Participation in Politics in Algeria, Morocco, and Tunisia.* Tunis: CAWTAR.

Hakimian, Hassan. 2011. "Iran's Free Trade Zones: Back Doors to the International Economy?" *Iranian Studies* 44(6):851–874.

Haouas, Ilham, and Mahmoud Yagoubi. 2008. *The Flexible Forms of Employment and Working Conditions: Empirical Investigation from Tunisia.* Working Paper No. 407. Cairo: ERF.

Harik, Iliya. 1992. "Privatization and Development in Tunisia." Pp. 210–231 in Iliya Harik and Denis Sullivan (Eds.), *Privatization and Liberalization in the Middle East.* Bloomington: Indiana University Press.

Harris, Kevan. 2013. "The Rise of the Subcontractor State: Politics of Pseudo-Privatization in the Islamic Republic of Iran." *International Journal of Middle East Studies* 45:45–70.

Hatem, Mervat. 1994. "Privatization and the Demise of State Feminism in Egypt 1977–1990." Pp. 40–60 in Pamela Sparr (Ed.), *Mortgaging Women's Lives: Feminist Critiques of Structural Adjustment.* London, UK: Zed Books.

Ilkkaracan, Ipek. 2012. "Why So Few Women in the Labor Market in Turkey?" *Feminist Economics* 18 (1): 1-37.

Islamic Republic of Iran. 2016 [1395]. *Natayej-e Amar-Geeri Neerooye Kar, Tabestan 1395 [Results of the Labor Force Survey, Summer 1395].* Tehran: National Planning and Budget Organization, Statistical Center of Iran.

Iversen, Torben, and Frances Rosenbluth. 2008. "Work and Power: The Connection Between Female Labor Force Participation and Female Political Representation." *Annual Review of Political Science* 11:479–495.

_____. 2006. "The Political Economy of Gender: Explaining Cross-National Variation in the Gender Division of Labor and the Gender Voting Gap." *American Journal of Political Science* 50(1):1–19.

Jaud, Mélise, and Caroline Freund. 2015. *Champions Wanted: Promoting Exports in the Middle East and North*

Africa. Washington, DC: World Bank Group, Directions in Development.

Karshenas, Massoud. 2001. "Economic Liberalization, Competitiveness, and Women's Employment in the Middle East and North Africa." Pp. 147–169 in Djavad Salehi-Esfahani (Ed.), *Labour and Human Capital in the Middle East*. Reading, UK: Ithaca Press.

_____. 1990. *Oil, State and Industrialization in Iran*. Cambridge, UK: Cambridge University Press.

Karshenas, Massoud, and Valentine M. Moghadam. 2001. "Female Labor Force Participation and Economic Adjustment in the MENA Region." Pp. 51–75 in Mine Cinar (Eds.), *The Economics of Women and Work in the Middle East and North Africa*. JAI Press.

Karshenas, Massoud, Valentine M. Moghadam, and Nadereh Chamlou. 2016. "Women, Work, and Welfare: Introduction and Overview." Pp. 1–30 in Massoud Karshenas and Nadereh Chamlou (Eds.), *Women, Work, and Welfare in the Middle East and North Africa*. London, UK: Imperial College Press.

Katouzian, Homa. 1981. *The Political Economy of Modern Iran: Despotism and Pseudo-Modernism*. New York: New York University Press.

Khosrokhavar, Farhad, and Mohammad Amin Ghaneirad. 2010. "Iranian Women's Participation in the Academic World." *Iranian Studies* 43(2):224–238.

Mahdavi, Hossein. 1972. "Patterns and Problems of Economic Development in Rentier States: The Case of Iran." Pp. 428–467 in Michael A. Cook (Ed.), *Studies in the Economic History of the Middle East*. Oxford, UK: Oxford University Press.

Mahfoudh Draoui, Dorra. 2016. *CREDIF Tunisiennes et Action Politique en Contexte Post-Révolutionnaire*. Tunis: CREDIF.

Meyer, John, John Boli, George Thomas, and Francisco Ramirez. 1997. "World Society and the Nation-State." *American Journal of Sociology* 103(1):144–181.

Moghadam, Fatemeh Etemad. 2009. "Undercounting Women's Work in Iran." *Iranian Studies* 42(1):81–95.

Moghadam, Fatemeh E., Farrokh Guiahi, and Rabia Naguib. 2016. "Women and Work in Dubai City: An Exploration in Institutional Barriers and Potentials." Pp. 351–382 in Nadereh Chamlou and Massoud Karshenas (Eds.), *Women, Work and Welfare in the Middle East and North Africa*. London, UK: Imperial College Press.

Moghadam, Valentine M. 2016. "Engendering Development Sociology: The Evolution of a Field of Research." Pp. 21–47 in Gregory Hooks (Ed.), *Handbook of the Sociology of Development*. Berkeley: University of California Press.

_____. 2013. *Modernizing Women: Gender and Social Change in the Middle East*, 3rd ed. Boulder, CO: Lynne Rienner.

_____. 2006. "Maternalist Policies vs. Economic Citizenship? Gendered Social Policy in Iran." Pp. 87–108 in Shahra Razavi and Shireen Hassim (Eds.), *Gender and Social Policy in a Global Context: Uncovering the Gendered Structure of "the Social."* Basingstoke, UK: Palgrave.

_____. 2005. "Women's Economic Participation in the Middle East: What Difference Has the Neoliberal Policy Turn Made?" *Journal of Middle East Women's Studies* 1(1):110–146.

_____. 2003. *Modernizing Women: Gender and Social Change in the Middle East*, 2nd ed. Boulder, CO: Lynne Rienner.

_____. 1998. *Women, Work, and Economic Reform in the Middle East and North Africa*. Boulder, CO: Lynne Rienner.

_____. 1995. "A Political Economy of Women's Employment in the Arab Region." Pp. 6–34 in N. Khoury and V. M. Moghadam (Eds.), *Gender and National Development*. London, UK: Zed Books.

_____. 1993. *Modernizing Women: Gender and Social Change in the Middle East*. Boulder, CO: Lynne Rienner.

_____. 1988. "Women, Work and Ideology in the Islamic Republic." *International Journal of Middle East Studies* 20(May):221–243.

Moghadam, Valentine M., and Fatemeh Haghighatjoo. 2016. "Women and Political Leadership in an Authoritarian Context: A Case Study of the Sixth Parliament in the Islamic Republic of Iran." *Politics & Gender* 12:168–197.

Mohaddes, Kamiar, and Hashem Pesaran. 2013. "One Hundred Years of Oil Income and the Iranian Economy: A Curse or a Blessing?" ERF Working Paper 771 (September). Cairo: Economic Research Forum.

National Democratic Institute. 2015. "Enquête D'Opinion Auprès Des Femmes Tunisiennes Sur Des Thèmes D'Importance." Tunis: National Development Institute (September).

Nomani, Farhad, and Sohrab Behdad. 2006. *Class and Labor in Iran: Did the Revolution Matter?* Syracuse, NY: Syracuse University Press.

République Tunisienne. 2016. "Synthèse du Plan du Développement 2016–2020" (23 Mai).

_____. 2014. *Recensement en Chiffres/Statistique Tunisienne*. Available at http://census.ins.tn/fr/recensement

Richards, Alan, and John Waterbury. 1996. *A Political Economy of the Middle East*, 2nd ed. Boulder, CO: Westview Press.

_____. 1990. *A Political Economy of the Middle East*. Boulder, CO: Westview Press.

Ross, Michael. 2008. "Oil, Islam, and Women." *American Political Science Review* 102:107–123.

_____. 2001. "Does Oil Hinder Democracy?" *World Politics* 53(3):325–361.

Roudi-Fahimi. 2002. "Iran's Family Planning Program: Responding to a Nation's Needs." *Population Reference Bureau*, MENA Policy Brief (June): www.prb.org

Sachs, Jeffrey D., and Andrew D. Warner. 2001. "The Curse of Natural Resources." *European Economic Review* 45(4–6):827–838.

Salehi-Esfahani, Hadi, and Parastoo Shajari. 2012. "Gender, Education, Family Structure, and the Allocation of Labor in Iran." *Middle East Development Journal* 4(2):1–40.

Seddon, David. 1993. "Austerity Protests in Response to Economic Liberalization in the Middle East." Pp. 88–113 in Tim Niblock and Emma Murphy (Eds.), *Economic and Political Liberalization in the Middle East*. London, UK: Academic Press.

Shalaby, Marwa, and Valentine M. Moghadam (Eds.). 2016. *Empowering Women After the Arab Spring*. London, UK: Palgrave Macmillan.

Sonbol, Amira al-Azhary. 2003. *Women of Jordan: Islam, Labour, and the Law*. Syracuse, NY: Syracuse University Press.

Spectorsky, Susan. 2009. *Women in Classical Islamic Law: A Survey of the Sources*. Leiden: E. J. Brill.

Standing, Guy. 1989. "Global Feminization Through Flexible Labor." WEP Labour Market Analysis Working Paper no. 31. Geneva: ILO.

Swiss, Liam. 2012. "The Adoption of Women and Gender as Development Assistance Priorities: An Event History Analysis of World Polity Effects." *International Sociology* 27(1):96–119.

Tohidi, Nayereh. 2010. "Iran." Pp. 121–156 in Sanja Kelly and Julia Breslin (Eds.), *Women's Rights in the Middle East and North Africa: Progress Amid Resistance*. Washington and Lanham: Freedom House and Rowman and Littlefield.

UNESCO. 2011. *EFA [Education for All] Global Monitoring Report 2011: Regional Overview—South and West Asia*. Paris: United Nations Educational, Scientific, and Cultural Organization.

United Nations Development Programme. 2013. *Human Development Report 2013: The Rise of the South: Human Progress in a Diverse World*. New York, NY: United Nations Development Programme.

Walby, Sylvia. 2009. *Globalization and Inequalities: Complexity and Contested Modernities*. London, UK: SAGE.

World Bank. 2018. *World Development Indicators*. Available at http://databank.worldbank.org.

World Bank/IFC, Women, Business and the Law. 2014. *Removing Restrictions to Enhance Gender Equality*. Washington, DC: World Bank.

_____. 2012. *Education Statistics*. http://data.worldbank.org/data-catalog/edstats

_____. 2006. *Morocco, Tunisia, Egypt, and Jordan After the End of the Multi-Fiber Agreement: Impact, Challenges, and Prospects*. Washington DC: World Bank.

_____. 2003. "Poverty in Iran: Trends and Structure, 1986–1998." Washington DC: The World Bank, Middle East and North Africa Region, Report no. 24414.

Zonis, Marvin. 1991. *Majestic Failure: The Fall of the Shah*. Chicago, IL: University of Chicago Press.

Chapter 6

Adika, V., J. Yabga, F. Apiyanteide, P. Ologidi, and K. Ekpo. 2011. "Perception and Behaviour on Use of Sanitary Pads During Menstruation Among Adolescent School Girls in Bayelsa State, Nigeria." *Advance in Applied Science Research* 2(6):9–15.

Alam, Mahbub-Ul, et al. 2017. "Menstrual Hygiene Management Among Bangladeshi Adolescent Schoolgirls and Risk Factors Affecting School Absence: Results From a Cross-Sectional Survey." *BMJ Open* 7:e015508.

Ali, T. S., and S. N. Rizvi. 2010. "Menstrual Knowledge and Practices of Female Adolescents in Urban Karachi, Pakistan." *Journal of Adolescence* 33:531–541.

Ali, T., N. Sami, A. K. Khuwaja, et al. 2007. "Are Unhygienic Practices During the Menstrual, Partum and Postpartum Periods Risk Factors for Secondary Infertility?" *Journal of Health, Population, and Nutrition* 25(2):189–194.

Amnesty International. 2010. "Risking Rape to Reach a Toilet: Women's Experience in the Slums of Nairobi, Kenya." http://www.amnesty.org/en/library/asset/ (accessed March 1, 2015)

Avotri. J., and V. Walters. 1999. "'You just look at our work and see if you have any freedom on Earth': Ghanaian Women's Accounts of Their Work and Their Health." *Social Science & Medicine* 48:1123–1133.

Baisley, K., J. Changalucha, H. A. Weiss, et al. 2009. "Bacterial Vaginosis in Female Facility Workers in North-Western Tanzania: Prevalence and Risk Factors." *Sexually Transmitted Infections* 85(5):370–375.

Bayo, S., F. X. Bosch, S. de Sanjosé, et al. 2002. "Risk Factors of Invasive Cervical Cancer in Mali." *International Epidemiological Association* 31(1):202–209.

Bisung, E., and S. J. Elliott. 2017. "Psychosocial Impacts of the Lack of Access to Water and Sanitation in Low- and Middle-Income Countries: A Scoping Review." *Journal of Water and Health* 15(1):17–30.

Boosey, R., G. Prestwich, and T. Deave. 2014. "Menstrual Hygiene Management Amongst Schoolgirls in the Rukungiri District of Uganda and the Impact on Their Education: A Cross-Sectional Study." *Pan African Medical Journal* 19(253).

Bukar, M., and Y. S. Jauro. 2013. "Home Births and Postnatal Practices in Madagali, North-Eastern Nigeria." *Nigerian Journal of Clinical Practice* 16(2): 232–237.

Cairncross, S., and J. L. Cuff. 1987. Water Use and Health in Mueda, Mozambique. *Transactions of the Royal Society of Tropical Medicine & Hygiene* 81:51–54.

Caruso, B. A., et al. 2017. "Understanding and Defining Sanitation Insecurity: Women's Gendered Experiences of Urination, Defecation and Menstruation in Rural Odisha, India." *BMJ Global Health* 2(4).

Chandler, Michael A. 2017. "Free Access to Tampons Gains Political Traction." *Washington Post*, Aug. 8.

Chandra, Swati. 2013. "No Proper Guidelines to Implement Menstrual Hygiene Scheme," *Times of India* Sep. 14. (accessed Sept. 16, 2013)

Chaouki, Noureddine, et al. 1998. "The Viral Origin of Cervical Cancer in Rabat, Morocco." *International Journal of Cancer* 75:546–554.

Corburn, Jason, and C. Hildebrand. 2015. "Slum Sanitation and the Social Determinants of Women's Health in Nairobi, Kenya." *Journal of Environmental and Public Health* Article ID 209505.

Coultas, M., J. Martin, C. Stephen, and S. Warrington. 2017. *Moving Forward: Findings From Menstrual Hygiene Management Formative Research in Bangladesh*. 40th WEDC International Conference, Loughborough, UK, 2017. Paper 2783.

Crichton, J., J. Okal, C. W. Kabiru, and E. M. Zulu. 2013. "Emotional and Psychosocial Aspects of Menstrual Poverty in Resource-Poor Settings: A Qualitative Study of the Experiences of Adolescent Girls in an Informal Settlement in Nairobi." *Health Care for Women International* 34(10):891–916.

Crofts, T., and J. Fisher. 2012. "Menstrual Hygiene in Ugandan Schools: An Investigation of Low-Cost Sanitary Pads." *Journal of Water, Sanitation and Hygiene for Development* 2(1):50–58.

Das, N. P., and U. Shah. 2007. *A Study of Reproductive Health Problems Among Men and Women in Urban Slums With Special Reference to Sexually Transmitted Infections*. Population Research Centre, Maharaja Sayajirao University of Baroda, India.

Das, Padma, et al. 2015. "Menstrual Hygiene Practices, WASH Access and the Risk of Urogenital Infection in Women from Odisha, India." *PLoS ONE* 10(6).

Dasgupta, A., and M. Sarkar. 2008. "Menstrual Hygiene: How Hygienic Is the Adolescent Girl?" *Indian Journal of Community Medicine* 33(2):77–80.

Economic Times. 2014. "Premium Condom Market in India May Collapse as Drug Pricing Authority Sets Cap Price at Rs.6.50." April 2.

Ensign, Josephine. 2001. "Reproductive Health of Homeless Adolescent Women in Seattle, Washington, USA." *Women & Health* 31(2–3).

Garg, S., and T. Anand. 2015. "Menstruation Related Myths in India: Strategies for Combating It." *Journal of Family Medicine and Primary Care* 4(2):184–186.

Garg, S., N. Sharma, and R. Sahay. 2001. "Socio-Cultural Aspects of Menstruation in an Urban Slum in Delhi, India." *Reproductive Health Matters* 9(17):16–25.

Gius, Mark, and R. Subramanian. 2015. "The Relationship Between Inadequate Sanitation Facilities and the Economic Well-Being of Women in India." *Journal of Economics and Development Studies* 3(1):11–21.

Graham, J., M. Hirai, and S. Kim. 2016. "An Analysis of Water Collection Labor Among Women and Children in 24 Sub-Saharan African Countries." *PLoS One* 11(6).

Grant, M. J., C. B. Lloyd, and B. S. Mensch. 2013. "Menstruation and School Absenteeism: Evidence From Rural Malawi." *Computer Education Review* 57(2):260–284.

Gujarat Water Supply and Sewerage Board. n.d. "Programs Being Taken Up by Water Supply Department." http://www.gwssb.org/

Hennegan, J., and P. Montgomery. 2016. "Do Menstrual Hygiene Management Interventions Improve Education and Psychosocial Outcomes for Women and Girls in Low and Middle Income Countries? A Systematic Review." *PLoS One* 11(2):e0146985.

Hennegan, J., et al. 2016. "Measuring the Prevalence and Impact of Poor Menstrual Hygiene Management: A Quantitative Survey of Schoolgirls in Rural Uganda." *BMJ Open* 6:e012596.

Hirai, M., J. P. Graham, and J. Sandberg. 2016. "Understanding Women's Decision Making Power and Its Link to Improved Household Sanitation: The Case of Kenya." *Journal of Water Sanitation and Hygiene for Development* 6(1):151–160.

Hirway, I. 2002. "Dynamics of Development in Gujarat." *Economic and Political Weekly* 35(35–36).

Hirway, I., and D. Mahadevia. 2004. *Human Development Report*. Mahatma Gandhi Labour Institute, Ahmedabad, India.

Howard, G., and J. Bartram. 2003. *Domestic Water Quantity, Service Levels and Health*. Geneva: World Health Organization.

Hulland, K. R., et al. 2015. "Sanitation, Stress, and Life Stage: A Systematic Data Collection Study Among Women in Odisha, India." *PLoS One* 10(11).

India Census. 2011. Primary Census Abstract. http://www.censusindia.gov.in/pca/default.aspx

International Institute for Population Sciences. 2010. *District Level Household and Facility Survey (DLHS-3), 2007–08: India*. Mumbai: IIPS.

Jasper, C., T. T. Le, and J. Bartram. 2012. "Water and Sanitation in Schools: A Systematic Review of the Health and Educational Outcomes." *International Journal of Environmental Research and Public Health* 9(8):2772–2787.

Jewitt, S., and H. Ryley. 2014. It's a Girl Thing: Menstruation, School Attendance, Spatial Mobility and Wider Gender Inequalities in Kenya. *Geoforum* 56:137–147.

Joint Monitoring Program. 2012. *Meeting Report of JMP, Post–2015 Global Monitoring Working Group on Hygiene: Sub-Groups on Menstrual Hygiene, Handwashing, and Food Hygiene*. May 15–16, Washington, DC.

Joshi, Deepa, Ben Fawcett, and Fouzia Mannan. 2011. "Health, Hygiene and Appropriate Sanitation: Experiences and Perceptions of the Urban Poor," *Environment and Urbanization* 23(1):91–111.

Kuhlmann, A. S., K. Henry, and L. L. Wall. 2017. "Menstrual Hygiene Management in Resource-Poor Countries." *Obstetrical & Gynecological Survey* 72(6):356–376.

Lennon, Shirley. 2011. "Fear and Anger: Perceptions of Risks Related to Sexual Violence Against Women Linked to Water and Sanitation in Delhi, India, A Briefing Note." http://www.shareresearch.org/LocalResources/VAW_India.pdf (accessed March 1, 2015)

Mani, G. 2014. "Prevalence of Reproductive Tract Infections Among Rural Married Women in Tamil Nadu, India: A Community Based Study." *Journal of Pioneer Medical Sciences* 4(1):18–24.

Mason, L., E. Nyothach, and K. Alexander. 2013. "'We Keep It Secret so No One Should Know'—A Qualitative Study to Explore Young Schoolgirls Attitudes and Experiences With Menstruation in Rural Western Kenya." *PLoS One* 8:e79132.

Massey, Keren. 2011. "Insecurity and Shame Exploration of the Impact of the Lack of Sanitation on Women in the Slums of Kampala, Uganda: A Briefing Note," Sanitation and Hygiene Applied Research for Equity. http://www.shareresearch.org/LocalResources/VAW_Uganda.pdf (accessed September 2014)

McMahon, S. A., P. J. Winch, B. A. Caruso, et al. 2011. "'The Girl With Her Period Is the One to Hang Her Head': Reflections on Menstrual Management Among Schoolgirls in Rural Kenya." *BMC International Health and Human Rights* 11:7.

Misra, P., et al. 2013. "A Community-Based Study of Menstrual Hygiene Practices and Willingness to Pay for Sanitary Napkins Among Women of a Rural Community in Northern India." *National Medical Journal of India* 26(6):335–337.

NextBillion. 2013. "The Female Sanitary Revolution." http://nextbillion.net/blogpost.aspx?blogid=3190, http://nextbillion.net/the-female-sanitary-revolution/

Nieves, Evelyn. 2017. "In Nepal, a Monthly Exile for Women." *New York Times*, Jan. 5. https://lens.blogs.nytimes.com/2017/01/05/in-nepal-monthly-exile-for-women/

Padhi, B. K., et al. 2015. "Risk of Adverse Pregnancy Outcomes Among Women Practicing Poor Sanitation in Rural India: A Population-Based Prospective Cohort Study." *PLOS One* (July 7).

Page, Ben. 1996. "Taking the Strain—the Ergonomics of Water Carrying." *Waterlines* 14(3):29–31.

Peng, H., et al. 1991. "Human Papillomavirus Types 16 and 33, Herpes Simplex Virus Type 2 and Other Risk Factors for Cervical Cancer in Sichuan Province, China." *International Journal of Cancer* 47(5):711–716.

Phillips-Howard, P. A., et al. 2015. "Menstrual Needs and Associations With Sexual and Reproductive Risks in Rural Kenyan Females: A Cross-Sectional Behavioral Survey Linked With HIV Prevalence." *Journal of Women's Health* 24(10):801–811.

Routray, P., et al. 2017. "Women's Role in Sanitation Decision Making in Rural Coastal Odisha, India." *PLOS One* 12(5):e0178042.

_____. 2015. "Socio-Cultural and Behavioural Factors Constraining Latrine Adoption in Rural Coastal Odisha: An Exploratory Qualitative Study." *BMC Public Health* 15:880.

Sahoo, K. C., et al. 2015. "Sanitation-Related Psychosocial Stress: A Grounded Theory Study of Women Across the Life-Course in Odisha, India." *Social Science and Medicine* 139(August):80–89.

Scott, L. M., C. R. Ryus, C. Dolan, S. Dopson, and P. Montgomery. 2013. *The Power of Ordinary Objects: Investigating Menstrual Care in Ghana.* Working paper. Cambridge, UK: Oxford University.

Scott, P. A., J. Charteris, and R. S. Bridger. 1998. *Global Ergonomics.* The Netherlands: Elsevier.

Sebastian, A., et al. 2013. "Menstrual Management in Low Income Countries: Needs and Trends." *Waterlines* 32(2).

Shah, S. P., R. Nair, and P. P. Shah. 2013. "Improving Quality of Life With New Menstrual Hygiene Practices Among Adolescent Tribal Girls in Rural Gujarat, India." *Reproductive Health Matters* 21(41):205–213.

Sheikh, Shahana. 2008. *Public Toilets in Delhi: An Emphasis on the Facilities for Women in Slum/Resettlement Areas.* CCS Working Paper No. 192. Delhi: Center for Civil Society.

Sikarwar, Deepshikha. 2017. "Government Adds Sanitary Napkins to the 12% Gst Slab. Here's Why." *Economic Times*, July 10.

Singh, A. J. 2006. "Place of Menstruation in the Reproductive Lives of Women of Rural North India." *Indian Journal of Community Med* 31(1):10–14.

Singh, M. M., R. Devi, S. Garg, and M. Mehra. 2001. "Effectiveness of Syndromic Approach in Management of Reproductive Tract Infections in Women." *Indian Journal of Medical Science* 55(4):209–214.

Sommer, M. 2010. "Where the Education System and Women's Bodies Collide: The Social and Health Impact of Girls' Experiences of Menstruation and Schooling in Tanzania." *Journal of Adolescence* 33(4):521–529.

Sommer, Marni, et al. 2017. "Beyond Menstrual Hygiene: Addressing Vaginal Bleeding Throughout the Life Course in Low and Middle Income Countries." *BMJ Global Health* 2:e000405.

Sommer, M., S. Chandraratna, S. Cavill, et al. 2016. "Managing Menstruation in the Workplace: An Overlooked Issue in Low- and Middle-Income Countries." *International Journal for Equity in Health* 15:86.

Sommer, M., et al. 2014. "A Comparison of the Menstruation and Education Experiences of Girls in Tanzania, Ghana, Cambodia, and Ethiopia." *Compare: A Journal of Comparative and International Education* 45(4):589–609.

Sommer, M., and M. Sahin. 2013. "Overcoming the Taboo: Advancing the Global Agenda for Menstrual Hygiene Management for Schoolgirls." *American Journal of Public Health* 103:1556–1559.

Srivastava, L. 2010. "Reproductive Tract Infections Among Women of Rural Community in Mewat, India." *Journal of Health Management* 12(4):519–538.

Sumpter, C., and B. A. Torondel. 2013. "Systematic Review of the Health and Social Effects of Menstrual Hygiene Management." *PLoS ONE* 8(4).

Tamiru, S., et al. 2015. Towards a Sustainable Solution for School Menstrual Hygiene Management: Cases of Ethiopia, Uganda, South-Sudan, Tanzania, and Zimbabwe. *Waterlines* 34:92–102.

Tegegne, T. K., and M. M. Sisay. 2014. Menstrual Hygiene Management and School Absenteeism Among Female Adolescent Students in Northeast Ethiopia. *BMC Public Health* 14:1118.

Thakre, S. B., S. S. Thakre, M. Reddy, et al. 2011. "Menstrual Hygiene: Knowledge and Practice Among Adolescent School Girls of Soannar, Nagpur District." *Journal of Clinical and Diagnostic Research* 5(5):1027–1033.

Thompson, John, et al. 2001. *Drawers of Water II: 30 Years of Change in Domestic Water Use and Environmental Health in East Africa.* London, UK: International Institute for Environment and Development.

Umeora, O. U. J., and V. E. Egwuatu. 2008. "Menstruation in Rural Igbo Women of South East Nigeria: Attitudes, Beliefs and Practices." *African Journal of Reproductive Health* 12(1):109–115.

UNESCO. 2014. *Puberty Education & Menstrual Hygiene Management.* Good Policy and Practice in Health Education Booklet 9.

van Eijk, A. M., et al. 2016. "Menstrual Hygiene Management Among Adolescent Girls in India: A Systematic Review and Meta-Analysis." *BMJ Open* 6(3):e010290.

Varghese, C., N. S. Amma, K. Chitrathara, et al. 1999. "Risk Factors for Cervical Dysplasia in Kerala, India." *Bulletin World Health Organization* 77(3):281–283.

Vaughn, J. G. 2013. "A Review of Menstruation Hygiene Management Among Schoolgirls in Sub-Saharan Africa." Paper in partial fulfillment of degree in Master of Public Health in the Department of Maternal and Child Health, the University of North Carolina at Chapel Hill.

Verdemato, Tania. 2005. *Responding to Women's Menstrual Hygiene Needs in Emergencies: A Case Study from Katakwi, Uganda*. MSc theses (Silsoe) Cranfield University, Silsoe. http://hdl.handle.net/1826/1319 (accessed January 2010)

WaterAid. 2016. "Girls' Menstrual Needs Neglected, New Journal Article Finds Wateraid at Women Deliver 2016." http://womendeliver.org/wp-content/uploads/2016/05/WATERAID-PRESS-RELEASE-Girls-menstrual-needs-neglected-FINAL3.pdf (accessed September 2016)

Weiss-Wolf, Jennifer. 2017. *Periods Gone Public: Taking a Stand for Menstrual Equality*. New York, NY: Arcade.

Winter, S. C., and F. Barchi. 2016. "Access to Sanitation and Violence Against Women: Evidence From Demographic Health Survey (DHS) Data in Kenya." *International Journal of Environmental Health Research* 26(3):291–305.

World Bank. 2017. *Changing the Lives of Women and Girls through Affordable Feminine Hygiene Products*. https://www.innovationpolicyplatform.org/system/files/6_Health%20Female%20Hygiene%20Case_Jun21.pdf (accessed October 20, 2017)

_____. 2011. *World Development Report, 2012: Gender Equity and Development*. Washington, DC: World Bank.

_____. 2008. *Economic Impacts of Sanitation in South-East Asia*. http://www.wsp.org/sites/wsp.org/files/publications/Sanitation_Impact_Synthesis_2.pdf

World Health Organization/United Nations Children's Fund Joint Monitoring Program. 2017. *Progress on Drinking Water, Sanitation and Hygiene: 2017 Update and SDG Baselines*. Geneva: World Health Organization and United Nations Children's Fund. http://www.who.int/mediacentre/news/releases/2017/launch-version-report-jmp-water-sanitation-hygiene.pdf (accessed September 2017)

_____. 2015. *Progress on Drinking Water, Sanitation and Hygiene: 2015 Update and MDG Assessment*. Geneva: World Health Organization and United Nations Children's Fund.

Yasmin, S., N. Manna, S. Mallik, et al. 2013. "Menstrual Hygiene Among Adolescent School Students: An In-Depth Cross-Sectional Study in an Urban Community of West Bengal, India." *Journal of Dental and Medical Sciences* 5(6):22–26.

Yasmin, S., and A. Mukherjee. 2012. "A Cyto-Epidemiological Study on Married Women in Reproductive Age Group (15–49 Years) Regarding Reproductive Tract Infection in a Rural Community of West Bengal." *Indian Journal of Public Health* 56(3):204–209.

Young, Iris Marion. 2005. *On Female Body Experience: "Throwing Like a Girl" and Other Essays*. New York, NY: Oxford University Press.

Zhang, Z. F., D. M. Parkin, and S.-Z. Yu. 1986. "Risk Factors for Cancer of the Cervix in a Rural Chinese Population." *International Journal of Cancer* 43(5):762–767.

Chapter 7

Achcar, Gilbert. 2013. *The People Want: Radical Exploration of the Arab Uprising*. London, UK: Saqi.

Alexander, Sally. 1995. *Becoming a Woman and Other Essays in 19th and 20th Century Feminist History*. New York: New York University.

Anker, Richard. 1998. *Gender and Jobs: Sex Segregation of Occupation in the World*. Geneva: International Labour Office.

Appleton, Simon, John Hoddinott, and Pramila Krishnan. 1999. "Gender Gap in Three African Countries." *Economic Development and Cultural Change* 47:289–312.

Baslevent, Cem, and Ozlem Onaran. 2004. "The Effect of Export-Oriented Growth on Female Employment in Turkey." *World Development* 32:1375–1393.

Becker, Gary. 1957. *Economics of Discrimination*. Chicago, IL: University of Chicago Press.

Bianchi, Suzanne, Melissa Milkie, Liana Sayer, and John Robinson. 2000. "Is Anyone Doing the Housework? Trends in the Gender Division of Labor." *Social Forces* 79:191–228.

Blood, Robert, and Donald Wolfe. 1960. *Husbands and Wives: Dynamics of Married Living*. Glencoe, IL: Free Press.

Blumberg, Rae Lesser, and Marion Tolbert Coleman. 1989. "Theoretical Look at the Gender Balance of Power in the American Couple." *Journal of Family Issues* 10:225–250.

Boserup, Esther. 1970. *Women and Economic Development*. New York, NY: St. Martin's Press.

Bridges, William. 1982. "Sexual Segregation of Occupations: A New Appraisal." *American Journal of Sociology* 88:270–295.

_____. 1980. "Industry Marginality and Female Employment: A New Appraisal." *American Sociological Review* 45:58–75.

Burt, Ronald. 1992. *Structural Holes: Social Structure of Competition*. Cambridge, MA: Harvard.

Catalyst. 2018. *Women in Management*. http://www.catalyst.org/knowledge/women-management

Cohn, Samuel. 1985. *Process of Occupational Sex-Typing: Feminization of Clerical Labor in Great Britain*. Philadelphia, PA: Temple.

Davidoff, Leonore and Catherine Hall. 1989. *Family Fortunes: Men and Women of the English Middle Class 1780–1850*. Chicago, IL: University of Chicago Press.

Dill, William. 1958. "Environment as an Influence on Managerial Autonomy." *Administrative Sciences Quarterly* 2:409–433.

Dimaggio, Paul and Walter Powell. 1983. "Iron Cage Revisited: Institutional Isomorphism and Collective Rationality in Organizational Fields." *American Sociological Review* 48:147–160.

Dunaway, Wilma. 2014. *Gendered Commodity Chains: Seeing Women's Work and Households in Global Production*. Stanford, CA: Stanford University Press.

El-Sahabary, Nagat. 2003. "Women and the Nursing Profession in Saudi Arabia." Pp. 71–83 in Suha Sabbagh (Ed.), *Arab Women: Between Defiance and Restraint*. New York, NY: Olive Branch.

Fernandez-Kelly, Patricia. 1983. *For We Are Sold, I and My People: Women and Industry in Mexico's Frontier*. Albany: SUNY.

Gereffi, Gary. 2007. *New Offshoring of Jobs and Global Production*. International Labor Office Social Policy Lecture. Geneva: International Labor Office.

Grusky, David, and Maria Charles. 2005. *Occupational Ghettoes: Worldwide Segregation of Women and Men*. Stanford, CA: Stanford.

Hammam, Mona. 1986. "Capitalist Development, Family Division of Labor and Migration in the Middle East." Pp. 158–173 in Eleanor Leacock, Helen Safa, et al. (Eds.), *Women's Work, Development and the Division of Labor by Gender*. South Hadley, MA: Bergin and Carvey.

Hammond, Laura. 2013. *Safety, Security and Socioeconomic Wellbeing in Somaliland*. Report for the Geneva Center for Demining and the Danish Demining Group.

Hartmann, Heidi. 1976. "Capitalism, Patriarchy and Job Segregation by Sex." Pp. 137–169 in Martha Blaxall and Barbara Reagan (Eds.), *Women and the Workplace: Implications of Occupational Segregation*. Chicago, IL: University of Chicago Press.

Heyzer, Noeleen. 1986. *Working Women in Southeast Asia: Development, Subordination and Emancipation*. Philadelphia, PA: Open University.

Honeyman, Katrina. 2000. *Women, Gender and Industrialization in England 1700–1870*. New York, NY: Saint Martins.

Kanter, Rosabeth Moss. 1977. *Men and Women of the Corporation*. New York, NY: Basic Books.

Kazeno, Sumiko. 2004. *Role of Women in Singapore: Collaboration and Conflict Between Capitalism and Asian Values*. Nagoya, Japan, Privately Published.

Kessler-Harris, Alice. 1993. *Women Have Always Worked: An Historical Overview*. New York, NY: Feminist Press.

Lane, A. T. 1987. *Solidarity or Survival: American Labor and European Immigrants 1830–1924*. Westport, CT: Greenwood.

Lee, Jean, Kathleen Campbell, and Audrey Chia. 1999. *Three Paradoxes: Working Women in Singapore*. Singapore: Association for Action and Research.

Lie, John. 1996. "From Agrarian Patriarchy to Patriarchical Capitalism: Gendered Capitalist Industrialization in Korea." Pp. 34–55 in Valentine Moghadam (Ed.), *Patriarchy and Development*. Oxford, UK: Clarendon.

Lown, Judy. 1990. *Women and Industrialization: Gender at Work in Nineteenth Century Britain*. Minneapolis: University of Minnesota Press.

Lucas, Rex. 1971. *Milltown, Minetown, Railtown: Life in Canadian Communities of Single Industry*. Toronto: University of Toronto Press.

Moghadam, Valentine. 1995. "Political Economy of Female Employment in the Arab Region." Pp. 6–34 in Nabil Khoury and Valentine Moghadam (Eds.), *Gender and Development in the Arab World: Women's Economic Participation Patterns and Policies*. Atlantic Highlands, NJ: Zed.

_____. 1993. *Modernizing Women: Gender and Social Change in the Middle East*. Boulder, CO: Lynne Rienner.

Ozler, Sule. 2000. "Export Orientation and Female Share of Employment: Evidence From Turkey." *World Development* 28:1239–1248.

Pfeffer, Jeffrey. 1981. *Power in Organizations*. Cambridge, UK: Ballinger.

Pinchbeck, Ivy. 1930. *Women Workers and the Industrial Revolution 1750–1850*. London, UK: Routledge.

Poster, Winifred. 2013. "Global Circuits of Gender: Women in High Tech Work in India and the United States." *Gender, Sexuality and Feminism* 1:37–52.

Rivera, Lauren. 2015. "Go With Your Gut: Emotion and Evaluation in Job Interviews." *American Journal of Sociology* 120:1339–1389.

———. 2012. "Hiring as Cultural Matching." *American Sociological Review* 77:999–1022.

Rivera, Lauren, Jayanti Owens, and Katherine Gan. 2014. "Glass Floors and Glass Ceilings: Effect of Matching Female Job Applicants With Female Interviewers on Hiring Decisions." Northwest University Department of Management and Organizations Working Essay.

Ross, Michael. 2008. "Oil, Islam and Women." *American Political Science Review* 102:107–134.

Safa, Helen. 1986. "Runaway Shops and Female Employment: Search for Cheap Labor." Pp. 58–71 in Eleanor Leacock and Helen Safa (Eds.), *Women's Work*. South Hadley, MS: Bergen and Gervey.

Seguino, Stephanie. 2000. "Gender Inequality and Economic Growth: a Cross-Country Analysis." *World Development* 28:1211–1230.

Sloane, Arthur and Fred Witney. 2009. *Labor Relations* Englewood Cliffs, NJ: Prentice-Hall.

Tanzania Gender Networking Programme. 1993. *Gender Profile of Tanzania*. Dar Es Salaam, Tanzania: Gender Networking Programme.

Torvik, Ragnar. 2009. "Why Do Some Resource-Abundant Countries Succeed While Others Do Not?" *Oxford Review of Economic Policy* 25:241–256.

Wallace, Michael and Arne Kalleberg. 1981. "Economic Organization of Firms and Labor Market Consequences: Towards a Specification of Dual Labor Market Theory." Pp. 77–118 in Iver Berg, (Ed.), *Sociological Perspectives on Labor Markets*. New York, NY: Academic.

Welter, Barbara. 1966. "Cult of True Womanhood 1820–1860" *American Quarterly* 18:151–174.

Williams, Christine. 1989. *Gender Differences at Work: Women and Men in Non-Traditional Occupations*. Berkeley: University of California Press.

Williams, Joan. 2015. "Five Biases Pushing Women Out of STEM." *Harvard Business Review.* March 24. https://hbr.org/2015/03/the-5-biases-pushing-women-out-of-stem

World Bank. 2011. *World Development Report 2012: Gender Equality and Development*. Washington, DC: World Bank.

Chapter 8

Ahmed, Sara. 2000. *Strange Encounters: Embodied Others in Postcoloniality*. London, UK: Routledge.

Albrecht, Scott, and Robert P. Korzeniewicz. 2018. "'Creative Destruction' From a World-Systems Perspective: Billionaires and the Great Recession of 2008." Pp. 94–115 in M. Boatcă, A. Komlosy, and H. Nolte (Eds.), *Global Inequalities in World-System Perspective*. London, UK: Routledge.

Arton Capital. 2017. *A Shrinking World: Global Citizenship for UHNW Individuals. Special Report.* Retrieved March 25, 2018, from https://www.artoncapital.com/documents/publications/Arton-Capital-Wealth-X-Reportweb.pdf

Bartky, Sandra Lee. 1990. *Femininity and Domination: Studies in the Phenomenology of Oppression*. New York, NY: Routledge.

Blakeley, Rhys, and Tom Parfitt. 2018. "Pregnant Russians Flock to Florida for Sun (and US Passport)," *The Times*, January 12, 2018, https://www.thetimes.co.uk/article/pregnant-russians-flock-to-florida-for-sun-and-us-passport-67c7395wf

Boatcă, Manuela. 2017." The Centrality of Race to Inequality Across the World-System." *Journal of World-Systems Research* 23(2):465–473. http://jwsr.pitt.edu/ojs/index.php/jwsr/article/view/729

———. 2016. "Exclusion Through Citizenship and the Geopolitics of Austerity." Pp. 115–134 in Stefan Jonsson and Julia Willén (Eds.), *Austere Histories in European Societies: Social Exclusion and the Contest of Colonial Memories*. London, UK: Routledge.

———. 2015. *Global Inequalities Beyond Occidentalism* (Global Connections). Farnham, Surrey, UK: Ashgate.

Boatcă, Manuela, and Julia Roth. 2016. "Unequal and Gendered: Notes on the Coloniality of Citizenship Rights." *Current Sociology*, monograph issue: "Dynamics of Inequalities in a Global Perspective," Manuela Boatcă and Vilna Bashi Treitler (Eds.), January 2016, 191–212.

Braun, Katharine. 2016. "Dekoloniale Perspektiven auf Alltagspraktiken Bolivianischer Migratinnen Zwischen Santa Cruz de la Sierra und Genf." *Feministische Studien* 34:207–225.

Butler, Judith. 2004. *Undoing Gender*. New York, NY: Routledge.

———. 1993. *Bodies That Matter: On the Discursive Limits of Sex*. London, UK: Routledge.

_____. 1990. *Gender Trouble, Feminism and the Subversion of Identity*. London, UK: Routledge.

De Beauvoir, Simone. 1953. *The Second Sex*. London, UK: Jonathan Cape.

Dobrowolsky, Alexandra, and Evangelia Tastsoglou. 2006. "Crossing Boundaries and Making Connections." Pp. 1–35 in Alexandra Dobrowolsky and Evangelia Tastsoglou (Eds.), *Women, Migration and Citizenship: Making Local, National, and Transnational Connections*. Farnham, UK: Ashgate.

Fanon, Frantz. 1963. *Black Skin, White Masks* (Trans. C. L. Markmann). New York, NY: Grove Press.

Fausto-Sterling, Anne. 2000. 'The Five Sexes: Why Male and Female Are Not Enough." *The Sciences* 33(2):20–25.

_____. 1992. *Myths of Gender: Biological Theories About Women and Men*. New York, NY: Basic Books.

Feere, Jon D. 2010. *Birthright Citizenship in the United States: A Global Comparison*. Washington, DC: Center for Immigration Studies.

Foucault, Michel. 1979. *Discipline and Punish*. New York, NY: Vintage.

Franco, Jean. 1999. "La Malinche: From Gift to Sexual Contract." Pp. 66–82 in M. L. Pratt and K. Newman (Eds.), *Critical Passions: Jean Franco: Selected Essays*. Durham, NC: Duke University Press.

Guevara González, Yaatsil. 2015. "Migración de tránsito y ayuda humanitaria: apuntes sobre las Casas de Migrantes en la ruta migratoria del Pacífico Sur en México." *Fiar* 8(1).

_____. n.d. *Transit Itineraries: Migrant's Experiences and Interactions in Mexico's Southern Border*. Dissertation project. Unpublished.

Halberstam, Judith. 1998. *Female Masculinity*. Durham, NC: Duke University Press.

Hasenbalg, Carlos. 2005. *Discriminação e Desigualdades Raciais no Brasil*. Rio de Janeiro: Graal.

Heading South (France/Canada 2006, director: Laurent Cantet).

hooks, bell. 1990. *Yearning: Race, Gender and Cultural Politics*. Boston, MA: South End Press.

Huffington Post. 2013. "Steve King Introduces Bill to Stop 'Anchor Babies,'" January 4. www.huffingtonpost.com/2013/01/04/steve-king-anchor-babies_n_2411989.html (accessed March 5, 2018)

Kamugisha, Aaron. 2007. "The Coloniality of Citizenship in the Contemporary Anglophone Caribbean." *Race & Class* 49(2):20–40.

Korzeniewicz, Roberto Patricio, and Patrick Timothy Moran. 2009. *Unveiling Inequality: A World-Historical Perspective*. New York, NY: Russell Sage Foundation.

Lacey, Marc. 2011. "Birthright Citizenship Looms as Next Immigration Battle," *New York Times*, January 4. www.nytimes.com/2011/01/05/us/politics/05babies.html?pagewanted=all&_r=0 (accessed March 5, 2018)

Lorde, Audre. 1984. *Sister Outsider: Essays and Speeches*. Freedom, CA: Crossing Press.

Lugones, Maria. 2008. "The Coloniality of Gender." *Worlds and Knowledges Otherwise* (Spring):1–17.

_____. 2007. "Heterosexualism and the Colonial/Modern Gender System." *Hypatia* 22(1):186–209.

McClintock, Anne. 1995. *Imperial Leather: Race, Gender and Sexuality in the Colonial Contest*. New York, NY: Routledge.

Messinger, Irene. 2013. There Is Something About Marrying . . . the Case of Human Rights vs. Migration Regimes Using the Example of Austria. *Laws* 2:376–391.

Mies, Maria. 1996. *Patriarchy and Accumulation on a World Scale*. London, UK: Zed Books.

Mignolo, Walter. 2000. *Local Histories/Global Designs: Coloniality, Subaltern Knowledges, and Border Thinking*. Princeton, NJ: Princeton University Press.

Mignolo, W., and M. Tlostanova. 2006. "Theorizing From the Borders: Shifting to Geo- and Body-Politics of Knowledge." *European Journal of Social Theory* 9(2):205–211.

Milanovic, Branko. 2016. *Global Inequality: A New Approach for the Age of Globalization*. Cambridge, MA: Harvard University Press

O'Connell Davidson, Julia. 2001. "The Sex Tourist, the Expatriate, His Ex-Wife and Her 'Other': The Politics of Loss, Difference and Desire." *Sexualities* 4(1):5–24.

O'Connell Davidson, Julia, and Jacqueline Sanchez Taylor. 1999. "Fantasy Islands. Exploring the Demand for Sex Tourism." Pp. 37–54 in Kampala Kempadoo (Ed.), *Sun, Sex and Gold: Tourism and Sex Work in the Caribbean*. London, UK: Boulder.

Oxfam. 2018. *Reward Work, Not Wealth: To End Inequality Crisis, We Must Build an Economy for Ordinary Working People, Not the Rich and Powerful*, January 2018. https://www.oxfam.org/sites/www.oxfam.org/files/file_attachments/bp-reward-work-not-wealth-220118-summ-en.pdf

Oyewumi, Oyeronke. 1997. *The Invention of Women: Making African Sense of Western Gender Discourses*. Minneapolis: University of Minnesota Press.

Padilla, Mark. 2007. *Caribbean Pleasure Industry: Tourism, Sexuality and AIDS in the Dominican Republic.* Chicago, IL: University of Chicago Press.

Paradies: Liebe (Austria 2012, director: Ulrich Seidel).

Pavey, Harriet. 2017. "Wealthy Russians Are Flocking to Give Birth at Trump's Luxury US Resorts so Their Kids Can Have Dual-Citizenship," *Evening Standard*, September 7, 2017, https://www.standard.co.uk/lifestyle/london-life/russians-flock-to-give-birth-at-trump-s-properties-in-the-us-so-their-kids-can-have-dualcitizenship-a3620971.html

Pendleton, Devon, and Christopher Cannon. 2018. "The World's Wealthiest Women Are a Rare Breed," *Bloomberg*, March 8. https://www.bloomberg.com/graphics/2018-female-billionaires/

Pew Research Center. 2013. "Unauthorized Immigrants: How Pew Research Counts Them and What We Know About Them," April 17. www.pewresearch.org/2013/04/17/unauthorizedimmigrants-how-pew-research-counts-them-and-what-we-know-about-them/ (accessed March 6, 2018)

Prado, Fernando, Susana Seleme, Isabella Prado, and Carmen Ledo. 2007. *Santa Cruz y su Gente.* Hrsg. von CEDURE. ABC Producciones, Santa Cruz de la Sierra, Bolivia.

Pruit, Deborah, and Suzanne LaFont. 1995. "For Love and Money: Romance Tourism in Jamaica." *Annals of Tourism Research* 22(2):422–440.

Quijano, Aníbal. 2000. "Coloniality of Power, Eurocentrism, and Latin America." *Nepantla: Views From South* 1(3):533–574.

Reid-Henry, Simon. 2015. *The Political Origins of Inequality: Why a More Equal World Is Better for Us All.* Chicago, IL: University of Chicago Press.

Rich, Adrienne. 1980. "Compulsory Heterosexuality and Lesbian Existence." *Signs* 5(4):631–660.

_____. 1979. *Of Women Born, Motherhood as Experience and Institution.* London, UK: Virago.

Roth, Julia. 2013. "Entangled Inequalities as Intersectionalities: Towards an Epistemic Sensibilization." desiguALdades.netWorkingPaperNo.43.www.desigualdades.net/bilder/Working_Paper/43_WP_Roth_Online.pdf?1367229865.

Roth, Julia, and Manuela Boatcă. 2016. "Staatsbürgerschaft, Gender und globale Ungleichheiten." *Feministische Studien* 34(2):189–206.

Rubin, Gayle. 1975. "The Traffic in Women: Notes on the 'Political Economy' of Sex." Pp. 157–210 in R. Reiter (Ed.), *Toward an Anthropology of Women.* New York, NY: Monthly Review Press.

Sand Dollars (Dominican Republic 2015, directors: Laura Amelia Guzmán and Israel Cárdenas).

Shachar, Ayelet. 2009. *The Birthright Lottery: Citizenship and Global Inequality.* Harvard, CT: Harvard University Press.

Stam, Robert, and Ella Shohat. 2012. *Race in Translation: Culture Wars around the Postcolonial Atlantic.* New York, NY: Atlantic.

Stoler, Ann Laura, and Frederick Cooper (Eds.). 1997. *Tensions of Empire: Colonial Cultures in a Bourgeois World.* Berkeley: University of California Press.

Stout, Noelle M. 2014. *After Love: Queer Intimacy and Erotic Economies in Post-Soviet Cuba.* Durham, NC: Duke University Press.

Texas Observer. 2015. Children of Immigrants Denied Citizenship. www.texasobserver.org/children-of-immigrants-denied-citizenship/

Tlostanova, Madina. 2010. *Gender Epistemologies and Eurasian Borderlands.* New York, NY: Palgrave Macmillan.

Von Werlhof, C., M. Mies, and V. Bennholdt-Thomsen. 1983. *Frauen, die letzte Kolonie.* Reinbek bei Hamburg: Rowohlt.

Wang, Jennifer. 2018. "The Richest Women in the World 2018," *Forbes*, March 6. https://www.forbes.com/sites/jenniferwang/2018/03/06/richest-women/#12d3d55881f1

Werbner, Pnina, and Nira Yuval-Davis. 1999. "Introduction: Women and the New Discourse on Citizenship." Pp. 1–38 in P. Werbner and N. Yuval-Davis (Eds.), *Women, Citizenship, and Difference.* New York and London: Zed Books.

Chapter 9

Abrams, Kathryn. 1993. "Gender in the Military: Androcentrism and Institutional Reform." *Law and Contemporary Problems* 56:217–241.

Baker, Phyllis L., and Kevin T. Leicht. 2017. "Globalization, Gender and Development: Toward a Theoretical Understanding of Public Gender-Based Violence Against Women and Girls." *Sociology of Development* 3:323–345.

Benson, Michael, and Greer Fox. 2002. "Economic Distress, Community Context, and Intimate Partner Violence: An Application and Extension of Social Disorganization Theory," document number 193434. Washington, DC: U.S. Department of Justice.

Bunch, Will. 2010. *The Backlash: Right-Wing Radicals, High Def Hucksters, and Paranoid Politics in the Age of Obama*. New York, NY: Harper-Collins.

Burgess, Robert L., and Ronald L. Akers. 1966. "A Differential Association-Reinforcement Theory of Criminal Behavior." *Social Problems* 14(2):128–147.

Castells, Manuel. 1998. *End of Millennium*. Oxford: Blackwell.

_____. 1997. *The Power of Identity*. Oxford, UK: Blackwell.

Castro, Carl Andrew, et al. 2015 "Sexual Assault in the Military." *Current Psychiatry Reports* 17:54.

Cherlin, Andrew. 2014. *Labor's Love Lost: The Rise and Fall of Working Class America*. New York, NY: Russell Sage Foundation.

Cohen, Dov. 1998. "Culture, Social Organization, and Patterns of Violence." *Journal of Personality and Social Psychology* 75:408–419.

Cooper, Helen. 2014. "Reports of Sexual Assaults in the Military on the Rise," *New York Times*, https://www.nytimes.com/2014/12/04/us/reports-of-sexual-assaults-in-military-on-rise.html?_r=0

Department of Defense. 2014. *Department of Defense Annual Report on Sexual Assault in the Military Fiscal Year*. Sexual Assault Prevention and Response. Washington, DC: Department of Defense.

Dobrow, Jason. 2016. "Differential Association Theory." In *The Encyclopedia of Crime and Punishment*. New York, NY: John Wiley and Sons.

Eberstadt, Nicholas. 2017. *Men Without Work: America's Invisible Crisis*. West Conshocken, PA: Templeton Press.

Epstein, Cynthia Fuchs. 2007. "Great Divides: The Cultural, Cognitive, and Social Bases of the Global Subordination of Women." *American Sociological Review* 72(February):1–22.

Ferner, Matt, and Alissa Scheller. 2016. "There Were More Muslim Hate Crimes Last Year Than Any Year Since 2001," *Huffington Post*, https://www.huffingtonpost.com/entry/hate-crimes-muslims-since-911_us_57e00644e4b04a1497b59970

Freilich, J. D., and W. A. Pridemore. 2005. "A Reassessment of State-Level Covariates of Militia Groups." *Behavioral Sciences and the Law* 23:527–546.

Gibbs, A. 2016. "'Post-Truth' Is the Word of the Year Thanks to Brexit, Trump's Election Campaigns," CNBC, November 16, https://www.cnbc.com/2016/11/16/post-truth-is-the-word-of-the-year-thanks-to-brexit-trumps-election-campaigns-says-oxford-dictionaries.html

Gibson, J. W. 1994. *Warrior Dreams: Violence and Manhood in Post-Vietnam America*. New York, NY: Hill and Wang.

Giddens, Anthony. 1991. *Modernity and Self Identity: Self and Society in the Late Modern Age*. Redwood City, CA: Stanford University Press.

Haegerich, Tamera M., et al. 2014. "Prevention of Injury and Violence in the USA." *The Lancet* 384:64–74.

Hawley, George. 2017. "The European Roots of the Alt-Right: How Far Right Ideas Are Going International," *Foreign Affairs*, https://www.foreignaffairs.com/articles/europe/2017-10-27/european-roots-alt-right

Heise, Lori. 1998. "Violence Against Women: An Integrated, Ecological Framework." *Violence Against Women* 4:262–290.

Hochschild, Arlie. 2016. *Strangers in Their Own Land: Anger and Mourning on the American Right*. New York, NY: New Press.

Jonas, Eva, Stefan Schulz-Hardt, Dieter Frey, and Norman Thelen. 2001. "Confirmation Bias in Sequential Information Search After Preliminary Decisions: An Expansion of Dissonance Theoretical Research on Selective Exposure to Information." *Journal of Personality and Social Psychology* 80(4):557–571.

Kandiyoti, Deniz. 1988. "Bargaining With Patriarchy." *Gender and Society* 2:274–290.

Kimmel, Michael, and Abby L. Ferber. 2000. "'White Men Are This Nation': Right-Wing Militias and the Restoration of Rural American Masculinity." *Rural Sociology* 65(4):582–604.

Lutz, Amy. 2008. "Who Joins the Military? A Look at Race, Class, and Immigration Status." *Journal of Political and Military Sociology* 36(2):167–188.

Nichols, Tom. 2017. *The Death of Expertise: The Campaign Against Established Knowledge and Why It Matters*. Oxford, UK: Oxford University Press.

Nickerson, Raymond S. 1998. "Confirmation Bias: A Ubiquitous Phenomenon in Many Guises." *Review of General Psychology* 2(2):175–220.

Pippenger, Nathan. 2017. "Know-Nothing Nation." *Chronicle of Higher Education*. https://www.chronicle.com/article/Know-Nothing-Nation/238873

Potok, Mark. 2016. "Anti-Muslim Crimes Surged Last Year, Fueled by Hateful Campaign." https://www.splcenter.org/hatewatch/2016/11/14/anti-muslim-hate-crimes-surged-last-year-fueled-hateful-campaign

Ridgeway, Cecelia. 2014. "ASA Presidential Address." *American Sociological Review* 79(1):1–16.

Rogers, Daniel. 2017. "When Truth Becomes a Commodity." *Chronicle of Higher Education*. https://www.chronicle.com/article/When-Truth-Becomes-a-Commodity/238866

Rose, J. 2017. "Brexit, Trump, and Post-Truth Politics." *Political Integrity*, 19:555–558.

Sampson, Robert J., and W. Byron Groves. 1989. "Community Structure and Crime: Testing Social-Disorganization Theory." *American Journal of Sociology* 94(4):774–802.

Simi et al. 2017. "Addicted to Hate: Identity Residual Among Former White Supremacists." *American Sociological Review* 82:1167–1187.

Southern Poverty Law Center. 2017. "Hate Groups Increase for the Second Consecutive Year as Trump Electrifies Radical Right." https://www.splcenter.org/news/2017/02/15/hate-groups-increase-second-consecutive-year-trump-electrifies-radical-right

Stiglitz, Joseph. 2013. *The Price of Inequality*. New York, NY: W. W. Norton.

Turchik, Jessica, and Susan Wilson. 2010. "Sexual Assault in the U.S. Military: A Review of the Literature and Recommendations for the Future." *Aggression and Violent Behavior* 15:267–277.

Van Dyke, Nella, and Sarah A. Soule. 2002. "Structural Social Change and the Mobilizing Effect of Threat: Explaining Levels of Patriot and Militia Organizing in the United States." *Social Problems* 49:497–520.

Vance, J. D. 2014. *Hillbilly Elegy: A Memoir of a Family and Culture in Crisis*. New York, NY: HarperCollins.

Vandello, Joseph, and Dov Cohen. 2003. "Male Honor and Female Fidelity: Implicit Cultural Scripts That Perpetuate Domestic Violence." *Journal of Personality and Social Psychology* 84:997–1010.

Vandello, Joseph, et al. 2008. "Precarious Manhood." *Journal of Personality and Social Psychology* 95:1325–1339.

Watts, Charlotte, and Cathy Zimmerman. 2002. "Violence Against Women: Global Scope and Magnitude." *The Lancet* 359:1232–1237.

Willer, Robb, Christabel L. Rogalin, Bridget Conlon, and Michael T. Wojnowicz. 2013. Overdoing Gender: A Test of the Masculine Overcompensation Thesis. *American Journal of Sociology* 118(4):980–1022.

Williams, Joan. 2016. "What So Many People Don't Get About the U.S. Working Class." *Harvard Business Review*. https://hbr.org/2016/11/what-so-many-people-dont-get-about-the-u-s-working-class

Williamson, Oliver. 1985. *The Economic Institutions of Capitalism*. New York, NY: Free Press.

_____. 1975. *Markets and Hierarchies: Analysis and Antitrust Implications, a Study in the Economics of Internal Organization*. New York, NY: Free Press.

Zhou, Yilu, et al. 2005. "U.S. Extremist Groups on the Web." *IEEE Intelligent Systems* 20:44–51.

Chapter 10

Adhikari, A. (2014). *The bullet and the ballot box: The story of Nepal's Maoist revolution*. Verso Books.

Annan, Jeannie, Christopher Blattman, Dyan Mazurana, and Khristopher Carlson. 2011. "Civil War, Reintegration and Gender in Northern Uganda." *Journal of Conflict Resolution* 55(6):877–908.

Aretxaga, B. 1997. *Shattering Silence: Women, Nationalism, and Political Subjectivity in Northern Ireland*. Princeton, NJ: Princeton University Press.

Bagić, A. 2006. "Women's Organizing in Post-Yugoslav Countries: Talking About 'Donors.'" P. 141 in M. M. Ferree and A. M. Tripp (Eds.), *Global Feminism: Transnational Women's Activism, Organizing, and Human Rights*. New York: New York University Press.

Bellows, J., and E. Miguel. 2009. "War and Local Collective Action in Sierra Leone." *Journal of Public Economics* 93(11–12):1144–1157.

Berry, M. E. 2018. *War, Women, and Power: From Violence to Mobilization in Rwanda and Bosnia-Herzegovina*. New York, NY: Cambridge University Press.

_____. 2017. "Barriers to Women's Progress After Atrocity: Evidence From Rwanda and Bosnia-Herzegovina." *Gender & Society* 31(6):830–853.

_____. 2015a. "From Violence to Mobilization: War, Women, and Threat in Rwanda." *Mobilization: An International Quarterly* 20(2):135–156.

_____. 2015b. "When 'Bright Futures' Fade: Paradoxes of Women's Empowerment in Rwanda." *Signs: Journal of Women in Culture and Society* 41(1):1–27.

Berry, Marie E., and Trishna Rana. n.d. "What Prevents Peace? Women and Peacebuilding in Bosnia and Nepal." Unpublished paper.

Björkdahl, A. 2012. "A Gender-Just Peace? Exploring the Post-Dayton Peace Process in Bosnia." *Peace & Change* 37(2):286–317.

Blattman, C. 2009. "From Violence to Voting: War and Political Participation in Uganda." *American Political Science Review* 103(2):231–247.

Bohara, Rameswar. 2015. "War-Makers to Peace-Keepers," *Nepali Times*, September 4–10, http://nepalitimes.com /article/nation/Nepal-from-war-makers-to-peace-keepers,2565.

Bop, C. 2001. "Women in Conflict: Their Gains and Their Losses." Pp. 19–35 in S. Meintjes, M. Turshen, and A. Pillay (Eds.), *The Aftermath: Women in Post-Conflict Transformation.* London, UK: Zed Books.

Burnet, J. E. 2008. "Gender Balance and the Meanings of Women in Governance in Post-Genocide Rwanda." *African Affairs* 107(428):361–386.

Cockburn, Cynthia (with Rada Stakic-Domuz and Meliha Hubic). 2001. *Women Organizing for Change: A Study of Women's Local Integrative Organizations and the Pursuit of Democracy in Bosnia-Herzegovina.* Zenica, Bosnia and Herzegovina: Medica Women's Association.

Cockburn, C. 1998. *The Space Between Us: Negotiating Gender and National Identities in Conflict.* London, UK: Zed Books.

De Luca, Giacomo, and Marijke Verpoorten. 2015. "Civil War and Political Participation: Evidence From Uganda." *Economic Development and Cultural Change* 64(1):113–141.

Des Forges, A. 1999. *"Leave None to Tell the Story": Genocide in Rwanda.* New York, NY: Human Rights Watch.

DiMaggio, P. J., and W. W. Powell. 1983. "The Iron Cage Revisited: Institutional Isomorphism and Collective Rationality in Organizational Fields." *American Sociological Review* 48(2):147–160.

Enloe, C. 1993. *The Morning After: Sexual Politics at the End of the Cold War.* Berkeley: University of California Press.

Falch, Åshild. 2010. *Women's Political Participation and Influence in Post-Conflict Burundi and Nepal.* Oslo: Peace Research Institute.

Fujii, L. A. 2009. *Killing Neighbors: Webs of Violence in Rwanda.* Ithaca, NY: Cornell University Press.

Gervais, M. 2003. "Human Security and Reconstruction Efforts in Rwanda: Impact on the Lives of Women." *Development in Practice* 13(5):542–551.

Goswami, Roshmi. 2015. "UNSCR 1325 and Female Ex-Combatants—Case Study of the Maoist Women of Nepal." New York: UN Women.

Halilovic-Pastuovic, M. 2018. "Segregated Education in Post-Conflict Bosnia." Marie Sklodowska Curie Project, Horizon 2020. https://cordis.europa.eu/project/rcn/201594_en.html (accessed October 2018)

Helms, E. 2013. *Innocence and Victimhood: Gender, Nation, and Women's Activism in Postwar Bosnia-Herzegovina.* Madison: University of Wisconsin Press.

_____. 2002. "Women as Agents of Ethnic Reconciliation? Women's NGOs and International Intervention in Postwar Bosnia-Herzegovina." *Women's Studies International Forum* 26(1):15–33.

Hughes, M. 2009. "Armed Conflict, International Linkages, and Women's Parliamentary Representation in Developing Nations." *Social Problems* 56(1):174–204.

Hughes, M., and A. M. Tripp. 2015. "Civil War and Trajectories of Change in Women's Political Representation in Africa, 1985–2010." *Social Forces* 93(4):1513–1540.

Human Rights Watch. 2017. "Nepal: Events of 2017." https://www.hrw.org/world-report/2018/country-chapters/nepal (accessed October 2018)

International Center for Not-for-Profit Law. 2011. NGO Law Monitor: Rwanda. http://www.icnl.org/research/monitor/rwanda.html (accessed February 2012)

Kagame, P. 2014. *Keynote Address by President Paul Kagame at the Women in Parliaments Global Forum Joint Session With MDG Advocacy Group.* Kigali, Rwanda: Office of the President.

Kampwirth, K. 2004. *Feminism and the Legacy of Revolution: Nicaragua, El Salvador, Chiapas.* Athens: Ohio University Press.

Kleiman, M. 2007. *Challenges of Activism and Feminism in Creation of Women's Space: Work of Žene Ženama in Local, National and Regional Context.* Sarajevo, Bosnia-Herzegovina: Žene Ženama.

Lake, Milli. 2018. *Strong NGOs, Weak States: Pursuing Gender Justice in the Democratic Republic of Congo and South Africa.* New York, NY: Cambridge University Press.

_____. 2014. "Organizing Hypocrisy: Providing Legal Accountability for Human Rights Violations in Areas of Limited Statehood." *International Studies Quarterly* 58(3):515–526.

Longman, T. 2006. "Rwanda: Achieving Equality or Serving an Authoritarian State?" Pp. 133–150 in G. a. H. B. Bauer (Ed.), *Women in African Parliaments.* Boulder, CO: Lynne Rienner.

Malcolm, Noel. *Bosnia: A short history.* NYU Press, 1996. APA.

Mamdani, M. 2001. *When Victims Become Killers: Colonialism, Nativism, and the Genocide in Rwanda.* Princeton, NJ: Princeton University Press.

Mertus, J. A. 2000. *War's Offensive on Women: The Humanitarian Challenge in Bosnia, Kosovo, and Afghanistan.* Bloomfield, CT: Kumarian Press.

Newbury, C., and H. Baldwin. 2000. *Aftermath: Women in Postgenocide Rwanda.* Working Paper No. 303, USAID Center for Development Information and Evaluation.

Poudel, Keshab. 2017. "Migrant Workers, Threatened Jobs." *New Spotlight*, July 8, https://www.spotlightnepal.com/2017/07/08/migrant-workers-threatened-jobs/

Prunier, G. 1995. *The Rwanda Crisis, 1959–1994: History of a Genocide.* London, UK: Hurst.

Republic of Rwanda. 2004. *Survey of Genocide Deaths.* Kigali, Rwanda: Ministry of Local Administration and Community.

Sharoni, S. 2001. Rethinking Women's Struggles in Israel-Palestine and in the North of Ireland. Pp. 85–98 in C. O. N. Moser and F. Clark (Eds.), *Victims, Perpetrators or Actors: Gender, Armed Conflict and Political Violence.* London, UK: Zed.

_____. 1995. *Gender and the Israeli-Palestinian Conflict: The Politics of Women's Resistance.* Syracuse, NY: Syracuse University Press.

Silber, Laura, and Allan Little. *The death of Yugoslavia.* London: Penguin Books, 1996.

Skjelsbæk, I. 2006. "Victim and Srvivor: Narrated Social Identities of Women Who Experienced Rape During the War in Bosnia-Herzegovina." *Feminism & Psychology* 16(4):373–403.

Stephen, L. 1997. *Women and Social Movements in Latin America: Power From Below.* Austin: University of Texas Press.

Stiglmayer, A. 1994. "The Rapes in Bosnia-Herzegovina." Pp. 82–169 in A. Stiglmayer (Ed.), *Mass Rape: The War Against Women in Bosnia-Herzegovina.* Lincoln: University of Nebraska Press.

Straus, S. 2006. *The Order of Genocide: Race, Power, and War in Rwanda.* Ithaca, NY: Cornell University Press.

Straus, S., and L. Waldorf. 2011. *Remaking Rwanda: State Building and Human Rights After Mass Violence.* Madison: University of Wisconsin Press.

Thomson, S. M. 2018. *Rwanda: From Genocide to Precarious Peace.* New Haven, CT: Yale University Press.

_____. 2013. *Whispering Truth to Power: Everyday Resistance to Reconciliation in Post-Genocide Rwanda.* Madison: University of Wisconsin Press.

Tripp, A. M. 2015. *Women and Power in Postconflict Africa.* New York, NY: Cambridge University Press.

UN Office of the High Commissioner for Human Rights. 2012. *Nepal Conflict Report.* Geneva: OHCHR. http://www.ohchr.org/EN/Countries/AsiaRegion/Pages/NepalConflictReport.aspx

UN Mission in Bosnia and Herzegovina (UNMIBH). 2003. *Mandate.* https://peacekeeping.un.org/mission/past/unmibh/mandate.html (accessed 2/2019).

Viterna, J. 2013. *Women in War: The Micro-Processes of Mobilization in El Salvador.* New York, NY: Oxford University Press.

Viterna, J., K. Fallon, and J. Beckfield. 2008. "How Development Matters: A Research Note on the Relationship Between Development, Democracy, and Women's Political Representation." *International Journal of Comparative Sociology* 49(6):455–477.

Walsh, M. 2000. *Aftermath: The Impact of Conflict on Women in Bosnia and Herzegovina.* Washington, DC: Center for Development Information and Evaluation, USAID.

Wood, E. J. 2003. *Insurgent Collective Action and Civil War in El Salvador.* New York, NY: Cambridge University Press.

Yuval-Davis, N. 1997. *Gender & Nation.* Thousand Oaks, CA: SAGE.

Zraly, M., and L. Nyirazinyoye. 2010. "'Don't Let the Suffering Make You Fade Away': An Ethnographic Study of Resilience Among Survivors of Genocide-Rape in Southern Rwanda." *Social Science & Medicine* 70(10):1656–1664.

Chapter 11

Acharya, Meena, and Lynn Bennett. 1985. *Women and the Subsistence Sector: Economic Participation and Household Decision-Making in Nepal* (World Bank Staff Working Papers Number 526). Washington, DC: World Bank.

_____. 1981. *The Rural Women of Nepal: An Aggregate Analysis and Summary of Eight Village Studies.* Philippines: Regional Service Center.

Blumberg, Rae Lesser. 2016. "Magic Potion/Poison Potion: The Impact of Women's Economic Empowerment vs. Disempowerment for Development in a Globalized World." Pp. 153–189 in Gregory Hooks (Ed.),

Handbook of the Sociology of Development. Berkeley: University of California Press.

_____. 2015. "'Dry' Versus 'Wet' Development and Women in Three World Regions." *Sociology of Development* 1(1):91–122.

_____. 1984. "A General Theory of Gender Stratification." *Sociological Theory* 2:23–101.

Central Bureau of Statistics. 2014. "National Planning Commission Secretariat." *Population Monograph of Nepal, Vol II (Social Demography).* Kathmandu: Government of Nepal.

Davison, Jean. 1996. *Voices From Mutira: Changes in the Lives of Rural Gikuyu Women, 1910–1995*, 2nd ed. London, UK: Lynne Rienner.

Gaha Magar, Santa, and Ramesh Kumar. 2015. "Nepalis Are Living Longer," *Nepali Times.* http://archive.nepalitimes.com/article/from-nepali-press/Nepalis-are-living-longer,2027

Gender Equality and Social Inclusion Working Group. 2017. *A Common Framework for Gender Equality & Social Inclusion.* Nepal: Gender Equality and Social Inclusion Working Group, International Development Partners Group, Nepal.

Ghosh A., A. Singh, and S. Chigateri. 2017. *A Trapeze Act: Balancing Unpaid Care Work and Paid Work by Women in Nepal.* New Delhi: Institute of Social Studies Trust.

Hill Collins, Patricia. 1990. *Black Feminist Thought: Knowledge, Consciousness, and the Politics of Empowerment.* Boston, MA: Unwin Hyman.

Luttrell, Wendy. 1993. "'The Teacher, They All Had Their Pets:' Concepts of Gender, Knowledge, and Power." *Signs* 18(3):505–546.

Maharjan, A., S. Bauer, and B. Knerr. 2012. "Do Rural Women Who Stay Behind Benefit From Male Out-Migration? A Case Study in the Hills of Nepal." *Gender, Technology and Development* 16(1):95–123.

Ministry of Health, New ERA, and ICF. 2017. *Nepal Demographic and Health Survey 2016.* Kathmandu: Ministry of Health, Nepal.

Ministry of Labour and Employment, Government of Nepal. 2015. *Labour Migration for Employment: A Status Report for Nepal: 2014/2015.* Kathmandu: Government of Nepal.

Smith, Dorothy. 1987. *The Everyday World as Problematic: A Feminist Sociology.* Toronto, Canada: University of Toronto Press.

United Nations Development Programme. 2016. *Human Development Report 2016.* (http://hdr.undp.org/sites/default/files/2016_human_development_report.pdf)

Chapter 12

Ahmed, Sara, and Jackie Stacey (Eds.). 2000. *Transformations: Thinking Through Feminism.* London, UK: Routledge.

Ally, Shireen A. 2010. *From Servants to Workers: South African Domestic Workers and the Democratic State.* Scottsville, South Africa: University of KwaZulu-Natal Press.

Anderson, Bridget. 2000. *Doing the Dirty Work? The Global Politics of Domestic Labor.* London, UK: Zed Books.

Bakan, Abigail, and Daiva Stasiulis. 1997. *Not One in the Family: Foreign Domestic Workers in Canada.* Toronto: University of Toronto Press.

Chaney, Elsa, Mary Garcia Castro, and Margo L. Smith. 1989. *Muchachas No More. Household Workers in Latin America and the Caribbean.* Philadelphia, PA: Temple University Press.

Chang, Grace. 2001. *Disposable Domestics: Immigrant Women in the Global Economy.* Cambridge, MA: South End Press.

Chen, Martha Alter. 2011. "Recognizing Domestic Workers, Regulating Domestic Work: Conceptual, Measurement, and Regulatory Challenges." *Canadian Journal of Women & the Law* 23(1):167–184.

Chin, Christine. 1998. *In Service and Servitude: Foreign Female Domestic Workers and the Malaysian 'Modernity' Project.* New York, NY: Columbia University Press.

Cock, Jacklyn. 1989. *Maids & Madams: Domestic Workers Under Apartheid*, 2nd ed. London, UK: Women's Press Limited.

Ferrara, Alessandro. 1998. *Reflective Authenticity: Rethinking the Project of Modernity.* New York, NY: Routledge.

Fish, Jennifer. 2017. *Domestic Workers of the World Unite! A Global Movement for Dignity and Human Right.* New York: New York University Press.

_____. 2006. *Domestic Democracy: At Home in South Africa.* New York, NY: Routledge.

Fish, Jennifer N., Rachel Crockett, and Robin Ormiston (Directors). 2012. *C189: Conventional Wisdom.* Norfolk, VA: Sisi Sojourner Productions.

Gamburd, Michele Ruth. 2000. *The Kitchen Spoon's Handle: Transnationalism and Sri Lanka's Migrant Housemaids.* Ithaca, NY: Cornell University Press.

Gill, Lesley. 1994. *Precarious Dependencies: Gender, Class and Domestic Service in Bolivia.* New York, NY: Columbia University Press.

Heyzer, N., G. Lycklama à Nijehold, and N. Weerakoon. 1994. *The Trade in Domestic Workers: Causes, Mechanisms and Consequences of International Migration.* London, UK: Zed Books.

Hondagneu-Sotelo, Pierette. 2001. *Domestica: Immigrant Workers Cleaning and Caring in the Shadows of Affluence.* Berkeley: University of California Press.

International Domestic Workers' Network. 2010. *Platform of Demands.* International Labour Conference, 99th session, Geneva. http://www.wiego.org/sites/default/files/resources/files/IDWN%20-Platform-of-Demands-English-2010.pdf

International Labour Office. 2013. "Domestic Workers Across the World: Global and Regional Statistics and the Extent of Legal Protection." Geneva: International Labour Organization. http://www.ilo.org/public/libdoc/ilo/2013/113B09_2_engl.pdf

Jaggar, Alison. 1989. "Love and Knowledge: Emotion in Feminist Epistemology." Pp. 145–171 in A. Jaggar and S. Bordo (Eds.), *Gender/Body/Knowledge: Feminist Reconstructions of Being and Knowing.* New Brunswick, NJ: Rutgers University Press.

Jones, Siân. 2010. "Negotiating Authentic Objects and Authentic Selves: Beyond the Deconstruction of Authenticity." *Journal of Material Culture* 15(2):181–203.

Parreñas, Rhacel Salazar. 2001. *Servants of Globalization: Women, Migration and Domestic Work.* Stanford, CA: Stanford University Press.

Rollins, Judith. 1985. *Between Women: Domestics and Their Employers.* Philadelphia, PA: Temple University Press.

Romero, Mary. 1992. *Maid in the U.S.A.* New York, NY: Routledge.

Shouse, Eric. 2005. "Feeling, Emotion, Affect." *M/C Journal* 8(6). http://journal.media-culture.org.au/0512/03-shouse.php

Solari, Cinzia. 2010. "Resource Drain vs. Constitutive Circularity: Comparing the Gendered Effects of Post-Soviet Migration Patterns in Ukraine." *Anthropology of East Europe Review* 28(1):215–238.

Taylor, Charles. 1992. *The Ethics of Authenticity.* Cambridge, MA: Harvard University Press.

Index

Centre de Recherches, d'Etudes, de Documentation, et de l'Information sur la Femme (CREDIF), 112
Chagnon, Napoleon, 75
Chanchaló, Ecuador, 80
Charfi, Mohamed, 112, 118 (note 22)
Chen, Marty, 239 (note 6)
Chiapas massacre, 42
Chicas de oro (golden girls), 168
Chigateri, S., 215
Chihuahua, murder/disappearance of women in, 46
Childbirth, as social mobility strategy, 171–173
Childe, V. Gordon, 73
Child malnutrition, 24–25, 83
Child marriage, 31, 102 (table), 213
Children
    domestic workers as parents of, 233, 236
    sexual violence against, 31–32, 64 (note 3)
    violence against in Colombia, 41–44
Chile, violence against women in, 52
Chimpanzees
    differences from bonobos, 68–70
    DNA overlap with humans, 65, 68, 87
    female control of food supply among, 65
    place of evolution of, 68, 70
    sexual taboos and, 89 (note 6)
China
    birth tourism and, 172
    fentanyl exports from, 86
    FLFP in, 85
    foot-binding in, 84
    increase in billionaires in, 163–164
    population of, 26 (note 10)
    research on agricultural projects in, 80
    sex-selective abortion in, 85
    wet agriculture in, 9
Chronic violence, definition of, 64 (note 7)
Citizenship, coloniality of, 165–167
    definition of, 169
    ethnicity and, 166
    gender and, 165–167
    race and, 165–166
    See also Embodied social mobility
Citizenship premium, 162–163, 164, 173, 174 (note 3)
Ciudad Juarez, violence against women in, 42, 46
Clan del Golfo (Autodefensas Gaitanistas de Colombia-Urabenos), 31, 53
Clignet, Remi, 74
Cockburn, Cynthia, 42, 45, 46
Collective agency, 238
Collective authenticity, 228, 231
Collective consciousness, 61, 63
Collective identity, 228
Collective legitimacy, 231

Collective violence, 32, 33, 180, 182
Collins, R., 92 (note 28)
Colombia, paramilitarism in
    capitalist class role in rise of, 35
    land dispossession and rise of, 35–41
    legal foundation for establishment of, 37–38
    paramilitaries as sexual predators, 52–53
    political–economic conditions from which, emerged, 35–37
    primary forms of aggression by, 39 (table)
    second wave of, 52
    targets of, 38
    third wave of, 53
Colombia, predatory sexuality/violence of capital of
    agribusiness in, 36–37, 39–40
    armed conflict in, background of, 37
    child marriage in, 31
    constitutional protection of women's rights in, 44
    cosmetic procedures and, 58
    depeasantization in, 28
    domestic/intimate partner violence, 43–44
    FARC-EP in, 37, 38, 61–62
    forced displacement, areas of, 40 (map)
    forced recruitment and, 43, 57
    gender-based violence toward men and boys in, 57–58
    human trafficking and, 43
    ideological dimension of, 57–59
    illegal drug trade and, 36
    informal economy in, 37
    internally displaced persons in, 32
    land dispossession, instrumental violence and, 41–42
    land dispossession, intersection of material/ideological and, 55–62
    land ownership by drug traffickers in, 36, 64 (note 8)
    mining in, 36, 39
    Peace Accords, 2016, 37
    political participation/activism/leadership, repression of, 42–43
    poverty rate in, 37
    primitive accumulation in, 49–52
    racial and class components of, 50–52
    rape of displaced persons in, 28
    sex-selective massacre, 57
    sexual violence against children in, 31–32
    sexual violence against women in, 32
    statistics on violence toward women and children in, 41
    unequal land distribution in, 37
    violence against women and children in, purpose of, 41–44
    women home-run businesses in, 15
    See also Colombia, paramilitarism in

Colonial capitalism, 50
Colonialism, 16, 17–20
Coloniality of citizenship. *See* Citizenship,
    coloniality of
Commercialization of women's home-based
    production/enterprise, 5, 14–15
Compassionate capitalism, 235
Comprehensive peace accord
    (CPA; Nepal), 194
Confirmation bias, 178–179, 186, 188
Confucism, 92 (note 30)
Congo-Brazzaville, gender equity in, 71
Consumption, globalization of, 59–60
Contraception
    access in Afghanistan, 24
    access in Sub-Saharan Africa, 24
    among !Kung, 71
    decisions in Northeast Thailand, 83
    natural methods for, 71, 90 (notes 10–12)
    See also Family planning
Convention on the Elimination of All Forms of
    Discrimination Against Women (CEDAW; 1979),
    20, 96, 110, 113, 201
Cordoba, Piedad, 42
Cosmetic procedures, 58
Cotopaxi Province, research on agricultural
    development projects in, 80–81
Created biology of gender stratification, 28–29
    affect on both genders, 65, 83–84
    bride burning/dowry deaths and, 85
    conclusions/lessons learned, 87–89
    endemic, frequent warfare and, 75–76
    extremes in Global South, 79–84
    foot-binding and, 84
    gender inequality in Afghanistan, 83
    groups close to gender equality, 79–83
    historical horror stories, 84–86
    hoe horticulture and, 72–76
    human history and geography, across, 70–79
    hunting-gathering and, 70–72
    hunting-gathering *vs.* bonobo/chimpanzee, 68, 70
    industry and, 78–79
    kin/property systems and, 75
    low-education U.S. white males and, 86–87
    negative *vs.* positive effects of, 75–77
    plow agriculture and, 76–78
    prerequisite for economic power and, 74–75
    sati–widow burning and, 84, 93 (note 39)
    wet *vs.* dry plow agriculture, 76–77
CREDIF (Centre de Recherches, d'Etudes, de
    Documentation, et de l'Information sur la
    Femme), 112
Credit discrimination, 15–16
Cuba, sex tourism in, 174 (note 5)

Cultivation
    beginnings of, 87–88
    See also Horticulture
Cult of domesticity, 155
Cultural taboos, in India, 122–123
Cultural universals, 71
Culture of manliness, 152–153

DACA program, 172
Dalit. *See* Nepal, gender inequality in
Das, Padma, 136, 138
Davidoff, Leonore, 155
Davidson, Julia O'Connell, 170, 171
Dayton Peace Agreement, 193, 202
Deaths and diseases of despair, 86
Deforestation, 25, 82
Denmark, 92 (note 29), 174 (note 6)
Derecho de pernada (landlord's right
    to sex), 59
Descriptive *vs.* substantive representation,
    118 (note 20)
Deserts, creation of major, 91 (note 19)
Development, the State, and gender. *See* Iran and
    Tunisia, contrasting
Diamond, Jared, 26 (note 11)
Dill, William, 154
Dimaggio, Paul, 154
Dirty War (Chile), violence against women during, 52
Discount factors, 23, 27 (note 22)
Diseases and deaths of despair, 86
Divorce
    economic power and, 23
    Islamic feminism and, 110
    male unilateral, 109
    in MENA, 100, 109, 110, 112
    wages for housework/child care
        and, 100
    See also Marriage
Domestic violence, 32, 49, 56, 113,
    115, 175
Domestic work, devalued nature of, 222
Domestic workers, 30
    children of, 233, 236
    education and, 235
    Nepalese, 216–217
    numbers and gender of, 222
    race/ethnicity of, 222
Domestic workers, activism and
    accountability of Convention delegates and,
        235–236
    authenticity and, 222, 231, 234, 237, 238
    conclusions, 237–238
    decency and human rights appeals, 224–225
    emotion, as vehicle for affective power, 231–232

MENA (Middle East and North Africa)
economic empowerment of Muslim women in,
92 (note 30)
education and FLFP in, 12–13
exporting activities, FLFP and, 116 (note 1)
fertility decline in, 94, 95, 110
FLFP rates in, 77, 84, 94–95, 99 (table)
male outmigration and FLFP in, 11
male unemployment in, 98–99
neoliberal economic policy in, 98–99
neopatriarchy of, 99
state-led industrialization in, 97–98
variations among, 94–95
women's political representation in, 94
See also Iran and Tunisia, contrasting
Mendez, Danna, 42
Menstrual hygiene management (MHM), 119–120
definition of, 143 (note 6)–144 (note 7)
lack of studies in low-resource countries,
144 (note 7)
See also Menstrual hygiene management (MHM)
study in India
Menstrual hygiene management (MHM) study in
India, 29
access to water/toilets/soap, 123, 136–137
addressing challenges to, 140–141
affordable sanitary pads and, 123, 136
conceptual framework of, 121–123, 122 (figure)
conclusions, 140–143
coping mechanisms and, 132–133
cultural taboos and, 122–123, 128, 132, 136
discussion, 135–140
education and, 139
fulani cloth use, 130, 131, 132, 133
gender roles and inequalities, 121
health risks and, 137–139, 144 (note 11)
hygiene practices, impact of, 137–140
hygiene practices, impact of, data from other
studies, 137–140, 144 (note 11)
livelihood and, 139
menstrual protection options, 128, 129–131
methods of study, 123–124
methods of study, supplement to, 141–143
overview of, 120–121
postpartum hygiene management, 121–123,
122 (figure), 132
results of study, 124–135
rural women, most burdensome aspects for,
130 (table)
rural women, practices of, 129 (table)
socioeconomic characteristics and,
124 (table)–125 (table)
socioeconomic status and rural/urban residence
and, 122, 135–136

statistics on, 143 (note 3)
strength and limitations of, 140
unmet need for menstrual protection and, 133–135
views on commercial sanitary napkins, 134 (table)
washing/drying/disposal practices and, 131
water/sanitation insecurity/hygiene and, 125–128,
127 (table)
well-being/dignity, 139–140
Mestizas, gender ideology of, 92 (note 33)
Methodism, 155
Mexico
Chiapas massacre in, 42
citizenship through childbirth in, 172
export orientation and FLFP in, 151
illegal migration, victimization and, 57
murder/disappearance of women in, 46
sex-trafficking and, 43
violence against women in, 51, 52
Microfinance institutions (MFIs), 5, 14, 18,
26 (note 19)
Micro level effects of economic power, 22–24
education, 22–23
family division of childcare/domestic labor, 23
family domestic well-being, 22–23
family economic affairs, 22
family fertility and composition, 23
gendered spending patterns, 23
health, 22–23
life options, 23
negative effects of power of the purse, 23–24
Middle East
Nepalese domestic workers in, 216–217
oil and FLFP in, 149
See also MENA (Middle East and North Africa)
Mierswa, Emily, 12
Miess, Maria, 14
Migrant workers. *See* Domestic workers, activism and
Migration
illegal, victimization and, 57, 172
international, economic benefits of, 162–163
male outmigration, effects on FLFP in MENA,
11, 98
Milanovic, Branko, 162, 164
Militias and hate groups, 183 (figure)–184
Millennium Development Goals (MDGs), 120
Minangkabau people, 7
Minifundistas, 36
Mining Code Law 685 (Colombia), 36
Missionaries, 19
Moghadam, Fatemeh Etemad, 105
Moghadam, Valentine, 96, 149
Mohaddes, Kamiar, 98
Mohanty, C., 45–46
Morocco, 20, 68, 94, 96, 116

Mossadegh, Mohammad, 95, 96, 117 (note 14)–118 (note 14)
Mosuo people, agricultural projects and, 80
Mozambique, water supply, impact on hygiene in, 136
Muñoz, C. B., 46
Muslim Family law (MFL), 98, 100–101
Muslims
  economic empowerment of women, 92 (note 30)
  economic organization of women, 17
  hate crimes against Muslim Americans, 184
Muta'a (temporary marriage), 109
Myanmar (Burma), gender equality in, 19

Nagarik Aawaz, 200
Narco-aesthetics, 64 (note 17)
National borders, 29
Nazeh people, agricultural projects and, 80
Ndebele people, 16, 18–19
Neoliberalism, in Bolivia, 167–168
Neo-Nazis, 185
Neopatriarchy, 99
Nepal, armed conflict and women's resilience case
  community level analysis, 200–201
  dead and displaced persons, statistics on, 189, 193
  household level analysis, 196–197
  national political analysis, 203–204
  overview of, 193–194
  conclusions and implications, 218–220
  dead ends to economic empowerment and, 214–218
  early marriage/pregnancy and, 213–214
  economic hardships, gender expectations and, 210–211
  economic opportunity, dearth in early life, 210–212
  education issues, 212, 219
  gender constraints across lifespan, 209–218
  introduction to, 206–207
  lack of economic agency after marriage, 212–213
  life expectancy, 220 (note 3)
  men's migration/control of remittance and, 217–218
  migration overseas for job opportunities and 216–217
  migration to urban areas for work opportunities and, 216
  NGO involvement and, 214–216, 218–219
  participants/methodology of study, 207–208
  social discrimination, intergenerational, 211
Nepal Demographic and Health Survey 2016, 214, 215, 217
New Guinea, 90 (note 16)
New Zealand, 7, 77, 91 (note 25)
Nigeria, 17, 50, 90 (note 17), 136

Non-governmental organizations (NGOs)
  in Bosnia, 196
  in Nepal, 214–216, 218–219
Non-irrigated (dry) agriculture. *See* Dry plow agriculture
Nordic countries, 78, 91 (note 22)
North Africa, oil and FLFP in, 149. *See also* MENA (Middle East and North Africa)
North America, FLFP rates in, 99 (table)
Northeast Thailand (Isan)
  family planning in, 82, 83, 93 (note 37)
  gender and math test scores in, 91 (note 22)
  research on agricultural projects in, 80, 81, 82
Northern Ireland, "positive" outcomes after conflict in, 190
Norway, 92 (note 29), 150, 202–203
Nuclear family, 68, 81
Nuclear power, 103, 108, 148

Obama, Barack, 183
Occupational sex-typing
  absence of strong antifeminist movements and, 155
  capital intensivity and, 148
  conclusions, 160
  economic dependence of women and, 147
  export-oriented industries and, 150–151
  geisha-ism and, 157–160
  general exclusion of women from work force and, 147–151
  introduction to, 145–146
  labor costs and, 147–148
  labor intensivity and, 148
  light industry and, 149
  opportunistic wolfism and, 156–157
  overcoming, 161
  patriarchy and, 147, 153
  petroleum/high value minerals and, 149–150
  scarcity of irreplaceable skills and, 150
  sense of own masculinity and, 152–153
  "show" feminism of isomorphism and, 153–154
  unionization and, 153
  varied hostility to employing women, 151–160
  wage control and, 153
  white-collar work and, 148–149
  women in management positions, worldwide, 146
Ochoa, Ernestina, 229–230
Oil/valuable minerals
  relationship to economic growth, 117 (note 4)
  resource curse and, 98, 117 (note 4), 149
  women's employment/economic power and lack of, 149–150
  See also Iran and Tunisia, contrasting
Onaran, Ozlem, 151

Opioid crisis, 86
Opportunistic wolfism, 156–157
Orienting theory, 96–97
Ozler, Sule, 151

Pacific region, FLFP rates in, 99 (table)
Pahlavi, Mohammad Reza, 102
Pair bonding, 68, 71
Palestine, women's rights in, 117 (note 8)
Palmer, Ingrid, 81, 82
Paraguay, femicide in, 52
Pashtun people, 83
Pashtunwali, 83
Path dependence, 178, 182, 186, 187
Patriarchal bargain, 77
Patriarchal belt
    female malnutrition in, 83
    fertility/family-planning in, 84
    gendered well-being in, 77
    inheritance in, 6
Patriarchal gender contract, 98, 99
Patriarchal kinship, 77, 210
Patriarchy
    global crisis of, 177, 188
    Iran and, 110
    link to oil industry, 149
    Nepal and, 210
    occupational sex-typing and, 147, 153
    predatory, 46
    rise of, 74, 88
    women's economic power and, 4, 6–7
Patrilineality, spatial abilities and, 75
Patrilocality, 4, 7, 84
Peace Accords
    Colombia, 37
    El Salvador, 20, 21
Pearce, J., 62, 64 (note 7)
People's Aid (Norway), 202–203
People's Army. *See* Nepal
Perra, 58
Peru, femicide in, 52
Pesaran, Hashem, 98
Pfeffer, Jeffrey, 154
PGEs, 72–73, 90 (note 14)
Philippines, Agta people in, 71
Physical violence, 32
PISA exam, 91 (note 22)
Plan Lazo (Colombia), 37
Plastic surgery, 17 (note 17)
Plow, invention of, 9, 66–67, 76, 88. *See also* Dry plow
    agriculture; Wet plow agriculture
Political opportunism, 179–180
Political violence, 32, 33

Polygamy, 100, 109
Polygyny, 74, 75
Poor Laws, 55
Populist political parties, 184–186
Postal Savings Bank, British, 10–11
Poster, Winifred, 153–154
Postpartum hygiene management, 121–123,
    122 (figure), 132
Potok, Mark, 183
Poverty, feminization of, 46
Powell, Walter, 154
Power of the purse, 23–24
Pratt, M., 45–46
Predatory patriarchy, 46
Pregnancy
    early, in Nepal, 213–214
    malnutrition during, 93 (note 38)
    maternal mortality, 24, 93 (note 38)
    postpartum hygiene management,
        121–123, 122 (figure), 132
Preindustrial Europe, financial
    independence of women in, 13
Preston, W. A., 46
Pridemore, W. A., 184
Primitive accumulation, 48–52
The Process of Occupational Sex-Typing
    (POST; Cohn), 146
Pro Femmes, 202
Prostitution, human trafficking for, 43
Pryce, Shirley, 228
Purdah (female exclusion), 14

Qatar, domestic workers in, 217
Queer individuals, 47
Quichua-speaking groups
    gender ideology of, 92 (note 33)
    research on agricultural projects, 80–81

Race/ethnicity
    investment citizenship and, 164–165
    See also Global gender violence/bigotry, low-status
        men and
Rainmaking, 16
Rape
    in Bosnia, 196
    of displaced persons in Colombia, 28
    transition to capitalism and, 50–51
    U.S. military and, 181, 182
    as weapon of war, 33, 44–45
Raven-Roberts, A., 43
Refugees, 21, 93 (note 41), 175, 196, 200
Remittances, 97, 98, 194, 207, 217–218
Rentier states, 98, 117 (note 4), 149

Resource curse, 98, 117 (note 4), 149
Revolutionary Armed Forces of Colombia (FARC-EP), 37, 38, 61–62
Rice farming. *See* Wet plow agriculture (irrigated rice)
Richani, N., 36
Riley, R., 45–46
Rivera, Lauren, 157, 158
Robots/automation, 5, 86, 88
Romania, horticulture in, 26 (note 7)
Ross, Michael, 149
Rotating savings and credit associations (ROSCAs), 17
Roth, Louise, 16
Rouhani, Hassan, 111, 118 (note 21)
RPF (Rwandan Patriotic Front), 191–192, 201, 202
Rubin, Gayle, 166, 168
Russia, birth tourism and, 171–172
Rwanda, armed conflict and women's resilience case
  community level analysis, 197–198
  dead and displaced persons, statistics on, 189, 191
  household level analysis, 195
  national political analysis, 201–202
  overview of, 191–192
Rwandan Patriotic Front (RPF), 191–192, 201, 202

Salzinger, L., 46
Samboni, Yuliana, 32
Saracule Muslim women, economic organization of, 17
Sati–widow burning, 84, 93 (note 39)
Saudi Arabia
  armed conflict, correlation with FLFP in, 24, 93 (note 41)
  domestic workers in, 217
  effects of education on FLFP in, 12–13
  labor migration and, 98
  oil and FLFP in, 149
Schachar, Ayelet, 164
Schlegel, Alice, 25 (note 3)
Seguino, Stephanie, 147
Self Employed Women's Association (SEWA), 130, 140, 142
Self-employment, 161
Separate purses, 7, 26 (note 17), 75
SEWA (Self Employed Women's Association), 130, 140, 142
Sex ratio
  among bonobos/chimpanzees, 70
  in China, 85
  in India, 85, 141–142
  in Singapore, 157
Sex-selective abortion, 23, 75, 77, 85
Sex tourism, 169–171
Sexual assault/harassment, U.S. military and, 181–182
Sexuality, feminism and, 47–48

Sexual taboos, bonobos/chimpanzees, 89 (note 6)
Sexual violence, 32
  in childhood, 64 (note 2)
  rise of capitalism and, 47–48, 50–52
  WHO definition of, 64 (note 5)
  See also Colombia, predatory sexuality/violence of capital of; Global South, overview of sexual violence literature on
Sharia law, inheritance under, 6
Sharoni, S., 190
Shona people, 16, 18–19
"Show" feminism of isomorphism, 153–154
Sierra Leone, violence against women in, 46
Singapore, 19, 79, 157
Singh, A., 215
Slash and burn, 8
Slavery, 166
Social class
  international marriage market and, 167–168
  intersection with gender ideology, 63
  paramilitarism and, 35
  violence against women/children and, 50–52
Social disorganization, 179, 184, 188
Social media. *See* Media
Social mobility. *See* Embodied social mobility
Solari, Cinzia, 222
Somalia, gender-based access to land in, 16
Somaliland, extreme physical work by women in, 148
Somavía, Juan, 229, 238
Sommer, M., 139
Sonbol, Amira al-Azhary, 100
South Asia
  child malnutrition in, 83–84
  economic empowerment of Muslim women in, 92 (note 30)
  effects of education on FLFP in, 12
  effects of lack of FLFP in, 84
  FLFP rates in, 84, 91 (note 26), 99 (table)
  gender and rice production in, 91 (note 27)
  low birth weight babies in, 24–25, 93 (note 38)
  malnutrition in, 91 (note 26)
  patrilocal residency in, 84
  See also individual country
Southeast Asia
  bilateral kinship/matrifocality in, 7, 77
  export orientation and FLFP in, 151
  gender and math test scores in, 91 (note 22)
  gender and rice production in, 77–78
  industrialization in, 79
  population of, 26 (note 10)
  women's economic organization in, 17
  See also individual country

World Health Organization
  definition of sexual violence, 64 (note 5)
  pregnancy weight gain guideline,
    93 (note 38)
World polity theory, 96
World War II, effect on FLFP, 12
Yacob, Halimah, 231
Yami, Hasila, 203
Yanomamo people, 75, 91 (note 23)
Yemen, 11, 98, 100

Yoruba people, 17
Yugoslav People's Army (JNA). *See* Bosnia
Yunnan Province, agricultural projects in, 80
Yunus, Mohammad, 18
Yuval-Davis, Nira, 166

Zald, Mayer, 3
Zambia, informal cross-border traders in, 18
Zheng He, 78
Zimbabwe, 16, 17–19